SAMS

Teach Yourself

DB2 Universal Database

in 21 Days

SECOND EDITION

SAMS

800 East 96th Street, Indianapolis, Indiana, 46240 USA

Sams Teach Yourself DB2 Universal Database in 21 Days

Copyright © 2004 by Sams Publishing

All rights reserved. No part of this book shall be reproduced, stored in a retrieval system, or transmitted by any means, electronic, mechanical, photocopying, recording, or otherwise, without written permission from the publisher. No patent liability is assumed with respect to the use of the information contained herein. Although every precaution has been taken in the preparation of this book, the publisher and author assume no responsibility for errors or omissions. Nor is any liability assumed for damages resulting from the use of the information contained herein.

International Standard Book Number: 0-672-32582-9

Library of Congress Catalog Card Number: 2003092626

Printed in the United States of America

First Printing: August 2003
Second printing with corrections: November 2003

07   06   05   04   4   3   2

Trademarks

All terms mentioned in this book that are known to be trademarks or service marks have been appropriately capitalized. Sams Publishing cannot attest to the accuracy of this information. Use of a term in this book should not be regarded as affecting the validity of any trademark or service mark.

IBM, DB2 and DB2 Universal Database are trademarks of IBM Corporation in the United States, other countries, or both. Windows is a trademark of Microsoft Corporation in the United States, other countries, or both.

Warning and Disclaimer

Every effort has been made to make this book as complete and as accurate as possible, but no warranty or fitness is implied. The information provided is on an "as is" basis. The authors and the publisher shall have neither liability nor responsibility to any person or entity with respect to any loss or damages arising from the information contained in this book or from the use of the CD or programs accompanying it.

Bulk Sales

Sams Publishing offers excellent discounts on this book when ordered in quantity for bulk purchases or special sales. For more information, please contact

U.S. Corporate and Government Sales
1-800-382-3419
corpsales@pearsontechgroup.com

For sales outside of the U.S., please contact

International Sales
1-317-428-3341
international@pearsontechgroup.com

ASSOCIATE PUBLISHER
Michael Stephens

ACQUISITIONS EDITOR
Loretta Yates

DEVELOPMENT EDITOR
Sean Dixon

MANAGING EDITOR
Charlotte Clapp

PROJECT EDITOR
Sheila D. Schroeder

COPY EDITOR
Geneil Breeze
Chuck Hutchinson

INDEXER
Erika Millen

PROOFREADER
Kellie Suesz

TECHNICAL EDITOR
Chris Fierros

TEAM COORDINATOR
Cindy Teeters

MULTIMEDIA DEVELOPER
Dan Scherf

INTERIOR DESIGNER
Gary Adair

COVER DESIGNER
Gary Adair

Contents at a Glance

Appendixes

Contents

About the Author

Susan Visser has worked on the DB2 product for more than 12 years. First as a technical writer creating product documentation, then as a service consultant answering customer questions on the phone, and finally as the leader of the DB2 certification program creating certification exams to validate DB2 product skills. Five years ago, Susan wrote and published the first edition of *Sams Teach Yourself DB2 Universal Database in 21 Days*. Since then she has helped other authors write and publish their books. In many cases, she has reviewed their books and provided guidance as to the style and topics to cover.

As part of her job as certification lead, Susan speaks to many people who are trying to learn DB2 either for the first time or for a new release. She has gathered ideas from them to learn how people like to learn and the books they like to learn from. She also helps people get the skills they need to pass the certification exams and understand what is necessary both in terms of content and the different styles of learning.

Bill Wong has spent the last 18 years working in various positions within IBM. Bill has worked with the DB2 product since its inception, working as a systems programmer, DBA, product planner, and as a technical sales specialist.

Bill has also spent time teaching courses on database technology, strategic I/T planning, systems analysis and design, and decision theory. He is the author of many articles on DB2 technology and speaks frequently at technical conferences and customer sites around the world.

Bill is currently the Program Director for Information Grid Solutions, and is responsible for helping customers understand IBM's latest directions in Grid computing, and how DB2 might fit into that environment.

Acknowledgments

Thanks to the many people who helped make this book a reality. Special thanks to Loretta Yates, Sean Dixon, Sheila Schroeder, Geneil Breeze, Dan Scherf, and Michael Stephens at Sams Publishing for helping with the update of this book.

Thanks to management and colleagues: Judith Escott, Melissa Montoya, and John Botsford. Thanks to the following individuals who assisted with technical reviews: Chris Fierros (President, Ten digit Consulting, Inc.), Bob Harbus, Dale Hagen, and Frank Fillmore (President, The Fillmore Group). Thanks also to everyone else we deal with on a regular basis who may have helped without even knowing that they helped.

The authors would also like to make the following acknowledgements to their families:

Susan Visser

Thanks to my husband Karl for helping me test the information and the samples and for looking after all the things I ignored. Thanks to my son Kevin for waiting patiently while I finished yet another chapter and for cheering me on as I made progress.

Bill Wong

I would like to thank my wife, Shirley, for having the patience and tolerance that allowed me to write two books this year. Thanks to my daughter and son, Dana and Austin, for telling me to complete my writing tasks each day, so that we could spend time playing together.

We Want to Hear from You!

As the reader of this book, *you* are our most important critic and commentator. We value your opinion and want to know what we're doing right, what we could do better, what areas you'd like to see us publish in, and any other words of wisdom you're willing to pass our way.

As an associate publisher for Sams Publishing, I welcome your comments. You can email or write me directly to let me know what you did or didn't like about this book—as well as what we can do to make our books better.

Please note that I cannot help you with technical problems related to the topic of this book. We do have a User Services group, however, where I will forward specific technical questions related to the book.

When you write, please be sure to include this book's title and author as well as your name, email address, and phone number. I will carefully review your comments and share them with the author and editors who worked on the book.

Email: feedback@samspublishing.com

Mail: Michael Stephens
          Associate Publisher
          Sams Publishing
          800 East 96th Street
          Indianapolis, IN 46240 USA

For more information about this book or another Sams Publishing title, visit our Web site at www.samspublishing.com. Type the ISBN (excluding hyphens) or the title of a book in the Search field to find the page you're looking for.

Introduction

Welcome to *Sams Teach Yourself DB2 Universal Database in 21 Days*! This book provides a practical, hands-on approach to learning how to use DB2 Universal Database quickly. DB2 Universal Database is a powerful relational database that can help you and your business become more successful. This book shows you how to exploit DB2 features to create world-class applications that can put your business ahead of your competition. You also learn how to use the tools provided with DB2 Universal Database to simplify the task of administering your database.

In addition to the 21 lessons there are two appendixes: one that gives you hints on getting certified on DB2 and one that provides answers to the quiz questions.

Scenarios and step-by-step examples are provided to help you build your skill in an easy-to-understand manner. The book focuses on the most commonly used tasks so that you can get started using DB2 immediately. You are taught how to use the DB2 graphical interfaces and wizards on the Windows platform.

This is the perfect book for you if you are learning about databases for the first time or if you are changing careers from another database product or platform.

The focus is on using the administration tools provided with the product. During a three-week period, you will be exposed to many aspects of database administration, through a scenario presented in the book to create a library database to store your CD collection. All steps required to create your CD library are provided, including

- Installing, configuring, and setting up DB2
- Designing a database, including normalizing data and choosing a primary key
- Using wizards to create the database, tables, and relationships between the tables
- Adding data to the tables using SQL or by loading or importing from other sources
- Accessing your data using SQL, Java, or your own applications
- Setting up security to protect your data
- Automating tasks such as creating monthly reports
- Scheduling tasks to run at specified times
- Backing up and restoring data
- Exporting data to other sources such as spreadsheets
- Replicating data to other databases
- Tuning performance parameters
- Solving problems

You are encouraged to perform the tasks as they are introduced and described in each lesson. After you have finished a lesson, you can make sure that you have retained the knowledge by answering the quiz questions at the end.

After reading this book, you will have the fundamental knowledge required to use the common features of DB2. You will also have all the information needed to be able to pass the entry-level DB2 Certification Exam (Exam 700). After you have mastered the tasks in this book, you will find it easy to move to more complicated tasks and books provided in the IBM Press series.

Assumptions

You'll get the most out of this book if you have the following level of experience:

- Some knowledge of the Windows environment
- Previous experience with relational database

This book steps you through installing the DB2 Universal Database Version 8 product provided on the CD-ROM included with the book. The DB2 Workgroup Server Edition is included on the CD-ROM. This edition enables you to use the product on a trial basis and allows you to connect clients to access the database on your server.

How to Use This Book

This book has been designed as a three-week teach-yourself course, complete with quizzes, exercises, and examples that you can try on your own. It's expected that you complete a lesson a day for a period of 21 days. Of course, you should work at your own pace, so if you can complete more than one lesson in a day, this is fine. Also if you think you need more time to complete a lesson, take all the time that you need.

Each week begins with a Week at a Glance section that briefly describes the tasks you will learn in the coming week. Each lesson ends with a question-and-answer section related to the day's lesson. There is also a quiz at the end of the day to test your grasp of the day's concepts and skills. We urge you to complete these sections to reinforce your new knowledge. If you can answer the questions without looking up the answers, you can be sure that you've learned the concepts rather than memorized them. Also at the end of each lesson is an exercise. The exercise is intended to give you an opportunity to build on the concepts learned in the lesson. For example, the lesson that discusses database design teaches you how to create a database to store information about a CD collection. The exercise at the end of the lesson challenges you to go use the steps presented in the lesson to design a database on your own.

Conventions Used in This Book

Menu names are separated from menu options by a vertical bar (|). For example, File|Open means that you should choose Open from the File menu.

- Input and Output—All code and other elements that you type in (input) and results of any input that you type in (output) appear in monospace. Commands and other code that you don't necessarily type in also appear in monospace.

- Note—Notes present tangential information that can help you understand the concepts and techniques.

- Tip—Tips are little pieces of information to begin to help you in real-world situations. They often offer shortcuts or information that makes a task easier or faster.

- Caution—Pay careful attention to Cautions. They provide information about detrimental performance issues or dangerous errors.

About the CD-ROM

As mentioned earlier, the CD-ROM that accompanies this book includes a try-and-buy version of DB2 Universal Database Workgroup Server Edition Version 8. You have 180 days to use this version of DB2 to gain critical hands-on knowledge of the product.

The CD-ROM also includes the sample data used in the examples in the book.

Preface

An ongoing challenge for today's computer professionals is reserving the time to develop new skills to keep up with changes in technology. It is, however, an imperative that we do so, because it is the very essence of our competitive edge as technical professionals. Our value to our customers, partners and teammates increases as we learn and develop new skills with industry-leading products. One of the most technologically advanced products in the industry is DB2 Universal Database, which is also the market leader on popular environments such as Linux, UNIX, and Windows.

More than 20 years ago, relational database technology was first invented at IBM Research, which resulted in the delivery of the first commercially available databases in the early 1980s. This invention created a powerful confluence of being able to represent data in a simple, efficient tabular form, access it through the very powerful SQL query language and make it readily available to the business community in a high availability environment. All this has helped power business applications to a whole new level. Today, tens of thousands of business all over the world rely on DB2 databases to store their key corporate data assets and run their businesses both traditionally and over the Web.

DB2 Universal Database provides virtually unlimited scalability, industry-leading performance, reliability, and availability whether you deploy on Windows, Linux, or Unix. DB2 continues to lead the industry by introducing innovations such as SMART technology (Self-Managing and Resource Tuning) that enables the database to manage itself! Several built-in wizards and advisors make DBAs more productive and allow our customers without a DBA staff to manage their database environments effectively with a minimum of effort.

This book guides the user to the many powerful features of DB2 in a user-friendly manner; many examples are illustrated using a graphical user interface. Also, should you decide to obtain a DB2 certification, this book will also address those needs. This book is an excellent way to be introduced to DB2 and develop new skills. I hope you use this book to its fullest potential and enjoy the benefits of being a DB2 professional.

Bob Picciano
Director of Database Technology
IBM Toronto Software Laboratory

WEEK 1

At a Glance

During Week 1, you learn many of the concepts of DB2 Universal Database. Later in the week, you learn how to install a server and a client and how to set up the communications between the two separate machines. The last lesson of the week teaches you to set up your system to be secure. Here's a day-by-day summary of Week 1:

- Day 1, "What DB2 Can Do for You"

    This lesson focuses on the many products that make up DB2 Universal Database version 8. The concepts of server and client are defined, and the role of the administration tools is discussed. You also learn how you can use the Internet, ODBC, or Java applications to access data in DB2 databases.

- Day 2, "Exploring the Capabilities of DB2 Universal Database"

    This lesson introduces the many concepts of a relational database and the way these concepts relate to DB2 Universal Database.

- Day 3, "Installing and Configuring DB2 Server"

    During this lesson, you install and configure the DB2 Universal Database Workgroup Server Edition product on a Windows system. This product acts as a server.

- Day 4, "Getting Started"

    After you install the product, you can use the instructions in this lesson to learn how to log on, work with passwords, start or stop DB2, and understand the objects that DB2 has added to your desktop.

1

2

3

4

5

6

7

- Day 5, "Setting Up DB2 Instances and Server Communications"

  This lesson discusses how you can use DB2's administration tools to set up or modify DB2 instances and the communications protocols that are used for client/server communications.

- Day 6, "Installing and Configuring DB2 Clients"

  After you install and configure your DB2 server, you can use the instructions in this lesson to install and set up a client workstation on Windows.

- Day 7, "Ensuring Data Security"

  During this lesson, you learn the ways you can guard your data against unauthorized use.

DAY 1

What DB2 Can Do for You

Today you will learn about the various DB2 products available and which one is right for you. You will learn the basic features available in the products and how these features can help you organize your data.

Today you learn the following:

- How to distinguish between the many editions of DB2
- How DB2 works with data
- How to administer DB2 databases using graphical tools
- How to access data stored in mainframe databases
- How to create applications that access DB2 data
- How Internet applications access DB2 data
- How extremely large amounts of data can be organized
- How DB2 enterprise host servers fit in with the DB2 family

In business environments today, the demand for information access is increasing while the volume and complexity of data and the variety of applications using data grow rapidly. Users once satisfied with simple rows and columns of data now require the ability to work with complex data such as images, video, formatted text, and other rich media formats. Simple transactions have grown into real-time decision making, data warehousing, and content management.

More and more, critical business applications are being moved to LANs because of the advances in hardware capacity, software function, and performance. Data may now be located across the office, across the country, or around the world. Decisions must be made on where best to store data, how to access it quickly, and how to set up production databases and applications on various platforms so that they can best interact.

This book focuses on setting up and using a DB2 server on a Microsoft Windows Server and a DB2 client on a Microsoft Windows Workstation. DB2 Universal Database (DB2 UDB) is a powerful Web-enabled relational database management system that helps you manage your data in complex and rapidly changing environments. This relational database management system (RDBMS) allows users to create, update, and control relational databases by using Structured Query Language (SQL).

Designed to meet the information needs of small and large businesses alike, DB2 is available on various platforms, including large systems such as zSeries; mid-sized systems such as iSeries, Linux, and Unix; and single or LAN-based systems such as Windows and Linux. Data managed by DB2 database servers can be accessed and manipulated by applications on PC workstations running Windows or Linux, and by applications developed for Unix workstations from IBM, HP, or SUN.

What Is DB2 Universal Database?

DB2 Universal Database is a Web-enabled relational database management system that supports data warehousing and transaction processing. It can be scaled from hand-held computers to single processors to clusters of computers and is multimedia-capable with image, audio, video, and text support.

DB2 is optimized for each platform to maximize performance. Internally, the DB2 products that run on the mainframe platforms (MVS, z/OS, iSeries, and so on) differ from the products that run on distributed platforms (Linux, Unix, and Windows). The DB2 products for the distributed platforms share the same source code.

DB2's Various Flavors

DB2 comes in the following editions: DB2 Express, DB2 Workgroup Server Edition, DB2 Enterprise Server Edition, and DB2 Personal Edition. All four editions provide the same full-function database management system, but they differ from each other in terms of connectivity options, licensing agreements, and additional function.

NOTE   DB2 Workgroup Server Edition and DB2 Enterprise Server Edition are commonly referred to as *DB2 servers* throughout this book.

To access data stored on mainframe computers, DB2 Connect is available in the following editions: DB2 Connect Enterprise Edition and DB2 Connect Personal Edition. For developers, the following editions are available: DB2 Universal Developer's Edition and DB2 Personal Developer's Edition. The products include DB2 plus a wide range of development tools.

DB2 Workgroup Server Edition

DB2 Workgroup Server Edition is licensed on a per-user basis. It's available for the AIX, HP-UX, Linux, Solaris, Windows Server 2003, Windows 2000, Windows XP, and Windows NT platforms.

The DB2 Workgroup Server Edition is ideal for smaller departmental applications or for applications that do not need access to remote databases on iSeries or zSeries.

DB2 Enterprise Server Edition

DB2 Enterprise Server Edition includes all the features provided in the DB2 Workgroup Server Edition, plus support for host connectivity, providing users with access to DB2 databases residing on iSeries or zSeries platforms. DB2 Enterprise Server Edition is available for the AIX, HP-UX, Linux, Solaris, and Windows platforms.

For very large databases, complex workloads, or increased parallelism, the DB2 Database Partitioning Feature (DPF) is available for the DB2 UDB Enterprise Server Edition. The DPF is ideal to handle the large amounts of data required for biotechnology and mapping genetic codes. This feature allows databases to be partitioned across multiple independent computers of a common platform. To end users and application developers, it still appears as a single database on a single computer.

DB2 Express Edition

DB2 Express Edition is the same full-function DB2 database as DB2 Workgroup Server Edition, but new features make it easy to transparently install within an application. DB2 Express Edition is available for the Linux and Windows platforms.

DB2 Personal Edition

DB2 UDB Personal Edition allows you to create and use local databases and access remote databases if they're available. DB2 Personal Edition is available for the Linux and Windows platforms.

DB2 Personal Developer's Edition

DB2 Personal Developer's Edition includes DB2 Universal Database Personal Edition, DB2 Connect Personal Edition, and DB2 Software Developer's Kits for Windows platforms.

The DB2 Personal Developer's Edition allows a developer to design and build single-user desktop applications. It provides all the tools needed to create multimedia database applications that can run on Linux and Windows platforms and can connect to any DB2 server. The kit includes Windows and Linux versions of DB2 Personal Edition plus all the DB2 Extenders.

DB2 Universal Developer's Edition

DB2 Universal Developer's Edition includes the full suite of DB2 products, including all DB2 server editions, DB2 Connect, the DB2 Extenders, Warehouse Manager, and Intelligent Miner, and application development tools for all supported platforms.

This kit gives you all the tools you need to create multimedia database applications that can run on any of the DB2 client or server platforms and can connect to any DB2 server. It includes the following complementary products: DB2 Everyplace Software Development Kit, WebSphere Application Server, WebSphere Studio Site Developer Advanced, WebSphere MQ and QMF for Windows.

DB2 Connect Enterprise Edition

DB2 Connect Enterprise Edition provides access from network clients to DB2 databases residing on iSeries or zSeries host systems. DB2 Connect Enterprise Edition is available for AIX, HP-UX, Solaris, Linux, and Windows platforms.

DB2 Connect Personal Edition

DB2 Connect Personal Edition provides access from a desktop computer to DB2 databases residing on iSeries or zSeries host systems. DB2 Connect Personal Edition is available for the Linux and Windows platforms.

DB2's Architecture

All members of the DB2 family have the same basic architecture as the original mainframe version and use many of the same key algorithms. It's important to understand, however, that these later products aren't just a port from the mainframe to other operating systems: Their internal components have been optimized to exploit each platform's specific features.

DB2 is an open system. In addition to client platforms provided by IBM, all DB2 database servers allow for open access from any product that supports the *Distributed*

Relational Database Architecture (DRDA). DRDA is a standard that allows applications to establish fast and transparent access to the tremendous amount of data stored in relational databases on mainframe computers. This support eliminates the need for expensive add-on components and gateways. IBM also offers a facility to access any other RDBMS that implements the DRDA application server specification. This support is offered by a companion product known as *DB2 Connect*.

In addition to its data management functions, DB2 includes tools that let you create customized applications for accessing and working with data. Support is available for the development of multimedia, object-oriented, Internet, and ODBC applications.

DB2 and Its Companion Products

If your organization has data spread across multiple databases, remote relational access can represent an important advantage in the way data can be designed, managed, and used. DB2 makes it possible for organizations to distribute and access data across a network of systems.

Users can query, add, delete, or update data in remote databases, letting you focus on the design of your database and the problems to be solved rather than on the complexities of gaining access to the data. Data is requested at one location and provided by another. The database serving the request maintains authorizations for remote requests in the same way as for local requests.

To understand how data is distributed, you must understand the components that make up such an environment. The key components include a *database server* and one or more *database clients*. The server controls one or more databases and handles requests from clients that want to access those databases. Each component is described in the following sections.

The DB2 Server

DB2 Universal Database is available in the following editions: Personal Edition, Express Edition, Workgroup Server Edition, and Enterprise Server Edition. The database engine in each version is identical. The engine is a full-function, robust database management system that includes optimized SQL support based on actual database usage and tools to help manage the data. The difference between these products is the capability to support remote clients, the licensing considerations, and the number of database partitions supported.

The Personal Edition can be accessed only from local applications; it does not support access from remote clients over a network. The Personal Edition supports any local applications that run on the same computer where the database resides. Figure 1.1 shows an example of a DB2 Personal Edition setup, with several local applications.

FIGURE 1.1

*A sample setup of
IBM's DB2 Personal
Edition.*

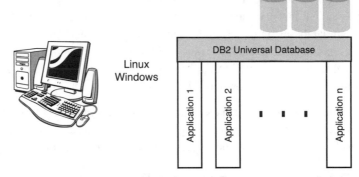

The Personal Edition includes the database engine plus the Administration Client that
provides the tools for administrative tasks such as configuring the system, replicating
data, tuning performance, backing up and recovering the system, and managing media
and the DB2 Run-Time Client component for access to remote servers. This environment
is ideal if you want a simple standalone system or if you perform database administration
tasks and need to have local databases to prototype applications. If you want to use an
application development environment, you should consider the DB2 Developer's
Editions.

The Express, Workgroup Server, and Enterprise Server Editions include functions that
allow DB2 to be accessed by local and remote clients. Remote clients must have the DB2
Run-Time Client component installed to access a database server. The Express,
Workgroup Server, and Enterprise Server Editions also include the database engine and
the Administration Client that provides tools for performing administrative tasks, as well
as the DB2 Run-Time Client component for access to remote database servers.

In addition to accepting requests from remote clients, the Enterprise Server Edition has
the DRDA Application Server feature built in. It accepts requests from z/OS, OS/400,
VM, and other DRDA clients.

The DB2 Database Partitioning Feature provides the capability of partitioning the database across multiple, independent computers by a LAN. It is available to use with DB2
Enterprise Server Edition, can handle extremely large databases, and can improve performance by adding more processing power to a given database operation.

The DB2 Database Partitioning Feature exploits large-scale SMP and multinode
(MPP/Cluster) configurations. Figure 1.2 shows an example of a possible configuration.

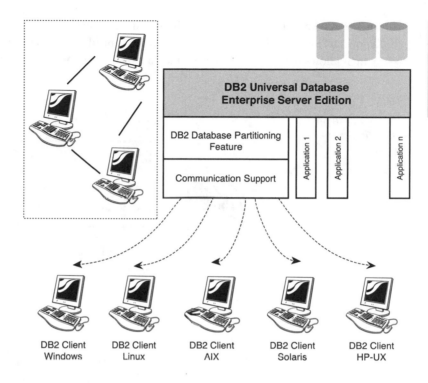

FIGURE 1.2

The DB2 Enterprise Server Edition with DB2 Database Partitioning Feature environment, with remote client support.

The DB2 Clients

The DB2 server can run applications locally and can be accessed by applications running on remote systems with the DB2 client installed. There are three types of DB2 clients:

- DB2 Run-Time Client
- DB2 Administration Client
- DB2 Application Development Client

DB2 clients are available for the following operating systems:

- Windows
- Linux
- Unix (AIX, HP-UX, and Solaris)

DB2 clients provide communication support plus support for application interfaces such as JDBC, SQLJ, ODBC, CLI, and OLE DB. They must be installed on each client that will connect to the server.

Figure 1.3 shows a DB2 server with local applications and applications running on remote clients. DB2 Workgroup Server Edition or Enterprise Server Edition is installed on the server and contains your databases. Any applications running on the server are known as *local applications*. The client systems need one of the DB2 clients installed, which allows applications to access the data on the remote server system.

FIGURE 1.3

*DB2 with local appli-
cations and remote
clients.*

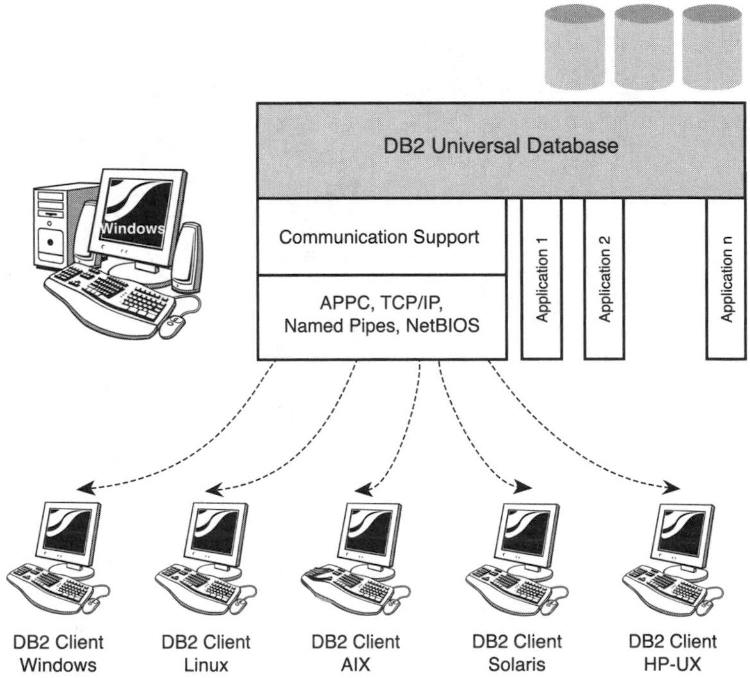

A DB2 client is built into each DB2 Universal Database product. A workstation with DB2 client installed can access any DB2 server with any of a number of supported communication protocols. For example, DB2 client for Windows supports the APPC, Named Pipes, NetBIOS, and TCP/IP protocols. (The same protocols are supported on DB2 for Windows servers.) This heterogeneous support protects your existing investment in client workstations and allows you to select a server machine that's most appropriate for your database environment.

The DB2 Run-Time Client provides a runtime environment that allows client applications to access one or more DB2 servers or DB2 Connect servers. This client requires the least amount of disk space.

A DB2 client provides the capability for workstations to access and administer DB2 databases. The DB2 Administration Client has all the features of the DB2 Run-Time Client and also includes all the DB2 administration tools. These tools are described later in the section "DB2 Tools for Administering Databases."

The DB2 Application Development Client is a collection of graphical and non-graphical tools and components designed to meet the needs of database application developers. It includes libraries, header files, documented APIs, and sample programs to build character-based, multimedia, and object-oriented applications. The DB2 Application Development Client also includes the Development Center and all the tools provided as part of the DB2 Administration Client product.

Understanding How DB2 Universal Database Works with Data

As well as providing a relational database to store your data, DB2 lets you administer requests to query, update, insert, or delete data from local or remote client applications.

DB2 includes the DB2 Administration Client that provides graphical tools for you to tune performance, access remote DB2 servers, manage all servers from a single site, develop powerful applications, and process SQL queries. These tools are described later in the section "DB2 Tools for Administering Databases."

When a network is operational and protocols are functional on the workstations, LAN-to-LAN connections between DB2 servers and clients require no additional software. For example, Figure 1.4 shows a DB2 server on a Windows workstation connected to a LAN in Montreal, and another DB2 server on a Linux workstation connected to a LAN located in Toronto. As long as a connection exists between the two LANs, clients on either network can access either server.

Within a single transaction, databases on both servers are accessed and updated, and the integrity of the data on both servers is maintained. This is commonly known as a *two-phase commit* or *distributed-unit-of-work access*. Transferring money from one bank account to another is a classic example of when two-phase commit is important. It is critical that both the debit from one account and the credit to the second account be completed as a single transaction.

DB2 Tools for Administering Databases

You can perform database administration tasks locally or remotely with the DB2 Administration Tools provided with the DB2 Administration Client. The General Administration Tools folder contains the Control Center, Journal, Replication Center, and Task Center to help you administer DB2 servers. These tools are described later in the section "Managing Databases with the Control Center."

FIGURE 1.4

Accessing data on multiple servers.

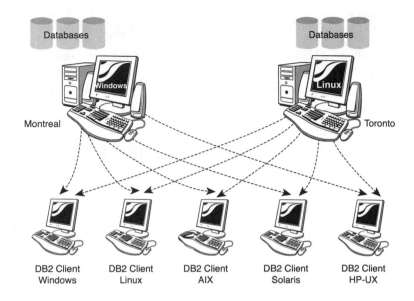

If you want to have a dedicated database administrator (DBA) system, which allows you to administer remote DB2 databases, you can use the DB2 Administration Client or the DB2 Personal Edition.

Managing Databases with the Control Center

The Control Center displays database objects (such as databases, tables, and packages) and their relationships to each other. It contains tools for performing common database administration tasks. With the Control Center, you can manage a local database server or multiple remote database servers (including databases in a partitioned environment) and the database objects within them, all from a single point of control. It provides seamless integration of the DB2 Administration Tools, gives you a clear view of all managed systems, lets you manage databases remotely, and provides step-by-step assistance for some tasks. Figure 1.5 shows the main Control Center window.

From the Control Center, you can perform the following tasks on database objects:

- Create and drop a database.
- Create, alter, and drop a table space or table.
- Create, alter, and drop an index.
- Back up and recover a database or table space.
- Define the replication sources and subscriptions to replicate data between systems.

FIGURE 1.5

The Control Center's main window.

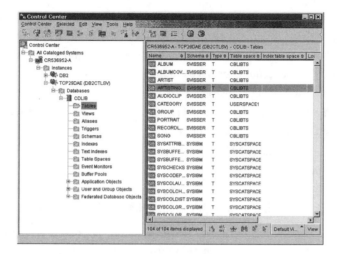

You can also manage database manager environments (known as *DB2 instances*) as follows:

- Maintain the communications protocols.
- Set database manager configuration values that affect performance.

Wizards are provided to help you perform complex tasks. For example, a wizard is available to load large amounts of data into your database. See Day 9, "Creating Databases and Tables," for instructions on using the Create Database Wizard.

The Control Center provides additional facilities to help you manage your DB2 servers. You can run these facilities from the Control Center toolbar or from IBM DB2 folders:

- The *Replication Center*, to create replication definitions and manage Capture, Apply, and Monitor programs to propagate data among database servers on the network.
- The *Information Catalog Center*, to find and access business information quickly and easily.
- The *Satellite Administration Center*, to set up and maintain satellites, groups, and the batches that the satellites execute when they synchronize.
- The *Data Warehouse Center*, to design, build, maintain, govern, and access DB2 data warehouses.
- The *Command Center*, to execute DB2 commands and SQL statements.
- The *Task Center*, to create mini-applications known as *scripts*, which you can store and schedule to run later.

- The *Health Center*, to identify, analyze, and improve key performance and resource problems.
- The *Journal*, to view all available information about tasks that are pending execution, are executing, or have completed execution; the recovery history log; the alerts log; and the messages log.
- The *License Center*, to display license status and usage information for DB2 products installed on your system.
- The *Development Center*, to create stored procedures, user-defined functions, and structured types.
- The *Tools Setting*, to change the settings for the Administration tools, replication tasks, Health Center notification, and default scheduling scheme.

The DB2 Administration Server (DAS) is a control point used to assist with tasks on DB2 servers. The DAS is required to use any of the administration tools described earlier.

Managing Communications on the Server

The Control Center's Setup Communications option allows you to view, update, and reset the server protocol settings. This tool helps database administrators do the following:

- Configure database manager communications parameters for a new instance or maintain the communication configuration of an existing instance. Many required steps are automated. You simply need to select the communication protocols you want supported on the server instance.
- Generate database information in a profile that can be used to configure clients.

Managing Connections to Databases with the Configuration Assistant

The Configuration Assistant helps you manage your database connections to remote database servers. It leads you through the necessary steps to configure and manage DB2 clients, while at the same time hides many of the steps required by automating them. With the Configuration Assistant, you can do the following:

- Use the Add Database Wizard to define local and remote databases that you can access from your system. The wizard catalogs nodes and databases while shielding you from the complexities of the tasks.

1

- Use the Change Database Wizard to change the database directory information associated with the local and remote databases that you can access from your system.
- Remove local and remote databases that you no longer need to access from your system.
- Bind applications to a database by selecting utilities or bind files from a list.
- Test connections to local or remote databases identified on your system to ensure that you can connect to the server you need.
- Change connection passwords for a database.
- Configure the settings for your DB2 databases that will be accessed by DB2 CLI applications. You can also connect to a data source to retrieve information about it.
- Tune the DBM configuration parameters on your system. Parameters are logically grouped, and hints are provided on the interface as parameters are selected.
- View and set the DB2 Registry values that set up your operating environment.
- Configure another local or remote instance.
- Reset the configuration associated with an instance.
- Import or export profiles allowing you to duplicate the environment. Profiles can include environment information such as database connections, communication settings, configuration parameters, and registry values.
- Add, change, or remove systems and instances that you can access remotely.
- Set up a connection to a DRDA server if DB2 Connect is installed.

Accessing Host Data from the Desktop

DB2 Connect provides connectivity to data stored in mainframe databases. It provides applications with transparent access to host data through a standard architecture for managing distributed data. This standard, known as Distributed Relational Database Architecture (DRDA), allows your applications to establish a fast connection to databases on iSeries or zSeries hosts.

DB2 manages a great deal of the data in large organizations on systems such as iSeries, OS/390, z/OS, VSE, and VM. Applications that run on any of the supported platforms can work with this data transparently, as if a local database server managed it.

DB2 Connect enables applications to create, update, control, and manage DB2 databases and host systems using SQL, DB2 Administrative APIs, ODBC, JDBC, SQLJ, or DB2 CLI. In addition, DB2 Connect supports Microsoft Windows data interfaces such as ActiveX Data Objects (ADO), Remote Data Objects (RDO), and Object Linking and Embedding (OLE) DB.

DB2 Connect comes in two versions: *DB2 Connect Personal Edition* and *DB2 Connect Enterprise Edition*. With DB2 Connect Personal Edition, local clients can directly access host and iSeries database servers. Figure 1.6 shows an example of the DB2 Connect Personal Edition.

Figure 1.6

A sample DB2 Connect Personal Edition setup.

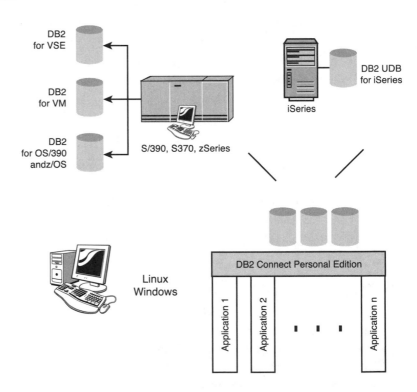

DB2 Connect Enterprise Edition allows multiple clients to connect to host data and can significantly reduce the effort required to establish and maintain access to enterprise data. Figure 1.7 shows an example of clients connecting to host and iSeries databases through DB2 Connect Enterprise Edition.

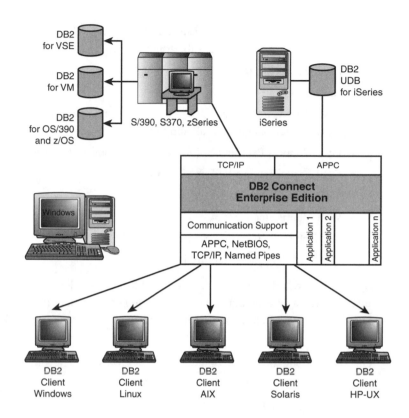

FIGURE 1.7

A sample DB2 Connect Enterprise Edition setup.

1

Developing Applications with the DB2 Developer's Editions

The DB2 Developer's Editions give you all the tools you need to create database applications that run on various platforms and connect to any DB2 database. There are two types of DB2 Developer's Editions:

- DB2 Personal Developer's Edition
- DB2 Universal Developer's Edition

The DB2 Personal Developer's Edition runs on the Linux and Windows platforms and includes the following products:

- DB2 servers and clients for Linux and Windows platforms
- DB2 Connect Personal Edition
- DB2 Extenders and DB2 XML Extender for Windows
- Visual Studio for Java, Entry Edition

The DB2 Universal Developer's Edition runs on AIX, HP-UX, Solaris, Linux, and Windows platforms and includes the following products:

- DB2 Personal Edition, DB2 Workgroup Server Edition, and DB2 Enterprise Server Edition for all supported platforms
- DB2 Run-Time Clients, DB2 Administration Clients, and DB2 Application Development Clients for all supported platforms
- DB2 Connect Personal Edition and DB2 Connect Enterprise Edition
- DB2 Extenders and DB2 XML Extender
- Visual Studio for Java, Entry Edition
- WebSphere Studio
- WebSphere Application Server, Standard Edition
- Query Management Facility (try and buy)

Applications developed with the DB2 Application Development Client can be ported to any platform where the equivalent DB2 Run-Time Client component is installed. Through the DB2 Run-Time Client, these applications can access all DB2 servers and, by using DB2 Connect, can also access other database servers that support DRDA.

The DB2 Application Development Client allows you to develop applications that use the following interfaces:

- Embedded SQL
- Call Level Interface (CLI) development environment (compatible with ODBC from Microsoft)
- Java Database Connectivity (JDBC)
- DB2 application programming interfaces to access database utilities

DB2 Application Development Client supports several programming languages (including COBOL, C, and C++) for application development and provides precompilers for the supported languages.

The Development Center allows you to develop stored procedures and user-defined functions. You can also map structured types from Enterprise JavaBeans. Wizards are available to simplify most development tasks.

Features include

- Support for multiple projects and database connections
- The Server view for seeing the development objects on the server

- SQL debugger for debugging routines; includes views for breakpoints, variables, and call stack
- Wizards for building user-defined functions for WebSphere MQSeries, OLE DB data sources, and XML documents
- Wizards for exporting, importing, and deploying routines and project information

Accessing DB2 Data from the Web

The popularity of the Internet and the World Wide Web has created a demand for Web access to enterprise data. For example, large retailers are using the Internet to create online stores where customers can access enterprise data to browse catalogs of products, compare prices, and place orders. Java Database Connectivity (JDBC) is provided with DB2 to allow you to create Web-based applications that access data in DB2 databases.

Using technology similar to that found in the Development Center, WebSphere Studio Application Developer also provides plug-ins for the stored procedure builder and user-defined function builder. If you work with WebSphere to develop applications, you can access many of the same features of the Development Center and take advantage of the WebSphere suite of products with the power of DB2.

XML Extenders support Web services with the Web services Object Runtime Framework (WORF), a set of tools for implementing Web services with DB2. The XML Extender also supports WebSphere MQSeries so that you can send XML documents to, or retrieve documents from, WebSphere MQSeries message queues.

Web services enable the development and deployment of loosely coupled applications within a company or across industries. You can create a Web service that allows people and applications to find and use the service over the Web. DB2 can be accessed as a Web service provider and is usually paired with IBM WebSphere family products to provide a complete services framework.

Using Java Database Connectivity

Use JDBC to create applications or applets that access data in DB2 databases. You can run JDBC applications from any system that has the DB2 Run-Time Client software installed; a Web browser and a Web server aren't required.

You can run JDBC applets inside HTML Web pages on any system with a Java-enabled browser, regardless of your client's platform. No additional software is required on your client system beyond this browser. The processing of JDBC applets is shared between the client and the server.

The JDBC server and the DB2 Run-Time Client must reside on the same machine as the Web server. The JDBC server calls in to the DB2 Run-Time Client to connect to local or remote databases, or into z/OS to connect to host databases. When a connection to a DB2 database is requested by the applet, the JDBC client opens a TCP/IP socket to the JDBC server on the machine where the Web server is running. Figure 1.8 shows an example of Java-enabled browsers remotely accessing data from DB2 databases.

FIGURE 1.8

Using JDBC to access Internet data stored on DB2.

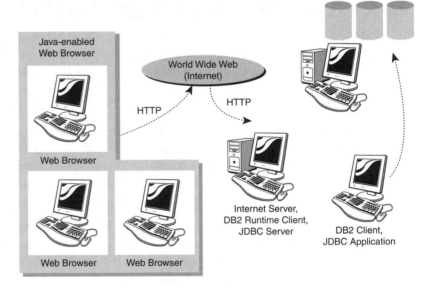

Using DB2 Parallelism

DB2 extends the database manager to the parallel, multinode environment. A *database partition* is part of a database that consists of its own data, indexes, configuration files, and transaction logs. A database partition is sometimes called a *node* or *database node*.

Because data is divided across database partitions, you can use the power of multiple processors on multiple physical database partition servers to satisfy requests for information. Data retrieval and update requests are decomposed automatically into subrequests and executed in parallel among the applicable database partitions. That databases are split across database partitions is transparent to users of SQL.

DB2 offers several parallel features to enhance the performance and efficiency of your databases. By using DB2 UDB Enterprise Server Edition and the DB2 Database Partitioning Feature, you can partition a database across multiple, independent computers connected by a LAN. This way, an application can use a database that's simply too large for a single computer to handle efficiently.

1

By using DB2 in a symmetric multiprocessor (SMP) environment, you can speed up the execution of a single SQL query by exploiting multiple processors, disks, and memory. This way, workload can be divided more evenly among processors, thereby achieving better scalability. This is possible because all processors have the choice to work on all data, which is analogous to a single queue serviced by multiple bank tellers.

Overview of the DB2 Enterprise Host Servers

This section presents a brief overview of the enterprise server members of the DB2 family: DB2 Universal Database for z/OS and OS/390, DB2 Universal Database for iSeries, and DB2 Server for VSE & VM. All DB2 Run-Time Clients described in this book provide access to these products with the help of DB2 Connect. DB2 Connect extends DB2 Call Level Interface, ODBC, and JDBC support to all DB2 platforms. These products are covered in the following three sections.

NOTE   Much of the discussion of the DB2 Universal Database products applies to DB2 host products as well, but not all. For more specific information about each product, refer to the product documentation.

DB2 Universal Database for z/OS and OS/390

Since its introduction, DB2 for z/OS and OS/390 (initially known simply as *DB2* before DB2 was available on other platforms) has been the database of choice for large companies and organizations. DB2 for OS/390 specializes in providing high-performance service for large-scale online transaction processing systems, complex decision support systems, data warehousing, and business intelligence needs. DB2 for z/OS and OS/390 also gives you support for client/server processing, stored procedures, object-oriented programming, and support for large objects. Highlights of DB2 for z/OS and OS/390 are as follows:

- It can manage terabytes of data on behalf of thousands of users.
- It enables data sharing, which makes it possible for a group of DB2 subsystems to have concurrent access to the same data without replication and keeps data available during outages.
- It extends network support to include native TCP/IP, which allows you to connect various DRDA clients without using an SNA gateway machine.

- It supports Microsoft Windows data interfaces such as ActiveX Data Object (ADO), Remote Data Objects (RDO), and Object Linking and Embedding (OLE) DB to access data through DB2 Connect.
- It can keep data available 24 hours a day, seven days a week. Many activities that would normally require a database manager to stop can be performed without affecting its operation.
- It achieves excellent performance through use of a cost-based optimizer, large buffer pools for efficient I/O processing, parallel query processing, and concurrency when running utilities and SQL applications.
- It uses sophisticated locking and logging methods and flexible authorization techniques to keep your data valid, accurate, and consistent across systems.
- It supports applications written in Java as well as stored procedures developed using Java or the SQL procedure language.

If you have large amounts of enterprise data that must be accessed from all your corporate locations, use DB2 for OS/390 on a System/390.

DB2 Universal Database for iSeries

Formerly known as the AS/400 database manager, DB2 Universal Database for iSeries is a fully-enabled 64-bit relational database that's integrated into the iSeries and AS/400. DB2 UDB is the transaction engine helping power the leading edge performance of the iSeries in Java and data-transaction workloads. This product is compatible with the entire DB2 product line, from DB2 on mainframes to DB2 for Windows. It enables an iSeries host to operate equally well with centralized database applications, or to act as a database server in a heterogeneous client/server network.

Some features of DB2 UDB for iSeries include the following:

- World Wide Web accessibility—With a standard browser and a Web connection, your company and customers can easily tap into your data warehouse.
- Replication—With DataPropagator Capture and Apply, you can define replication solutions that maintain consistent and synchronized information throughout your enterprise, even if the majority of your staff is mobile.
- Parallel database—DB2 symmetric multiprocessing, DB2 multisystem, and parallel I/O are some of the choices available on an iSeries to improve performance of very large databases.
- Standard features—All standard DB2 functions are available, including declarative referential integrity, data replication, advanced SQL optimizer, and Java support.

With state-of-the-art database functions, reliable performance, and conformance to open standards, DB2 UDB for iSeries provides stable and mature support in a client/server environment.

DB2 Server for VSE & VM

Like z/OS and iSeries, the VSE and VM database platforms let you store large amounts of enterprise data. DB2 Server for VSE & VM is easy to use, conforms to standards across multiple platforms, offers flexible application development, and provides excellent performance. It can be used as a server with a number of clients on the workstation platforms.

Some other benefits are that it

- Implements DRDA2 Distributed Unit of Work (DUOW) Application Server support. This way, you can read and update in multiple locations within a single unit of work. Integrity of data is protected with a two-phase commitment.

- Supports DataPropagator Capture. You can track logged activity on specified tables so that the DataPropagator Apply product can distribute those changes across multiple replicas of the tables throughout your enterprise.

- Includes an uncommitted read option that improves productivity for database users. Multiple users can access data in read-only mode, thus improving their access time. All data can be accessed in read-only mode, including data that may have been changed.

- Improves database administration by automating many routine database administration tasks through the IBM SQL Master for VSE and VM program.

- Is shipped with a copy of the DB2 development editions to enable application development on common workstation and Internet platforms.

You can achieve high performance and exploit the ESA technology with support for VM data spaces on the VM/ESA platform and the virtual disk feature on the VSE/ESA platform. For more information on the DB2 Server for VSE & VM product, see the Web site at http://www.software.ibm.com/data/db2/vse-vm.

Summary

Today you saw that DB2 Universal Database is a relational database management system that supports a variety of client and server platforms and communication protocols. DB2 Universal Database is made of several administration tools such as the Control Center and the Command Center, that simplify the task of managing your environment and data.

Data stored in enterprise database management systems such as DB2 UDB for z/OS or OS/390 and DB2 UDB for iSeries can be accessed directly from a DB2 client workstation through the DB2 Connect product.

You can create or use many different types of applications to access DB2 data. You can write your own applications by using languages such as C, C++, or COBOL; create Web-based applications by using Java; or use existing applications such as Microsoft Access.

What Comes Next?

On Day 2, "Exploring the Capabilities of DB2 Universal Database," you learn about the relational concepts that make up DB2 Universal Database.

Q&A

Q On what platforms can I run DB2 Universal Database?

A The server edition of DB2 Universal Database Version 8 runs on AIX, Linux, HP-UX, Solaris, and Windows platforms. The client edition of DB2 runs on the same platforms as the server. The personal edition of DB2 runs on Linux and Windows platforms.

Q What tools are available to help me administer and manage DB2 databases?

A The main tool available with DB2 is the Control Center, from which you can launch the Command Center, Task Center, Journal, Health Center, Tools Setting, Development Center, and Replication Center. Also available is the Configuration Assistant.

Q I need to access data on enterprise systems. What software is required?

A You need one of the DB2 Connect products to access data on enterprise systems including DB2 UDB for z/OS, DB2 UDB for OS/390, DB2 Server for VSE & VM, and DB2 Server for iSeries. You can use the DB2 Connect Personal Edition product to directly access the enterprise data from your workstation. You can use the DB2 Connect Enterprise Edition as a gateway to have many clients in your network access enterprise data.

Q I need to create stored procedures. What tool should I use?

A Use the DB2 Development Center to create stored procedures, user-defined functions, and structured types.

Q I need to create a warehouse to store my data. What tool should I use?

A Use the DB2 Data Warehouse Center to design, build, maintain, govern, and access DB2 data warehouses.

Workshop

The purpose of the Workshop is to allow you to test your knowledge of the material covered in the lesson. See whether you can successfully answer the questions in the quiz before you continue with the next lesson. The answers appear in Appendix B, "Answers to Quiz Questions and Exercises."

Quiz

1. What's a local application? What's a remote application?

2. What are the two ways to use Java Database Connectivity to access DB2 data?

3. What's the name of the DB2 product feature that provides a parallel, partitioned database server environment?

4. Name the interfaces that you can use when creating applications with the DB2 Application Development Client.

5. DB2 Workgroup Server Edition and DB2 Enterprise Server Edition are largely the same, except for two differences. What are the differences? When would you use one edition over the other?

DAY 2

Exploring the Capabilities of DB2 Universal Database

To effectively use DB2, you should have a basic understanding of the features available in this function-rich product. Today you learn the basics elements of DB2, including

- The major components of DB2
- The elements of a relational database
- How DB2 ensures data integrity
- The many types of application programs you can create to access data in DB2
- The power of the many tools and system management facilities available with DB2

Major Components of DB2

The major components of the DB2 Universal Database relational database management system include the database engine and facilities to access data such as the Command Center, Command Line Processor, the Control Center, and application interfaces. A rich suite of tools also is available for the DB2 environment.

The database engine provides the base functions of the DB2 relational database management system. It manages the data, controls all access to it, generates packages, generates optimized paths, provides transaction management, ensures data integrity and data protection, and provides concurrency control. All data access takes place through the SQL interface. The basic elements of a database engine are database objects, system catalogs, directories, and configuration files. These elements are described in the next section.

You can manage the database and access data through several facilities:

- The *Control Center* is the central point of administration for DB2. The Control Center provides a graphical interface to administrative tasks such as recovering a database, defining directories, configuring the system, managing media, and more. See Day 4, "Getting Started," for details.

- The *Command Center* provides a graphical interface to the Command Line Processor, enabling access to data through the use of database commands and interactive SQL. See Day 11, "Accessing the Data," for more information.

- The *Configuration Assistant* automates protocol configuration for clients accessing remote database servers. See Day 6, "Installing and Configuring DB2 Clients," for more information.

- *Wizards* provide step-by-step guidance to functions such as creating a table or tuning performance. See Day 9, "Creating Databases and Tables," for instructions on using the Create Database Wizard. The other wizards are covered throughout this book.

- *Applications* access data by using embedded SQL, the Call Level Interface, Open Database Connectivity (ODBC), Java Database Connectivity (JDBC), or application programming interfaces (APIs). DB2 Universal Database provides many APIs to manipulate the database environment. External tools supported by DB2 Universal Database also use these APIs. These interfaces are described later in the section "Application Programming Interfaces (APIs)."

- *External tools* provide a variety of additional functions. For an example, see Day 11.

The server versions of DB2 contain communication support that allows access and administration from remote workstations in a network environment.

What Is a Relational Database?

A *relational database* presents data as a collection of tables. A *table* is a collection of rows and columns. SQL is used to retrieve or update data by specifying columns, tables, and the various relationships between them.

SQL, or Structured Query Language, is a standardized language for defining and manipulating data in a relational database. SQL statements are executed by DB2, which in general terms is known as a *database manager*.

The following sections describe the basic elements used by DB2 Universal Database to define and manage databases:

Database objects   Directories

Data integrity   Storage objects

Object relational capabilities   Configuration files

System catalog tables   Recovery objects

Instances   Database objects

Figure 2.1 shows the major relational database objects in a DB2 Universal Database server. Examples of objects are databases, table spaces, tables, views, indexes, packages, functions, or data types.

Each database includes a set of *system catalog tables* to describe the logical and physical structure of the data, a *configuration file* to contain the parameter values allocated for the database, and a *recovery log* to log ongoing transactions and archivable transaction logs.

Tables, Columns, and Rows

A *table* consists of data logically arranged in columns and rows. Figure 2.2 shows a simple table with several rows and columns. Data in the table is logically related, with relationships defined between different tables in a database. Data is viewed and manipulated based on mathematical principles and operations called *relational algebra*, and table data is accessed via SQL.

A regular table can contain up to 500 columns, any number of rows, and up to 64GB of data (not including large objects). A *column* is a set of values of the same data type. A *row* consists of a sequence of values, one for each column. The rows aren't necessarily ordered within the table. To order the resultset, you have to explicitly specify ordering in the SQL statement that selects data from the table. At the intersection of every column and row is a specific data item called a *value*.

FIGURE 2.1

Basic elements: relational database objects.

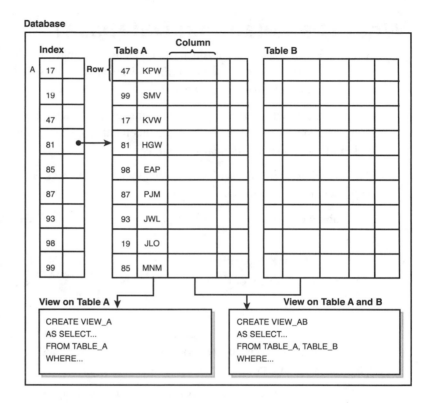

Views

A *view* is the result of a query of one or more tables. A view looks like a real table, but actually it is just a representation of the data from one or more tables. You can think of a view as a logical or virtual table. It only exists as a result of a query. A view can include all or some of the columns contained in the tables on which it's defined. Figure 2.3 shows the view called Deptname, created by combining some columns from the EMPLOYEE table and others from DEPARTMENT table.

A view efficiently represents data without having to maintain it. A view isn't an actual table and requires no permanent storage; instead, a *virtual table* is created and used.

Views allow multiple users to see different presentations of the same data. For example, several users may be accessing a table of data about some employees but not others, and other users may see some data about all employees but not their salaries. Each user is operating on a view derived from the real table. Each view appears to be a table and has a name of its own.

FIGURE 2.2

Tables consist of data arranged by columns and rows.

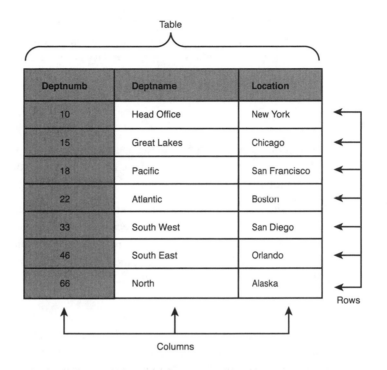

FIGURE 2.3

A simple view.

EMPLOYEE				
Empno	Firstname	Midinit	Lastname	Deptno
10	Kevin	P	Weckworth	A00
20	Melissa	M	Montoya	B01

DEPARTMENT	
Deptno	Deptname
A00	Research
B01	Marketing

Employee Department View showing employee last names from
the EMPLOYEE table and department names from the DEPARTMENT table.

Empno	Lastname	Deptname
10	Weckworth	Research
120	King	Research
110	Wong	Research
20	Montoya	Marketing

> **TIP** _____ | One advantage to using views is that you can use them to control access to sensitive data. Different people can have access to different columns or rows of the data.

Schemas

A *schema* is a set of database objects in the database and is used to logically group the objects in the database. It can contain database objects such as tables, views, indexes, packages, distinct types, functions, or triggers.

It is used as the first part of a two-part object name. When an object is created, you can assign it to a specific schema. If you don't specify a schema, the object is assigned to the default schema, whose name is usually the username of the person who created the object. The second part of the name is the name of the object. For example, a user named Smith might have a table called SMITH.PAYROLL.

Keys

A *key* is a set of columns that identify a particular row. For example, the employee number column would be a good choice for the key of a table that holds data about employees. Without a key, you will be unable to identify or access a row of data. A key composed of more than one column is called a *composite key*.

Unique and Primary Keys

An optional *unique key* is defined to have no two of its values the same. The columns of a unique key can't contain null values. This constraint is enforced by the database manager when data is inserted or updated. A table can have multiple unique keys. Unique keys are defined when the table is created or altered. Within a company, no two employees are assigned the same employee number. Therefore an employee number column can be defined as a unique key in an EMPLOYEE table.

A *primary key* is a special kind of unique key that uniquely identifies a row of a table. The columns of a primary key can't contain null values. In the EMPLOYEE table mentioned earlier, the employee number column would be defined as the primary key. Consider the PAYROLL table that would contain a record for each pay period. The primary key for this table would be a combination of the date of pay column plus the employee number column.

A table can have only one primary key, but it can have multiple unique keys. You can define additional unique keys by creating unique indexes (see the later section "Indexes").

TIP

> Defining a primary key for a new table is recommended because uniquely identifying each row speeds row access. For example, it is faster to access an account by its unique account number than it is to search through all the accounts. It's best to define a primary key at the time you create a table, although you can add a primary key to an existing table.

Primary keys support updates from many ODBC applications. When you choose a column as the primary key, the database checks each new row for a unique value in that column, rejecting any duplicates.

You can choose multiple columns as the primary key. For example, you might want to create a primary key on the first name and last name columns of an employee table to ensure uniqueness. A unique index is created automatically for the columns that make up the primary key.

Foreign Keys

A *foreign key* defines a relationship between two or more tables: the *parent table* and the *child table*. The relationship between the tables is based on matching a set of columns of the parent table (called the *parent key*) and a set of columns of the child table (called the *foreign key*). The parent key must be either a primary key or a unique key of the parent table. For example, a typical foreign key constraint might state that an employee cannot be assigned to a department unless the department already exists. To establish this relationship, define the DEPTNO column of the EMPLOYEE table as the foreign key and the DEPTNO column of the DEPARTMENT table as the parent key.

A table can have zero or more foreign keys. The value of the composite foreign key is null if any component of the value is null. Foreign keys are optional and are defined when a table is created or altered.

Indexes

An *index* is a list of the locations of rows, sorted by the contents of one or more specified columns. When you create a unique key or a primary key, an index is created. An index is a set of keys, each pointing to a row in a table. The EMPLOYEE table in Figure 2.4, for example, has an index based on the employee numbers in the table. This key value provides a pointer to a single row in the table; for example, employee number 81 points to employee Wells.

An index is a separate object from the table data. When an index is created, the database manager builds this structure and maintains it automatically.

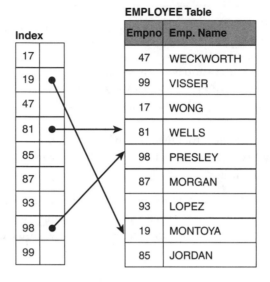

FIGURE 2.4

Indexes and keys.

Indexes are typically used to speed up access to rows in a table by creating a direct path to the data through these pointers. The optimizer takes indexes into consideration when determining the fastest access path to data.

Unique indexes can be created to ensure uniqueness of the index key. An *index key* is a column or ordered collection of columns on which an index is defined. A unique index does not allow the entry of duplicate values in the columns, thereby guaranteeing that no two rows of a table are the same. For example, if you define a unique index on the column Lastname in the EMPLOYEE table, it means that each employee in the table must have a different last name.

Packages

A *package* is an object that includes all the information needed to process specific SQL statements from a single source file. Created during the binding of an application program, a package contains the information needed by the database manager to access data in the most efficient way for a given program.

Data Types

Data types define acceptable values for constants, columns, host variables, functions, expressions, and special registers.

The data types supported by DB2 include the following:

- A *character string* is a sequence of bytes. The length of the string is the number of bytes in the sequence. If the length is zero, the value is called the empty string. This value should not be confused with the null value. The data types in this category include fixed-length character strings and varying-length character strings (VARCHAR, LONG VARCHAR, and CLOB).

- All *numbers* have a sign and a precision. The sign is considered positive if a number is zero. *Precision* is the number of bits or digits excluding the sign. For example, the precision of the number 125 is 3. The data types in this category include small integer (SMALLINT), large integer (INTEGER), big integer (BIGINT) single-precision floating point (REAL), double-precision floating point (DOUBLE or FLOAT), and decimal (DECIMAL or NUMERIC).

- The *date/time* data types aren't strings or numbers: date, time, timestamp, string representations of date/time values, date strings, time strings, and timestamp strings.

- The term *large object* refers to any BLOB, CLOB, or DBCLOB data type, including character large object (CLOB) strings, double-byte character large object (DBCLOB) strings, and binary large objects (BLOB).

- A *graphic string* is a sequence of bytes representing double-byte character data. Graphic strings include fixed-length graphic strings, variable-length graphic strings (VARGRAPHIC, LONG VARGRAPHIC, and DBCLOB), and NUL-terminated graphic strings.

- A *binary string* is a sequence of bytes. Unlike character strings, which usually contain text data, binary strings are used to hold non-traditional data such as pictures.

Data types are defined when a table is created.

Distinct Types

Application developers can create distinct types to represent their unique data. A *distinct type* is a user-defined data type that shares its internal representation with an existing type but is considered to be a separate and incompatible type for semantic purposes. For example, distinct types can be created for different currencies. The different currencies can't be compared directly, but a function can be written to convert one to the other before comparing.

Distinct types, like built-in types, can be used for columns of tables as well as parameters of functions. For example, you can define a data type such as ANGLE (which varies between 1 and 360) and a set of user-defined functions (UDFs) to act on it such as SINE, COSINE, and TANGENT.

Large Object (LOB) Support

Large object data types allow multimedia objects such as documents, video, image, and voice to be stored in the database and manipulated like other database objects. Figure 2.5 shows some of the many large objects that you can store and manipulate in DB2 Universal Database.

FIGURE 2.5

Basic elements: large objects.

Type	Name	
jpg	vacation photos	
bmp	family photos	
gif	fun photos	
pcx	portraits	
map	destinations	
jpg	postcards	

Type	Name	
chart	status	
email	letter	
doc	announcement	
pdf	chapter	
scan	resume	
graphic	certificates	

Type	Name	
movie	vacation	
audio	school play	
music	karioke	
film	favorite	
radio	talk show	
music	song	
plays	shaw	
books	e-novel	
art	favorite	

Multiple LOB columns, with a maximum size of 2GB each, can be defined per table. The exact number depends on the size defined for each column. LOB data is maintained directly in the database, and SQL is used for storage and retrieval.

Examples of LOB usage include the following:

- Banks storing customer's signatures
- Resumes kept on file with data and photos
- Voice prints for authentication
- Audio clips for a CD collection

Because LOB values can be very large, transferring them from the database server to client application programs can be time-consuming. LOB values are typically processed one piece at a time, however, rather than as a whole. For those cases where an application doesn't need (or want) the entire LOB value to be stored in application memory, it can reference this value by using a large object locator variable. Subsequent statements can then use the locators to perform operations on the data without necessarily retrieving the entire large object.

DB2 provides mechanisms to allow application programs to manage large object data in efficient ways. One of these mechanisms is *locator variables*, used to reduce memory requirements for applications and improve performance by reducing the data flow between the client (where the application resides) and the server (where the database resides). For example, you can use locator variables to retrieve a single chapter from a 35-chapter book stored as a large object. After you retrieve the chapter, you can edit it as required and then replace it. All this is accomplished without the need to retrieve the entire book.

Another mechanism is *file reference variables*, which retrieve a large object directly to a file or update a large object in a table directly from a file. File reference variables are used to reduce the storage requirements for the applications because they don't need to hold the large object data in memory.

The combination of distinct types and LOBs gives you considerable power. You're no longer restricted to using the built-in data types provided by DB2 to model your business data and to capture that data's semantics. You can use distinct types to define large, complex data structures for advanced applications.

Functions

A *function* is a subroutine that performs a distinct set of tasks and usually returns a single set of values. DB2 provides column functions (such as COUNT, MIN, and MAX) and scalar functions (such as SUBSTR, DATE, and DAYS).

Application developers can create their own suite of functions oriented to specific applications or domains such as scientific and business functions. This expands the availability of common functions, allows greater flexibility to the system, and allows the database manager to capture more of the data's semantics. These functions can operate over all database types, including LOBs and distinct types.

User-defined functions (UDFs) are particularly flexible, as they can operate on data managed within or outside DB2 Universal Database. For example, a function can be enabled to send an electronic message, update a flat file, or perform some other operation. Figure 2.6 shows an example of how UDFs work.

FIGURE 2.6

Basic elements: user-defined functions.

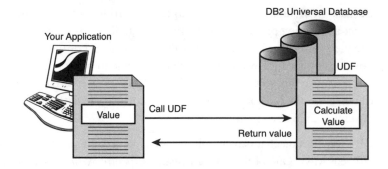

A retail store could define a price data type for tracking the cost of items it sells. This store might also want to define a sales_tax function, which would take a given price as input, compute the applicable sales tax, and return this data to the requesting user or application.

DB2 provides a rich library of UDFs. The library includes a set of mathematical functions such as SIN, COS, and TAN; scientific functions such as RADIANS, LOG10, and POWER; general-purpose functions such as LEFT, DIFFERENCE, and UCASE; and many more.

User-defined functions also support object-oriented programming in your applications. User-defined functions provide the *abstraction* of the object, which defines its behavior and central characteristics. Defining scalar functions to use with distinct types enables the creation of *methods*. The creation of methods is a central concept of object orientation.

With user-defined functions, you also can overload. *Overloading* allows you to use the same name for different actions against data but have the system examine the parameters to determine how to execute the function. For example, you can create a length function on AUDIO, TEXT, and PICTURE data types. For the AUDIO data type, you want length to return the number of seconds; for TEXT, the number of words; and for PICTURE, the number of bytes.

User-defined functions also provide encapsulation of objects. *Encapsulation* is the means of controlling access to the underlying data of an object. Data is hidden or protected from direct manipulation and, therefore, protected from corruption.

Data Integrity

Data integrity is fundamental to any database management system. Whenever data is shared, there is a need to manage and control operations that ensure the accuracy of the values within database tables. DB2 Universal Database ensures data integrity through the previously mentioned transaction support and concurrency control, as well as through the features described in the following sections.

Roll-Forward Recovery

When you lose online data due to a media failure, such as a hard disk crash, roll-forward recovery enables you to recover it by applying log journal information against the restored database. Log journals contain the changes made to the database since the last backup. After these journals are applied, the database will be in the same state as it was before the failure.

Constraints

To protect data and to define relationships between your data, you usually define *business rules*. Rules define what data values are valid for a column in a table, or how columns in one or more tables are related to each other.

DB2 provides constraints as a way to enforce those rules with the database system. A *constraint* is a mechanism that ensures that certain conditions relating to columns and tables are maintained—for example, an employee number must be unique from person to person and, as such, is under some constraint. By using the database system to enforce business rules, you don't have to write code in your application to enforce them. If a business rule applies to only one application, however, you should code it in the application rather than use a global database constraint.

DB2 provides different kinds of constraints:

- Unique constraints
- Referential constraints and relationships such as NOT NULL, PRIMARY KEY, and FOREIGN KEY
- Table check constraints
- Informational constraints

You define constraints when you create or alter a table.

Unique Constraints

Unique constraints ensure that the values in a set of columns are unique and not null for all rows in the table (not-null constraints prevent null values from being entered into a column). For example, a typical unique constraint on a DEPARTMENT table may be that the combination of the location number and department number be unique. These constraints are added to the database through the definition of primary keys or unique indexes.

You can optionally define unique constraints when you create or alter a table. The database manager enforces constraints during insert and update operations, ensuring data integrity.

Referential Constraints and Relationships

Another important feature that provides robust data integrity is *referential integrity*, which lets you define required relationships between and within tables. Referential constraints, declared when a table is defined, ensure the consistency of data values between related columns in different tables. DB2 Universal Database maintains these relationships, so you don't need to program this function into applications.

Relationships are expressed as *referential constraints*, which require that all values of a given attribute or column of a table also exist in some other table or column. For example, a typical referential constraint might require that every employee be a member of an existing department. By defining unique constraints and foreign keys, you can define a relationship between the EMPLOYEE and DEPARTMENT tables and consequently enforce this business rule (see Figure 2.7). With this relationship, you can control updates to the employee table by ensuring that the department number is valid, as defined in the DEPARTMENT table. The database can reject any employee record with an invalid department number. This ensures data integrity.

FIGURE 2.7

Enforcing referential integrity.

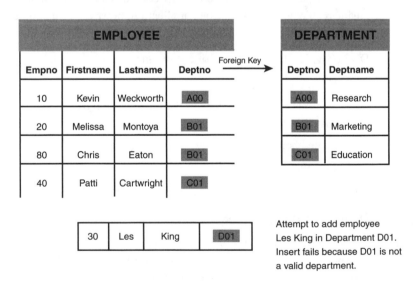

To establish a referential constraint, you define the department number in the EMPLOYEE table as the foreign key, and the department number in the DEPARTMENT table as the primary key. A foreign key in the EMPLOYEE table references the primary key of the DEPARTMENT table. This creates a constraint so that any value in the foreign key must match an existing value in the referenced key.

You can also choose the action to be taken when rows of the parent table are deleted. In the preceding example, you can decide that when a department is deleted, all employees in that department are also deleted. Conversely, you could decide that if any employees are still members of the department, the department can't be deleted.

Table Check Constraints

Table check constraints are generally used to enforce business rules not covered by key uniqueness or referential integrity constraints. A *table check constraint* is a rule in the database that specifies the values allowed in one or more columns of every row of a table. This includes specifying a range or domain that valid entries must exist in. For example, you can define constraints on the EMPLOYEE table that specify that the job of an employee can be only one of Sales, Manager, or Clerk. Each entry in this column must exist in this domain to be valid.

Table check constraints also allow you to have a single constraint defined at the table level involving multiple columns in the table. For example, on a table that contains columns for an employee's salary, bonus, and date of hire, you can define a single constraint to ensure that no employees with more than one year of service can receive a total annual income (including salary and bonus) of less than $35,000.

Table check constraints specify evaluated conditions for each row of a table. You can specify check constraints on individual columns.

Informational Constraints

An *informational constraint* is a rule that can be used by the SQL compiler but is not enforced by DB2. The SQL compiler includes a rewrite query stage, which transforms SQL statements into forms that can be optimized and improves the access path to the required data. The purpose of the constraint is not to have additional verification of data by DB2, rather it is to improve query performance.

Informational constraints are defined when a table is created or altered. You can specify whether you want DB2 to enforce the constraint and whether you want the constraint to be used for query optimization.

User-Defined Types (UDTs)

Every data element in the database is stored in a column of a table, and each column is defined to have a data type. The data type places limits on the types of values you can put into the column and the operations you can perform on them. For example, a column of integers can contain only numbers within a fixed range. DB2 includes a set of built-in data types with defined characteristics and behaviors: character strings, numerics, date/time values, and large objects.

Sometimes, however, the built-in data types might not serve the needs of your applications. DB2 provides user-defined types that enable you to define the distinct data types you need for your applications. The ability to define distinct types gives you freedom beyond the system-provided types. Distinct types are just one building block for object-oriented extensions.

UDTs are based on the built-in data types. When you define a UDT, you also define its valid operations. For example, you might define a money data type based on the decimal data type. For the money data type, however, you might allow only addition and subtraction operations between two money data types, not multiplication and division operations.

User-defined distinct types ensure data integrity through *strong typing*, which guarantees that only functions and operations defined on the distinct type can be applied to the type. For example, the system doesn't allow you to directly compare a Canadian dollar type with an American dollar type even though they share the same underlying type. If you want to do such a comparison, you can *cast* or convert one or both of the values to a common value by using a UDF. Encapsulation ensures that the behavior of distinct types is restricted by the functions and operators that can be applied to them.

Triggers

A *trigger* defines a set of actions executed or triggered by an update, insert, or delete operation on a specified base table. When such a SQL operation is executed, the trigger is said to be *activated*. You can activate the trigger before or after the SQL operation. Triggers can be used to perform validation of input data, automatically generate a value for a newly inserted row, read from other tables for cross-referencing purposes, or write to other tables for audit-trail purposes.

The use of triggers promotes faster application development, because they're stored in the relational database. The actions triggers perform don't have to be coded in each application. Maintenance of applications and databases is easier because if a business policy changes, only a change in the corresponding trigger is needed instead of changes in each application program. Multiple triggers per table can be set up, and one trigger can cascade and initiate other triggers. Figure 2.8 gives you an example of how triggers work. There are two tables: one for employees of the sales department and another that lists the total number of employees. When a new employee is added to the sales department, a trigger is activated that updates the information in the table showing the total number of employees. If you didn't have a trigger, you would have to perform a query that goes through the sales department and counts each employee.

FIGURE 2.8

Basic elements: triggers.

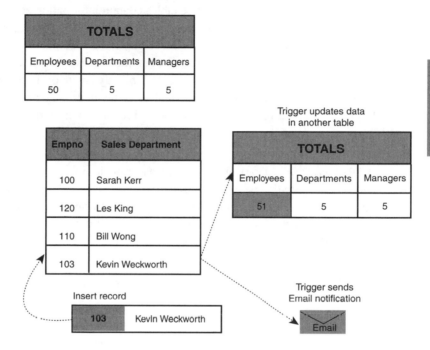

2

Triggers provide integrity checking by doing complex, cross-table validation of data beyond the scope of referential integrity and check constraints.

One powerful use of a trigger is to globally enforce a business rule. For instance, a trigger could be used to ensure that a manager of a department earns more than the maximum salary of his employees.

Triggers allow greater flexibility within the system and allow the database manager to capture more of the data semantics. For example, a trigger could be written to verify that orders don't exceed a customer's credit limit. If it does, the trigger could refuse to place the order.

When combined with UDFs, triggers can be used to implement alerts that signal users or other applications that a given event has occurred within the database manager. For example, if you want to notify a certain member of the personnel department whenever an engineer's salary is changed to exceed $100,000, DB2's triggering mechanism can support this function. Such support provides considerable power and flexibility.

System Catalog Tables

Each database includes a set of system catalog tables, which describe the logical and physical structure of the data. These tables contain information about database objects such as tables, views, packages, referential integrity relationships, functions, distinct types, triggers, and indexes, as well as security information about the authority users have for these objects. They're created when the database is created and are updated in the course of normal operation. You can't explicitly create or drop them, but you can query and view their contents. Some tables can be modified through views and Visual Explain to update statistics that can help you model different data characteristics.

Instances

A DB2 *instance* is a logical database manager environment where you catalog databases and set configuration parameters. Depending on your needs, you can create more than one instance on a single server. This means that you can create several instances of the same product on a physical machine and have them running concurrently. This provides flexibility in setting up environments. You can use multiple DB2 instances to do the following:

- Use one instance for a development environment and another instance for a production environment.
- Separately tune a database instance for a particular environment.
- Protect access to sensitive information. For example, you may want to have your payroll database protected on its own instance so that owners of other instances can't see payroll data.
- Control the assignment of SYSADM, SYSCTRL, and SYSMAINT authority for each instance.
- Optimize the database manager configuration for each database instance.
- Limit the impact of an instance crash. In the unlikely event of an instance crash, only one instance is affected. The other instance may continue to function normally.

However, multiple instances have some minor disadvantages:

- Additional system resources (virtual memory and disk space) are required for each instance.
- More administration is required because you have additional instances to manage.

DB2 program files are physically stored in one location on a particular machine. The instance directory is located in the /sqllib subdirectory, in the directory where DB2 was installed. As part of your installation procedure, you create an initial instance of DB2 called "DB2". Several related databases can be located within a single instance. Figure 2.9 shows how databases, instances, and systems relate to one another.

FIGURE **2.9**

Basic elements: instances.

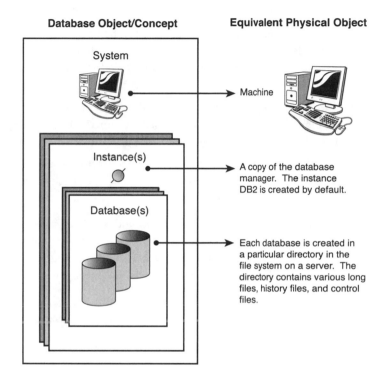

You can connect to more than one database at the same time. These databases can be in multiple instances on the same or different machines. Instances are cataloged as local or remote in the node directory. When you attempt to access a database not in your default instance, the node directory is used to determine how to communicate with the database.

You can *attach* to an instance to perform maintenance and utility tasks that can be done only at an instance level such as creating a database, forcing applications, issuing database monitor commands, or performing database manager configuration updates.

Directories

Directories are necessary for accessing local and remote databases. They ensure that access to a database is transparent to users and applications, regardless of where the database physically resides.

DB2 Universal Database uses three types of database directories, which identify the location of databases, and a node directory, which contains network connection information for remote databases. The database directories are as follows:

- The *system database directory* identifies the name, alias, and physical location of each cataloged database. For a user or application to access a database, an entry for that database must be in this directory. All clients and servers must have a system database directory.

- A *local database directory* contains the name of a database and the subdirectory pathname in which the database files are stored. One directory exists in every path that contains a database. An entry is added to it when a database is created.

- The *database connection services (DCS)* directory is used only if DB2 Connect is installed on your system. It contains an entry for each distributed relational database that your node can access.

The node directory contains an entry for all nodes to which your database client and protocol can connect. Each entry contains the node's name, communication information, and instance information. A database server's node must be cataloged in this directory before remote database clients can access it or a DB2 Connect gateway.

The system database directory, local database directory, DCS directory, and node directory can be cataloged through the Client Configuration Assistant or the Control Center.

Figure 2.10 shows how the various directories interact. It shows a client connecting to the DB2DB on a DB2 server.

Storage Objects

Table spaces, containers, and buffer pools let you define how you'll store the data on your system and how you can improve performance related to accessing the data. You aren't required to create a table space, container, or buffer pool to be able to add data to tables in a database. You can accept the defaults for each when you create a database and a table. Use the information in this section to understand how you can tune these storage objects for your environment.

Table Spaces

Databases are made up of storage structures called *table spaces*. Essentially, a table space is a place to store tables. When creating a table, you can decide to have certain objects, such as indexes and large object data, kept separately from the rest of the table data. Figure 2.11 shows some of the flexibility you have in spreading data over table spaces.

FIGURE 2.10

Basic elements: example of directories interacting.

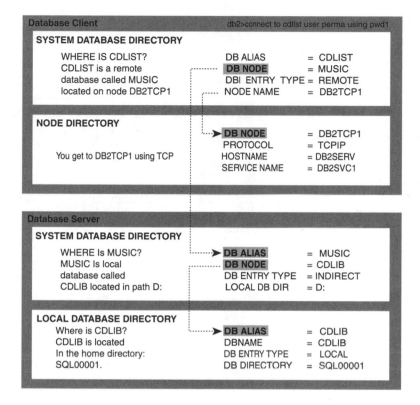

It's easier to manage large databases by separating them into table spaces. A table space allows you to assign the location of table and index data directly onto media storage devices or containers, and allows a database to exceed the size of the file system. A single table space can span several file systems or devices. For example, if you have a 10GB database, you'll need to spread this database over several containers. You could spread the data over five containers, with each being 2GB in size.

You have the flexibility to assign portions of a table (such as data, indexes, and long field data) to different table spaces. You can then assign different storage devices depending on the contents of each table space. If additional space is required for any of these table spaces, you can increase the size by adding more devices or storage space. This can increase the size without stopping the database, and the data in the table space is automatically rebalanced for maximum performance.

Table spaces can also be backed up or restored as a unit. Backing up only the changed data reduces the time needed to perform a backup, enabling you to back up frequently changed data more often.

FIGURE 2.11

Basic elements: table spaces.

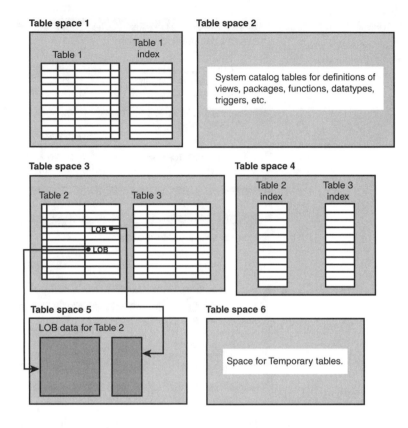

A table space can be a *system managed space (SMS)* or a *database managed space (DMS)*. For an SMS table space, each container is a directory in the file space of the operating system, and the operating system's file manager controls the storage space. (Containers are described in the next section.) For a DMS table space, each container is a fixed-size preallocated file or a physical device, such as a disk, and the database manager controls the storage space. Figure 2.12 illustrates the differences between SMS and DMS table spaces.

Tables containing user data exist in the regular table spaces. By default, a table space known as USERSPACE1 is created. Indexes and system catalog tables are also stored in regular table spaces. The default system catalog table space is known as SYSCATSPACE. Tables containing long field data or long object data, such as multimedia objects, can be optionally placed into long table spaces. The temporary table space is used during SQL operations for things such as sorting or reorganizing tables, creating indexes, and joining tables. A database should have one temporary table space. You can create more, although for most situations only one is required. By default, a table space called TEMPSPACE1 is created. Figure 2.13 shows the different types of table spaces.

FIGURE 2.12

Basic elements: SMS or DMS table spaces.

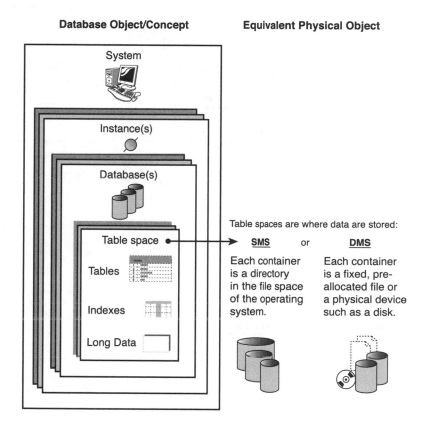

Database Object/Concept   **Equivalent Physical Object**

System

Instance(s)

Database(s)

Table spaces are where data are stored:

Table space

SMS   or   **DMS**

Tables

Each container is a directory in the file space of the operating system.

Each container is a fixed, pre-allocated file or a physical device such as a disk.

Indexes

Long Data

Containers

A *container* is a physical storage device that can be identified by a directory name, a device name, or a filename. A container is assigned to a table space (all database and table data is assigned to table spaces). A table space's definitions and attributes are recorded in the database system catalog. When a table space is created, you can then create tables within this table space.

A container isn't explicitly shown in the Control Center, but it's listed when you view table spaces in the Journal, which is one of the DB2 database administration tools. A single table space can span many containers, but each container can belong to only one table space. Figure 2.14 shows the HUMANRES table space spanning five containers.

FIGURE 2.13

Basic elements: types of table spaces.

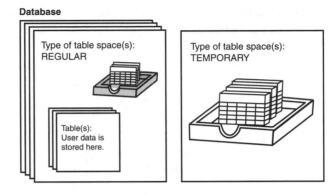

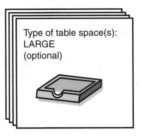

FIGURE 2.14

Basic elements: containers.

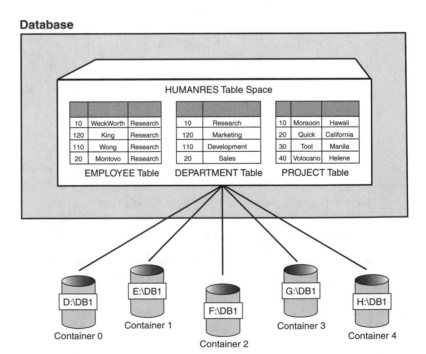

Data for any table is stored on all containers in a table space in a round-robin fashion. This way, data is balanced across the containers that belong to a given table space. The number of pages that the database manager writes to one container before a different one is used is called the *extent size*.

Buffer Pool

A *buffer pool* is an allocation of main memory allocated to cache table and index data pages as they're being read from a disk or being modified. The purpose of the buffer pool is to improve database system performance. Data can be accessed much faster from memory than from a disk; therefore, the fewer times the database manager needs to read from or write to a disk, the better the performance. (You can create more than one buffer pool, although for most situations only one is required.) Figure 2.15 shows the relationship between the buffer pool and the other database objects.

FIGURE 2.15

Basic elements: Buffer pools.

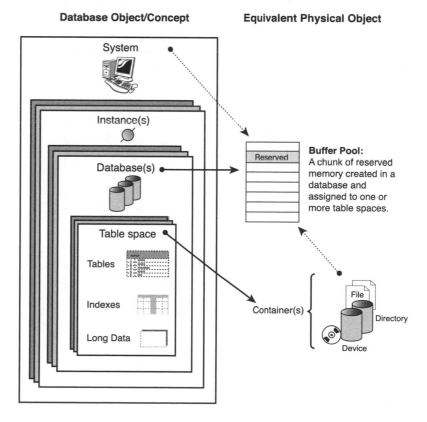

Configuration Files

Configuration files contain parameter values that define the resources allocated to DB2 and to individual databases. There are three types of configuration files:

- The Database Manager Configuration file for DB2 as a whole
- The Database Configuration file for each individual database
- The Administration Configuration file for the DB2 Administration Server

The Database Manager Configuration file is created when DB2 is installed or when an instance of DB2 is created. The parameters it contains affect system resources at a global (product or instance) level, independent of any one database stored on the system. Many of these parameters can be changed from the system default values to improve performance or increase capacity, depending on your system's configuration. Figure 2.16 shows the relationship between the various configuration files.

FIGURE 2.16

Basic elements:
Configuration files.

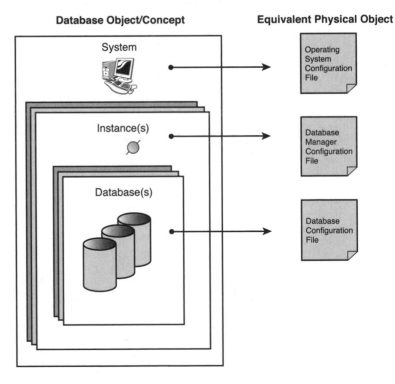

There's one Database Manager Configuration file for each installation of a client as well. This file contains information about the client enabler for a specific workstation. A subset of the parameters available for a server is applicable for the client.

A Database Configuration file is created when a database is created and resides where that database physically resides. There's one configuration file per database. Its parameters specify the amount of resources to be allocated to that database; many of the parameters can be changed to improve performance or increase capacity. Different changes may be required, depending on the type of activity in that specific database.

The Administration Configuration file is created when DB2 Universal Database is installed or when the DB2 Administration Server is created. The parameters it contains affect the remote administration of DB2 servers.

Recovery Objects

Log files and the recovery history file are created automatically when a database is created. You can't modify them; however, they are important should you need to use your database backup to recover lost or damaged data.

Log Files

Each database includes recovery logs, which are used to recover from application or system errors. With the database backups, they're used to recover the consistency of the database right up to the point in time when the error occurred. Figure 2.17 shows the interaction between the active and offline log files.

FIGURE 2.17

Basic elements: Log files.

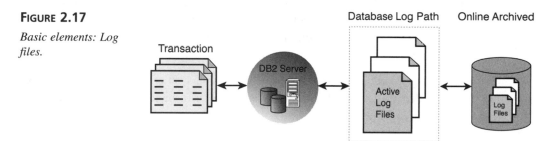

Should you lose online data due to a media failure, such as a hard disk crash, roll-forward recovery enables you to recover it by applying log journal information against the restored database. Log journals contain the changes made to the database since the last backup. After these journals are applied, the database will be in the same state as it was before the failure.

Circular Logging

Circular logging is the default when a database is created. As the name suggests, circular logging uses a circle (ring) of online logs to provide recovery from transaction failures and system crashes (see Figure 2.18). The logs are used and retained only to the point of ensuring the integrity of current transactions.

FIGURE **2.18**

Basic elements:
Circular logging.

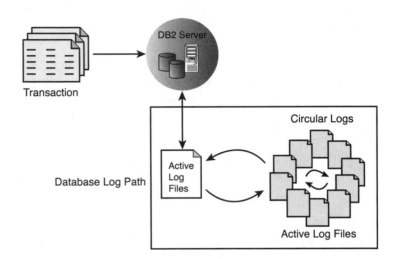

Circular logging doesn't allow you to roll forward a database through prior transactions from the last full backup. You recover from media failures and disasters by restoring a full, offline backup. All changes since the last backup are lost. The database must be offline (inaccessible to users) when a full backup is taken. Because this type of restore recovers your data to the specific point in time of the full backup, it's sometimes called *version recovery*.

Circular logging records the changes to your database in a set of logs. When the last log file series is filled, the first log file is reused in a circular fashion. Circular logging supports restore-only recovery.

Archive Logging

Archive logging doesn't overwrite older log files. Instead, it continuously creates additional logs to record every transaction since your last backup. This type of logging supports roll-forward recovery.

This complete recovery option allows for all logs up to the last complete transaction to be replayed. Archive logging is activated when the LOGRETAIN parameter is set to YES. When archive logging is activated, a full offline backup is required. If LOGRETAIN is turned off, logging reverts to circular, and the online logs are automatically deleted. If it's necessary to back out of the changes from an errant application that damaged data, a database can use the logs to roll forward to any point in time between the full, offline backup and the last completed transaction.

With archive logging, it becomes necessary to pay more attention to the handling of the logs and to ensure their safety. The ability to perform roll-forward recovery of your database depends on the integrity of the logs. Consideration should be given to backing up log data and to keeping it on disk arrays or mirrored volumes.

Active Logs

Active logs contain transactions that haven't yet been committed or rolled back, or whose changes haven't yet been written to disk. Active logs are located in the database log path directory.

Online Archived Logs

When all changes in the active log are no longer needed for normal processing, the log is closed and becomes an archived log. An archived log is said to be *online* when it's stored in the database log path directory. Figure 2.19 shows an example of active logs that are archived.

FIGURE 2.19

Basic elements: archive logging.

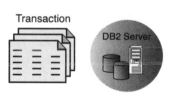 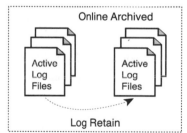

Offline Archived Logs

You also can store archived logs in a location other than the database log path directory by using a user exit program. An archived log is said to be *offline* when it's not stored in the database log path directory.

Recovery History File

The *recovery history file* contains a summary of the backup information that can be used in case all or part of the database must be recovered to a given point in time. It's used to track recovery-related events such as backups, restores, and loads. A recovery history file is created with each database and is automatically updated when certain actions are performed such as database or table space backup or restore.

Application Programs

DB2 provides several different ways to access and manipulate data in DB2 databases through application programs. You can use embedded SQL, the DB2 CLI, Java, or ODBC end-user tools. To perform administrative functions, you can use the DB2 Administrative APIs.

A client application that needs to access a DB2 database sends a request to the server. The request is coded in SQL (the language used to access DB2 databases). The server processes the request and returns the data to the client application. In this context, DB2 programming is the development of client applications that access DB2 databases to retrieve, store, or manipulate data.

DB2 programming also includes developing user-defined functions and stored procedures that run on the server. DB2 also provides many features to build advanced applications: triggers, constraints, stored procedures, user-defined functions, user-defined data types, and support for large objects (such as audio, video, and image) to build multimedia applications.

You can develop client applications by using the following:

- Personal Developer's Edition
- Universal Developer's Edition
- Java Development Kit
- WebSphere Studio Application Developer
- An Open Database Connectivity (ODBC) or OLE DB end-user tool such as Microsoft Access

Application programs that can access DB2 databases include those created by an end user or developer in your company, as well as those commercially available. All applications, including query products such as Microsoft Access and fourth-generation languages such as Borland Delphi, use the same SQL interface described here.

You can choose several different ways to access DB2 databases. The way your application accesses DB2 databases depends on the type of application you want to develop. For example, if you want a data-entry application, you might choose to embed static SQL statements in your application. If you want an application that performs queries over the World Wide Web, you would probably choose to develop Java applications. Or if you just want a simple application to query a database, you might code it by using Microsoft Visual Studio.

Embedded SQL

SQL is the database interface language used to access and manipulate data in DB2 databases. You can embed SQL statements in your applications, enabling them to perform any task supported by SQL such as retrieving and storing data. With DB2, you can code your embedded SQL applications in the C, C++, COBOL, FORTRAN, Java (SQLJ), and REXX programming languages.

An application in which you embed SQL statements is called a *host program*. A programming language that you compile and in which you embed SQL statements is called a *host language*. The program and language are defined this way because they *host* or accommodate SQL statements.

Static and Dynamic SQL

Embedded SQL may be static or dynamic. The method of compiling a SQL statement and the persistence of its operational form distinguish static SQL from dynamic SQL. Static SQL statements are ones where you know, before compile time, the SQL statement type and the table and column names. The only unknowns are the specific data values the statement is searching for or updating. You can represent those values in the host language variables. You prepare or build static SQL statements before you run your application.

In contrast, dynamic SQL statements are those statements that your application builds and executes at runtime. An interactive application that prompts users for key parts of a SQL statement, such as the names of the tables and columns to be searched, is a good example of dynamic SQL. The application builds the SQL statement while it's running, and then submits the statement for processing.

Generally, static SQL statements are well suited for high-performance applications with predefined transactions. A reservation system is a good example of such an application. Generally, dynamic SQL statements are well suited for applications that run against a rapidly changing database where transactions need to be specified at runtime. An interactive query interface is a good example of such an application. You can write applications that have only static SQL statements, only dynamic SQL statements, or a mix of both.

Precompiling and Binding

When you embed SQL statements in your applications, you must *precompile* and *bind* your applications to a database. The precompiler converts the SQL statements in each source file into DB2 runtime API calls to the database manager. The precompiler also produces an access package in the database and an optional bind file, if you specify that you want one created. The access package contains access plans selected by the DB2 optimizer for the static SQL statements in your application. The access plans contain the information required by the database manager to execute the static SQL statements in the most efficient manner as determined by the optimizer.

For dynamic SQL statements, the optimizer creates access plans when you run your application. The bind file contains the SQL statements and other data required to create an access package. You can use the bind file to rebind your application later without having to precompile it first. Rebinding optimizes access plans for current database conditions. You need to rebind your applications if your application will access a different database from the one against which it was precompiled.

With static SQL applications, you can limit the access users have to data. For example, you can grant a user permission to run an application that updates a table without giving that user general access to the table. You do this by granting authorizations to execute an access package when you bind your application. This encapsulates access authority in the package, giving selected users permission only to run a package, not to access the entire table. In dynamic SQL applications, authorizations are validated at runtime on a per-statement basis. Therefore, to run a dynamic SQL statement, users must have explicit access privileges for each database object.

Open Database Connectivity (ODBC)

In some cases, you might need an application to perform a basic task such as querying a database. You can use ODBC end-user tools such as Lotus Approach, Microsoft Access, or Microsoft Visual Basic to create these applications. Microsoft developed a callable SQL interface specification called Open Database Connectivity (ODBC) for Microsoft operating systems to provide a simpler alternative to developing applications than using a high-level programming language.

Lotus Approach provides two ways to access DB2 data:

- You can use the graphical interface to perform queries, develop reports, and analyze data.
- You can develop applications by using LotusScript, an object-oriented programming language that comes with a wide array of objects, events, methods, and properties, along with a built-in program editor.

DB2 Call Level Interface (DB2 CLI)

DB2 CLI is a programming interface that your C or C++ applications can use to access DB2 databases. DB2 CLI is based on the Microsoft ODBC specification and the ISO CLI standard. Through this interface, applications use standard function calls at execution time to connect to a database and issue SQL statements to access and update data.

You don't need to precompile or bind DB2 CLI applications because they use common access packages provided with DB2. You simply compile and link your applications. Therefore, applications developed with this interface are independent of any particular database server. This independence means a DB2 CLI application doesn't have to be recompiled to access different database servers, but instead selects the appropriate one at runtime.

Before your DB2 CLI or ODBC application can access DB2 databases, however, the DB2 CLI bind files must be bound on each DB2 database that will be accessed. This occurs automatically on the first connection to the database, but it's recommended that the database administrator bind the bind files from one client on each platform that will access a DB2 database. Suppose that you have Linux, AIX, and Windows clients that each access two DB2 databases. The administrator must bind the bind files from one Linux client on each database that will be accessed. Next, the administrator must bind the bind files from one AIX client on each database that will be accessed. Finally, the administrator must do the same on one Windows client.

When you use DB2 CLI, your application passes dynamic SQL statements as function arguments to the database manager for processing. As such, DB2 CLI is an alternative to embedded dynamic SQL, providing another way to access DB2 databases by using dynamic SQL.

Application Programming Interfaces (APIs)

When writing your applications, you might need to perform some database administration tasks such as creating, activating, backing up, or restoring a database. DB2 provides numerous APIs so that you can perform these tasks from your applications, including embedded SQL and DB2 CLI applications. This way, you can program the same administrative functions into your applications that you can perform by using the DB2 administration tools.

You also might need to perform specific tasks that can be performed only by using the DB2 APIs. For example, you might want to retrieve the text of an error message so that your application can display it to users. To retrieve the message, you must use the Get Error Message API.

System Management Facilities

DB2 provides many facilities in addition to the Control Center to aid in the management of a large, diverse database system. You can administer database clients from one central location, perform database administration tasks remotely from a client workstation, monitor database activity, spread databases across multiple file systems, force users off the system, and diagnose problems.

Online Administrative Capability

A number of database administration tasks can be performed while the database is still operational (while users or applications are still connected). This provides for greater availability of data to users. Some tasks that can be done online include loading data, backing up data, reorganizing data, creating tables or table spaces, and altering tables or table spaces.

Lightweight Directory Access Protocol (LDAP)

Lightweight Directory Access Protocol (LDAP) is an industry standard access method to directory services. A *directory service* is a repository of resource information about multiple systems and services within a distributed environment, and it provides client and server access to these resources.

Each database server instance publishes its existence to an LDAP server and provides database information to the LDAP directory. Each client is no longer required to store catalog information locally on each computer. Client applications search the LDAP directory for information required to connect to the database.

Summary

Today you learned that a relational database presents data as a collection of tables. The basic elements used by DB2 Universal Database include database objects, data integrity, object relational capabilities, system catalog tables, instances, directories, storage objects, configuration files, and recovery objects.

DB2 provides a rich development environment through the DB2 Personal Developer's Edition and the DB2 Universal Developer's Edition. These kits allow you to access and manipulate DB2 data by using embedded SQL, DB2 CLI, Java, ODBC end-user tools, or DB2 APIs.

DB2 provides several system-management facilities to help you manage very large databases and large networks. These facilities include being able to perform many administration tasks while users are still connected to the database, allowing client code to be shared to simplify configuration, and a governor to help you define how applications behave.

What Comes Next?

On Day 3, "Installing and Configuring DB2 Server," you learn how to install the DB2 Universal Database Workgroup Server Edition product provided in demonstration mode on the CD-ROM included with this book.

Q&A

Q What different kinds of constraints does DB2 provide to enforce business rules?

A DB2 provides unique constraints to ensure that the values in a set of columns are unique and not null for all rows in the table. Referential constraints let you define relationships between and within tables by requiring that all values of a given column of a table also exist in some other table or column. Check constraints are provided to enforce rules not covered by uniqueness or referential integrity. Check constraints allow you to specify a range of values allowed in one or more columns of every row of a table.

Q What are the two types of table spaces?

A A table space can be system managed space (SMS) or database managed space (DMS). For SMS table spaces, the operating system manages the directories that contain the data files and controls the storage space. For DMS table spaces, the DB2 controls the storage space, and the data is stored in preallocated files or physical devices.

Q How does roll-forward recovery work?

A To use roll-forward recovery, you must make an initial backup of your database and set the LOGRETAIN parameter to YES. As you make changes to the data in your database, the transactions are stored in log journals. If you have a media failure, you must first restore the database image and then use roll-forward recovery to reapply the transactions stored in the log journals. You can choose to roll data forward to a specific point in time or to the end of the logs.

Workshop

The purpose of the Workshop is to allow you to test your knowledge of the material covered in the lesson. See whether you can successfully answer the questions in the quiz and complete the exercise before you continue with the next lesson. The answers appear in Appendix B, "Answers to Quiz Questions and Exercises."

Quiz

1. What's the advantage of using a view?

2. Give some reasons why you would want to define a primary key for a table.

3. What is the difference between unique keys and primary keys?

4. What's an instance? What's the advantage of using an instance?

5. What's the difference between static and dynamic SQL?

Exercise

1. The sample database used throughout this book is an inventory of a music library. Start thinking about the types of information that should be stored in such a database, what tables will be needed, what the keys should be for each table, and the types of relationships needed between the various tables. The design of the sample database is covered in detail at the end of Week 1.

DAY **3**

Installing and Configuring DB2 Server

Although the DB2 documentation covers the installation and configuration of DB2 servers and clients, today provides more detailed instructions on installing the server. (Day 6, "Installing and Configuring DB2 Clients," shows how to install the DB2 clients.) I also explain each decision you'll be faced with when installing.

As you know from Day 1, "What DB2 Can Do for You," the DB2 server runs on many different operating systems. Because this book focuses primarily on the Windows platform, however, the examples are specific to that interface, as are the installation instructions in this lesson.

Today you see how to perform an interactive Typical, Custom, or Compact install of the DB2 server product. Typical and Compact installs require fewer questions to answer, but to see exactly what the install program adds to your system, you'll also look at the Custom install.

> **NOTE**
>
> If you're migrating from previous versions of DB2, you must complete certain procedures before installing DB2 UDB Version 8. The instructions for migrating from a previous version are beyond the scope of this book.

Preparing for the Install

Go through the steps in this section before you begin installing to ensure that you have the required items and information.

Hardware and Software Requirements

Before installing the DB2 product, check to see that you have the proper hardware and software components available on your system:

- Disk space—The amount of disk space required to install DB2 depends on the options that you choose to install. Typically, you should have between 260–600 MB of free disk space to install DB2. You also need additional disk space to store the applications and databases that you'll use with DB2 (this amount depends on the amount and type of data you store in your databases).

- Processor—You can run DB2 on a Pentium-based computer. For 64-bit DB2 products, an Itanium-based computer is required.

- Memory—To run the DB2 graphical tools, you need at least 128 MB of memory installed. The more memory you have, the faster the tools will run. Additional memory is required for any clients connecting to your system and to run other programs on your computer.

- Operating systems—DB2 can be installed on Windows NT Version 4 with Service Pack 6a or higher, Windows 2000 with Service Pack 2, Windows XP (32-bit), and Windows Server 2003 (32-bit and 64-bit).

> **NOTE**
>
> The DB2 Personal Edition product runs on all Windows operating systems. It has the same function as the DB2 server, but it can't accept requests from remote clients.

- Software—You will need Java Runtime Environment (JRE) Version 1.3.1 to run DB2's Java-based tools such as the Control Center. During installation, the correct level of the JRE is installed if it is not already. An Internet browser is required to view the online help.

- User accounts—You must have one user account to install DB2, and two user accounts for setup. The user accounts can be created before you install DB2, or you can have the DB2 Setup Wizard create them for you.

- Communications—You need communications software only if you want to access remote databases or have remote clients access your databases. Regardless of the operation, you have several communication protocols to choose from: TCP/IP, NetBIOS, and Named Pipes. All these protocols are installable options in Windows operating systems. You don't need to purchase separate products to provide this support. Make sure that you've installed and configured the protocol support that you intend to use.

NOTE Lightweight Directory Access Protocol (LDAP) is supported for DB2, but the use of LDAP is beyond the scope of this book.

Creating a User Account for Installing DB2 Products

You need a local or domain user account to install DB2. The user account must belong to the Administrators group on your computer, and it must adhere to DB2 naming rules and have the Act as Part of the Operating System advanced user right.

To create a user account on a Windows 2000 system, choose Start|Settings|Control Panel|Administrative Tools|Computer Management. Expand Local Users and Groups, right-click on Users, and choose New User. Create a new user by filling in the details in the New User dialog box.

To grant advanced user rights on Windows, you must be logged on as a local administrator. On a Windows 2000 system, choose Start|Settings|Control Panel|Administrative Tools|Local Security Policy. Expand the Local Policies object and select User Rights Assignment. In the right window pane, select the Act as Part of the Operating System policy to open the Local Security Policy Setting dialog box. Click Add to open the Select User or Groups dialog box. Click the user account that you will use for the install procedure and click Add. Click OK to finish.

A valid DB2 user account can contain up to 30 characters and complies with DB2's naming rules:

- The username must begin with A through Z, @, #, or $.
- It cannot contain accented characters.

- It can contain alphanumeric characters, in lowercase, uppercase, or mixed case, and special characters @, #, $, or _.
- You can't use these special words: USERS, ADMINS, GUESTS, PUBLIC, or LOCAL or any SQL reserved word.
- You can't begin the username with IBM, SQL, or SYS.

TIP

> Windows Server 2003, Windows 2000, and Windows XP currently have a practical limit of 20 characters.

Performing a Typical Install

Use the Typical install type if you want to install the DB2 components used most often, and if you want to have the DB2 instance and DB2 Administration Server configured to use the communications protocols detected on your system. The Typical install type sets up the DB2 components used most often, including all required components, ODBC support, and commonly used DB2 tools such as the Control Center and the Configuration Assistant. The DB2 instance and the DB2 Administration Server are created and customized to use the protocols detected on your system.

NOTE

> You can't selectively uninstall components after the DB2 Setup Wizard completes the installation. If you don't want to install all the components mentioned in the preceding paragraph, see the sections on the Compact and Custom installs later in today's lesson.

To do a Typical DB2 server install on a Windows 2000 workstation, follow these steps:

1. Log on as a user that meets the requirements for installing DB2. (For more information, see the previous section "Creating a User Account for Installing DB2 Products.")

2. Shut down any other programs so that the DB2 Setup Wizard can update files as required.

3. Insert the CD-ROM into the drive. The autorun feature automatically starts the DB2 Setup Wizard. The DB2 Setup Wizard determines the system language and launches the DB2 Setup Wizard for that language.

TIP

> To run the DB2 Setup Wizard in a different language, you need to manually invoke the DB2 Setup Wizard. Choose Start|Run. In the Open text box, type `x:\setup /i=LANGUAGE`, where `x:` represents your CD-ROM drive, and *LANGUAGE* represents the two-character country code for your language (for example, EN for English). Click OK.

4. In the Welcome to DB2 dialog box (see Figure 3.1), you can choose to see the installation prerequisites, the release notes, and an interactive presentation of the product, or you can launch the DB2 Setup Wizard to install the product. Click Install Products to open the Select the Product You Would Like to Install dialog box (see Figure 3.2).

FIGURE 3.1

The Welcome to DB2 dialog box.

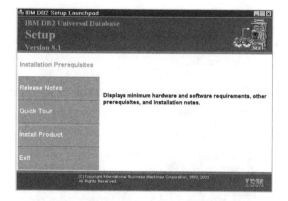

FIGURE 3.2

The Select the Product You Would Like To Install dialog box.

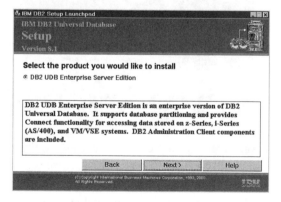

5. Choose a DB2 product depending on the type of license you've purchased (the installation instructions are the same whether you're installing the Workgroup or Enterprise Server Edition):

    *   Choose DB2 Universal Database Enterprise Server Edition if you want the DB2 server plus the capability of having your clients access enterprise servers such as DB2 for z/OS.

    *   Choose DB2 Universal Database Workgroup Server Edition if you want the DB2 server.

TIP

> Although you can install a DB2 client by following the instructions in this section, it's best if you follow Day 6 when installing a client. The instructions vary slightly.

6. Click Next. The Welcome to the DB2 Setup Wizard dialog box appears (see Figure 3.3). Click Next to continue.

FIGURE 3.3

The Welcome to the DB2 Setup Wizard dialog box.

The License Agreement opens (see Figure 3.4). Read the agreement carefully, and if you agree, click I Accept the Terms in the License Agreement to continue with the install. Click Next to continue.

8. Select the installation type you prefer by clicking the appropriate button—for these steps, the Typical button (see Figure 3.5). An estimate of the amount of disk space for each option is shown.

FIGURE 3.4

The License Agreement dialog box.

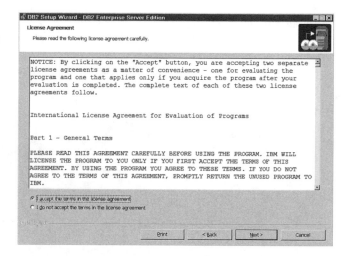

FIGURE 3.5

The Select Installation Type dialog box.

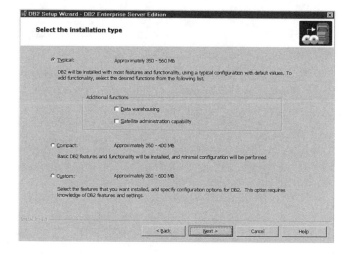

You also can install the Data Warehousing or Satellite Administration capability options. For the purposes of this book, these features will not be installed. Click Next to continue.

9. In the Select the Installation Action dialog box, you have a choice to install DB2 on this computer or to save your choices in a response file (see Figure 3.6). Select to install on this computer and click Next to continue.

10. In the Select Installation Folder dialog box, select a directory and a drive where DB2 is to be installed (see Figure 3.7). Click the Disk Space button to help you select a directory with enough available disk space. (The amount of space required

for the product also appears onscreen.) Click the Change button if you need to change the current destination folder. Click Next to continue.

FIGURE 3.6

The Select the Installation Action dialog box.

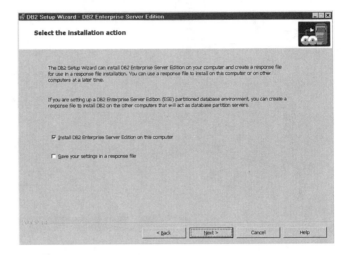

FIGURE 3.7

The Select Installation Folder dialog box.

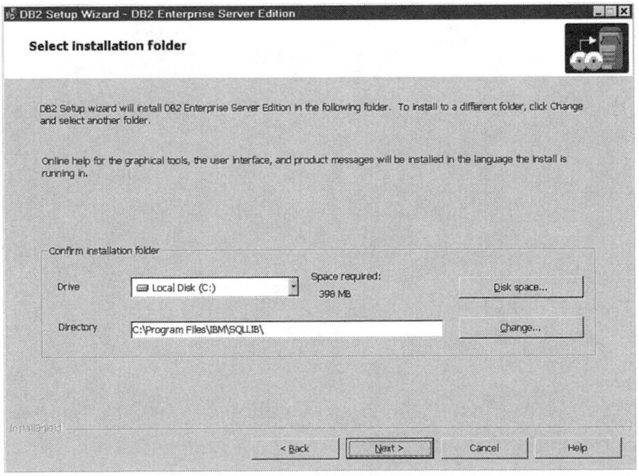

NOTE   If a DB2 Version 8 product is already installed on this computer, you must install subsequent products and components in the same path. The Directory and Drive boxes are disabled if this is the case.

11. In the Set User Information for the DB2 Administration Server dialog box, enter a username and password that will be used for the DB2 Administration Server (see Figure 3.8).

FIGURE 3.8

The Set User Information for the DB2 Administration Server dialog box.

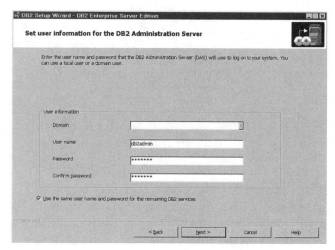

The DB2 Administration Server uses the username and password provided here to log on to the system and start itself as a service. (You use the DB2 Administration Server to enable remote administration.) The DB2 Setup Wizard checks to see whether the username specified for the DB2 Administration Server exists. If it doesn't, you'll be asked whether you want it created, provided that the username you're using to install DB2 has the Act as Part of the Operating System advanced user right. If it does exist, the DB2 Setup Wizard verifies that the username is a member of the Administrators group and verifies that the password is valid. By default, the Use the Same User Name and Password for the Remaining DB2 Services option is selected. Click Next to continue.

12. In the Set up the Administration Contact List dialog box (see Figure 3.9), you can indicate where a list of administrator contacts is to be located. The list will consist of the people who should be notified if the database requires attention. Choose Local if you want the list to be created on your computer or Remote if you plan to use a global list for your organization. For the purposes of this book, choose Local.

This dialog box also allows you to enable notification to an SMTP server that will send email and pager notifications to people on the list. For the purposes of this book, do not enable the SMTP server. (This option can be changed after the product is installed.)

FIGURE 3.9

*The Set Up the
Administration
Contact List dialog
box.*

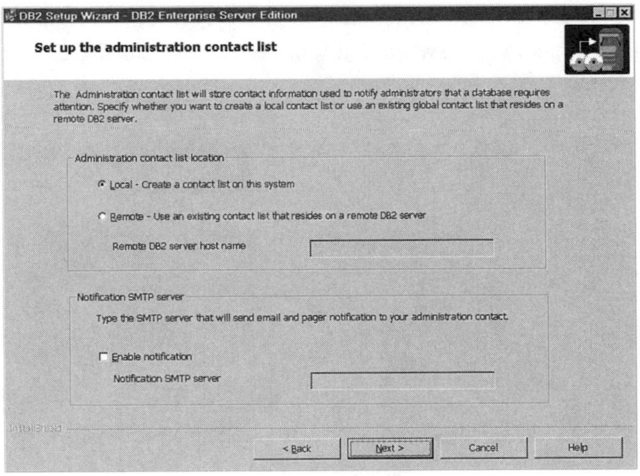

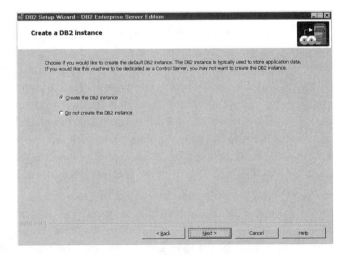

13. In the Create a DB2 Instance dialog box (see Figure 3.10), choose to create the
    default DB2 instance. The DB2 instance is typically used to store application data.
    Select the Create the DB2 Instance option and click Next to continue.

FIGURE 3.10

*The Create a DB2
Instance dialog box.*

14. In the Configure DB2 Instances dialog box (see Figure 3.11), you can modify the
    protocol and startup settings for the DB2 instances. For this step, choose to leave
    the settings at their default values. The Custom install section gives details on
    modifying these settings.

FIGURE 3.11

The Configure DB2 Instances dialog box.

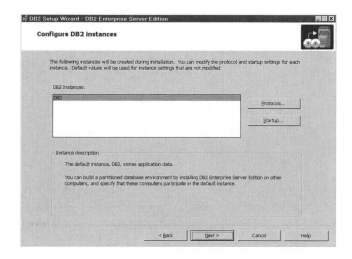

15. In the Prepare the DB2 Tools Catalog dialog box (see Figure 3.12), you can select to prepare the tools catalog to enable tools such as the Task Center and Scheduler. Although this step can be performed after the installation, it is best to have it done during the installation. Select Prepare the DB2 Tools Catalog in a Local Database.

FIGURE 3.12

The Prepare the DB2 Tools Catalog dialog box.

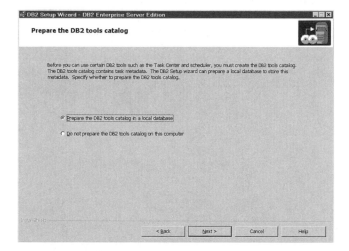

16. In the Specify a Contact for Health Monitor Notification dialog box (see Figure 3.13), you can specify the name of the person to be contacted in case your system needs attention. This name can be added and changed after the installation, so select to Defer the Task Until After Installation is Complete. Click Next to continue.

FIGURE 3.13

The Specify a Contact for Health Monitor Notification dialog box.

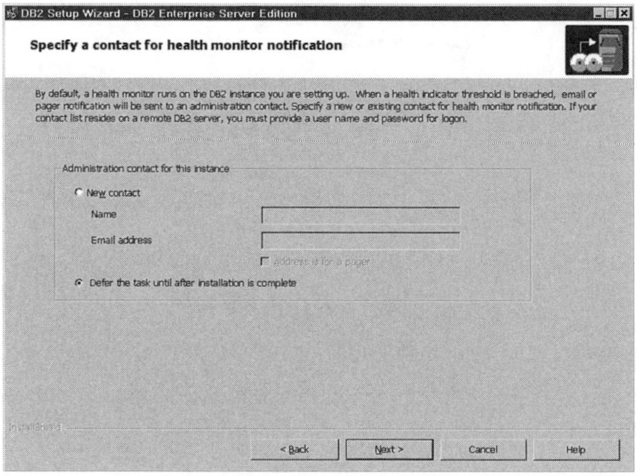

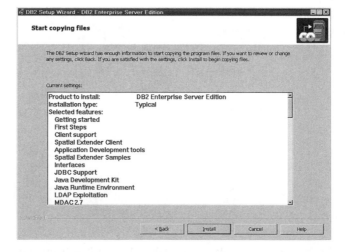

17. You've given DB2 all the information required to install the product on your system. In the Start Copying Files dialog box (see Figure 3.14), you're given one last chance to verify the values you've entered. Click Install to have the files copied to your system. You also can click Back to return to the dialog boxes that you've already completed to make any changes.

FIGURE 3.14

The Start Copying Files dialog box.

18. The installation progress bars appear onscreen while the product is being installed. After the product is installed, a reboot of your computer is not required, but you do need to stop all programs and restart them. Click the Finish button, as shown in the Setup Is Complete dialog box in Figure 3.15, to complete the installation.

Figure 3.15

The Setup Is Complete dialog box.

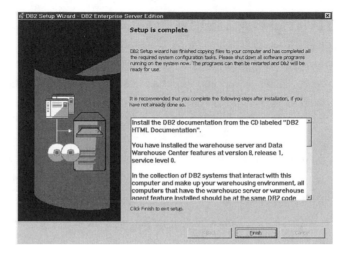

3

TIP

For information on errors encountered during product installation, see the `db2.log` file, which stores general information and error messages resulting from install and uninstall activities. By default, this file is located in the `'Documents and Settings'\<user_account>\'My Documents'\DB2LOG` directory.

The installation program has completed the following:

- Created DB2 program groups and items (or shortcuts).
- Registered a security service.
- Updated the Windows Registry.
- Created a default instance named DB2, added it as a service, and configured it for communications.
- Created the DB2 Administration Server, added it as a service, and configured it so that DB2 tools can administer the server. The service's start type was set to Automatic.
- Activated DB2 First Steps to start automatically following the first boot after installation.

You've completed all the installation steps. Proceed to Day 4, "Getting Started," to verify the installation and to get the system ready for general use.

Performing a Custom Install

Use the Custom install type if you want to choose which DB2 components to install and to configure the DB2 instance and DB2 Administration Server. Through a Custom install, only those components that you select are installed. The DB2 instance and the Administration Server are created and customized to use the protocols detected on your system. The default for a Custom install is to set up all available components and sub-components.

To set up DB2 server on a Windows 2000 workstation by doing a Custom install, follow steps 1–7 as described in the section "Performing a Typical Install," and then continue with the following steps:

8. Select the installation type you prefer—for these steps, the Custom option (see Figure 3.16).

FIGURE 3.16

The Select Installation Type dialog box.

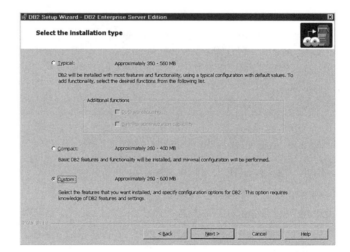

9. Select the installation action you prefer (see Figure 3.17). For these steps, choose to have the product installed on this computer. Click Next to continue.

10. The list of features to be installed on your computer is shown on the Select the Features You Want to Install dialog box (see Figure 3.18). These features are divided into the following categories:

    • Administration tools, including the Control Center, Client Tools, Command Center, Configuration Assistant, Database Tools, Event Analyzer, and DB2 Web Tools.

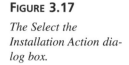

FIGURE **3.17**

The Select the Installation Action dialog box.

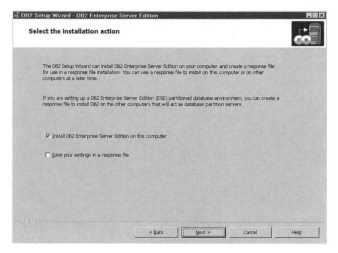

3

- Application Development tools, including Development Center, Warehouse Samples, Spatial Extender Samples, Information Catalog Manager Samples, Java Development Kit, Sample Applications, SQLJ Application Development Tools, and SQLJ Samples.

- Server support, including Apply, Capture, Connect Support, Satellite Control Server, Relational Connect for Informix Data Sources, and Communication protocols.

- Client support, including Interfaces, Base Client Support, System Bind Files, Satellite Synchronization, Spatial Extender Client, Java Runtime Environment, LDAP Exploitation, XML Extender, and Communication protocols.

- Business Intelligence, including Data Warehouse tools and Information Catalog Manager Tools.

- Getting started, including First Steps, Sample Database, Warehouse Sample Database Source, and XML Extender Samples.

To select the features that you want to install, first expand the category by clicking on the plus sign. Next click on the triangle next to a feature to open the Selection dialog box. If the feature is to be installed, it will have an indicator symbol next to the option name. To deselect the feature, click on the This Feature Will Not be Available option. You will see the indicator symbol turn to an X to indicate that the feature will not be installed. For purposes of this book, simply accept the defaults.

FIGURE 3.18

The Select the Features You Want to Install dialog box.

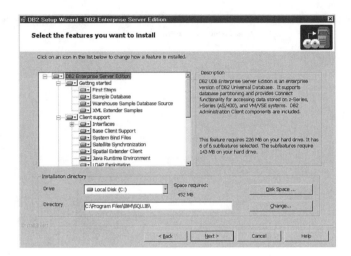

TIP

Be sure to install the Graphical Tools. This book primarily discusses how to use these tools to maintain your databases. If you don't install the tools, you must use the command-line processor to perform these tasks.

In the lower section of this dialog box, you must select a directory and a drive where DB2 is to be installed. Click the Disk Space button to help you select a directory with enough available disk space. (The amount of space required for the product also appears onscreen.) Click the Change button if you need to change the current destination folder. Click Next to continue.

11. In the Select the Languages to Install dialog box, you can select to install the online help, user interfaces, and product messages in multiple languages (see Figure 3.19). For the purpose of this book, only the default language is selected. Click Next to continue.

12. In the Set User Information for the DB2 Administration Server dialog box, enter a username and password that will be used for the DB2 Administration Server (see Figure 3.20).

The DB2 Administration Server uses the username and password provided here to log on to the system and start itself as a service. (You use the DB2 Administration Server to enable remote administration.) The DB2 Setup Wizard checks to see whether the username specified for the DB2 Administration Server exists. If it doesn't, you'll be asked whether you want it created, provided that the username you're using to install DB2 has the Act as Part of the Operating System advanced user right. If it does exist, the DB2 Setup Wizard verifies that the username is a member of the Administrators group and verifies that the password is valid. Click the Use the Same User Name and Password for the Remaining DB2 Services option if you prefer to have one user account for all DB2 services. Click Next to continue.

FIGURE 3.19

The Select the Languages to Install dialog box.

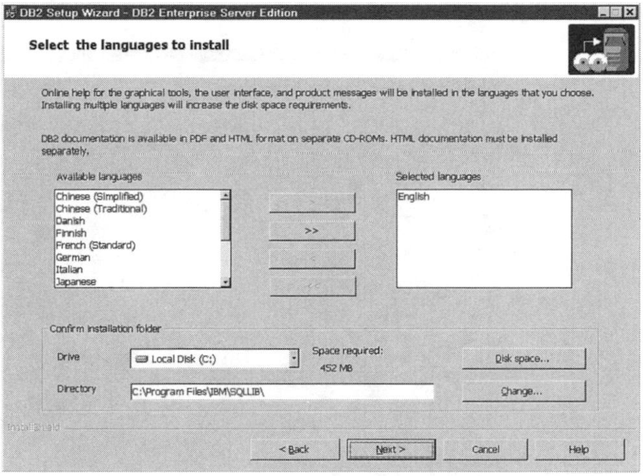

FIGURE 3.20

The Set User Information for the DB2 Administration Server dialog box.

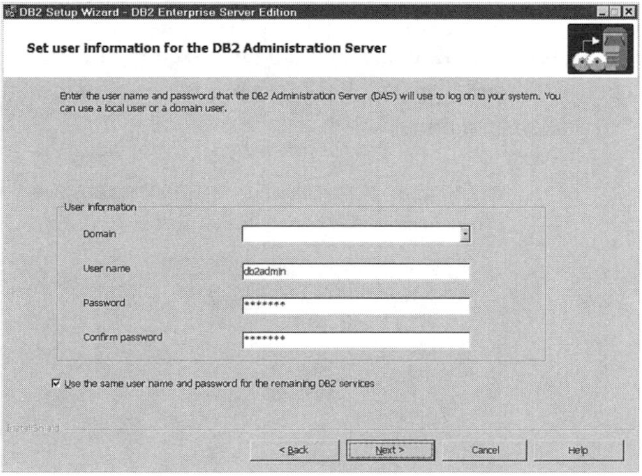

13. In the Set Up the Administration Contact List dialog box (see Figure 3.21), you can indicate the location of the administrator contact list to be local on this computer or global to your organization. The list will consist of the people who should

be notified if the database requires attention. Choose to have the list local to your computer.

This dialog box also allows you to enable notification to an SMTP server that will send email and pager notifications to people on the list. The enablement of the notification of SMTP server is beyond the scope of this book. Click Next to continue.

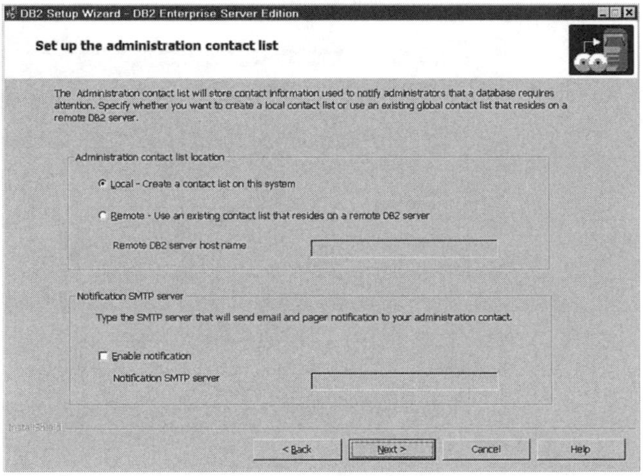

FIGURE 3.21

The Set Up the Administration Contact List dialog box.

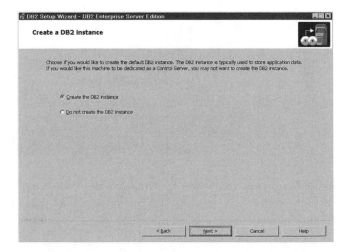

14. In the Create a DB2 Instance dialog box (see Figure 3.22), choose to create the default DB2 instance. The DB2 instance is typically used to store application data. Click Next to continue.

FIGURE 3.22

The Create a DB2 Instance dialog box.

15. In the Configure DB2 Instances dialog box (see Figure 3.23), you can modify the protocol and startup settings for the DB2 instances. By default, DB2 detects the protocols available on your system and assigns values for each required parameter. To see what DB2 has detected and configured, select an instance and click the Protocols button.

FIGURE 3.23

The Configure DB2 Instances dialog box.

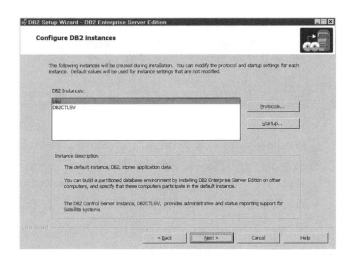

The Instance Communication Protocols dialog box opens. There are three or more tabbed pages on this dialog box, each corresponding to a protocol that was detected on your computer. Figure 3.24 shows the default settings for the TCP/IP protocols. Click on NetBIOS or Named Pipes to see the settings for those protocols.

NOTE

The protocol dialog boxes for the DB2 instance and the DB2 Administration Server are similar (only the DB2 Instance dialog boxes are shown here). If you want to customize the values, customize them for both the DB2 instance and the DB2 Administration Server.

As you can see in the Instance Communication Protocols dialog box in Figure 3.24, DB2 has detected that NetBIOS, TCP/IP, and Named Pipes are installed and configured on this computer. Figure 3.24 shows an example of values assigned to TCP/IP.

FIGURE 3.24

The Instance Communication Protocols dialog box.

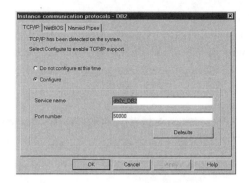

The following parameters are required for the TCP/IP protocol:

- Hostname—A systemwide TCP/IP parameter that is used to uniquely identify the system in the network. You cannot change this value through DB2.
- Service name—This is arbitrary and must be unique within the TCP/IP services file. It is used to identify the connection port used by DB2.
- Port number—This must be unique within the TCP/IP services file.

The following parameters are required for the NetBIOS protocol:

- Adapter number—The logical network adapter that is to be used for the NetBIOS connection. The server uses adapter 0 by default.
- Workstation name—The NetBIOS name of the server workstation. It is chosen arbitrarily, but must be unique among all NetBIOS nodes in the network.

The Named Pipes protocol requires only one parameter, computer name, which is a systemwide parameter and is assigned when Windows is installed on the system. You cannot change this value through DB2.

TIP

> For simplicity, keep the values that DB2 assigns for the parameters, but deselect any of the protocols that you don't intend to use by clicking the Do not Configure at this Time option. It takes extra time to start each protocol; if they aren't needed, this is wasted time.

16. On the Configure DB2 Instances dialog box, you can also set the autostart option. Click the Startup button to open the Startup Options dialog box (see Figure 3.25). By default, the DB2 instance is set to start automatically as a Windows service. For simplicity, keep the default option.

FIGURE 3.25

The Startup Options dialog box.

TIP

If you intend to use DB2 each time you boot your system, choose to have the DB2 instance started automatically (to reduce the number of steps you need to perform each time you boot your system). If you'll use DB2 only occasionally, choose to have it manually started. (To learn how to start the DB2 instance, see Day 4.)

3

17. In the Select the Metadata You Want to Prepare dialog box (see Figure 3.26), you can choose to prepare the tools catalog and the warehouse control database. Choose to prepare the DB2 tools catalog to enable the Task Center and Scheduler.

FIGURE 3.26

The Select the Metadata You Want to Prepare dialog box.

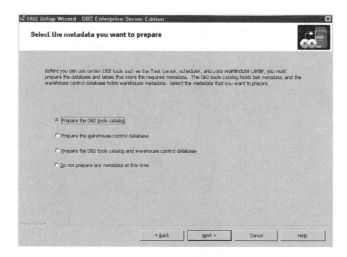

Accept the defaults for the location of the DB2 tools catalog, as shown in Figure 3.27. Click Next to continue.

18. In the Specify a Contact for Health Monitor Notification dialog box, you can specify the name of the person to be contacted in case your system needs attention.

This name can be added and changed after the installation, so select the Defer the Task Until After Installation Is Complete option (see Figure 3.28).

FIGURE 3.27

The Specify a Local Database to Store the DB2 Tools Catalog dialog box.

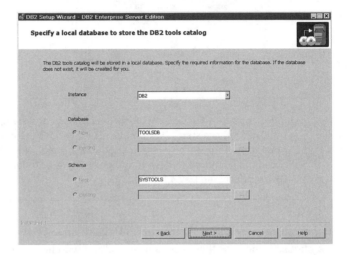

FIGURE 3.28

The Specify a Contact for Health Monitor Notification dialog box.

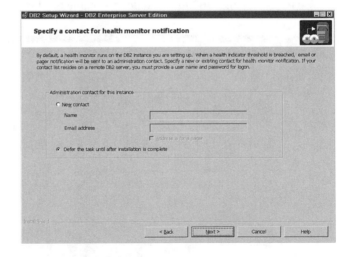

19. In the Request Satellite Information dialog box, you can provide information to set up the satellite server. Setting up the satellite server is beyond the scope of this book. Click Next to continue.

20. You've given DB2 all the information required to install the product on your system. In the Start Copying Files dialog box (see Figure 3.29), you're given one last chance to verify the values you've entered. Click Install to have the files copied to

your system. You also can click Back to return to the dialog boxes that you've already completed to make any changes.

FIGURE 3.29

The Start Copying Files dialog box.

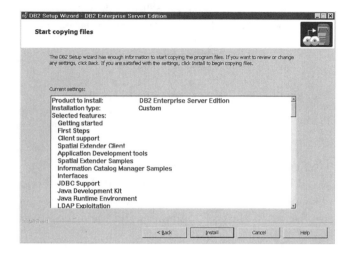

21. The installation progress bars appear onscreen while the product is being installed. After the product is installed, a reboot of your computer is not required, but you should stop all active programs before starting DB2. Click Finish, as shown in the Setup Is Complete dialog box in Figure 3.30, to complete the installation.

FIGURE 3.30

The Setup Is Complete dialog box.

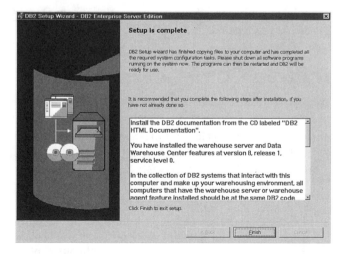

3

TIP
> For information on errors encountered during product installation, see the db2.log file, which stores general information and error messages resulting from install and uninstall activities. By default, this file is located in the 'Documents and Settings'\<user_account>\'My Documents'\DB2LOG directory.

The installation program has completed the following:

- Created DB2 program groups and items (or shortcuts).
- Registered a security service.
- Updated the Windows Registry.
- Created a default instance named DB2, added it as a service, and configured it for communications. If you selected to automatically start the DB2 instance at boot time, the service's startup type was set to Automatic; otherwise, it was set to Manual.
- Created the DB2 Administration Server, added it as a service, and configured it so that DB2 tools can administer the server. The service's start type was set to Automatic.
- Activated DB2 First Steps to start automatically following the first boot after installation.

You've completed all the steps for a Custom install. Go to Day 4 to verify the installation and to get the system ready for general use.

Performing a Compact Install

The steps to perform a Compact installation are the same as for performing a Typical installation, except for the installed product components. During a Compact installation, only the required components are installed, which greatly reduces the amount of disk space required for the product but also greatly reduces the functionality available. For example, the Graphical Tools aren't installed during a Compact installation.

TIP
> Use Compact installation on systems where you use another application to interface to the database. For example, if you're planning to use Microsoft Access as the interface to DB2, you might not want to use the DB2 tools or online documents.

Now that you've successfully installed DB2, see Day 4 to get started with DB2 databases.

Installing the Product Information library

Before you can view the product documentation, you must install the DB2 HTML documents using these steps:

1. Double-click on the setup.exe icon located in the DOC folder. This launches the IBM DB2 Setup Launchpad.

2. Click the Install Products option to open the Select the Product you Would Like to Install dialog box. Click DB2 HTML Documentation. Click Next to continue.

3. On the Welcome to DB2 Setup Wizard dialog box, click Next to continue.

4. On the Select the Installation Action dialog box, choose the Install DB2 HTML Documentation on this Computer option and click Next to continue.

5. On the Select the HTML Documentation Components that you Want to Install dialog box, you can choose the books that you want to install on your system. If you have unlimited disk space, it is recommended to install all the HTML books. This is the default. The entire set of books requires 141 MB of free disk space. Choose a destination folder and click Next to continue.

6. On the Select Languages to Install dialog box, you can select one or more language options for the HTML documentation. For the purposes of this book, leave the default language selected and click Next to continue.

7. On the Start Copying Files dialog box, you are shown a complete list of the HTML documents that will be installed on your computer. Click Install to continue.

8. The Setup Is Complete dialog box appears when the installation of the HTML documents is complete. Click Finish to continue. You do not need to reboot your computer after installation.

Modifying, Repairing, or Removing DB2

If you start the DB2 Setup Wizard on a computer where DB2 Version 8 is already installed, you are presented with the Program Maintenance dialog box, as shown in Figure 3.31.

From this screen, you can change the program features that are currently installed, repair any installation errors in the program, or remove DB2 from your computer.

FIGURE 3.31

The Program Maintenance dialog box.

Summary

Today you saw that you must use a valid DB2 username when using and installing DB2. The username must be fewer than 20 characters long or have the Act as Part of the Operating System advanced user right.

The three different installation types are Custom, Compact, and Typical. Normally, you would use the Typical install type, but you should understand what the options are to ensure that this install type is right for you.

DB2 requires a username and password to be specified for the Administration Server.

What Comes Next?

On Day 4, "Getting Started," you learn about what to do immediately following the installation of the product.

Q&A

Q I have a limited amount of disk space available. Which install type should I use?

A Normally if you have a limited amount of disk space available on your machine, you would select the Compact installation type. This installation type installs the basic components of the product. The DB2 tools are *not* installed if you use this installation type, so it will be difficult—if not impossible—to complete the rest of the examples in this book. If you have a limited amount of space, try to free up space or find another computer.

Q Do I have to customize the communication protocols during the installation?

A If you choose the Typical or Compact installation type, your system is automatically set up to use the default values for the communication protocols detected on your system. You don't need to do anything additional. If you want to see or modify the default values, you must choose the Custom installation type. It's recommended that you don't change the default values, but if you must, make sure that you keep a record of the values you've used.

Q Where can I find information about the success or failure of the installation?

A During installation, DB2 keeps all information, warning, or error messages in the `db2.log` file. This file is located in the `'My Documents'\DB2LOG` folder on your computer.

Workshop

The purpose of the Workshop is to allow you to test your knowledge of the material covered in the lesson. See whether you can successfully answer the questions in the quiz before you continue with the next lesson. The answers appear in Appendix B, "Answers to Quiz Questions and Exercises."

Quiz

1. What's the one difference concerning the default instance when using the Custom install type rather than the Typical install type?

2. Under what circumstances would you need to manually invoke the installation program?

3. How do you know which subcomponents are installed on your system when using the Custom install type?

4. When would you want the default instance to automatically start each time you boot your system?

5. What installation steps can be deferred until the installation of the product is complete?

DAY 4

Getting Started

So, now that DB2 Universal Database is installed, what's next? Where do you begin? Today you learn everything you should do immediately following the installation:

- Logging on to the system
- Changing passwords
- Starting and stopping DB2
- Using First Steps
- Granting privileges to other users

You don't need to perform these steps in the order presented, but you should consider each step before proceeding to later days in this book. Today also introduces you to DB2's desktop and folders.

Logging On to the System

When you start your system, log on with a username that belongs to the Administrators group and meets DB2's naming rules so that you can create databases and set up the security for the users on your system.

NOTE

In many cases, the username db2admin was created during installation. You may choose to log on with this username because it has the highest level of authority. The password for this username was set during installation.

By default, any user belonging to the Administrators group has DB2 System Administration (SYSADM) authority on the instance created during the installation. To change the group that has SYSADM authority on the default instance, see the later section "Changing Default Privileges for Users." To use DB2, log on with a valid username that has the appropriate authority level for the commands you want to execute. The section "Changing Default Privileges for Users" later in today's lesson lists the authority level required to execute certain commands.

TIP

Most database administration tasks described in this book require that you have DBADM or SYSADM authority, so you should log on with a user account that's a member of the Administrators group.

Understanding the Desktop

This section describes each program you'll see on the desktop and in folders following an install. On a Windows system, all the DB2-related programs are found in Start| Programs|IBM DB2 folders, as shown in Figure 4.1.

FIGURE 4.1

The IBM DB2 desktop and folders.

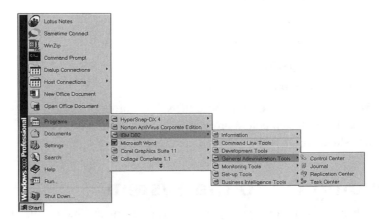

Here is what you'll see:

- Choose the Business Intelligence Tools folder to launch the Data Warehouse Center and Information Catalog Center.
- Choose the Command Line Tools folder to launch the Command Center, Command Line Processor, or Command Window as shown in Table 4.1.

TABLE 4.1 Command Line Tools

Tool	Description
	Choose Command Center to enter DB2 commands and SQL statements in an interactive window and see the execution result in a result window. You can scroll through the results and save the output to a file. You can also create access plan graphs by using the Command Center. Each function is described in this book.
	Choose Command Line Processor to enter commands and SQL statements at a DB2 command prompt.
	Choose Command Window to enter commands and SQL statements at a Windows command prompt. These tools are useful if you know the commands you want to execute and prefer using the command line rather than the graphical tools.

- Choose the Development Tools folder to launch the Development Center and Project Deployment Tool. These tools help you create stored procedures and user-defined functions.
- Choose the General Administration Tools folder to launch the tools shown in Table 4.2. Information on how to use each tool is covered throughout this book.

TABLE 4.2 General Administration Tools

Tool	Description
	The Control Center manages systems, instances, databases, and database objects such as tables and views. In the Control Center, you can display all your systems, databases, and database objects and perform administration tasks on them. From the Control Center, you can also open other centers and tools to help you work with DB2 commands, tasks, and scripts, optimize queries, and monitor performance.
	Use the Journal to view all historical information generated within the Control Center and its components. The Journal gives information about tasks that are pending execution, are executing, or have completed execution, database history, performance monitor alerts, and notification log messages. The Journal also allows you to review the results of tasks that run unattended.

4

Use the Replication Center to launch the Replication Center Launchpad that describes the required tasks to create and operate the DB2 replication environment and subsequently the Replication Center to manage your replication environment.

 Use the Task Center to create mini-applications known as *tasks*, which can be stored and invoked at a later time. These tasks can contain DB2 commands, SQL statements, and operating-system commands. You can schedule tasks to run unattended. These tasks can be run once or set up to run on a repeating schedule. (A repeating schedule is particularly useful for tasks such as backups.)

- Choose Information folder to launch the Information Center allowing you to browse the DB2 online library in HTML format and to access task help, samples, and useful external Web links. The Information Center is described later in today's lesson.
- Choose the Monitoring Tools folder to launch the tools listed in Table 4.3.

TABLE 4.3   Monitoring Tools

Tool	Description
	Use the Event Analyzer to collect information on database activities over a period of time. The information collected by the Event Analyzer provides a good summary of the activity for a particular database event. This information can be used to determine how well the activity was performed.
	Use the Health Center to analyze and improve the health of DB2 in areas such as sufficient resources, efficient use of resources, completion of tasks, and states of objects.
	Use the Indoubt Transaction Manager to perform actions on any global transactions that were left in an indoubt state.
	Use the Memory Visualizer to graphically monitor the memory-related performance of an instance and its databases.

- Choose the Set-up Tools folder to launch the tools listed in Table 4.4.

TABLE 4.4   Set-up Tools

Tool	Description
	Choose Configuration Assistant to manage and maintain database connections and database manager configuration parameters. With the Configuration Assistant, you can define connections to databases, remove cataloged databases, modify the properties of a cataloged database, test connection to local or remote databases, bind applications, and tune configuration parameters. Each function is described throughout this book.

TABLE 4.4   continued

Tool	Description
	Choose First Steps to create the SAMPLE database, work with the data in the database, and launch the Information Center. First Steps, discussed more fully later in this lesson, is automatically launched after DB2 is installed, so you may have noticed it already.
	Choose Register Visual Studio Add-Ins to run an application that registers the add-in products that you may use.
	Choose Satellite Synchronizer to synchronize data with satellites with the satellite control server.
	Choose Warehouse Control Database Management to change the warehouse control database that you are using.

Changing Passwords

During installation, you entered a password for the default user account db2admin. If you want to change this password, follow these steps:

1. Choose Start|Settings|Control Panel|Administrative Tools|Computer Management.

2. In the left-hand panel, expand the Local Users and Groups tool.

3. Choose Users to have a list of current users appear in the right-hand panel.

4. Choose the db2admin user account and click Action|Set Password from the main menu. The Set Password dialog box opens.

5. Enter a new password and confirm. Click OK when finished.

Then follow these steps to change the password for the DB2-DB2DAS00 service to match the new password for the db2admin username:

1. Choose Start|Settings|Control Panel|Administrative Tools|Services.

2. In the Services dialog box, select the DB2-DB2DAS00 service and click Actions| Properties from the main menu.

3. In the Properties dialog box, select the Log On tab, change the password, and confirm the new password. Click OK when finished.

4

Starting or Stopping DB2

During installation, a default instance named DB2 and the DB2 Administration Server named DB2DAS00 were created, added as services, and configured for communications. If you performed a Typical install, these services are set to start automatically each time you boot your system. If you performed a Custom install, you chose whether to have these services started automatically or manually. In either case, to change how the service is started, follow these steps:

1. Choose Start|Settings|Control Panel|Administrative Tools|Services.
2. In the Services dialog box, select the DB2-DB2 service and click Actions| Properties from the main menu. The Startup type can be set to Automatic, Manual, or Disabled. It is best to have this service set to Automatic to ensure that DB2 works when you need it to.
3. Repeat step 2 for the DB2-DB2DAS00 service.
4. Click OK to exit the Services dialog box.
5. To modify whether the services are started automatically or manually, click the Startup icon on the Services dialog box. Select the radio button that corresponds with Automatic, Manual, or Disabled.

If you select Manual, users wanting to launch DB2 as a service must have certain privileges:

- They must belong to one of the following groups: SYSADM_GROUP, SYSCTRL_GROUP, or SYSMAINT_GROUP. These privileges are specified in the database manager configuration file.
- They must have the correct privileges as defined by Windows. They must belong to one of the following Windows groups Administrators, Server Operators, or Power Users group.

Using DB2 First Steps

When your system restarts the first time after installation, DB2 First Steps starts automatically (see Figure 4.2). To invoke DB2 First Steps at any time, choose Start|Programs |IBM DB2|Setup Tools|First Steps.

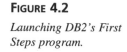

FIGURE 4.2

Launching DB2's First Steps program.

Use DB2 First Steps to perform the following (each task is described in detail in the following sections):

- Choose Create Sample Database to create a sample database (named, of course, SAMPLE) against which you can issue commands to verify that the system is working correctly. The product documentation and sample programs refer to the tables and fields of this database.

- Choose Work with Sample Database to start the Control Center (a DB2 Administration Tool). From the Control Center, you can perform various actions on the SAMPLE database and its objects. Using the Control Center is explored in greater detail throughout this book.

- Choose Work with Tutorials to display the list of tutorials available to learn how to use DB2. To use these tutorials, you must install the DB2 documentation.

- Choose View the DB2 Product Information Library to start the Information Center. This enables you to view and search the DB2 online library with your Web browser and to access task help, samples, and useful external Web links. You must install the DB2 documentation to enable this option.

- Choose Launch DB2 UDB Quick Tour to start an interactive presentation to help you understand the features available in DB2.

- Choose Find Other DB2 Resources on the World Wide Web to start a browser that links to several locations on the IBM Web site. You must have a browser and be connected to the Internet to use this option.

- Choose Exit First Steps to stop the First Steps program.

Creating the Sample Database

To help you verify that the system is installed and configured correctly, create the SAM-PLE database (click the Create Sample Database button in First Steps) and issue a few commands against it. After selecting this option, you are given a dialog box to choose to install the DB2 Samples or the Warehouse Database samples. For the purposes of this book, choose the DB2 Samples.

It takes a few minutes for this database to be created. When it's created, you'll receive the message shown in Figure 4.3.

FIGURE 4.3

The message indicating that the database is created.

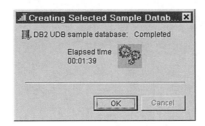

The product documentation and the sample programs use the tables in the SAMPLE database to demonstrate DB2's features. This book uses examples that call these tables as well. Some tables and columns that the SAMPLE database contains are shown in Table 4.5.

TABLE 4.5   Tables and Columns in the SAMPLE Database

Table	Columns Included
EMPLOYEE	EMPNO, FIRSTNME, MIDINIT, LASTNAME, WORKDEPT, PHONENO, HIREDATE, JOB, EDLEVEL, SEX, BIRTHDATE, SALARY, BONUS, and COMM
STAFF	ID, NAME, DEPT, JOB, YEARS, SALARY, and COMM
DEPARTMENT	DEPTNO, DEPTNAME, MGRNO, ADMRDEPT, and LOCATION
ORG	DEPTNUMB, DEPTNAME, MANAGER, DIVISION, and LOCATION
EMP_PHOTO	EMPNO, PHOTO_FORMAT, and PICTURE
EMP_RESUME	EMPNO, RESUME_FORMAT, and RESUME

Each table is described in detail in the SQL Reference. Later in today's lesson, you'll see how to access this information in the HTML version of the book.

Viewing and Working with the Sample Database

To ensure that DB2 was installed correctly, you can start the graphical administration tools. The primary tool is the Control Center, a graphical tool used for DB2 administration tasks. Use the Control Center to

- Manage databases
- Manage tables, views, and indexes
- Configure DB2 systems and instances
- Perform database backup and recovery tasks
- Schedule jobs
- Replicate data

To start the Control Center at this point, click the Work with Sample Database button in the First Steps window. The Control Center allows you to see the objects that make up the SAMPLE database (see Figure 4.4).

FIGURE 4.4

The Control Center.

4

To view the data in the SAMPLE database, right-click on the EMPLOYEE table in the SAMPLE database and choose the Sample Contents option. Several rows of the EMPLOYEE table are shown in the Sample Contents dialog box (see Figure 4.5).

TIP

You can also start the Control Center by choosing Start|Programs|IBM DB2| General Administration Tools|Control Center.

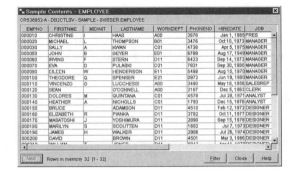

FIGURE 4.5

The Sample Contents – EMPLOYEE dialog box.

First, you should know the terminology used to describe the various Control Center elements. The Control Center interface has five elements that help you define and manage systems and databases: a menu bar, a toolbar, an object tree, the contents pane, and the contents pane's toolbar (see Figure 4.6).

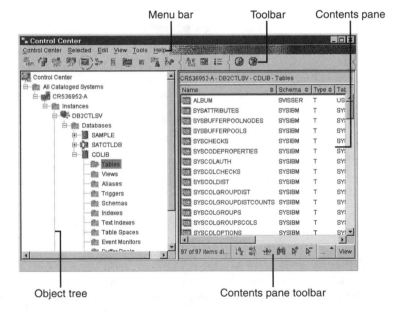

FIGURE 4.6

The elements of the Control Center interface.

The Menu Bar

Use the menu bar to work with objects in the Control Center, open other administration centers and tools, and access online help:

- With the Control Center menu, you can open another Control Center or close all the tools now open.

- With the Selected menu, you can see the actions that can be performed on the currently highlighted object. This menu provides the same options as the right-click pop-up menu.

- The Edit menu helps you find an object or select all the objects within the currently highlighted folder.

- Use the View menu to refresh the objects displayed in the object tree and contents pane, and customize the look of the contents pane. Some of the functions in this menu are also available by clicking icons in the Control Center toolbar and contents pane toolbar.

- Use the Tools menu to open any of the DB2 tools. Some functions in this menu are also available by clicking the icons in the Control Center toolbar.

- The Help menu gives you access to online help or the Information Center.

The Control Center Toolbar

Use the toolbar icons above the object tree to open DB2 tools, view the legend for Control Center objects, and view DB2 information.

Table 4.6 shows the toolbar icons.

TABLE 4.6   Control Center Toolbar Icons

Icon	Description
	Opens another Control Center to display your systems, instances, databases, and database objects and perform administration tasks on them.
	Opens the Replication Center for you to design and set up your replication environment.
	Opens the Satellite Administration Center for you to set up and administer satellites and information in control tables.
	Opens the Data Warehouse Center for you to manage data warehouse objects.
	Opens the Command Center for you to work with database commands, their results, and access plans.
	Opens the Task Center for you to create and run scripts that contain DB2 and operating system level commands.
	Opens the Information Catalog Center for you to manage your business metadata.
	Opens the Health Center that can be set up to alert you to potential problems and provides recommendations to resolve these problems.

TABLE 4.6 continued

Icon	Description
	The Journal for you to run, schedule, and delete jobs and view the recover history log and messages log.
	Opens the License Center so that you can display the status of your DB2 license and to configure your system for license monitoring.
	Opens the Development Center for you to develop stored procedures, user-defined functions, and structured types.
	Opens the Contacts window where you can specify contact information for individual users or groups.
	Opens the Tools settings notebook for you to customize settings and properties for the administration tools.
	Opens the Legend window that displays all the object icons available in the Control Center by icon and name.
	Opens the Information Center for you to search for help on tasks, commands, and information in the DB2 library. You can also use the Information Center to update local documentation.
	Displays help for getting started with the Control Center.

The Object Tree

Use the object tree to display and work with systems and database objects. The top-level objects are Systems, Instances, and Databases. Click the + sign in front of an object to reveal the objects it contains. For example, clicking the + sign in front of the Databases folder reveals a list of databases that you have access to within the selected instance.

The Contents Pane

Use the contents pane to display and work with systems and database objects. The contents pane displays those objects that make up the contents of the selected object in the object tree. For example, when you click the Databases folder, you'll see a list of the databases available in the selected instance.

The Contents Pane's Toolbar

Use the toolbar below the contents pane to tailor the view of objects and information in the contents pane to suit your needs. You can choose to sort, filter, or customize columns, find, select all, or deselect all objects, or view the objects in details, icon, or text formats. (You also can select these functions from the Edit and View menus.)

Table 4.7 shows the toolbar icons.

TABLE 4.7   Icons for the Control Center Contents Pane Toolbar

Icon	Description
	Choose Sort to select the order in which objects appear in the contents pane. You can sort on any column or multiple columns in the contents pane.
	Choose Filter to filter the objects that appear in the contents pane.
	Choose Customize Columns to select the order of the informational columns in the contents pane and reorder, include, or exclude them.
	Choose Find to search for a string in the columns that appear in the contents pane.
	Choose Select All to select all the objects in the contents pane.
	Choose Deselect All to deselect all the objects in the contents pane.

One thing you might want to do right now is view the contents of a database table, such as EMPLOYEE. Follow these steps:

1. Click the + (plus sign) in front of the Systems folder. This shows you the systems, instances, and databases you have on your system.

2. Click the SAMPLE folder to see the objects available within the SAMPLE database.

3. Click Tables to see a listing of all the tables in the contents pane. Scroll down until you see the EMPLOYEE table as shown in Figure 4.7.

FIGURE 4.7

The list of tables in the contents pane.

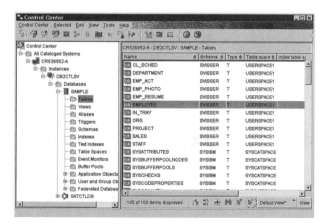

4

Notice the table names that begin with SYS. These are system catalog tables. The system maintains the contents of these tables, but you can view them. Also notice the columns shown in the contents pane. You can see the schema and table space that each table belongs to.

4. Right-click the EMPLOYEE table and select Sample Contents from the pop-up menu to see the first 50 rows of the EMPLOYEE table. The Sample Contents window appears as shown in Figure 4.8.

FIGURE 4.8

The Sample Contents window.

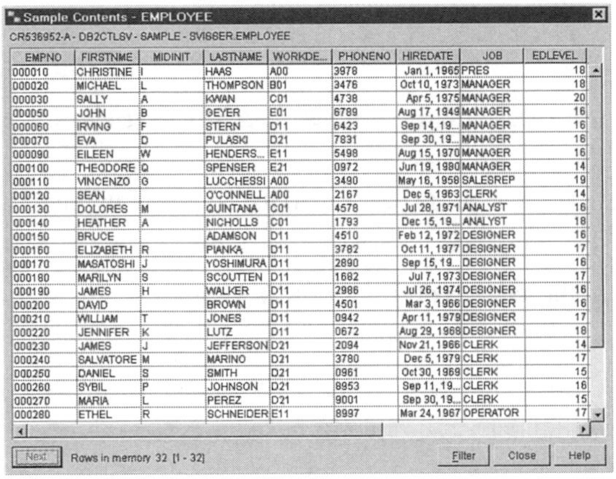
Sample Contents - EMPLOYEE
CR536952-A - DB2CTLSV - SAMPLE - SVISSER.EMPLOYEE

EMPNO	FIRSTNME	MIDINIT	LASTNAME	WORKDE...	PHONENO	HIREDATE	JOB	EDLEVEL
000010	CHRISTINE	I	HAAS	A00	3978	Jan 1, 1965	PRES	18
000020	MICHAEL	L	THOMPSON	B01	3476	Oct 10, 1973	MANAGER	18
000030	SALLY	A	KWAN	C01	4738	Apr 5, 1975	MANAGER	20
000050	JOHN	B	GEYER	E01	6789	Aug 17, 1949	MANAGER	16
000060	IRVING	F	STERN	D11	6423	Sep 14, 19...	MANAGER	16
000070	EVA	D	PULASKI	D21	7831	Sep 30, 19...	MANAGER	16
000090	EILEEN	W	HENDERS...	E11	5498	Aug 15, 1970	MANAGER	16
000100	THEODORE	Q	SPENSER	E21	0972	Jun 19, 1980	MANAGER	14
000110	VINCENZO	G	LUCCHESSI	A00	3490	May 16, 1958	SALESREP	19
000120	SEAN		O'CONNELL	A00	2167	Dec 5, 1963	CLERK	14
000130	DOLORES	M	QUINTANA	C01	4578	Jul 28, 1971	ANALYST	16
000140	HEATHER	A	NICHOLLS	C01	1793	Dec 15, 19...	ANALYST	18
000150	BRUCE		ADAMSON	D11	4510	Feb 12, 1972	DESIGNER	16
000160	ELIZABETH	R	PIANKA	D11	3782	Oct 11, 1977	DESIGNER	17
000170	MASATOSHI	J	YOSHIMURA	D11	2890	Sep 15, 19...	DESIGNER	16
000180	MARILYN	S	SCOUTTEN	D11	1682	Jul 7, 1973	DESIGNER	17
000190	JAMES	H	WALKER	D11	2986	Jul 26, 1974	DESIGNER	16
000200	DAVID		BROWN	D11	4501	Mar 3, 1966	DESIGNER	16
000210	WILLIAM	T	JONES	D11	0942	Apr 11, 1979	DESIGNER	17
000220	JENNIFER	K	LUTZ	D11	0672	Aug 29, 1968	DESIGNER	18
000230	JAMES	J	JEFFERSON	D21	2094	Nov 21, 1966	CLERK	14
000240	SALVATORE	M	MARINO	D21	3780	Dec 5, 1979	CLERK	17
000250	DANIEL	S	SMITH	D21	0961	Oct 30, 1969	CLERK	15
000260	SYBIL	P	JOHNSON	D21	8953	Sep 11, 19...	CLERK	16
000270	MARIA	L	PEREZ	D21	9001	Sep 30, 19...	CLERK	15
000280	ETHEL	R	SCHNEIDER	E11	8997	Mar 24, 1967	OPERATOR	17

Next Rows in memory 32 [1 - 32] Filter Close Help

Further details about the tasks you can perform with the Control Center are covered throughout this book.

TIP

It is recommended that you keep the SAMPLE database (if disk space allows) because it provides a good place for you to test ideas without damaging data in your own databases. If, after you finish using and testing the SAMPLE database, you want to remove it to free up disk space, right-click the SAMPLE folder and select Drop to remove the database.

Viewing the Product Information library

You can view the DB2 product library through the Information Center. The Information Center launches the complete set of DB2 information separated into the categories Tasks, Concepts, Reference, Troubleshooting, Samples, and Tutorials.

To see how to use the Information Center, you can locate information that describes the tables of the SAMPLE database by following these steps:

1. Click the View the DB2 Product Information Library button in the First Steps window. The Information Center appears (see Figure 4.9).

FIGURE 4.9

The Information Center.

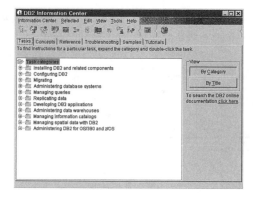

TIP

You can also start the Information Center by choosing Start I Programs I IBM DB2 I Information I Information Center.

4

2. Because you want to view information that is considered reference, click the Reference tab. You can sort the list of information items by category or title. Sort by title and scroll down until you see the SAMPLE database. Double-click on this item to open a window giving details about the SAMPLE database (see Figure 4.10).

FIGURE 4.10

The Information Center showing information about the SAMPLE database.

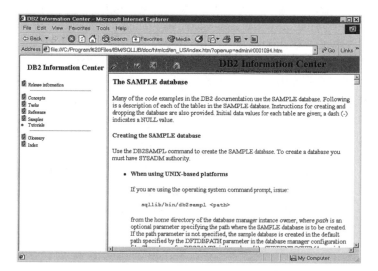

3. Click the Search icon to open the Search dialog box allowing you to set the search scope and to begin searching the entire set of DB2 HTML information installed on your computer.

4. In the Search field, enter the search words `sample database` and click Search. A list of the documents that contain this information appears in Figure 4.11.

FIGURE 4.11

The Search dialog box showing information about the SAMPLE database.

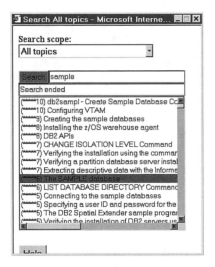

5. Double-click an entry to read the online information about the sample database.

Organizing and Viewing Objects by Schema

The objects in a relational database are organized into *schemas*, which provide a logical classification of objects in the database. The schema object is identified in the first part of a two-part object name. When an object such as a table, view, alias, distinct type, function, index, package, or trigger is created, it's assigned to a schema. This assignment is done explicitly or implicitly.

Use the following instructions to explicitly create a schema:

1. Start the Control Center.

2. Expand the objects until you see the Schemas folder.

3. Right-click the Schemas folder and select Create from the pop-up menu.

4. Type a schema name. The name must be fewer than 30 characters in length and begin with any letter from A through Z. (A schema name can't begin with SYS.)

5. For the Authorization Name field, select the owner of the schema from the drop-down list of users.

6. Click OK to have the schema created.

As you create objects with the Control Center, you can select from a list of existing schema names. To implicitly create a schema, simply type a valid name in the Schema Name text box, overwriting the default schema name. For example, when using the wizard to create a table, the first field allows you to choose or enter a schema name. The default name is the username you're signed in as.

Before creating your own objects, you need to consider whether you want to create them in your default schema (identified by your username) or by using a separate schema (such as PAYROLL for database objects relating to the payroll function) that logically groups the objects. If you're creating objects that will be shared, using a different schema name can be beneficial.

Connecting to a Database

You need to connect to the database before you can use SQL statements to query or update it. The CONNECT statement associates a database connection with a username.

A database is created in an instance through one of two different authentication types: CLIENT or SERVER. If an authentication type isn't specified when the instance is created, the default SERVER authentication is used.

Use the following instructions to connect to a database with the Control Center:

1. Start the Control Center.

2. Expand the objects until you see the database you want, for example, SAMPLE.

3. Right-click the database and select Connect from the pop-up menu.

4. Enter a username and password. If the authentication type is CLIENT, you must enter a valid username and password on the client system. If the authentication type is SERVER, you must enter a valid username and password on the server system.

Granting Privileges to Other Users

To give privileges to the SAMPLE database to other users on the system, follow these steps:

1. Start the Control Center, if it isn't already started.

2. Expand the objects until you see the SAMPLE database.

3. Right-click the SAMPLE database folder and select Authorities from the pop-up menu.

4. In the Database Authorities – SAMPLE window, click Add User, select one or more users from the list, and then click Add. Click Close when you're finished selecting users.

5. A window showing the privileges now assigned to each user opens (see Figure 4.12). A check mark in a column means that the user has the privilege; an x means that the user doesn't have the privilege. You can grant access to CREATETAB, BINDADD, CONNECT, NOFENCE, and IMPLICITSCHEMA privileges. Table 4.8 lists the definitions for each privilege.

FIGURE 4.12

Privileges assigned to each user.

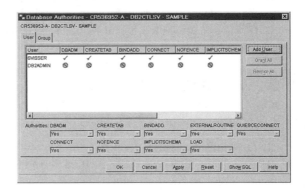

TABLE 4.8   Available User Privileges

Privilege	Definition
CREATETAB	Grants the authority to create base tables within the database. The creator of a base table automatically has the CONTROL privilege on that table. The creator retains this privilege even if CREATETAB is subsequently revoked.
BINDADD	Grants the authority to create packages in the database. The creator of a package automatically has the CONTROL privilege on that package and retains this privilege even if the BINDADD authority is subsequently revoked.
CONNECT	Grants the authority to access the database.
NOFENCE	Grants the authority to register functions that execute in the database manager's process (NOFENCE authority). After users register a function as not-fenced, the function continues to run in the database manager's process even if NOFENCE authority is revoked.

TABLE 4.8   continued

Privilege	Definition
IMPLICITSCHEMA	Grants the authority to create a schema for an object by specifying the schema's name in the definition of the object.
LOAD	Grants the authority to load data into a table if the user also has INSERT privilege on the table.
EXTERNALROUTINE	Grants the authority to register external routines such as stored procedures.
QUIESCECONNECT	Grants the authority to access the database while it is inactive.

Authorities provide a way both to group privileges and to control mainte-
nance and utility operations for instances, databases, and database objects.
The two authorities that you need to know about at this point are SYSADM and
DBADM:

- SYSADM—Grants the highest level of authority within the database manager; it
  controls all database objects. SYSADM authority is given to all users in the
  Administrators group; all other authorities are implicit. This authority level
  cannot be assigned through DB2. It is assigned through Windows' security
  system. DB2 simply assigns SYSADM authority to all users who are members of
  the Administrator group. See the next section, "Changing Default Privileges
  for Users," for instructions on changing the members of this group.

- DBADM—Grants all privileges against all objects in the database and may grant
  these privileges to other users or groups. CREATETAB, CONNECT, BINDADD, and
  NOFENCE authorities are automatically granted to an authorization name
  granted DBADM authority.

TIP

> To create databases and assign authorities to others, you must have SYSADM
> authority.

6. To grant privileges to an entire group, use the Windows Computer Management
   tool to assign users to a group. Click the Group tab in the Authorities window to
   grant access to the group.

TIP

> You may want to assign privileges to users according to their jobs. For exam-
> ple, a query user will need CONNECT on one or more databases, and SELECT,
> INSERT, and DELETE on some tables and views.

4

Changing Default Privileges for Users

By default, SYSADM privileges are granted to any valid DB2 username that belongs to the Administrators group in Windows. You can change the users who have administrator privileges for each DB2 instance by changing the SYSADM_GROUP parameter; before you do, however, make sure that the group exists. To check to see whether this group exists, use the Windows Computer Management tool. If the group exists, it's listed in the Group section of the Local Users and Groups branch.

To use another group as the System Administration group (SYSADM_GROUP), update the database manager configuration file. To change the System Administration group (SYSADM_GROUP) on the server instance, follow these steps:

1. Start the Control Center.
2. Click the + sign for the system that contains the instance you want to update.
3. Right-click the instance that you want to change—for example, DB2—and select Configure Parameters from the pop-up menu.
4. In the DBM Configuration dialog box, find the System Administration Authority Group (SYSADM_GROUP) parameter in the Administration section. Click on the icon in the Value column to open the Change DBM Configuration Parameter window. Type the name of an existing group that you want to assign this privilege.
5. Click OK when finished.
6. Stop all applications that are using DB2, including the Control Center. When restarted, the new value for SYSADM_GROUP is used.

Summary

In today's lesson, you saw that when using DB2, you must log on to Windows with a username that complies with DB2's naming rules. This username must have DBADM or SYSADM authority to perform most of the tasks described in this book. You may want to use the db2admin username created during installation.

You can reach most of the DB2-related programs through the Control Center. The Control Center can be started by choosing Start|Programs|IBM DB2|General Administration Tools|Control Center.

Use the DB2 First Steps program to create the SAMPLE database, work with the database, or access the product library. Each function is available separately as well.

If you're planning to have other users on your system who are required to have more privileges, you can create groups of usernames and use the Control Center to grant authorities.

What Comes Next?

On Day 5, "Setting up DB2 Instances and Server Communications," you learn how to manage instances, view or modify communication parameters, and set configuration parameters.

Q&A

Q What username should I use to log on to Windows if I want to use DB2?

A To use DB2, you must log on to Windows with a username that complies with DB2's naming rules. The most important rule is that the username must have 20 characters or fewer. The username db2admin is usually created during installation, so you may want to log on with this username.

Another factor you should consider is the authority the username has. Many things can be performed only by a username with SYSADM authority. By default, if your username is a member of the Administrators group, it has SYSADM authority. The db2admin username is created in the Administrators group and therefore has SYSADM authority.

Q What DB2 programs start automatically following a reboot?

A Following the first reboot after installation, DB2 First Steps is automatically started to allow you to create the SAMPLE database, work with the database, and access the DB2 product library.

Another choice you had during Custom install was whether you wanted the default instance (DB2) and the DB2 Administration Server (DB2DAS00) started automatically. If you used the Typical install type, both instances are started automatically.

Q How can I view data in the SAMPLE database?

A DB2 uses SQL to query tables in a database and returns the results to you in the form of a table. You can use SQL in many ways to view the information in a table. First, you can use the Control Center and select to sample the contents of a selected table. By using the Command Center, you can type in SQL statements to CONNECT to a database and SELECT data from a table. If you're registered for ODBC, you can use ODBC-enabled applications such as Lotus Approach or Microsoft Access to view the data. You can view the data in other ways as well.

4

Workshop

The purpose of the Workshop is to allow you to test your knowledge of the material covered in the lesson. See whether you can successfully answer the questions in the quiz and complete the exercises before you continue with the next lesson. The answers appear in Appendix B, "Answers to Quiz Questions and Exercises."

Quiz

1. Why would you want to create and use a schema?
2. What authority do you need to create databases?
3. What's the name of the tool that you use to view the DB2 product library?
4. What are the two ways you can start administration tools such as the Task Center?
5. What is the default authentication type and what is required to connect to a database instance created with this authentication type?

Exercise

1. The Control Center introduced in this lesson is the main administration tool that you'll use with DB2. Much of the rest of this book discusses what you can do with the Control Center and the various tools associated with it. At this time, explore various options available with the Control Center to get a feel for how the tool works.

DAY 5

Setting Up DB2 Instances and Server Communications

Today you learn about DB2 server instances and how to view or change protocol information associated with each instance.

An *instance* is a logical database environment that can be customized for the group of databases contained within the instance. For example, it is common to have an instance for test databases and an instance for production databases. Today you will learn how to set the instance that is used as a default, how to create and set up instances, how to update protocol information, how to remove instances, and how to start or stop instances.

The DB2 UDB for Windows product allows you to use TCP/IP, NetBIOS, Named Pipes, and APPC protocols to communicate with client workstations. Today you learn how to update information for the TCP/IP, NetBIOS, and Named Pipes protocols for each instance. (Updating the information for the APPC protocol is beyond the scope of this book.)

During the installation of DB2 servers, a default instance is created, and the protocols detected on your system are configured automatically so that DB2 can use them. Usually, you don't need to do anything further to enable your server to accept requests from clients.

You will learn about the DB2 Administration Server and how it helps clients discover databases on your system. You will also learn how to set configuration parameters and registry variables especially where they affect the discovery parameters. After your environment is set, you are shown how to create profiles that can help set up the remote clients in your environment.

Working with DB2 Instances

You can create one or more instances of DB2 on your system. DB2 program files are physically stored in one location on a particular computer. Each created instance points back to this location, so the program files are not duplicated for each instance created. Databases are stored in instances. Several related databases can be located within a single instance.

TIP

> If possible, create each database in a separate instance. This allows you to specifically tune the instance for a single database.

Setting Up Instances

A default instance, known as DB2, is created when you install DB2. The instance name is used to set up the directory structure. To support the immediate use of this instance, the following are set during installation:

- The environment variable DB2INSTANCE is set to DB2.
- The DB2 Registry value DB2INSTDEF is set to DB2.

These settings establish DB2 as the default instance. You can change the instance that's used by default, but first you have to create an additional instance.

Listing Available Instances

You can list all the database instances cataloged on your system through the Control Center as follows:

1. Open the Control Center if not already open.
2. Expand the object tree until you see the Instances folder.
3. Right-click the Instances folder and choose Refresh from the pop-up menu.

The list of available instances will be shown in the details pane. Alternatively, you can list the available instances by running the db2ilist system command at a command prompt.

Adding Additional Instances

You can add database instances to your system through the Control Center as follows:

1. Open the Control Center if not already open.
2. Expand the object tree until you see the Instances folder.
3. Right-click the Instances folder and choose Add from the pop-up menu.
4. The Add Instance dialog box opens as shown in Figure 5.1.

FIGURE 5.1

The Add Instance dialog box.

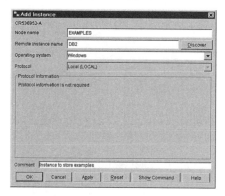

5. Enter the name of the new instance—for example, EXAMPLES.

Alternatively, if you're a user in the Administrators group, you can create additional DB2 instances by using the db2icrt system command at a command prompt. The command syntax is

```
db2icrt instance_name
```

where *instance_name* is a string up to eight alphanumeric characters long.

For example, to create an instance called EXAMPLES, use the following command:

```
db2icrt examples
```

How DB2 Selects an Instance

The value of the DB2INSTANCE variable determines which instance is started or stopped by default. During installation, DB2 sets the DB2INSTANCE variable in the Windows System Properties panel. This sets the variable for all sessions on the system. You can also set the DB2INSTANCE variable for an individual session, or globally for the system.

Setting DB2INSTANCE for the Current Session

The current session's environment variables are examined to see whether DB2INSTANCE is set. You can set it in a session by issuing the following command at a command prompt:

```
set db2instance=new_instance_name
```

To see the value currently set for the session, issue the following command at a command prompt:

```
set db2instance
```

Setting DB2INSTANCE for All Sessions

If DB2INSTANCE is not set in the current session, DB2 examines the system environment variables to see whether it's set for all sessions. On Windows, system environment variables are set in the System Properties panel. Change the value of the DB2INSTANCE variable as follows:

1. Choose Start|Settings|Control Panel and double-click the System icon.
2. In the System Properties dialog box, select the Advanced tab and select the Environment Variables button to list all environment variables in the System Variables list.
3. To change the name of the default instance, select the DB2INSTANCE environment variable and click Edit.
4. Change the Variable Value text box to the instance name—for example, examples.
5. Click OK on the Edit System Variable dialog box.
6. Click OK on the Environment variable dialog box, and then click OK on the System Properties dialog box.

You may have to reboot your system for these changes to take effect.

Setting DB2INSTANCE Globally

If DB2INSTANCE isn't set at all, DB2 uses the registry variable, DB2INSTDEF. It's set at the registry's global level with the following command:

```
db2set db2instdef=new_instance_name -g
```

Remember, a value set for the environment variable DB2INSTANCE at the session or system level overrides the DB2INSTDEF setting.

To determine which database instance applies in the current session, enter the following command at a command prompt:

INPUT   `db2set db2instance`

See "Viewing and Modifying Registry Variables" later in this lesson for instructions on setting registry variables using the Configuration Assistant.

Starting and Stopping a DB2 Server Instance

You must start a DB2 server instance before you can perform the following tasks:

- Connect to a database on the instance.
- Precompile an application.
- Bind a package to a database.

To start a single database instance, log in with a username that has SYSADM authority on the instance and is a member of the Administrators or Power Users groups. Then use one of these methods to start the database instance:

- From the Control Center, right-click the instance that you want to start and select Start from the pop-up menu.
- From a command line, enter the db2start system command.

The db2start system command resolves the DB2INSTANCE value as described earlier in the section "How DB2 Selects an Instance."

To stop an instance, use one of these methods:

- From the Control Center, right-click the instance you want to stop and select Stop from the pop-up menu.
- From a command line, enter the db2stop system command.

NOTE

If command-line processor sessions are attached to an instance, you must issue the terminate system command to end each session before issuing the db2stop system command.

5

Running Multiple Instances Concurrently

You can start multiple DB2 instances as long as they belong to the same level of code (such as DB2 version 8). To run multiple instances concurrently, use one of the following methods:

- From the Control Center, right-click another instance that you want to start and select Start.
- From the command line, set the DB2INSTANCE variable to the name of the other instance that you want to start by using the command set db2instance=*another_instance_name*. Start the instance by entering the db2start system command, and then stop and restart the DB2 Administration Server by entering the following commands at a command prompt:

INPUT
```
db2admin stop
db2admin start
```

See Day 7, "Ensuring Data Security," for information on configuring each instance with different environment variables.

If instances aren't shown when you refresh the Control Center, you must right-click the Instances folder and select Refresh from the pop-up menu.

If you have databases that no longer appear, right-click the Databases folder and select Refresh to see a list of databases that you can recatalog.

Attaching to Instances

You can attach to other instances to perform maintenance and utility tasks that can be done only at an instance level such as creating a database, forcing off applications, monitoring a database, or updating Database Manager Configuration files. When you attempt to attach to an instance that's not your default instance, the node directory is used to determine how to communicate with that instance.

To attach to another instance, which may be remote, use the attach system command:

```
attach to examples
```

This command attaches you to the instance called examples that was previously cataloged in the node directory.

To use the Control Center to attach to another instance, which may be remote, follow these steps:

1. In the Control Center, right-click the Instances folder and select Attach from the pop-up menu.
2. Enter the username and password for the system and click OK.

Removing Instances

To remove a DB2 instance, follow these steps:

1. End all applications now using the instance.

2. Stop the instance by right-clicking the instance and selecting Stop from the pop-up menu.

3. Back up files in the \sqllib*instance_name* directory, if needed. For example, you might want to save the Database Manager Configuration file, db2systm.

NOTE
> If the DB2INSTPROF environment variable is set, these files will be in a different location than the one used in this example.

4. Delete the instance by right-clicking the instance and selecting Remove from the pop-up menu.

Modifying the DB2 Communication Configuration of Server Instances

You use the Control Center's Setup Communications function to configure communications on the server. The Control Center allows you to display the protocols and configuration parameters that a server instance is configured to use. With the Control Center, you also can maintain the configured protocols by

- Modifying the parameter values of a configured protocol
- Adding or deleting a protocol

When you add support for a new protocol to the server system, the Setup Communications function detects and generates parameter values for the new protocol; you can accept or modify them before use. When you remove support for an existing protocol from the server system, the Setup Communications function detects the protocol that has been removed and disables its use by the instance. You also can use the Setup Communications function to maintain communications of both local and remote server instances.

To view or modify the configuration of the communication protocols for a DB2 instance, follow these steps:

5

1. To start the Control Center on a Windows system, choose Start|Programs|IBM DB2|General Administration Tools|Control Center.

2. Click the + sign beside the system name to get a list of that system's database instances.

3. Right-click the instance you want to configure and select the Setup Communications option from the pop-up list.

4. In the Setup Communications dialog box (see Figure 5.2), select a protocol that you want to view or update and click the associated Properties button.

FIGURE 5.2

The Setup Communications dialog box.

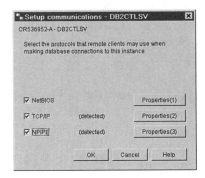

Click on Properties next to NetBIOS to open the Configure NetBIOS dialog box. For NetBIOS, you can enter values for workstation name and adapter number. The workstation name is the name of this system and must be unique on the network. The adapter number is the LAN adapter number that you want the instance to use for NetBIOS connections. Click on Default to have DB2 assign values for these parameters as shown in Figure 5.3. Click OK to have these values saved and to return to the Setup Communications dialog box.

FIGURE 5.3

The Configure NetBIOS dialog box.

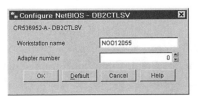

Click on Properties next to TCP/IP to open the Configure TCP/IP dialog box. For TCP/IP, you can enter values for service name and port number. The hostname is displayed for information only and cannot be changed through DB2 because it is a systemwide value. The service name is the name used in the services file to map to the port number used for this server instance. The port number is the TCP/IP port number used by this server instance to listen for connection requests from remote clients. Click on Default to have DB2 assign values for these parameters as shown in Figure 5.4. Click OK to have these values saved and to return to the Setup Communications dialog box.

FIGURE 5.4

The Configure TCP/IP dialog box.

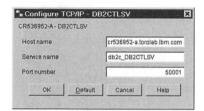

Click on Properties next to NPIPE to open the Configure Named Pipe dialog box. For Named Pipes, you are shown the computer name of your system. This is shown for your information only and cannot be changed through DB2 because it is a systemwide value. Figure 5.5 shows an example of the Configure Named Pipe dialog box as it is on my system. Click OK to have these values saved and to return to the Setup Communications dialog box.

FIGURE 5.5

The Configure Named Pipe dialog box.

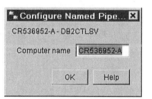

If you have APPC installed on your computer, and it is detected by DB2, click on Properties next to APPC to open the Configure APPC dialog box. For APPC, you can enter a value for the transaction program name. Enter the name of the transaction program that will be executed when a client connects to this server instance using the APPC protocol.

If DB2 detects an APPC stack that it can configure, you can enter the information that is needed, and DB2 will configure it. If it has been configured already, you are allowed to change only the LU name.

NOTE   If a new protocol is installed on the server's system, it will be detected and parameter values will be generated; you can accept these values or change them.

Click OK when you've completed the changes. Stop and start the instance for these changes to take effect. To stop the database manager instance, right-click the instance, and select Stop from the pop-up menu. To start the database manager instance, right-click the instance, and select Start from the pop-up menu.

Modifying an instance's communications settings might require you to update the database connection configuration on the client. Use the Configuration Assistant to update the connection information on the client, as discussed on Day 6, "Installing and Configuring DB2 Clients."

NOTE

> If clients are having trouble connecting to the server, make sure that the DB2COMM registry value is defined to use the protocol that you intend to use for the client and server communications. To check the DB2COMM value on the server, type db2set db2comm at a command window prompt.
>
> Also make sure that the database manager at the server is started. A client can't access the server unless a db2start has been issued. The database manager is usually set up to start each time you boot your system by default.

Viewing and Modifying Configuration Files

You can control your database environment through configuration parameters at either the instance or database levels. A Database Manager Configuration file is created for each instance created on your computer. The parameters in the Database Manager Configuration file affect system resources at an instance level. A Database Configuration file is created when a database is created, and its values affect the resources specific to this database.

Your environment can also be controlled through the registry variables stored in the DB2 Profile Registry. These variables can be set at the global or instance level.

Viewing and Modifying Database Manager Configuration Files

Configuration parameters set at the database manager or instance level affect all databases within this instance. You can set more than 90 configuration parameters at an instance level. The configuration parameters are split into six categories: Administration, Communications, Diagnostic, Environment, Miscellaneous, and Performance.

You can use the Control Center to view and update the values in the Database Manager Configuration file, as follows:

1. Start the Control Center, if not already started.

2. Right-click the DB2 instance and choose Configuration Parameters from the pop-up menu. The DBM Configuration dialog box opens as shown in Figure 5.6. You'll need to scroll down to see all the values in this file because it is long.

FIGURE 5.6

DBM Configuration dialog box.

3. Click on a configuration parameter keyword to receive hint information as to how the parameter is used.

4. To change values in this file, click on the icon in the Value column. A Change DBM Configuration Parameter dialog box opens allowing you to change or add a parameter. A hint is given to help you make your choice. For example, to change the DISCOVER value from Search to Known, click the radio button next to Known (see Figure 5.7).

FIGURE 5.7

Change DBM Configuration Parameter – DISCOVER dialog box.

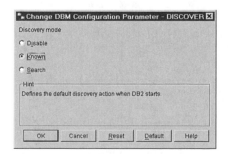

5

5. Click OK to close the Change DBM Configuration – DISCOVER dialog box.

6. Click OK to close the DBM Configuration dialog box.

Viewing and Modifying Database Configuration Files

Setting configuration parameters at a database level allows you to tune each database independently of all others on your computer. There are 87 database configuration parameters, which are divided into six categories: Applications, Environment, Logs, Performance, Recovery, and Status.

You can use the Control Center to view and update the values in the Database Manager Configuration file, as follows:

1. Start the Control Center, if not already started.

2. Right-click the SAMPLE database and choose Configuration Parameters from the pop-up menu. The Database Configuration - SAMPLE dialog box opens as shown in Figure 5.8. You'll need to scroll down to see all the values in this file because it is long.

FIGURE 5.8

Database Configuration – SAMPLE dialog box.

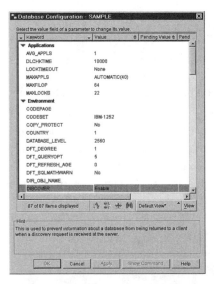

3. Click on a configuration parameter keyword to receive hint information as to how the parameter is used.

4. To change values in this file, click on the icon in the Value column. A Change Database Configuration Parameter dialog box opens allowing you to change a parameter value. A hint is given to help you make your choice. For example, to

change the DISCOVER value from Enable to Disable, click the radio button next to Disable (see Figure 5.9).

FIGURE 5.9

Change Database Configuration Parameter – DISCOVER dialog box.

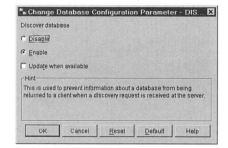

5. Click OK to close the Change Database Configuration Parameter – DISCOVER dialog box.

6. Click OK to close the Database Configuration dialog box.

Viewing and Modifying Registry Variables

Registry variables can also help to control your environment at the global or instance level. Registry variables are stored in the DB2 Profile Registry. You can use the Configuration Assistant to view and update the variables in the registry, as follows:

1. Start the Configuration Assistant, if not already started.

2. Click DB2 Registry from the Configure menu to open the DB2 Registry as shown in Figure 5.10.

5

FIGURE 5.10

DB2 Registry opened from the Configuration Assistant.

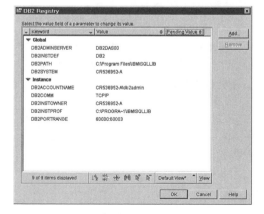

3. To change values in this file, click on the icon in the Value column. A Change
   Registry dialog box opens allowing you to change the value. For example, to
   change the DB2COMM registry value, open the Change Instance Registry –
   DB2COMM and add NETBIOS to the list (see Figure 5.11).

FIGURE 5.11

*Change Instance
Registry – DB2COMM
dialog box.*

4. Click OK to close the Change Instance Registry – DB2COMM dialog box.

5. The DB2 Registry only shows the registry variables that are currently set. To set
   registry variables that are not listed, click the Add button, select a variable, and
   give a value. For example, choose DB2DISCOVERYTIME and set the registry value to 35
   seconds as shown in Figure 5.12. This parameter specifies that the searched discovery will wait 35 seconds for a response from servers.

FIGURE 5.12

*Add Registry dialog
box setting the
DB2DISCOVERY-
TIME registry vari-
able.*

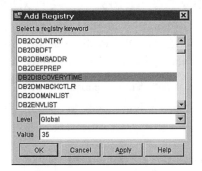

6. Click OK to set this value and to close the Add Registry dialog box. You'll see that
   this variable was added to the list of registry variables.

7. Click OK to close the DB2 Registry.

NOTE

DB2 Registry values can also be set using db2set commands in the DB2
Command Window.

Adding Systems Through the Control Center

You can use the Control Center to administer databases on remote servers as well as the databases you have on your local system. To access instances and databases on other servers, you must first add the system to the Control Center object tree.

DB2 needs to catalog the system in the admin node directory of the client. Adding a system adds an entry to the admin node directory giving DB2 the information it needs to communicate with the remote system. All systems that you access will have an entry in the admin node directory. Use the Add System dialog box to specify information about the computer you want to connect to.

On a server, the Control Center displays local and remote systems under the Systems icon in the object tree. You can work with objects from the local system such as instances and databases, but you cannot change or remove the local system because it represents your local computer. Figure 5.13 shows the Control Center with two systems. VUE-SERVER1 is the local system, and CERTSRVR is a remote system.

FIGURE 5.13

The Control Center showing local and remote systems.

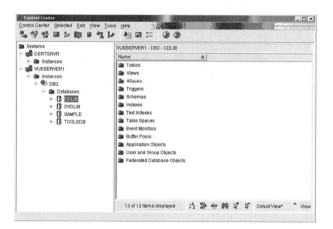

5

To add a remote system, instance, and database using the Control Center, right-click the SYSTEM folder and select Add from the pop-up menu. The Add System dialog box opens. In this dialog box, you must provide the system name, hostname, and node name of the remote system you want to access as follows:

System name: The name of the physical machine where the target database is located. This is defined by the DB2SYSTEM DAS configuration parameter on the server.

NOTE   If you are using TCP/IP, you may be able to complete the remaining entries by using Discover.

Hostname:	TCP/IP requires you to enter the hostname of the remote system. (If the system was discovered, click the View Details button to view protocol information.)The protocol information needed depends on the protocol you are using to communicate with the remote server.
Node name:	A local nickname for the remote server. This name must be unique on your system.
Operating system:	Of the remote server.

If the remote system you are trying to access is known to your computer, you can click the Discover button to automatically fill in this information. The fields are filled in after the information is retrieved from the remote system. Figure 5.14 shows the VUE-SERVER1 system on my computer being discovered by a remote DB2 Client.

FIGURE 5.14

The Discovery Search dialog box launched through the Add System window in the Control Center.

Click OK to have the remote system added to the object tree in the Control Center.

Now that you have a remote system listed in the Control Center, you must add the instances and databases you intend to use on the remote system. To add an instance, expand the objects within the remote system and right-click the Instances folder. Choose Add from the pop-up menu. The Add Instance dialog box opens (see Figure 5.15).

FIGURE 5.15

*The Add Instance dia-
log box launched
through the Control
Center.*

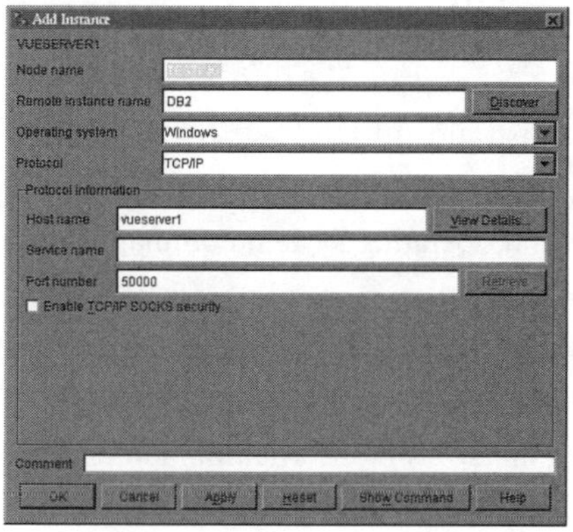

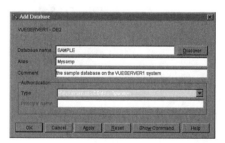

Click Discover to have information about the remote instances returned to your system.
Select an instance you want to add and click OK to have it added to the object tree in the
Control Center.

The last step is to add the databases from the remote system. The databases will stay on
the remote system, but you can view the data and perform administration tasks for this
database. To add a database, expand the objects below the instance you have just added.
Right-click on the Databases folder and choose Add from the pop-up menu. The Add
Database dialog box opens (see Figure 5.16).

FIGURE 5.16

*The Add Database
dialog box launched
through the Control
Center.*

5

Click Discover to have the remote databases listed on the screen. Click OK to have the
database added to the object tree in the Control Center. You can now administer the
remote database.

The DB2 Administration Server

The DB2 Administration Server (DAS) is a control point used only to assist with tasks
on DB2 servers. You must have a running DAS if you want to use available tools such as
the Configuration Assistant, the Control Center, or the Development Center. DAS assists

the Control Center and Configuration Assistant when working on the following administration tasks:

- Enabling remote administration of DB2 servers.
- Providing the facility for job management, including the capability to schedule the running of both DB2 and operating system command scripts. These command scripts are user-defined.
- Defining the scheduling of jobs, viewing the results of completed jobs, and performing other administrative tasks using the Task Center.
- Providing a means for discovering information about the configuration of DB2 instances, databases, and other DB2 administration servers in conjunction with the DB2 Discovery utility. This information is used by the Configuration Assistant and the Control Center to simplify and automate the configuration of client connections to DB2 databases.

You can only have one DAS on a computer. The DAS is configured during installation to start when the operating system is booted.

Typically, the DB2 Setup Wizard creates a DAS on the instance-owning machine during DB2 installation. If, however, the DB2 Setup Wizard failed to create it, you can manually create a DAS or reinstall DB2. If you want to manually create the DAS service on Windows, follow these steps:

1. Log on to the computer you want to create the DAS on using a user account that has local administrator authority.
2. Enter the command

```
db2admin create /user: myusername /password: mypassword
```

When creating the DAS, specifying a username and password is optional. If valid, the username and password will identify the user account to start the DAS service. Set the password for the account name to "Password Never Expires."

After you create the DAS, you can establish or modify its ownership by providing a username and password with the db2admin setid system command.

Setting Discovery on the Server

Network searches can be customized to meet the needs of individual organizations. Network searching uses the DB2 Discovery facility to obtain information from DB2 servers. This information is used to configure clients for database connections. Two discovery methods are available for searching the network: Known and Search.

Known discovery allows you to find instances and databases on systems known to your client, and to add new systems so that their instances and databases can be discovered. However, it does not support searching the network for servers. *Search discovery* provides all the functions described for the Known discovery mode, but allows your local network to be searched for DB2 servers.

TIP

> The Search discovery mode may appear to be a simpler method. In larger networks, however, network routers and bridges can filter the messages Search uses to find DB2 servers on the network, resulting in an incomplete or even empty list. In this case, use the Add System method; its messages are not filtered by routers and bridges. If in doubt, contact your network administrator for assistance.

A DB2 client uses the Discovery feature either through the Control Center or Client Configuration. In either case, you must enable discovery on the server for DB2 clients to find the system, instances, and databases on the server. By default, all the required parameters are set to enable discovery.

Three configuration levels control discovery parameters: DAS, instance, and database. The examples earlier in this lesson showed how you set the discovery parameters at the instance and database levels.

Setting Discovery Parameters at the DAS Level

The DISCOVER parameter for the DAS can be set to SEARCH, KNOWN, or DISABLE:

- KNOWN—To have the server support Known discovery, set DISCOVER to KNOWN.

- SEARCH—To have the server support Search discovery, set DISCOVER to SEARCH.

- DISABLE—To prevent discovery of the server, and all its instances and databases, set DISCOVER to DISABLE.

The DAS must be running and enabled for Discovery to work. By default, the DAS is set to automatically start, and the DISCOVER parameter is set to SEARCH.

View the DAS configuration file with the Command Line Processor as follows:

```
get admin cfg
```

Update the DAS configuration file with the Command Line Processor as follows:

```
update admin cfg using discover [ DISABLE | KNOWN | SEARCH ]
```

5

> Servers configured with DISCOVER set to KNOWN will not respond to search requests from clients. It is important that you consider this when changing the DISCOVER parameter, which was set to SEARCH during installation.

Setting Discovery Parameters at the Instance Level

Three discovery parameters that can be set at the instance level: DISCOVER, DISCOVER_COMM, and DISCOVER_INST.

- DISCOVER—Set to DISABLE, KNOWN, or SEARCH. This parameter defines the discovery action when DB2 starts.
- DISCOVER_COMM—Set to any combination of TCP/IP and NetBIOS. This parameter defines the communication protocol that clients use to issue discovery requests and servers use to listen for search discovery requests.

> On the server, the values specified by DISCOVER_COMM must be equal to or a subset of the values set by DB2COMM Registry value.

- DISCOVER_INST—To allow clients to discover server instances on a system, set this parameter in each server instance on the system to ENABLE (the default value). Set this parameter to DISABLE to hide this instance and its databases from discovery.

Use the Control Center to view or update the instance level parameters, as follows:

1. Start the Control Center, if not already started.
2. Right-click the DB2 instance and choose Configuration Parameters from the pop-up menu. The DBM Configuration dialog box opens.
3. Click on a configuration parameter keyword to receive hint information as to how the parameter is used.
4. To change values in this file, click on the icon in the Value column. The Change DBM Configuration dialog box opens.
5. Click OK to close the Change DBM Configuration dialog box.
6. Click OK to close the DBM Configuration dialog box.

Setting Discovery Parameters at the Database Level

To allow a database to be discovered from a client, set the DISCOVER database configuration parameter to ENABLE (the default value). Set this parameter to DISABLE to hide the database from discovery.

Use the Control Center to view or update the database level parameters, as follows:

1. Start the Control Center, if not already started.
2. Right-click the database and choose Configuration Parameters from the pop-up menu. The Database Configuration dialog box opens.
3. Click on a configuration parameter keyword to receive hint information as to how the parameter is used.
4. To change values in this file, click on the icon in the Value column. The Change Database Configuration dialog box opens.
5. Click OK to close the Change Database Configuration dialog box.
6. Click OK to close the Database Configuration dialog box.

Server Profiles

Server profiles can be generated for a DB2 server. They contain information about instances on the server system and databases within each instance. The information for each instance includes the protocol information required to connect a client to databases in that instance.

To generate server profiles, use the Export Server Profile function provided in the Control Center. When a profile is generated for a DB2 server system, it includes server instances that have the DISCOVER DBM configuration parameter set to ENABLE and databases with the DISCOVER database configuration parameter set to ENABLE. For information on setting the DISCOVER_INST, DISCOVER_DB, and DISCOVER configuration parameters, see "Setting Discovery on the Server" earlier in this lesson.

Generating a Server Profile

You need to generate a server profile only if you want to set up clients to access this server. At least one database should be created on your server before creating a profile.

To generate an access profile, perform the following steps on the machine where your databases are located:

1. Start the Control Center.
2. Click the + sign beside the Systems folder to list the systems.

5

3. Right-click the system to be profiled and select Export Server Profile from the pop-up menu. The Export Server Profile dialog box appears (see Figure 5.17).

FIGURE 5.17

The Export Server Profile dialog box.

4. Select the path and type in a filename for the profile, and then click OK. You should put the file in a location that your clients can access such as a network drive or an FTP site. For the example in this lesson, I used the name `e:\profile\enterprise.prf`.

To process a server profile and add its databases to the client's connection configuration list, use the Configuration Assistant's Add functions on the remote client machine to select the database connection data in the server profile that you want to add to the client. (This function invokes the Add Database Wizard, covered in Day 6.)

Summary

Today you saw that you can create one or more instances of DB2 on your system. DB2 program files are physically stored in one location on a particular machine, and each created instance points back to this location.

Databases are stored in instances. You can have several related databases located within a single instance.

A default instance called DB2 is created when you install the product. The instance name is used to set up the directory structure where the data files are stored.

You saw that the Control Center is used to view and modify the communications on the server. The server is configured automatically to use the protocols detected on your system when DB2 is installed.

You can use one or more of the following protocols to listen for requests from clients if your server is on Windows: APPC, Named Pipes, NetBIOS, or TCP/IP.

Usually, you should accept the default values used to configure the supported communications. If you want to change any of the values, you should proceed with caution.

You saw that you can view and update database manager and database configuration parameters using the Control Center. Parameters set in the Database Manager Configuration file affect all databases within the instance. Parameters set in the Database Configuration file affect only the specific database. You can use the Configuration Assistant to change DB2 registry variables that can affect your system at either a global or an instance level.

You saw that to allow clients to discover the systems, instances, or databases on your computer, several discovery parameters must be enabled. In this lesson, you learned that by default these parameters are set to enable discovery and that you can disable this function at one of three levels.

You also saw that a profile can be created that can include database connections, configuration parameters, and registry variables. These profiles can be used to provide the necessary information to set up the clients that need to access your databases.

What Comes Next?

On Day 6, "Installing and Configuring DB2 Clients," you learn how to install and set up DB2 clients on a Windows computer.

Q&A

Q The default instance is determined by the value of the DB2INSTANCE environment variable. What are the different ways this variable can be set?

A You can set the DB2INSTANCE environment variable for an individual session by entering set db2instance=*new_instance_name* at a command prompt. The environment variable can be set for all sessions by using the System Properties dialog box. And, finally, you can use the DB2INSTDEF profile registry value to set the DB2INSTANCE environment variable globally. If you have all three values set, the two environment variable settings override the registry value.

Q Can I run multiple instances at one time?

A If you have multiple instances defined on your system and they're all at the same level of product code, you can run multiple instances at one time. You might want to do this if you have a production database in one instance and a test database in another, and you want to query the data in both instances at the same time.

5

Q What's the difference between starting an instance and attaching to an instance?

A You attach to an instance when you want to perform maintenance such as creating a database, forcing off applications, or updating a Database Manager Configuration file. You can perform these same actions if you start the instance as well. Attaching to an instance allows you to perform maintenance on several instances that may not be defined as your default instance.

Q When should I install communications support on my system?

A If you're installing a new system from scratch, it's best to have any communication protocols you intend to use with DB2 installed and fully configured before you install DB2. Then, when you install DB2, the installation program will detect that these protocols are available and will proceed to configure DB2 to use these protocols. If you install protocols after installing DB2, you'll need to manually configure the protocols so that DB2 can use them.

Q How many protocols can I use at the same time?

A You can use all supported protocols at the same time. This means that if you have three different clients each set up to use a different protocol, you can configure the DB2 server to accept requests from each client concurrently. The only thing that you have to ensure is that all protocols are installed and configured on the server.

If, however, you only intend to use one protocol, you should configure your system to use only this protocol. It takes additional resources to have each protocol configured and started each time DB2 is used.

Q What are the two available discovery methods?

A You can choose the KNOWN or SEARCH discovery method. With KNOWN, your client can find only the instances and databases on the network that are known to the client. You can add systems if you know what protocol is used and the specific protocol information of the remote server. Using the SEARCH discovery method allows your client to search all the systems on the local network for databases.

Q When would I use a server profile?

A A server profile is generated at the server workstation and contains information about the databases cataloged on the server. After you generate a profile of the databases on the server, you can store the profile on a network drive that all your clients can access. Each client user can import this profile so that each client can easily set up the information needed to connect to the database. This ensures that each client uses the same database information, thereby reducing problems when connecting clients to servers.

Workshop

The purpose of the Workshop is to allow you to test your knowledge of the material covered in the lesson. See whether you can successfully answer the questions in the quiz and complete the exercises before you continue with the next lesson. The answers appear in Appendix B, "Answers to Quiz Questions and Exercises."

Quiz

1. What properties can you change if you're modifying the TCP/IP protocol?

2. Do you configure communications for an entire instance or for each individual database?

3. What three configuration methods are available with the Configuration Assistant?

4. What's the command that you use if you want to view the configuration parameters set for the DB2 Administration Server (DAS)?

5. What drive and subdirectory structure is created when you create an instance?

6. What's the command to use if you want to change the ownership of the DB2 Administration Server after it's created?

7. How do you change the instance that's started as a default?

8. What types of information can you export to a profile from a server computer?

9. If you don't want your clients to be able to search the network for databases, how can you turn off this option?

10. What protocols are supported by the SEARCH discovery method?

11. What profile registry variables can be used to tune the search discovery on the client?

Exercises

1. Create a few instances, attach to the instances, and create databases in each. Look at the directory structure that's created when an instance is created. Start multiple instances and connect to more than one database at a time. Drop the instances that you no longer need.

2. Use the Control Center to view the protocol values set during installation. Don't change any of the values—just look at them. Then, use the Configuration Assistant to make sure that the values are the same in both locations.

3. Change the discovery parameters to disable network searching and test that it works as expected.

5

DAY 6

Installing and Configuring DB2 Clients

Today you learn how to perform an interactive installation of a DB2 client on a Windows system. DB2 clients can be installed on any of the following Windows operating systems:

- Windows Me
- Windows NT version 4 with Service Pack 6a or later
- Windows 2000
- Windows XP (32-bit and 64-bit editions)
- Windows Server 2003 (32-bit and 64-bit)

Instructions for installing a DB2 client are identical for all these operating systems. DB2 clients are also available for AIX, HP-UX, Solaris, and Linux. This book covers how to install on Windows platforms.

Understanding the Different Types of DB2 Clients

There are three types of DB2 clients:

- DB2 Run-Time Client—A lightweight client that provides the functionality required for an application to access DB2 servers. Functionality includes communication protocol support and support for application interfaces such as JDBC, SQLj, ODBC, CLI, and OLE DB. Because no administration tools are installed, the DB2 Run-Time Client has the least disk requirements.

- DB2 Administration Client—Provides the capability for workstations to access and administer DB2 databases. The DB2 Administration Client has all the features of the DB2 Run-Time Client and also includes all the DB2 administration tools.

- DB2 Application Development Client—A collection of graphical and non-graphical tools and components for developing character-based, multimedia, and object-oriented applications. Special features include the Development Center and sample applications for all supported programming languages. The Application Development Client also includes the tools and components provided as part of the DB2 Administration Client product.

The installation instructions are identical for each of these types of clients.

NOTE You cannot create a database on a DB2 client. You can only access remote databases that were created on a DB2 server.

The DB2 Run-Time Client is automatically installed with every DB2 version 8 product. If a DB2 version 8 product currently exists on your computer, the DB2 Run-Time Client has already been installed, and there's no need to reinstall it. To configure your client to access remote servers, see the section "Configuring Client-to-Server Communications with the Configuration Assistant" later in this lesson.

You can install DB2 clients on any number of workstations; there are no licensing restrictions for installation. DB2 Enterprise Server Edition allows an unlimited number of users to connect to the server. DB2 Workgroup Server Edition has user-based entitlement restrictions for the number of concurrent users that can connect to the server.

TIP

> It is best to connect DB2 version 8 clients to DB2 version 8 servers to ensure that you have the full range of functions that are available.

Preparing for the Install

Today's lesson shows how to install the DB2 Administration Client on Windows workstations by using the Typical, Custom, and Compact installation types. Before you begin the install, however, read and complete the following sections to make sure that you have the required items and information you'll need.

Hardware and Software Requirements

Before installing the DB2 client, check to see that you have the proper hardware and software components available on the workstation:

- Disk space—You need 110MB of free disk space to install DB2 Administration Client. You also need additional disk space to store the applications that you'll use with DB2; this amount depends on the size of your applications. The DB2 Setup Wizard provides an estimate of the amount of disk space required to install the chosen options.

- Processor—You can run DB2 clients on Pentium-based computers.

- Memory—To run the entire set of DB2 graphical tools included in the DB2 Administration Client, you need at least 64MB of memory in addition to the memory that is needed for the operating system. The more memory you have, the faster the tools will run. A DB2 Run-Time Client will run with the minimum required by the operating system.

- Operating systems—You need to have Windows 98, Windows Me, Windows NT version 4 with Service Pack 6a or later, Windows 2000, Windows XP (32-bit and 64-bit editions), or Windows Server 2003 (32-bit and 64-bit).

- Software—You will need Java Runtime Environment (JRE) version 1.3.1 to run DB2's Java-based tools such as the Control Center. During installation, the correct level of the JRE is installed if it is not already. An Internet browser is required to view the online help.

- User accounts—To install DB2, you must have a user account to install and set up DB2. The user account may be created before you install DB2, or you can have the DB2 Setup Wizard create it for you.

6

- Communications—You need to use communications to access remote databases. You have a wide selection of communication protocols to choose from: TCP/IP, NetBIOS, Named Pipes, and APPC. All these protocols, except APPC, are installable options on the Windows-based operating systems. You don't need to purchase separate products to provide this support. Make sure that you've installed and configured the protocol support that you intend to use.

TIP

> If you plan to administer databases remotely, make sure that you are using TCP/IP.

Creating a User Account for Installing DB2 Products

You need to have a valid DB2 username to install DB2. A valid DB2 username is 20 characters or fewer and complies with DB2's naming rules. To comply with DB2's naming rules, the username must begin with letter A through Z, @, #, or $, and can contain characters A through Z, 1 through 9, @, #, $, or _. Don't use the special words USERS, ADMINS, GUESTS, PUBLIC, or LOCAL, and don't begin the username with IBM, SQL, or SYS.

The username must belong to the Administrators group. It must also be a valid DB2 username or have the Act as Part of the Operating System advanced user right.

TIP

> If installing on Windows 98 or Windows Me, any valid username can be used to install the DB2 client. If installing on Windows Terminal Server, Windows NT, Windows 2000, Windows XP, or Windows Server 2003, you need a user account that belongs to a group with more authority than the Guests group such as the Users group.
>
> To perform an installation on Windows 2000 servers and Windows Server 2003 as part of the Users group, the registry permissions have to be modified to allow Users write access to the HKEY_LOCAL_MACHINE\Software registry branch. In the default Windows 2000 and Windows Server 2003 environment, members of the Users group only have read access to the HKEY_LOCAL_MACHINE\Software registry branch.

You can create a username on a Windows 2000 system in the User Manager dialog box. You can access this dialog box by choosing Start|Settings|Control Panel|Administrative Tools|Computer Management. Expand Local Users and Groups, right-click on Users, and choose New User. Create a new user by filling in the details in the New User dialog box.

If the username doesn't comply with DB2's naming rules but has the Act as Part of the Operating System advanced user right, the setup program will create the username db2admin to perform the installation.

Performing a Typical Install

Use the Typical install type if you want to install the DB2 components used most often and to have the DB2 instance created. A Typical install installs all required components, ODBC support, documentation, and commonly used DB2 tools such as the Configuration Assistant.

NOTE You can't selectively uninstall components after the setup program completes the installation.

To install the DB2 Administration Client using the Typical Install type, follow these steps:

1. Log on as a user that meets the requirements for installing DB2. (For more information, see the earlier section "Creating a User Account for Installing DB2 Products.")

2. Shut down any other programs so that the DB2 Setup Wizard can update files as required.

3. Insert the CD-ROM into the drive. The autorun feature automatically starts the DB2 Setup Wizard. The DB2 Setup Wizard determines the system language and launches the DB2 Setup Wizard for that language. This launches the IBM DB2 Setup Launchpad (see Figure 6.1).

FIGURE 6.1

The Welcome dialog box.

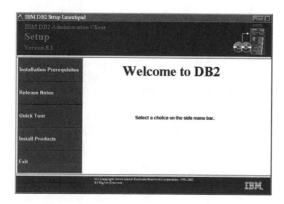

6

TIP

The setup program determines the system language and launches itself for that language. If you want to run the setup program in a different language, you need to invoke the program manually. Choose Start I Run. In the Open text box, type x:\setup /i=*LANGUAGE*, where x: represents your CD-ROM drive, and *LANGUAGE* represents the two-character country code for your language (for example, EN for English). Click OK.

4. In the Welcome to DB2 dialog box, you can choose to see the installation prerequisites, the release notes, or an interactive presentation of the product, or you can launch the DB2 Setup Wizard to install the product. Click Install Products to open the Select the Product You Would Like to Install dialog box (see Figure 6.2).

FIGURE 6.2

The Select the Product You Would Like to Install dialog box.

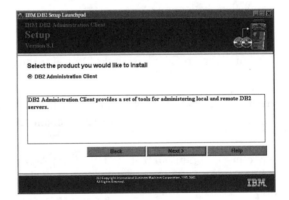

5. On the Select Products page, choose the DB2 Administration Client and click Next to continue.

6. The Welcome to the DB2 Setup Wizard page opens. Click Next to continue.

7. The License Agreement page opens (see Figure 6.3). Read the agreement carefully, and if you agree, click I accept the terms in the license agreement to continue with the install. Click Next to continue.

8. Select the installation type you prefer by clicking the appropriate button—for these steps, the Typical button (see Figure 6.4). An estimate of the amount of disk space for each option is shown.

   You also have the option to install the Data Warehousing option. For the purposes of this book, this feature will not be installed. Click Next to continue.

FIGURE 6.3

The License Agreement dialog box.

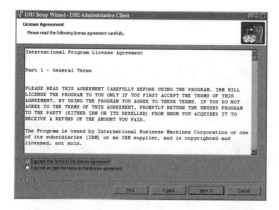

FIGURE 6.4

The Select Installation Type dialog box.

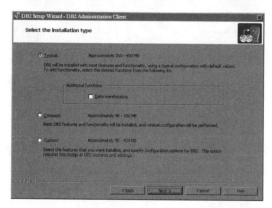

9. In the Select Installation Folder dialog box, select a directory and a drive where DB2 is to be installed (see Figure 6.5). Click the Disk Space button to help you select a directory with enough available disk space. (The amount of space required for the product also appears onscreen.) Click the Change button if you need to change the current destination folder. Click Next to continue.

10. You've given DB2 all the information required to install the product on your system. In the Start Copying Files dialog box (see Figure 6.6), you're given one last chance to verify the values you've entered. Click Install to have the files copied to your system. You also can click Back to return to the dialog boxes that you've already completed to make any changes.

11. The Setup is Complete dialog box appears when the installation of the DB2 client is complete (see Figure 6.7). Click Finish to continue. You should reboot your computer after installation.

6

FIGURE 6.5

The Select Installation Folder dialog box.

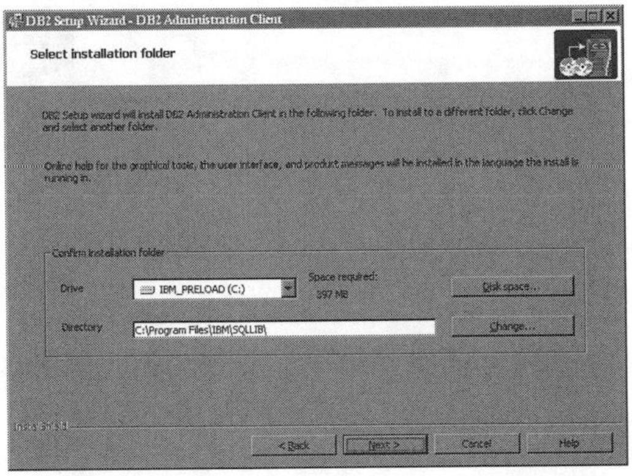

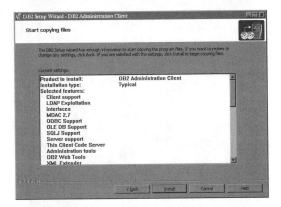

FIGURE 6.6

The Start Copying Files dialog box.

FIGURE 6.7

The Setup Is Complete dialog box.

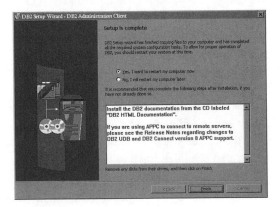

TIP

> For information on errors encountered during product installation, see the db2.log file, which stores general information and error messages resulting from install and uninstall activities. By default, the file is located in the db2log subdirectory found in the My Documents folder of the logged on user.

The DB2 Setup Wizard has completed the following:

- Created DB2 program groups and items (or shortcuts)
- Configured all protocols detected and supported by DB2
- Updated the Windows Registry
- Registered a security server
- Created a default instance named DB2

You've completed all the installation steps. See the section "Verifying the Connection" later in this lesson to verify the installation and get the workstation ready for general use.

Performing a Custom Install

Use the Custom install type if you want to choose the installed DB2 components. Through a Custom install, only those components that you select are installed, and the DB2 instance is created. The default for a Custom install is to install those components and subcomponents you would get in a Typical install.

To set up a DB2 client on a Windows computer by doing a Custom install, follow steps 1–7 as described in the earlier section "Performing a Typical Install" and then continue with the following steps:

8. Select the installation type you prefer by clicking the appropriate button—for these steps, the Custom button (see Figure 6.8).

9. Select the installation action you prefer by clicking to install the DB2 client on this computer or to save the choices in a response file (see Figure 6.9). Choose to have the product installed on this computer and click Next to continue.

10. The list of features to be installed on your computer is shown on the Select the Features You Want to Install dialog box (see Figure 6.10) and divided into the following categories:

   - Client support, including Interfaces, Base Client Support, System Bind Files, Spatial Extender Client, Java Runtime Environment, LDAP Exploitation, XML Extender, and Communication protocols.

6

- Server support, including Thin Client Code Server
- Administration tools, including the Control Center, Client Tools, Command Center, Configuration Assistant, Event Analyzer, and DB2 Web Tools
- Business Intelligence, including Data Warehouse tools and Information Catalog Manager Tools
- Getting started, including First Steps

FIGURE 6.8

The Select Installation Type dialog box.

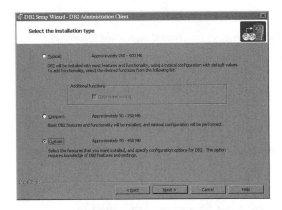

FIGURE 6.9

The Select the Installation Action dialog box.

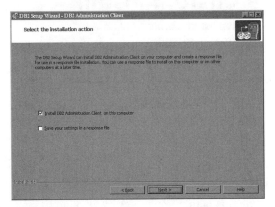

To select the features that you want to install, first expand the category by clicking on the plus sign. Next click on the triangle next to a feature to open the Selection dialog box. If the feature is to be installed, it will have an indicator symbol next to the option name. To deselect the feature, click on the This feature Will Not Be Available option. The indicator symbol turns to an X to indicate that the feature will not be installed. For purposes of this book, simply accept the defaults.

FIGURE 6.10

The Select the Features You Want to Install dialog box.

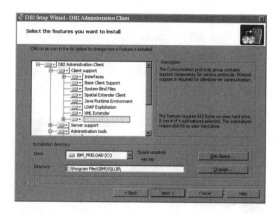

TIP

Be sure to install the administration tools. This book primarily discusses how to use these tools to maintain your databases. If you don't install the tools, you must use the Command Line Processor to perform these tasks.

In the lower section of this dialog box, you must select a directory and a drive where DB2 is to be installed. Click the Disk Space button to help you select a directory with enough available disk space. (The amount of space required for the product also appears onscreen.) Click the Change button if you need to change the current destination folder. Click Next to continue.

11. In the Select the languages to install dialog box, you can select to install the online help, user interfaces, and product messages in multiple languages (see Figure 6.11). For the purpose of this book, only the default language is selected. Click Next to continue.

FIGURE 6.11

The Select the Languages to Install dialog box.

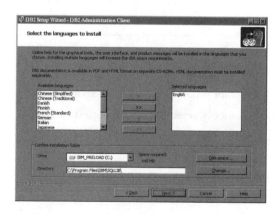

6

12. You've given DB2 all the information required to install the product on your system. In the Start Copying Files dialog box (see Figure 6.12), you're given one last chance to verify the values you've entered. Click Install to have the files copied to your system. You also can click Back to return to the dialog boxes that you've already completed to make any changes.

FIGURE 6.12

The Start Copying Files dialog box.

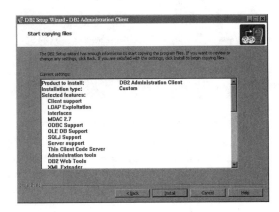

13. The installation progress bars appear onscreen while the product is being installed. After the product is installed, a reboot of your computer is not required, but you should stop all active programs before starting DB2. Select the Finish option to complete the installation.

TIP

> For information on errors encountered during product installation, see the db2.log file, which stores general information and error messages resulting from install and uninstall activities. By default, this file is located in the db2log subdirectory found in the My Documents folder of the logged on user.

The installation program has completed the following:

- Created DB2 program groups and items (or shortcuts)
- Configured all protocols detected and supported by DB2
- Registered a security service
- Updated the Windows Registry
- Created a default instance named DB2

You've completed all the installation steps. See the later section "Verifying the Connection" to verify the installation and to get the workstation ready for general use.

Performing a Compact Install

The steps to perform a Compact installation are the same as performing a Typical installation, except for the installed product components. During a Compact installation, only the required components are installed. This greatly reduces the amount of disk space required for the product, but it also greatly reduces the available functionality. For example, the graphical tools aren't installed during a Compact installation.

Compact installation should be used on systems where you use another application to interface to the database. For example, if you're planning to use Microsoft Access as the interface to DB2, you may not want to use the DB2 tools or online documents.

Configuring Client-to-Server Communications with the Configuration Assistant

Use the Configuration Assistant (CA) to configure your DB2 client to access remote databases on DB2 servers.

With the CA, you can do the following:

- Configure database connections that applications can use.
- Update or delete existing configured database connections.
- Display the information for existing configured connections.
- Test a connection to a database.
- Enable or disable database connections to be configured as CLI/ODBC data sources.
- Import or export client profiles, which contain information for the setup of a client.
- Update client configuration settings.
- Discover remote databases (if enabled).
- Bind user applications and utilities to databases.

6

Configuring Database Connections

You can configure database connections through the Add Database Wizard by

- Using a profile as a source of information to add database connections
- Searching the network for databases
- Adding database connections manually

Each of these techniques is covered in more detail in the following sections.

NOTE

> To complete the steps in the following sections, you must be logged on to the local system as a user with system administration (SYSADM) authority on the instance.

Configuring Database Connections Using a Profile

An *access profile* contains all the necessary information for a client to access a remote server. Using a profile to set up access allows you to create a single profile for access and easily propagate this information to other clients in your network. You can use a Server profile or a Client profile to configure database connections on a client. Instructions for creating an access profile were covered in Day 5, "Setting Up DB2 Instances and Server Communications."

If your administrator provided you with a file containing database access information, use the following steps to configure your workstation to access remote servers using an access profile:

1. Start the CA by choosing Start|Programs|IBM DB2|Setup Tools Configuration Assistant.

NOTE

> The Welcome panel opens each time you start the CA, until you've added at least one database to your client. Click Yes to start the Add Database Wizard for the first time.

2. Open the Add Database Wizard by selecting Add Database Wizard from the Selected menu option.
3. On the Source page, select the Use a Profile radio button and click the Next button (see Figure 6.13).

FIGURE 6.13

The Source page in the Add Database Wizard.

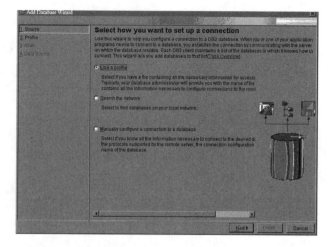

4. On the Profile page, click the Browse button to select an access profile, or enter the path and name of the file in the Profile name field (see Figure 6.14). Click Load to continue.

FIGURE 6.14

The Profile page in the Add Database Wizard.

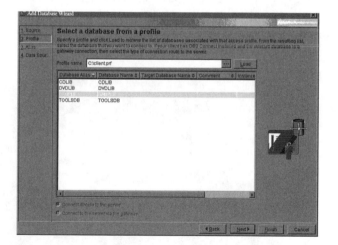

5. You're presented with a list of systems, instances, and databases. Select the database that you want to use and click Next.

6. On the Alias page, specify the database alias name or add a description of the database (see Figure 6.15). If you don't specify a database alias name, the default will be the same as the database name. Click Next to continue.

6

FIGURE 6.15

The Alias page in the Add Database Wizard.

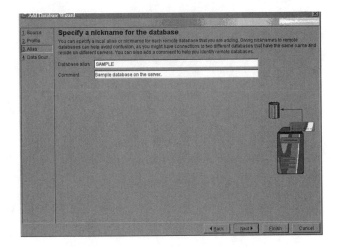

7. On the Data Source page, specify whether you plan to use applications such as Microsoft Access to access data in this database (see Figure 6.16). Click the Register This Database for ODBC check box, select the radio button that describes the type of data source that you want to register this database as, and select from the Optimize for Application drop-down box the application that you want to use (for example, Microsoft Access). It is best to register the database as a system resource.

FIGURE 6.16

The Data Source page in the Add Database Wizard.

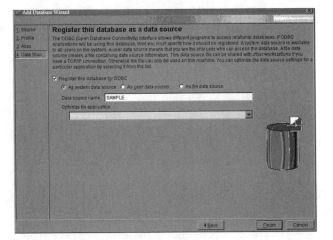

8. Click the Finish button to add the database and close the Add Database Wizard.

9. In the Test Connection dialog box, select a connection type: Standard, CLI, ODBC, OLEDB, JDBC, or ADO. For our example, choose CLI (see Figure 6.17).

Enter your username and password to access the database and click Test Connection. If the connection is successful, a message confirming the connection appears. If the connection fails, click the Help button for more information. For example, if the username or password that you entered is not known on the server, the connection will fail. The help message that appears will ask you to enter a valid username and password.

FIGURE 6.17

The Test Connection page in the Configuration Assistant.

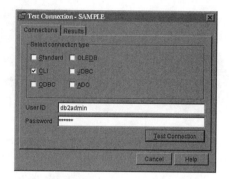

10. You now can use the database. If you want to access another database, relaunch the Add Database Wizard.

Searching the Network for Databases

Rather than enter protocol information to make a connection to remote database servers, you can use the CA to find all the databases on your local network.

NOTE

> The following scenario assumes that the installation defaults on the client and the server have not been changed, and that messages used by the SEARCH method of discovery aren't filtered by your network.

6

To search the network for databases, follow these steps:

1. Start the CA.

2. Open the Add Database Wizard by selecting Add Database Wizard from the Selected menu option.

3. On the Source page, select the Search the Network radio button and click Next.

4. On the Network page, click the Known Systems folder to list all the systems known to your client (see Figure 6.18).

FIGURE 6.18

*The known systems in
the Add Database
Wizard.*

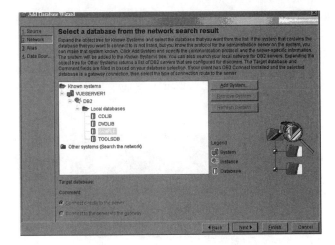

5. Click the + sign beside the system to get a list of the instances and databases on it. Select the database that you want to add and proceed to step 9.

6. If the system that contains the database that you want isn't listed, click the Other Systems (Search the Network) folder to search the network for additional systems.

> **TIP**
> The Other Systems (Search the Network) folder appears only if the client's DISCOVER parameter is set to SEARCH.

7. Click the + sign beside the system to get a list of the instances and databases on it. Select the database that you want to add and proceed to step 9.

8. If the system you want is still not listed, you can add it to the list of systems by clicking the Add Systems button. On the Add System page (see Figure 6.19), enter the required communication protocol parameters and click OK. Select the database that you want to add and proceed to step 9.

FIGURE 6.19

*The Add System page
of the Add Database
Wizard.*

9. On the Database page, specify the name of the database and the alias of the database.

10. On the Data Source page, specify whether you plan to use applications such as Microsoft Access to access data in this database.

11. Click the Finish button to add the database and close the Add Database Wizard.

12. In the Test Connection dialog box, select a connection type, enter your username and password to access the database, and click Test Connection. If the connection is successful, a message confirming the connection appears.

13. You now can use the database.

Manually Configure a Connection to a DB2 Database

Manually configuring a database connection requires you to know

- One of the protocols supported by the server instance containing the database
- The protocol connection information required to configure the connection to the server instance
- The name of the database on the server system

With this information, the wizard guides you through the steps necessary to add the database connection. Follow these steps:

1. Start the CA.

2. Open the Add Database Wizard by selecting Add Database Wizard from the Selected menu option.

3. On the Source page, select the Manually Configure a Connection to a DB2 Database radio button and click Next.

4. Select the radio button that corresponds to the protocol you want to use from the Protocol list (see Figure 6.20). Click Next.

5. Enter the required communication protocol parameters and click Next.

    The following parameters are required for the TCP/IP protocol:

    - Hostname—The hostname of the server where the target database resides.
    - Service Name—The service name of the server that matches the entry in the server's TCP/IP services file.
    - Port Number—The port number associated with the DB2 instance on the server that contains the target database.

    The following parameters are required for the NetBIOS protocol:

    - Adapter Number—The adapter number is the logical network adapter to be used for the NetBIOS connection. The client uses adapter 0 by default.

6

- Server Workstation Name—The workstation name of the server machine where the target database resides.
- Local Workstation Name—The workstation name of the local machine. One is assigned by DB2 if you don't currently have one. You can accept the value that DB2 assigns, or you can change the value to another name.

FIGURE 6.20

The Protocol page of the Add Database Wizard.

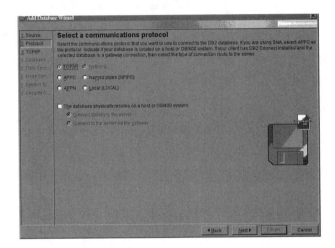

The following parameters are required for the Named Pipes protocol:

- Computer Name—The computer name of the server where the target database resides.
- Instance—The DB2 instance where the target database resides.

The APPC protocol requires the symbolic destination name parameter, which is the symbolic destination name found in the CPIC side information in the SNA subsystem.

6. On the Database page, specify the name of the database and the alias of the database.

7. On the Data Source page, specify whether you plan to use applications such as Microsoft Access to access data in this database.

8. Click the Finish button to add the database and close the Add Database Wizard.

9. In the Test Connection dialog box, select a connection type, enter your username and password to access the database, and click Test Connection. If the connection is successful, a message confirming the connection appears.

10. You now can use the database.

Verifying the Connection

You've already tested the connection to your database after adding the system using the Configuration Assistant. You can also test the connection to your database by using the Control Center or the Command Center.

To test your connection using the Control Center, follow these steps:

1. Start the Control Center, if not already started. As you learned earlier, to start the Control Center, choose Start|Programs|IBM DB2|General Administration Tools| Control Center.

2. Click the + (plus sign) in front of the Systems folder. This shows you the systems, instances, and databases you have on your system.

3. Click the SAMPLE folder to see the objects available within the SAMPLE database.

4. Click Tables to see a listing of all the tables in the contents pane. Scroll down until you see the EMPLOYEE table.

5. Right-click the EMPLOYEE table and select Sample Contents from the pop-up menu to see the first 20 rows of the EMPLOYEE table.

To test the connection using the Command Center, follow these steps:

1. Start the Command Center by choosing Start|Programs|IBM DB2|Command Line Tools|Command Center.

2. Connect to the SAMPLE database on your server by clicking the button on the right side of the Database connection field and select the SAMPLE database. The Connect to Sample command is automatically placed in the command area and executed. You will be asked for a username and password before the connection is completed.

TIP

> The values for *username* and *password* must be valid for the system on which they're authenticated. By default, authentication takes place on the server. If the database manager is configured for client authentication, the *username* and *password* must be valid on the client.

6

If the connection is successful, you'll get a message showing the name of the database to which you've connected:

OUTPUT
```
Database product     = DB2/NT 8.1.0
SQL authorization ID = DB2ADMIN
Local database alias = SAMPLE
```

If you receive an error message, make sure that the SAMPLE database exists on the server and the database manager was started on the server.

3. You can now retrieve data from the database. For example, to select data from the EMPLOYEE table, you must enter the appropriate schema name. For example, the schema name for my tables is DB2ADMIN. I use the following command to see the data from the EMPLOYEE table on my computer:

INPUT   `select * from DB2ADMIN.EMPLOYEE`

4. When you're finished using the database connection, issue the `connect reset` command to end the database connection.

You're ready to start using the DB2 client to communicate with a DB2 server. See Day 11, "Accessing the Data," for details.

Creating Client Profiles

You generate client profiles from clients by using the CA's Export function. Database connections configured on one client are exported and used to set up one or more additional clients. Export can be used to generate a customized profile that can be imported on another client to set it up initially, or to update it.

The information contained in a client profile is determined during the export process. Depending on the settings chosen, it can contain the existing client's

- Database connection information, including CLI/ODBC settings
- Client settings, including database manager configuration parameters
- CLI/ODBC common parameters
- Configuration data for the local APPC communications subsystem

Exporting a Client Profile

Follow these steps to export the information from your fully configured client:

1. Start the Configuration Assistant.
2. Click Configure|Export Profile to open the menu of export choices: All, Database Connections, or Customize. Choose All to export the client's configuration settings as well as database connection settings. Choose Database Connections to export only the information needed to connect to remote databases. Choose Customize to choose or change parts of the configuration profile.

   Figure 6.21 shows an example of the options you can customize.

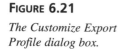

FIGURE 6.21

The Customize Export Profile dialog box.

3. In the File name text box, enter a path and filename for the client profile—for example, `e:\profile\client1.prf`.

4. Select the database connections to be exported from the Available DB2 Database Aliases list, and click the right arrow to add them to the Selected Database Aliases list.

5. Select the check boxes that correspond to the options that you want to set for the target client:

   - Nodes without an associated database
   - Admin nodes
   - DBM configuration parameters
   - DB2 registry
   - Common CLI parameters
   - APPC configuration
   - NetBIOS parameter

   You can click the Customize buttons next to DBM Configuration parameters or APPC Configuration to change the current values before exporting them to the profile. Figure 6.22 shows the DBM configuration parameters that you can customize.

   The settings that you customize affect only the profile to be exported; no changes will be made to your workstation. Use the onscreen hints to help you set the

6

various client settings. Click OK to return to the Customize Export Profile dialog box when you complete any customization.

FIGURE 6.22

DBM Configuration dialog box.

6. Click Export in the Customize Export Profile dialog box when you've customized the settings. The values will be saved in the file indicated. It is a good idea to store this file on a network drive that can be accessed by all other clients in your area.

7. The Results page of the Customize Export Profile notebook opens to show the results of the export. Use these messages to fix any problems that may have occurred.

Importing a Client Profile

Perform the following steps at the client that you want to set up. You can use this process to initially set up a new client or to update an existing one.

1. Start the CA.

2. Click Configure|Import Profile to open the menu of import choices: All or Customize. Choose All to import all the settings in the profile, or choose Customize to make changes to the settings that you want from the profile. Choose Customize to see the options that are available.

3. Select the path and filename of the client profile you want to import and click OK. For example, to import the profile that was exported in the previous section, select e:\profile\client1.prf. Click Load to see the Profile options (see Figure 6.23).

FIGURE 6.23

The Customize Import Profile dialog box.

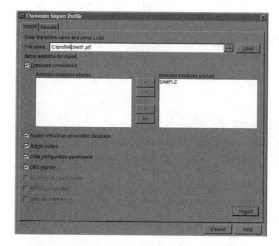

4. The items available to import are limited by the items that were exported in the first place. Select the items you want to import:

   - Database Connections—Select the database connections to be imported from the Available DB2 Database Aliases list, and click the right arrow to add them to the Selected Database Aliases list.

   - Nodes Without an Associated Database—Check this option to import all the nodes in the export file.

   - Admin Nodes—Check this option to import the admin nodes that are in the profile.

   - DBM Configuration Parameters—Configuration parameter settings found in the export file replace existing ones on the client.

   - DB2 Registry—Registry values found in the export file replace existing ones on the client.

   - Common CLI Parameters—Values found in the exported file replace those on the client.

   - APPC Configuration—If it's not already configured, this information is used to configure the APPC communications subsystem.

   - NetBIOS Name—If it's not already configured, this information is used to configure the NetBIOS protocol.

5. Click Import to import the settings.

6. The Results page of the Customize Import Profile dialog box opens to show the results of the import. Use these messages to fix any problems that may have occurred.

6

7. Test the connection to the database by selecting the database that was imported and clicking the Test Connection button from the Selected menu in the Configuration Assistant.

Summary

Today you saw that there are three different types of DB2 clients to meet your needs: DB2 Run-Time Client, DB2 Administration Client, and DB2 Application Development Client.

You can acquire the DB2 client software by using the DB2 Client Pack CD-ROM included with DB2's Workgroup and Enterprise Server Editions. You can also download the latest DB2 client software from the IBM Data Management Web site.

If you want your server to also act as a client, you don't need to install the DB2 client software separately on the server. The DB2 client software is already built into each DB2 product. You need to install this software only on a remote system that's to act as a client.

This day showed you how to install the clients using the Typical and Custom installation types. After the client software is installed, you can use the Configuration Assistant to find databases on the network.

What Comes Next?

On Day 7, "Ensuring Data Security," you learn how to set up your database so that your data is protected against unauthorized use.

Q&A

Q When are the graphical tools installed with the client?

A You can install the DB2 Administration Client if you're using DB2 Administration Client on Windows or Linux platforms. The administration tools aren't provided with the clients for the other platforms.

For the purposes of this book, you need to have the tools. If you intend to perform the exercises from the server, you don't need the tools on the client.

Q Where can I install the product?

A If you already have a DB2 version 8 product installed on your computer, you must install any subsequent product on the same drive in the same directory. If this is your first DB2 version 8 product, you can install on any drive that has the required amount of space.

Q What about communications?

A The protocols that you need on a client to communicate with a remote server are detected and configured during installation. You use the Configuration Assistant after the client software is installed to view or modify the protocol information. Four protocols are supported for the Windows client: APPC, Named Pipes, NetBIOS, and TCP/IP. You must use a protocol that matches one of the protocols set up on the server you intend to access.

Q What are the two available discovery methods?

A You can choose the KNOWN or SEARCH discovery method. With KNOWN, your client can find only the instances and databases on the network that are known to the client. You can add systems if you know what protocol is used and the specific protocol information of the remote server. Using the SEARCH discovery method allows your client to search all the systems on the local network for databases.

Q When would I use a client profile?

A A client profile is generated at a client computer and contains information about the database's connections cataloged on the client as well as configuration information. After you generate a profile, you can store the profile on a network drive that all your clients can access. Each client user can import this profile so that each client can easily set up the information needed to connect to the database. This ensures that each client uses the same database information, thereby reducing problems when connecting clients to servers.

Q What three methods can I use to catalog databases on my client with the Configuration Assistant?

A You can use a pregenerated profile generated at the server or the client. The profile contains information about the database. You can search the network for systems that contain DB2 databases. You can manually enter the specific protocol information for the server system that you want to access.

6

Workshop

The purpose of the Workshop is to allow you to test your knowledge of the material covered in the lesson. See whether you can successfully answer the questions in the quiz and complete the exercises before you continue with the next lesson. The answers appear in Appendix B, "Answers to Quiz Questions and Exercises."

Quiz

1. When should the client's DISCOVER parameter be set to SEARCH?

2. Why would you want to register a database for ODBC?

3. If you can't connect to the server, what's the most likely problem?

4. What types of information can you export to a profile from a client workstation?

5. What are the three types of clients you can choose from, and when would you use each?

Exercise

1. Because this is the first time that the Configuration Assistant was introduced, try out the different panels and options to see what's available with this tool.

DAY 7

Ensuring Data Security

Three security levels control access to DB2 Universal Database data and functions. The first level of security checking is authentication, where the operating system verifies a user through a user ID and password. Once authenticated by the operating system, authorization is the next level of security where the user must be identified to DB2 using a SQL authorization name or authid. The authid can also be the same as the user ID and is normally used for identifying users to maintain the database and instances. Finally, privileges are rights granted to users to work with objects within a database, such as a view or table.

Today you will learn the following:

- How to use authentication types to determine where and how user identities are verified
- How to modify the authentication level for a DB2 instance
- How to grant database access authorities and privileges
- Security consideration for Windows groups

Authentication

Access to a database or instance is first validated outside DB2. This process, known as *authentication*, verifies that the user is who he claims to be.

Authentication Types

An authentication type is specified for a database instance when it's created or cataloged at the server, and when it's cataloged on a remote node that will be accessing the database. The authentication type determines where and how users are verified for access to databases on the server. The authentication type is stored in the database manager configuration file at the server and can be Client, Server, Server encrypt, Kerberos, Kerberos encrypt. There is one authentication type per instance, which covers access to that database server and all the databases under its control.

SERVER

This is the default authentication type. If the type is SERVER, the user will be verified at the server where the database resides, using local operating system security. If a username and password are specified during the connection attempt, they're compared to the valid username and password combinations at the server to determine whether the user is permitted to access the instance.

SERVER_ENCRYPT

This authentication behaves similarly to SERVER, except that passwords are encrypted by DB2 at the client before they are sent to the server. At the server, the password is decrypted and authenticated.

CLIENT

If CLIENT is specified, it's assumed that the user was verified on the client, where the application resides. No further authentication will take place at the server.

Specify Trusted Clients in the Database Manager Configuration file to choose whether to trust all clients (the default) or trust only those clients that come from systems where security is inherent in the operating system. Trusted clients are clients that have a reliable, local security system.

KERBEROS

If the DB2 client and server are using operating environments that support Kerberos, this security protocol performs authentication as a third-party authentication service by using cryptography to create a shared secret key. The Kerberos security protocol enables the use of a single sign-on to access a remote DB2 server.

KERBEROS_ENCRYPT

KERBEROS_ENCRYPT specifies that the server accepts Kerberos authentication or encrypted Server authentication schemes. If the client authentication is Kerberos, the client is authenticated using the Kerberos security protocol. If the client authentication is not Kerberos, the system will authenticate in the same manner as SERVER_ENCRYPT.

Setting the Authentication Level

The authentication level is set at the instance level. To view or modify the authentication level for the DB2 instance, follow these steps:

1. In the Control Center, right-click the DB2 instance object and select Configure Parameters from the pop-up menu.

2. Scroll down to the Authentication parameter and select it. A set of radio buttons appear to allow you to select either Server, Client, Server Encrypt, Kerberos, or Kerberos Encrypt authentication (see Figure 7.1). The default is SERVER authentication. Click Cancel.

FIGURE 7.1

DBM Configuration authentication options.

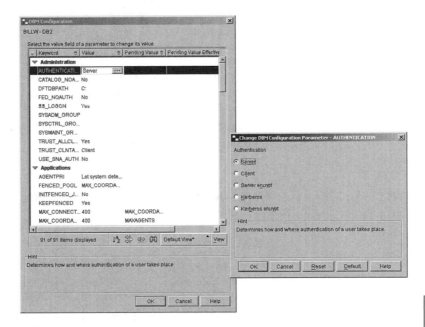

3. Continue to work with other DBM configuration parameters by scrolling to the Trust all Clients parameter (TRUST_ALLCLNTS) and choosing whether to trust all the clients. Leave this parameter at its default value for this example.

7

4. Select the Trusted Client Authentication parameter to specify whether a trusted client is authenticated at the client or the server. This parameter is only active when CLIENT authentication is selected. Leave this parameter at its default value for this example.

5. Click OK to save your settings and close the dialog box.

6. For your changes to take effect, you must stop the instance and restart it. Right-click the instance and select Stop from the pop-up menu to stop the instance. Right-click the instance and select Start from the pop-up menu to start the instance.

Access to DB2 Universal Database

DB2 uses external facilities to provide a set of user and group validation and management functions. Users must log on through the external facilities by providing a username and a password. The security facilities validate the username and password provided to ensure that access for this user is allowed.

You need to have a Windows username that will be used to administer DB2. The username must belong to the Administrators group and be a valid DB2 username. In many cases, DB2 creates a username during installation called db2admin that can be used for administering DB2 and setting up the security for the users on your system.

After successful authentication, access to objects within a DB2 instance is controlled by granting authorities or privileges to users or groups. Authorities are granted to users to perform administrative tasks on DB2 objects such as loading or backing up data. Privileges are granted to users to access or update data. See Figure 7.2 for the possible DB2 authorities and privileges allowed.

NOTE　　　 By default, System Administration (SYSADM) privileges are granted to any valid DB2 username that belongs to the Administrators group on Windows.

You can change the users who have administrator privileges for each DB2 instance by changing the SYSADM_GROUP parameter. Before you do, however, you need to ensure that the group exists. To check whether this group exists, use the Windows User Manager administrative tool (choose Start|Programs|Administrative Tools|User Manager). If the group exists, it's listed in the lower section of the User Manager window.

FIGURE 7.2

Hierarchy of authorities and privileges.

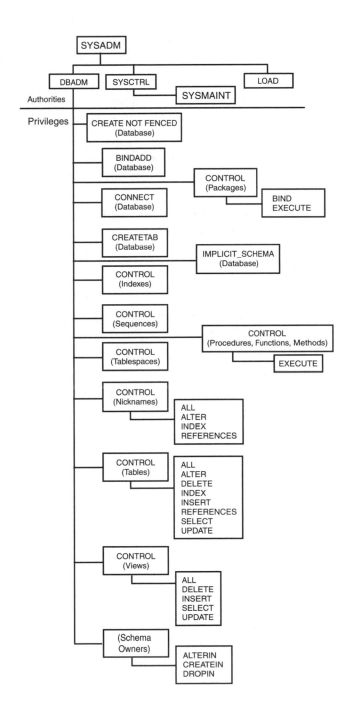

To use another group as the System Administrative group (SYSADM_GROUP), update the
Database Manager Configuration file. To change SYSADM_GROUP on the server instance,
follow these steps:

1. In the Control Center, click the + sign beside the Systems icon to list all the systems known to your workstation, and then click the + sign for the system containing the instance you want to update.

2. Right-click the instance that you want to change—for example, DB2—and select
   Configure Parameters from the pop-up menu. The DBM Configuration dialog box
   opens.

3. The Administration section shows the configuration parameters associated with
   administration. In the System Administration Authority Group text box, type the
   name of an existing group to which you want to assign this privilege. The Change
   DBM Configuration Parameter dialog box appears as you begin to type (see
   Figure 7.3).

FIGURE 7.3

*DBM Configuration –
SYSADM_GROUP options.*

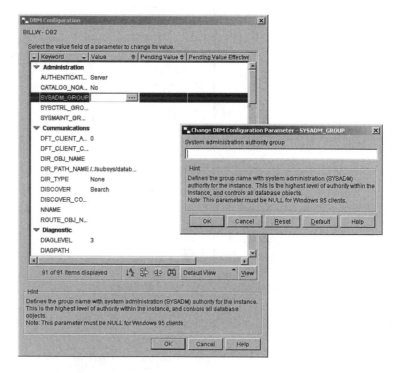

4. Click OK.

5. Stop all applications that are using DB2, including the Control Center. When the application or the Control Center is restarted, the new value for SYSADM_GROUP is used.

You can use these same steps to change the SYSCTRL_GROUP and SYSMAINT_GROUP parameters.

Access Within DB2

Access within DB2 is managed by the administrative authorities and user privileges within the database manager. Database authorities involve actions on a database as a whole. When a database is created, some authorities are automatically granted to anyone who accesses the database. For example, CONNECT, CREATETAB, BINDADD, and IMPLICIT_SCHEMA authorities are granted to all users.

Authorities

Privileges enable users to create or access database resources. *Authority levels* provide a method of grouping privileges and higher-level database manager maintenance and utility operations. Together, these act to control access to the database manager and its database objects. Users can access only those objects for which they have the appropriate *authorization*—that is, the required privilege or authority. A user or group can have one or more of the following levels of authority: SYSADM, DBADM, SYSCTRL, SYSMAINT, and LOAD. Figure 7.4 shows the relationship between the authorities and their span of control.

SYSADM

SYSADM, the highest level of administrative authority, provides control over all resources created and maintained by DB2 Universal Database. It includes all the privileges on all databases within the DB2 instance and the authority to grant or revoke authority. When using DB2 on a Windows system, SYSADM authority is assigned and managed by using the Windows security facilities.

SYSADM authority is assigned to the group specified by the SYSADM_GROUP configuration parameter.

DBADM

The second highest level of administrative authority, DBADM applies only to a specific database and lets users run utilities, issue database commands, and access any data in any table in the database. When DBADM authority is granted, database privileges (described shortly) are granted as well.

7

FIGURE 7.4

DB2 authorities.

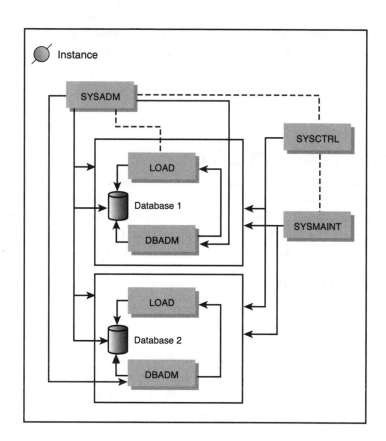

Only users with SYSADM authority can grant or revoke DBADM authority. Users with DBADM authority can grant privileges on the database to others and can revoke any privilege from any user regardless of who granted it. Some privileges include loading tables; reading log files; and creating, dropping, and activating event monitors.

SYSCTRL

SYSCTRL, the highest level of system control authority, allows operations that affect system resources only. Direct access to data isn't allowed. SYSCTRL authority is meant for users to administer a database instance that contains sensitive data.

SYSCTRL authority is assigned to the group specified in the SYSCTRL_GROUP configuration parameter. Some privileges include creating and dropping databases and table spaces; updating directory, history, and configuration files; and dropping, creating, or altering table spaces.

SYSMAINT

SYSMAINT, the second level of system control authority, allows system maintenance operations on all databases associated with an instance. Direct access to data isn't allowed. SYSMAINT authority is meant for users to administer a database instance that contains sensitive data.

SYSMAINT authority is assigned to the group specified in the SYSMAINT_GROUP configuration parameter. Some privileges include updating database configuration files; backing up and restoring databases and table spaces; and issuing roll-forward, trace, and database monitor commands.

LOAD

Users having LOAD authority at the database level, as well as INSERT privilege on a table, can use the LOAD command to load data into a table.

When a new database is created, or when a database is migrated from the previous release, PUBLIC is given IMPLICIT_SCHEMA database authority.

With this authority, any user can create a schema by creating an object and specifying a schema name that does not already exist. SYSIBM becomes the owner of the implicitly created schema, and PUBLIC is given the privilege to create objects in this schema.

The table shown in Figure 7.5 shows some of the valid tasks for the various DB2 privilege levels. The DBADM column has an asterisk (*) beside entries related to LOAD authority.

Schemas

A *schema* is a collection of named objects. Schemas provide a logical classification of objects in the database. A schema can contain tables, views, nicknames, triggers, functions, packages, and other objects.

A schema is also an object in the database. It is explicitly created using the CREATE SCHEMA statement with the current user recorded as the schema owner. It can also be implicitly created when another object is created, provided that the user has IMPLICIT_SCHEMA authority.

A *schema name* is used as the high-order part of a two-part object name. If the object is specifically qualified with a schema name when created, the object is assigned to that schema. If no schema name is specified when the object is created, the default schema name is used.

For example, a user with DBADM authority creates a schema called C for user A:

```
CREATE SCHEMA C AUTHORIZATION A
```

7

FIGURE 7.5

DB2 authorities and functions.

Function	SYSADM	SYSCTRL	SYSMAINT	DBADM
UPDATE DBM CFG	YES			
GRANT/REVOKE DBADM	YES			
ESTABLISH/CHANGE SYSCTRL	YES			
ESTABLISH/CHANGE SYSMAINT	YES			
FORCE USERS	YES	YES		
CREATE/DROP DATABASE	YES	YES		
RESTORE TO NEW DATABASE	YES	YES		
UPDATE DB CFG	YES	YES	YES	
BACKUP DATABASE/TABLE SPACE	YES	YES	YES	
RESTORE TO EXISTING DATABASE	YES	YES	YES	
PERFORM ROLL FORWARD RECOVERY	YES	YES	YES	
START/STOP INSTANCE	YES	YES	YES	
RESTORE TABLE SPACE	YES	YES	YES	
RUN TRACE	YES	YES	YES	
OBTAIN MONITOR SNAPSHOTS	YES	YES	YES	
QUERY TABLE SPACE STATE	YES	YES	YES	YES*
PRUNE LOG HISTORY FILES	YES	YES	YES	YES
QUIESCE TABLE SPACE	YES	YES	YES	YES*
LOAD TABLES	YES			YES*
SET/UNSET CHECK PENDING STATUS	YES			YES
CREATE/DROP EVENT MONITORS	YES			YES

User A can then issue the following statement to create a table called X in schema C:

```
CREATE TABLE C.X (COL1 INT)
```

Some schema names are reserved. For example, built-in functions belong to the SYSIBM schema, and the preinstalled user-defined functions belong to the SYSFUN schema.

When a database is created, all users have IMPLICIT_SCHEMA authority. This allows any user to create objects in any schema not already in existence. An implicitly created schema allows any user to create other objects in this schema. The ability to create aliases, distinct types, functions, and triggers is extended to implicitly created schemas. The default privileges on an implicitly created schema provide backward compatibility with previous versions.

If the IMPLICIT_SCHEMA authority is revoked from PUBLIC, schemas can be explicitly created using the CREATE SCHEMA statement, or implicitly created by users (such as those with DBADM authority) who have been granted IMPLICIT_SCHEMA authority. Although revoking IMPLICIT_SCHEMA authority from PUBLIC increases control over the use of schema names, it can result in authorization errors when existing applications attempt to create objects.

Schemas also have privileges, allowing the schema owner to control which users have the privilege to create, alter, and drop objects in the schema. A schema owner is initially given all these privileges on the schema, with the ability to grant them to others. An implicitly created schema is owned by the system, and all users are initially given the privilege to create objects in such a schema. A user with SYSADM or DBADM authority can change the privileges held by users on any schema. Therefore, access to create, alter, and drop objects in any schema (even one that was implicitly created) can be controlled.

Privileges

Database privileges involve actions on specific objects within the database. When a database is created, some privileges are automatically granted to anyone who accesses the database. For example, SELECT privilege is granted on catalog views, and EXECUTE and BIND privileges on each successfully bound utility are granted to all users. Figure 7.6 illustrates the database privileges.

FIGURE 7.6

Database privileges.

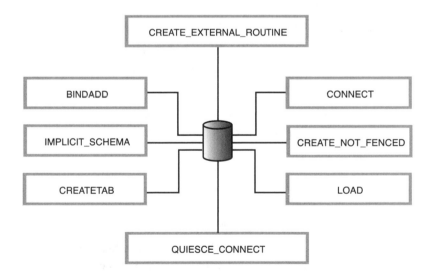

A *privilege* is the right to access a specific database object in a specific way. These rights are controlled by users with SYSADM or DBADM authority or by creators of objects. Authorized users can create database objects and have access to the objects they own. They can also give privileges for their own objects to other users by using the Control Center. Only users with SYSADM or DBADM authority can grant and revoke these privileges to and from other users.

7

Database privileges involve actions on a database as a whole:

- CONNECT allows a user to access the database.
- BINDADD allows a user to create new packages in the database.
- CREATETAB allows a user to create new tables in the database.
- CREATE_NOT_FENCED allows a user to create a user-defined function (UDF) or procedure that is "not fenced." UDFs or procedures that are "not fenced" can execute within the database kernel and should be tested extremely well; otherwise, it can cause severe problems. In contrast, fenced procedures are safer to execute when developing and executing procedures.
- IMPLICIT_SCHEMA allows any user to create a schema implicitly by creating an object using a CREATE statement with a schema name that does not already exist. SYSIBM becomes the owner of the implicitly created schema, and PUBLIC is given the privilege to create objects in this schema.
- LOAD allows a user to load data into a table.
- QUIESCE_CONNECT allows a user to access the database while it is quiesced.
- CREATE_EXTERNAL_ROUTINE allows a user to create a procedure for use by applications and other users of the database.

Privileges can be held on the following database objects: databases, tables, views, packages, and indexes. The following privileges, for example, can be held on a database and are granted to PUBLIC when a database is created:

- Connect to the database (CONNECT)
- Create packages (BINDADD)
- Create tables (CREATETAB)
- Create a schema implicitly when creating another object (IMPLICIT_SCHEMA)
- Query data in the system catalog views (SELECT)
- USE privilege on USERSPACE1 table space (USE)

Privileges not requiring specific authority include reading system and database configuration files, directories, and history files, and attaching to a DB2 instance. Individual privileges may be set to allow users to perform specific functions on selected objects.

A *package* is a database object that contains the information needed by the database manager to access data in the most efficient way for a particular application program. By granting privileges to execute a package, users do not need to be granted explicit privileges on the database objects referenced within the package. Figure 7.7 illustrates the possible object privileges.

FIGURE 7.7

Object privileges.

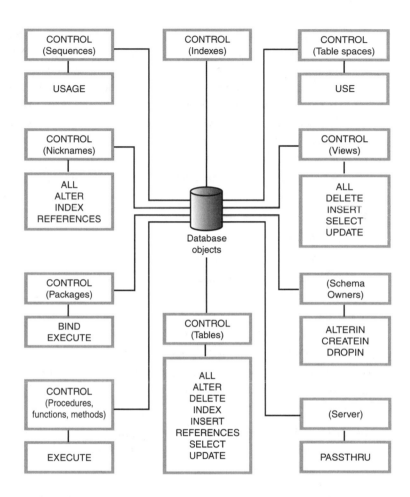

Table and view privileges involve actions on tables or views in a database. A user must have CONNECT privilege on the database to use any of the following privileges:

- CONTROL provides the user with all privileges for a table or view including the ability to drop it, and to grant and revoke individual table privileges. You must have SYSADM or DBADM authority to grant CONTROL. The creator of a table automatically receives CONTROL privilege on the table. The creator of a view automatically receives CONTROL privilege only if he has CONTROL privilege on all tables and views referenced in the view definition or has SYSADM or DBADM authority.
- ALTER allows the user to add columns to a table, to add or change comments on a table and its columns, to add a primary key or unique constraint, and to create or drop a table check constraint. The user can also create triggers on the table,

7

although additional authority on all the objects referenced in the trigger (including SELECT on the table if the trigger references any of the columns of the table) is required. A user with ALTER privilege on all the descendent tables can drop a primary key; a user with ALTER privilege on the table and REFERENCES privilege on the parent table, or REFERENCES privilege on the appropriate columns, can create or drop a foreign key. A user with ALTER privilege can also add comments to a given table. (These comments are stored in the database catalog and often used to describe a column or constraint.)

- DELETE allows the user to delete rows from a table or view.

- INDEX allows the user to create an index on a table. Creators of indexes automatically have CONTROL privilege on the index.

- INSERT allows the user to insert a row into a table or view, and to run the IMPORT utility.

- REFERENCES allows the user to create and drop a foreign key, specifying the table as the parent in a relationship. The user might have this privilege only on specific columns.

- SELECT allows the user to retrieve rows from a table or view, to create a view on a table, and to run the EXPORT utility.

- UPDATE allows the user to change an entry in a table, a view, or for one or more specific columns in a table or view. The user may have this privilege only on specific columns.

Together, privileges and authorities act to control access to an instance and its database objects. Users can access only those objects for which they have the appropriate authorization—that is, the required privilege or authority.

Granting and Revoking Privileges and Authorities

You can grant authorities at the database level and privileges for most other objects. To grant or revoke privileges or authorities to other users on the system, follow these steps:

1. In the Control Center, expand the objects until you see the CDLIB database.

2. Right-click the CDLIB database icon and select Authorities from the pop-up menu. The Authorities – CDLIB dialog box opens, listing the users that now have privileges assigned to work with objects in the CDLIB database. By default, the instance owner has privileges on all objects.

3. To add additional users to the list, click Add User, select one or more users from the list, and click Add. Click Close when you've finished selecting users to return to the Authorities CDLIB dialog box.

The Database Authorities dialog box shows the users you've just added with the privileges each has. A check mark in a column means that the user has the privilege; an X means that the user doesn't have the privilege (see Figure 7.8). You can grant access to DBADM, CREATETAB, BINDADD, CONNECT, NOFENCE, and IMPLICITSCHEMA.

FIGURE 7.8

The Database Authorities dialog box.

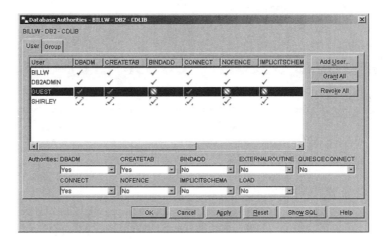

> **TIP**
>
> You can also grant privileges to an entire group. First, use the Windows User Manager to assign users to a group. Then, use the Group page of the Database Authorities dialog box to grant access to the group.

Administration of privileges can also be accomplished by issuing the GRANT and REVOKE SQL statements through the command-line tools.

Authorization is controlled in three ways:

• Explicit authorization is controlled through privileges controlled with the GRANT and REVOKE statements (by clicking the Show SQL button in the Database Authorities dialog box, you can see the GRANT or REVOKE statement that is generated).

• Implicit authorization is controlled by creating and dropping objects.

• Indirect privileges are associated with packages.

7

NOTE   Packages may include both static and dynamic SQL. To process a package
               with static SQL, a user need only have EXECUTE privilege on the package.
               This user can then indirectly obtain the privileges of the package binder for
               any static SQL in the package, but only within the restrictions imposed by
               the package.

Windows Security Considerations

An account containing other accounts, also called *members*, is a *group*. Groups give
Windows administrators the ability to grant rights and permissions to the users within the
group at the same time, without having to maintain each user individually. Groups, like
user accounts, are defined and maintained in the Security Access Manager (SAM) database.

Once authenticated

- The user must be identified to DB2 using a SQL authorization name or authid.
  This name can be the same as the user ID, or a mapped value.
- A list of groups to which the user belongs is obtained. Group membership may be
  used when authorizing the user. Groups are security facility entities that must also
  map to DB2 authorization names. This mapping is done in a method similar to that
  used for user IDs.

DB2 UDB allows you to specify either a local group or a global group when granting
privileges or defining authority levels. A user is determined to be a member of a group if
the user's account is defined explicitly in the local or global group, or implicitly by being
a member of a global group defined to be a member of a local group.

DB2 for Windows NT supports the following types of groups:

- Local groups
- Global groups
- Global groups as members of local groups

DB2 for Windows NT enumerates the local and global groups that the user is a member
of, using the security database where the user was found. DB2 Universal Database provides an override that forces group enumeration to occur on the local Windows NT
server where DB2 is installed, regardless of where the user account was found. This
override can be achieved using the following commands:

- For global settings:

  ```
  db2set -g DB2_GRP_LOOKUP=local
  ```

- For instance settings:

  ```
  db2set -i <instance name> DB2_GRP_LOOKUP=local
  ```

After issuing these commands, you must stop and start the DB2 instance for the change to take effect. Then create local groups and include domain accounts or global groups in the local group.

To view all DB2 profile registry variables that are set, type

```
db2set -all
```

If the DB2_GRP_LOOKUP profile registry variable is not set, the following occurs:

1. DB2 first tries to find the user on the same machine.
2. If the username is defined locally, the user is authenticated locally.
3. If the user is not found locally, DB2 attempts to find the username on its domain and then on trusted domains.

If DB2 is running on a machine that is a primary or backup domain controller in the resource domain, it can locate any domain controller in any trusted domain. This occurs because the names of the domains of backup domain controllers in trusted domains are only known if you are a domain controller.

If DB2 is not running on a domain controller, issue the following command:

```
db2set -g DB2_GRP_LOOKUP=DOMAIN
```

This command tells DB2 to use a domain controller in its own domain to find the name of a domain controller in the accounts domain. That is, when DB2 finds out that a particular user account is defined in domain x, instead of attempting to locate a domain controller for domain x, it sends that request to a domain controller in its own domain. The name of the domain controller in the account domain will be found and returned to the machine DB2 is running on. There are two advantages to this method:

- A backup domain controller is found when the primary domain controller is unavailable.
- A backup domain controller is found that is close when the primary domain controller is geographically remote.

7

Summary

In this lesson, you saw that DB2 includes levels of security that control the access to the database and within the database. Access to DB2 for Windows is controlled by the Windows operating system security mechanism. Access within DB2 is controlled through authorities and privileges that are set for most objects in the database.

What Comes Next?

On Day 8, "Designing the CDLIB Database," you will learn how to design an application to track a library of music CDs.

Q&A

Q What authentication types can I set for an instance?

A The default authentication type is SERVER. This means that users are verified at the server where the database resides. CLIENT authentication can be used to verify users at the client machine with no further authentication occurring at the server. KERBEROS authentication is used when both the DB2 client and server are on operating systems that support the Kerberos security protocol. The Kerberos security protocol performs authentication as a third-party authentication service by using conventional cryptography to create a shared secret key. This key becomes a user's credential and is used to verify the identity of users during all occasions when local or network services are requested. The key eliminates the need to pass the username and password across the network as clear text. Using the Kerberos security protocol enables the use of a single sign-on to a remote DB2 server.

Q What are the five levels of authority?

A DB2 uses five levels of authority to group privileges and control over database objects. SYSADM, the highest level of authority, provides control over all resources created and maintained by DB2. DB2ADM authority provides the second highest level of authority and applies only to a specific database. The SYSCRTL and SYSMAINT authorities are provided to allow access to the system resources but not the data. LOAD authority allows users to load data into the database.

Q What is the difference between authorization and privileges?

A Two types of permissions are recorded by DB2: privileges and authority levels. A *privilege* defines a single permission for an authorization name, enabling a user to create or access database resources. Privileges are stored in the database catalogs. *Authority levels* provide a method of grouping privileges and control over higher-level database manager maintenance and utility operations. Database-specific authorities are stored in the database catalogs; system authorities are associated with group membership and are stored in the Database Manager Configuration file for a given instance.

Q What are groups?

A Groups provide a convenient means of performing authorization for a collection of users without having to grant or revoke privileges for each user individually. Unless otherwise specified, group authorization names can be used anywhere that authorization names are used for authorization purposes.

Workshop

The purpose of the Workshop is to allow you to test your knowledge of the material covered in the lesson. See whether you can successfully answer the questions in the quiz and complete the exercise before you continue with the next lesson. The answers appear in Appendix B, "Answers to Quiz Questions and Exercises."

Quiz

1. If you want to create databases and assign authorities to other users, what authority should you have?
2. Describe the importance of implicit versus explicit privileges.
3. What authorities are granted to all users when the database is created?
4. What is the default for the Trusted Clients option? What does this mean?

Exercise

1. Create several users who have different levels of authorities and attempt to access data from each user. Set up different views for each user to see how you can restrict access to certain pieces of information.

7

WEEK 2

At a Glance

During Week 2, you learn how to logically design a relational database by designing the sample database that is used throughout the book. Subsequent lessons teach you how to create this database and its tables and table spaces, and how to access data in your tables. These are the tasks that you will perform in your day-to-day work as a database administrator. Here's a day-by-day summary of Week 2:

- Day 8, "Designing the CDLIB Database"

  This lesson introduces the database that is used throughout the rest of the book to demonstrate the concepts and features of the DB2 Universal Database product. As the sample database is being introduced, the theory of logically designing a database is explained.

- Day 9, "Creating Databases and Tables"

  During this lesson, you use a wizard to create a database called CDLIB. After you create the database, you use a wizard to create several tables in the database.

- Day 10, "Creating Table Spaces"

  This lesson teaches you the concepts of table spaces and the ways to use them. You also learn how to create table spaces to store your tables.

- Day 11, "Accessing the Data"

  This lesson describes the many choices you have to access the data stored in DB2 databases.

- Day 12, "SQL Concepts"

  This lesson teaches you to use basic SQL to access the data in your tables.

8

9

10

11

12

13

14

- Day 13, "Advanced SQL"

  This lesson teaches you how to use SQL statements to implement business functionality. A number of the IBM Relational Extenders, all written using the object-oriented features of DB2, are also examined.

- Day 14, "Design Considerations"

  This lesson covers several ways you can affect the performance of your system simply through the design of your databases, tables, and applications.

DAY 8

Designing the CDLIB Database

Today you go through the steps of designing a database, tables, and referential constraints to hold the data for a CD collection. Today focuses on planning and designing a database structure; the actual creation of the database and its tables is covered tomorrow. Planning a database structure is as important as actually creating the database—in fact, good planning helps prevent hard-to-fix problems down the road.

I'll take you through the usual steps for designing a database to show you the structure of the database for the CD collection. These steps include deciding what data to store in the database, choosing appropriate columns and data types, defining relationships between the tables, identifying the primary key of the table, identifying constraints and foreign keys, and normalizing tables.

Today you learn the following:

- How to decide what data to store in your database
- How to define tables for each type of relationship

- How to choose a column to be the primary key
- How to identify constraints and foreign keys
- How to normalize your table

Deciding What Data to Store in the Database

As you learned in Day 2, "Exploring the Capabilities of DB2 Universal Database," a table is a collection of rows and columns. Each row contains information about one object such as the information for one CD. Each column contains the same type of information such as the title of the CD. A table is a group of information regarding one subject—for example, a collection of songs. One or more tables are related to each other through the addition of foreign keys that link information, such as the song title, to a particular album.

For a CD collection, you might want to record information such as the name of the artist or group, the title of the CD, the names of each song on the CD, the length of each song, the length of the CD, the year the CD was released, members of the group, type of music, record label, and perhaps an audio clip or photo of the artist. Before you design your tables, however, you must understand each entity and its relationship to other entities. Artist, album, and song are examples of entities. The artist records one or more albums, each of which contains one or more songs. The relationship between artists, songs, and albums applies to each row of the tables.

The information contained within a table depends on the relationships to be expressed, the amount of flexibility needed, and the data retrieval speed desired. The following sections describe each table and the attributes for each column within the table.

For each column, you need to provide the following information:

- Column name—You can have up to 500 columns in a table using 4KB page size and 1012 columns if using 8KB, 12KB, or 32KB page size. Each column name can contain up to 30 characters and must be different from all other columns in the table. Choose a column name that describes the data you intend to put in the column. For example, you may choose the column name album_title for the column that will contain the title of each album in the table.
- Type of data and length—You must analyze the data that you intend to store in the column. This is often difficult to do because you don't always know in advance what data will need to be put into the table. Data usually falls into the categories of character, numeric, or large object. There are many data types for each category.

The following data types can be used for the columns in the table. Some size restrictions are inherent in the data types, so it is important to choose the data type that gives you the flexibility you need.

Data Type	Description
INTEGER	For a large integer.
SMALLINT	For a small integer.
DOUBLE	For a floating-point number.
DECIMAL	For a decimal number.
CHARACTER	For a fixed-length character string.
VARCHAR	For a varying-length character string with a maximum length of 4000.
LONG VARCHAR	For a varying-length character string with a maximum length of 32700.
BLOB	For a binary large object string.
CLOB	For a character large object string.
DBCLOB	For a double-byte character large object string.
GRAPHIC	For a fixed-length graphic string.
VARGRAPHIC	For a varying-length graphic string with a maximum length of 2000.
LONG VARGRAPHIC	For a varying-length graphic string with a maximum length of 16350.
DATE	For a date.
TIME	For a time.
TIMESTAMP	For a time stamp.
Distinct type	For a type you want to create based on your specific needs. Distinct types are listed in the form of schema.type.

- Whether the column has a default value or is null—If a column in the table is likely to contain a certain value, you can define the value as the default for the column. For example, if you have a table containing addresses and most of the people in your table are from the same city or state, you can define this as the default value so that if you don't enter a value for the column, the default value is automatically used.

Some columns may never contain a value. In this case, you should define the column as being nullable. A null value is a special value that indicates that the column value is unknown or not applicable. For example, if you have a column for email addresses in your address table, you should make the column null to accommodate those people in your table who don't currently have an email address.

The CATEGORY Table

The CATEGORY table contains the musical categories for the CD collection (see Figure 8.1). This table includes the following attributes:

Column Name	Data Type, Size, and Whether Nullable
CATEGORYID	SMALLINT; not null
DESCRIPTION	VARCHAR, 50; not null

FIGURE 8.1

A sample CATEGORY table.

The primary key of this table, CategoryID, contains a unique ID number for each category type. Category types include rock, classical, country, and soundtrack.

The RECORDLABEL Table

The RECORDLABEL table contains the names of each record label for the CD collection (see Figure 8.2). Examples of record labels include MCA Records, EMI/Capitol Records, and WEA Music. The table includes the following attributes:

Column Name	Data Type, Size, and Whether Nullable
RECORDERLABELID	SMALLINT; not null
NAME	VARCHAR, 50; not null

The primary key of this table, RECORDLABELID, contains a unique ID number for each record company.

FIGURE 8.2

A sample RECORD-LABEL table.

The ARTIST Table

The ARTIST table contains information about each person who is a performer on an album (see Figure 8.3). Artist names could include John Lennon, Bono of U2, and David Bowie. This table includes the following attributes:

Column Name	Data Type, Size, and Whether Nullable
ARTISTID	SMALLINT; not null
NAME	VARCHAR, 50; not null
PORTRAITID	SMALLINT; null

FIGURE 8.3

A sample ARTIST table.

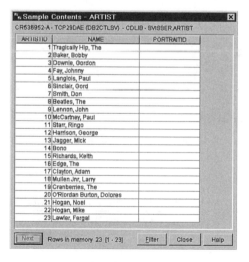

The primary key of this table, ARTISTID, contains a unique ID number for each artist. PORTRAITID is a foreign key to the PORTRAIT table, where a photo of the artist may be stored.

The GROUP Table

The GROUP table contains information regarding a musical group that performs on an album (see Figure 8.4). Group names could include the Beatles, U2, and the Rolling Stones, as well as solo artists, such as John Lennon or Loreena McKennitt, or composers, such as Vivaldi. This table includes the following attributes:

Column Name	Data Type, Size, and Whether Nullable
GROUPID	SMALLINT; not null
NAME	VARCHAR, 50; not null

The primary key of this table, GROUPID, contains a unique ID number for each group.

FIGURE 8.4

A sample GROUP table.

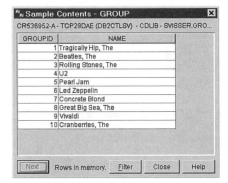

The ALBUM Table

The ALBUM table contains information about a musical recording on CD (see Figure 8.5). Album titles could include *Pop*, *Abbey Road*, and *Four Seasons*. This table includes the following attributes:

Column Name	Data Type, Size, and Whether Nullable
ALBUMID	SMALLINT; not null
CATEGORYID	SMALLINT; not null
GROUPID	SMALLINT; not null
TITLE	VARCHAR, 50; not null
RELEASEYEAR	SMALLINT; not null
RECORDLABELID	SMALLINT; not null
ALBUMCOVERID	SMALLINT; null
LENGTH	SMALLINT; null

FIGURE 8.5

A sample ALBUM table.

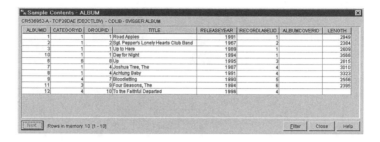

The primary key of this table, AlbumID, contains a unique ID number for each CD in the collection.

For each album, the year it was released and the length of the album are included. A check constraint is defined on the ReleaseYear to ensure that the date is entered accurately.

This table has several foreign keys: CATEGORYID is a foreign key to the CATEGORY table, GROUPID is a foreign key to the GROUP table, RECORDLABELID is a foreign key to the RECORDLABEL table, and ALBUMCOVERID is a foreign key to the ALBUMCOVER table.

The SONG Table

The SONG table contains information regarding each song on an album (see Figure 8.6). This table includes the following attributes:

Column Name	Data Type, Size, and Whether Nullable
SONGID	SMALLINT; not null
ALBUMID	SMALLINT; not null
TITLE	VARCHAR, 50; not null
LENGTH	SMALLINT; not null
AUDIOCLIPID	SMALLINT; null

The primary key of this table is a combination of SONGID and ALBUMID. The same song can be recorded by many artists, but typically a CD contains only a single version of the song. (There are exceptions, but this lesson ignores these cases for simplicity.)

The TITLE column contains the title of each song such as "Cordelia," "On the Verge," and "With or Without You." The length of each song is also included. AUDIOCLIPID is a foreign key to the AUDIOCLIP table, where a sample of the song may be stored.

FIGURE 8.6

A sample SONG table.

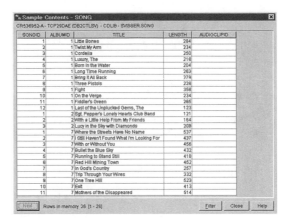

The ARTISTINGROUP Table

The ARTISTINGROUP table associates each artist with a group (see Figure 8.7). This table takes into account that a group is made of several members, and these members may actually be parts of different groups throughout their careers. For example, Paul McCartney was a member of the Beatles and Wings.

FIGURE 8.7

A sample ARTISTIN-GROUP table.

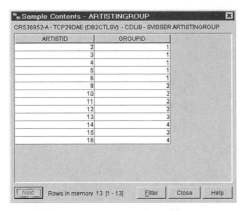

The primary key of this table is a combination of ARTISTID and GROUPID. ARTISTID is a foreign key to the ARTIST table, and GroupID is a foreign key to the GROUP table:

Column Name	Data Type, Size, and Whether Nullable
ARTISTID	SMALLINT; not null
GROUPID	SMALLINT; not null

The PORTRAIT Table

The optional PORTRAIT table contains GIF images of some artists. This table includes the following attributes:

Column Name	Data Type, Size, and Whether Nullable
PORTRAITID	SMALLINT; not null
PORTRAIT	BLOB, 1MB; not null

The primary key is the PORTRAITID.

The AUDIOCLIP Table

The optional AUDIOCLIP table contains WAV samples of songs. This table includes the following attributes:

Column Name	Data Type, Size, and Whether Nullable
AUDIOCLIPID	SMALLINT; not null
AUDIOCLIP	BLOB, 1MB; not null

The primary key is AUDIOCLIPID.

The ALBUMCOVER Table

The optional ALBUMCOVER table contains GIF samples of CD covers. This table includes the following attributes:

Column Name	Data Type, Size, and Whether Nullable
ALBUMCOVERID	SMALLINT; not null
ALBUMCOVER	BLOB, 1MB; not null

The primary key is the ALBUMCOVERID.

Defining Tables for Each Type of Relationship

In a database, you can express several types of relationships. The type of relationship can vary, depending on the specific environment. You'll want to define separate tables for different types of relationships:

- *One-to-one relationships* are single valued in both directions. For example, each song has one title. This type of relationship can be assigned to the album table or the song table. This sample database associates song titles with the SONG table.

- *One-to-many relationships* are multivalued in one direction. For example, the relationship between categories and albums is one-to-many, because each category has many albums, and each album has one category defined. (In reality, an album may belong to many categories, but for simplicity I've associated a single category per album.) The many side in the album/category relationship is album, so this example defines a table for albums.

- *Many-to-one relationships* are also multivalued in one direction. For example, an album has many songs. The many side of the songs/album relationship is songs, so this example defines a SONG table.

- *Many-to-many relationships* are multivalued in both directions. For example, it usually takes many performers to record one song, and each performer usually records many songs. This type of relationship can be expressed in a table with a column for each entity.

Figure 8.8 shows the many types of relationships in the CDLIB database.

FIGURE 8.8

Structure of the CDLIB database.

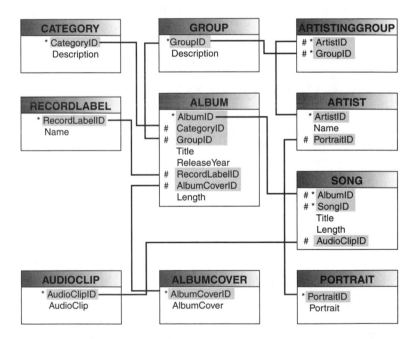

Identifying the Primary Key

Determine whether you want to define a primary key for your table. As you learned in Day 2, a primary key is one of the unique keys defined on a table but is selected as the column of first importance on the table. The table can have only one primary key, but the

8

primary key can be made up of one or more columns. An asterisk (*) next to the column name in Figure 8.8 indicates that it's a primary key.

The key columns you should consider should have the following qualities:

- Persistence—A value must always be present in the row. The columns of a primary key can't contain null values.

- Uniqueness—Each key value is and always will be different for each row. A primary key is a special kind of unique key that uniquely identifies a row of a table. You can choose multiple columns as the primary key. For example, you might want to create a primary key on the song ID and album ID columns of a song table to ensure uniqueness.

- Stability—The key value is one that should never change to another value. For example, you don't want to define a person's name as the primary key because the person may change his name as Richard Starkey changed his name to Ringo Starr. It is common to use an identifier column such as employee number as the primary key because this number is unlikely to change.

If you have more than one table describing properties of the same entity, make sure that equal values represent the same entity. For example, if you add an ADDRESS table to contain the Web site and email addresses for each group, you would have a column for the GroupID that would match the GROUPID column in the GROUP table. The connecting columns can have different names or the same name. For example, you can call the column GROUPID in the GROUP table and GRPID in the ADDRESS table.

Identifying Constraints and Foreign Keys

You can define several types of constraints on your table, including foreign key constraints, table check constraints, and triggers.

Foreign key constraints let you define relationships tables and require that all values of a given column of a table also exist in some other table. For example, the DEPTNO column of the EMPLOYEE table has a foreign key defined on the DEPTNO column of the DEPARTMENT table. This means that an employee cannot be assigned to a department unless the department already exists.

A number sign (#) next to the column name in Figure 8.8 indicates that it's a foreign key. Foreign keys are defined on the dependent table and rely on the data in the parent table.

Table check constraints enforce business rules that you define in your database design. These constraints specify conditions that are enforced for each row of the table and are automatically activated when data is updated or inserted in the table.

A table check constraint can be used for validation. For example, you can define a constraint to check the validation of the RELEASEYEAR of an album. You can make sure that the entered value is greater than 1900 and less than the current year.

You can also define triggers to help support business rules. A trigger is activated when data is inserted, updated, or deleted from the table. For example, you can create a trigger that sends you an email message whenever a business rule such as a credit limit is exceeded.

Normalizing Your Table

Normalizing helps you avoid redundancies and inconsistencies in your data. The main idea behind normalizing is to reduce tables to a set of columns in which all the non-key columns depend on the entire primary key of the table.

You may think that normalizing your tables sacrifices performance because querying data from normalized tables requires joining one or more of the tables. The actual performance difference between accessing data in tables that are normalized as opposed to tables that aren't normalized is minimal. In fact, the benefits of avoiding redundancies and inconsistencies far outweigh the minimal differences in performance.

The process of normalizing your tables involves analyzing your tables to see whether they violate a series of normalization rules. These rules are called first normal form, second normal form, third normal form, and so on. The following sections briefly describe the rules for first, second, and third normal forms and provide examples of tables that violate the rules and how they can be normalized. The fourth and fifth normal forms are beyond the scope of this book.

First Normal Form

In first normal form, one value exists in each row and column position, never a set of values. For example, the Table 8.1 violates first normal form because the ARTIST column contains several values for each occurrence of GROUP.

TABLE 8.1   Violation of First Normal Form

Group ID (Primary Key)	Group Name	Artist
1	Rolling Stones	Mick Jagger, Keith Richards, Charlie Watts, Ronnie Woods, Bill Wyman, Brian Jones
2	The Beatles	John Lennon, Paul McCartney, George Harrison, Ringo Starr

Table 8.2 shows the table in first normal form.

TABLE 8.2   Satisfying First Normal Form

Group ID (Primary Key)	Group Name	Artist ID (Primary Key)	Artist Name
1	Rolling Stones	1	Mick Jagger
1	Rolling Stones	2	Keith Richards
1	Rolling Stones	3	Ronnie Woods
1	Rolling Stones	4	Charlie Watts
1	Rolling Stones	5	Bill Wyman
1	Rolling Stones	6	Brian Jones
2	The Beatles	7	John Lennon
2	The Beatles	8	Paul McCartney
2	The Beatles	9	George Harrison
2	The Beatles	9	Ringo Starr

Second Normal Form

In second normal form, each column not in the key depends on all columns in the key. This reduces repetition among database tables.

Second normal form is violated when a non-key column depends on a subset of a composite key, as in Table 8.3.

TABLE 8.3   Violation of Second Normal Form

Song ID (Primary Key)	Album ID (Primary Key)	Album Title	Song Title
1	1	Sgt. Pepper's Lonely Hearts Club Band	Fixing a Hole
2	2	Pop	Please
3	1	Sgt. Pepper's Lonely Hearts Club Band	Being for the Benefit of Mr. Kite!

The key consists of the ALBUMID and SONGID columns together. Because the album title depends only on the value of the ALBUMID column (a subset of the composite key), the table violates the rule for second normal form.

The problems with this design are as follows:

- The album name is repeated for each song. An album like *Sgt. Pepper's Lonely Hearts Club Band* has 13 songs, so the album title will be repeated 13 times.
- The album title won't change, but when you're inserting data into the table, you must make sure that you spell the album title correctly each time you enter it.

To satisfy second normal form, the information in Table 8.3 should be split into Tables 8.4 and 8.5 with the non-key columns depending on the entire key in each table.

TABLE 8.4   Satisfying Second Normal Form

Song ID (Primary Key)	Album ID (Primary Key)	Song Title
1	1	Fixing a Hole
2	2	Please
3	1	Being for the Benefit of Mr. Kite!
4	1	Getting Better

TABLE 8.5   Satisfying Second Normal Form

Album ID (Primary Key)	Album Title
1	Sgt. Pepper's Lonely Hearts Club Band
2	Pop

Third Normal Form

In third normal form, each non-key column is independent of other non-key columns and depends only on the key. Table 8.6 violates the third normal form.

TABLE 8.6   Violation of Third Normal Form

Album ID (Primary Key)	Album Name	Record Label	Phone Number
1	Abbey Road	Apple	555-1234
2	Pop	MCA	555-5678
3	Let It Be	Apple	555-1234

8

Third normal form is violated in Table 8.6 because a non-key column such as PHONE NUMBER depends on another non-key column such as RECORDLABEL. Changing the phone number for the record label of a single album won't change the phone number for all other rows that refer to the same record label. The inconsistency after an update is shown in Table 8.7.

TABLE 8.7 Inconsistent Data

Album ID (Primary Key)	Album Name	Record Label	Phone Number
1	Abbey Road	Apple	555-9999
2	Pop	MCA	555-5678
3	Let It Be	Apple	555-1234

You can normalize this table by providing a new table with columns for record labels and phone numbers. In this case, updating a phone number is much easier because the update has to be made only to the new table. A SQL query that shows the phone number with the name of an album is more complex to write because it requires joining the two tables. Tables 8.8 and 8.9 are defined as a result of normalizing the tables.

TABLE 8.8 Satisfying Third Normal Form

Album ID (Primary Key)	Album Name	Record Label ID
1	Abbey Road	1
2	Pop	2
3	Let It Be	1

TABLE 8.9 Satisfying Third Normal Form

Record Label ID (Primary Key)	Name	Phone Number
1	Apple	555-9999
2	MCA	555-5678

Summary

Today, you saw the several requirements behind designing a database. You must decide what you want to store in the database, define tables for each relationship, identify the primary key for each table, identify constraints and foreign keys, and finally normalize your tables.

Today's lesson also introduced the sample database used in this book. It's introduced while describing the steps that must take place when designing a database. The database is called CDLIB and contains the information for a collection of CDs.

No matter how carefully you plan for your database, you can't anticipate some situations. For this reason, you should go through a scenario with as much different data as you can think of to see whether your design works. Remember, the more flexible you try to make your database, the more difficult it can become.

Normalizing tables is a common topic for relational databases. This book covers up to third normal form.

What Comes Next?

On Day 9, "Creating Databases and Tables," you learn how to use the Control Center to create the CDLIB database and the tables introduced in this lesson.

Q&A

Q How do I choose a primary key?

A You must look at all the columns in your table and choose the column that's always present, always unique, and rarely changes. Most often you'll decide to introduce a new column to your table that holds these properties. For example, in a table containing information about employees, an employee number is assigned to each employee. The number is unique for each person, and the employee uses the number for the entire time she is employed at the company. Often when an employee leaves, the number isn't reassigned, so if the employee returns, she is assigned the same number as before.

Q How many columns can I have in a table?

A DB2 allows you to have 500 columns in a single table.

Q How do I choose a data type?

A You must analyze the data that you intend to store in the column. This is often difficult to do because you don't always know in advance what data will need to be
put into the table. Data usually falls into the categories of character, numeric, or
large object. There are many data types for each category.

Workshop

The purpose of the Workshop is to allow you to test your knowledge of the material covered in the lesson. See whether you can successfully answer the questions in the quiz and
complete the exercise before you continue with the next lesson. The answers appear in
Appendix B, "Answers to Quiz Questions and Exercises."

Quiz

1. What different types of relationships can you represent in a table?
2. Where are foreign keys defined?
3. Why should you normalize your tables?
4. Is it a good idea to use a phone number as a primary key? Why or why not?
5. What data types should be used for data such as photos or movies?
6. What is the difference between data types CHARACTER and VARCHAR?

Exercise

1. Go through the lesson and define a database that you have an idea for. Perhaps you
    can modify the database described in this lesson to suit your personal CD collec-
    tion. Or you could create a new database design that contains an inventory of
    movies or books in your collection.

DAY 9

Creating Databases and Tables

The easiest way to create a database is to use the Create Database Wizard. A *wizard* is a graphical interface that walks you through a task with several steps. Wizards make performing a complex task easier to accomplish. You can use the Create Database Wizard to create a simple database that uses the default values for table spaces or a sophisticated database that has separate table spaces defined for different data types and spans different containers.

Today, you create a few databases to see the available choices. You'll create the sample CDLIB database (defined on Day 8, "Designing the CDLIB Database") to store information about a collection of CDs. The example continues when you create tables and set up the referential constraints.

Today, you learn the following:

- How to create a simple database
- How to create tables

- How to add data to tables
- How to set up referential integrity
- How to alter tables

Creating a Simple Database

First, you create a simple database where you accept most of the available defaults. To create a database with the Create Database Wizard, follow these steps:

TIP

> You must have SYSADM authority to create a database. Your username must belong to the Administrators group to have SYSADM authority.

1. Start the Control Center, if not already started. As you learned earlier, to start the Control Center, choose Start|Programs|IBM DB2|General Administration Tools| Control Center.

2. Expand the object folders until you see the Databases folder. Right-click the folder and select Create from the pop-up menu.

3. The Create Database Wizard appears, open at the first page (see Figure 9.1).

FIGURE 9.1

The Create Database Wizard.

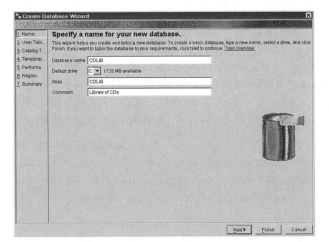

4. Fill in the first page as follows:
   - Database Name—Enter a name to identify your database. This name must be different from any other database names cataloged on this drive. The name

must contain no more than eight characters; use characters A through Z, 0 through 9, @, #, or $; and can't begin with a number. For this example, enter CDLIB.

> **TIP**
>
> If you're planning to use the database in a communications environment or outside North America, avoid using the @, #, and $ symbols in the name.

9

- Default Drive—Select the drive that you want to use. Make sure that you'll have enough space on this drive to contain all the data you'll eventually have in your database. All associated database files will be stored in this drive. (Later, you'll see how to create and spread data over table spaces.)

> **TIP**
>
> To estimate the size of a database, you must include the size of the system catalog tables (initially 1600KB, but grow as objects and privileges are added to the database), the size of each user table in the database, the index space, the log file space, and the temporary work space.

- Alias—An alias is a nickname given to the database. If you leave this text box blank, it will default to the name of the database. Leave this blank so that it will default to CDLIB.

- Comment—In this text box, enter an optional description for your database. The comment can contain up to 30 characters. Enter a comment such as Library of CDs.

5. Click the Finish button to create the database. (Pages 2 through 7 are more advanced topics and are covered in the next section.)

After a few minutes, you'll get a message stating that the database is created and that you should run the Configuration Advisor Wizard to tune your database. Click No to skip this step. This topic is covered in the next section. Check the main panel of the Control Center to see a folder added for the CDLIB database.

At this point, the database is empty. To make it useful, you need to create tables, add data, and set up referential constraints.

Creating Tables

You can create tables with the Control Center through the Create Table Wizard. The Create Table Wizard allows you to create simple tables as well as more complicated ones with referential constraints.

For this example, you'll use the Create Table Wizard to create a simple table and add the constraints in a later step. To create the CATEGORY table, which will contain the music categories of the CDs in this collection, follow these steps:

1. Start the Control Center, if it's not already started.
2. Expand the object folders under the CDLIB database folder until you see the Tables folder. Right-click that folder.
3. Select Create from the pop-up menu to start the Create Table Wizard (see Figure 9.2).

FIGURE 9.2

The Create Table Wizard's Name page.

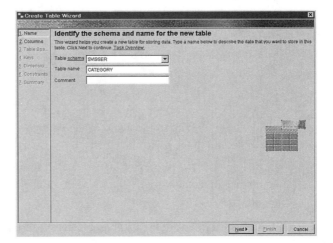

4. On the Name page, enter the following information:
   - Table Schema—Specify the schema for the table you're creating. The initial value is the username that you're using. My username is SVISSER, so tables I create with my username are named SVISSER.*TABLE_NAME*. This is fine if you're the only user of the database. You might want to have a more universal schema name such as a department or function name. For example, the Payroll department might want to use the schema PAYROLL instead of someone's username.

Select an existing schema or type the name of a new schema. (You must have IMPLICIT_SCHEMA authority to be able to create new schemas.) Rather than use my username, I use ADMINISTRATOR.

- Table Name—The name of your table must be unique within the schema and can contain up to 128 characters and cannot be SYSIBM, SYSCAT, SYS-FUN, or SYSSTAT. For this example, name the table CATEGORY.

- Comment—In this text box, enter an optional description for your table. The comment can contain up to 30 characters.

5. Click Next to continue.

6. On the Columns page, you can click the Add Predefined button to add a column from the list of predefined columns on the Select Columns dialog box to use for your table (see Figure 9.3). For example, if you're keeping a list of addresses, click the Addresses item in the Column Categories list to see all the predefined columns for an address list. Each column is defined with preset column sizes and characteristics. The selected column moves to the Columns to Create list.

FIGURE 9.3

Use the Select Columns dialog box to add a predefined column to your table.

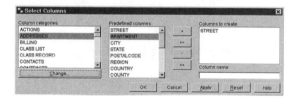

For this example, you want to create two columns that aren't in any of these predefined lists. To create these, click the Add button on the Columns page of the Create Table Wizard. This opens the Add Column dialog box, as shown in Figure 9.4.

7. On the Add Column dialog box, you must define the characteristics of the new column. For our example, enter the details as follows:

TIP

Plan carefully when setting the characteristics for each column. Most columns can't easily be altered after you finish creating the table unless you drop the table and re-create it.

- Column Name—Enter a unique name for the column. The name can contain up to 30 characters. For this example, enter CATEGORYID.

- Data Type—Many data types are available in DB2, and you also can make your own unique data types. Examples of some predefined data types include

INTEGER, BIGINT, SMALLINT, DOUBLE, DECIMAL, CHARACTER, and VARCHAR. For this example, select SMALLINT because you want CATEGORYID to be a small integer.

FIGURE 9.4

The Add Column dialog box of the Table Wizard.

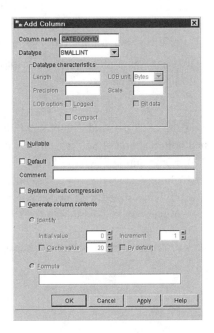

- Data Type Characteristics—The data type characteristics that you need to define depend on the data type that you selected. You selected the SMALLINT data type, so you have no additional characteristics to define.

- Default—You can enter an optional value that you want used as a default whenever a value isn't entered. For example, if for a field named COUNTRY the most common entry is UNITED STATES, you should set the default to this value so that when you don't enter a value, DB2 will fill in this value. For this example, leave it blank.

- Nullable—Select the Nullable check box if you want to allow this field to be blank. Nullable is the default. For this example, you want CATEGORYID to be the primary key, so clear the Nullable check box.

TIP

If the column will be a primary key column, it can't be nullable. A primary key cannot be nullable because the primary key must exist in every row in the table. This guarantees that the row can be found.

8. Click OK when finished. You'll return to the Columns page of the Create Table Wizard and see that the column has been added. Click Add to create a second column with the following information:

- Column Name—Enter the name DESCRIPTION for this column.

- Data Type—For this example, select VARCHAR because you want the description to contain characters and the length to be variable.

TIP

Using the VARCHAR data type is more efficient than using the CHARACTER data type to store character values. Because VARCHAR is variable, it uses only the necessary space to store the value, whereas the CHARACTER data type reserves a block of space for the value regardless of its actual size.

- Data Type Characteristics—An upper value must still be specified for VARCHAR. For a category description, 30 characters should be enough.

- Default—Don't define a default for this field.

- Nullable—Make the description field required even though it won't be the primary key.

9. Click OK to add the column and to exit the Add Column dialog box. The second page of the Create Table Wizard now shows the two columns created as shown in Figure 9.5.

FIGURE 9.5

The Create Table Wizard's Columns page.

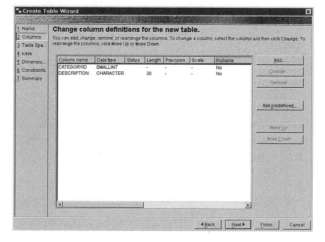

10. On the Table Space page, you can create table spaces for storing the table data. This topic is important for more sophisticated databases, but because you are creating a simple and small database, leave this topic for later. This topic is covered in Day 10, "Creating Table Spaces;" leave the default values for these fields for now and click Next to move to the Keys page.

11. On the Keys page (see Figure 9.6), you can define a primary key, unique key, or foreign key for the new table.

FIGURE 9.6

The Create Table Wizard's Keys page.

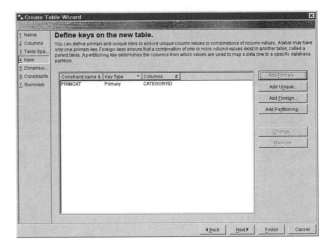

Click Add Primary to create a primary key from the list of columns that you have in the table. In this example, you want to have CATEGORYID as the primary key. Move CATEGORYID into the Primary key columns list (see Figure 9.7) and click OK to create the primary key. You learn how to create a unique key and foreign key in a later section. Click Next to continue.

TIP

> If the column selected to be the primary key was defined as nullable in the previous page, you'll get an error message saying that you can't use this column as part of the primary key. If you get this message, click Back to return to the previous page, select the column that you need to modify, click Change, and make the column not nullable.

12. On the Dimensions page, you can set up data clustering. Defining more than one dimension on the table enables multidimensional clustering. For example, defining a dimension on a YEAR column and another on a MONTH column causes all data

rows from the same year and month to be co-located on the disk. This can lead to performance gains for queries that involve YEAR, MONTH, or both. Click Next to continue.

FIGURE 9.7

The Define Primary Key dialog box launched from the Create Table Wizard's Keys page.

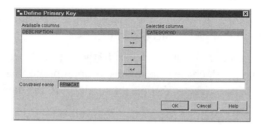

9

13. On the Constraints page, you can define check constraints, or business rules, that specify the values for every row in the table. Check constraints are checked whenever data is inserted or updated. This topic is covered later in today's lesson. Click Next to continue.

14. On the Summary page, you are shown a summary of all the choices you made while using the Create Table Wizard. Click the Show SQL button to show the SQL code that will be used to create the table. Click Finish to create the table as defined in the summary page.

If you want to look at your empty table, use the Control Center. Click the Tables folder in the main Control Center panel. In the right panel, you'll see all the tables now in the database. Most of these are DB2 system tables that you can view but can't change. Scroll down until you see the CATEGORY table just created. Right-click CATEGORY and choose Sample Contents from the pop-up menu. You'll see the two table columns that you added, with no data. Next, you'll add data to this table. Now close this window by clicking Close button.

Adding Data to Tables

You can add data to tables in several ways in DB2. Most likely you'll have an application from which you can enter data into DB2 databases. As mentioned in earlier lessons, you can create your own applications by using many popular programming languages such as C++, C, Visual Basic, Power Builder, or Java, or applications such as Microsoft Access to help you enter data.

If you don't have an application, you can enter data by using the Command Center and simple SQL statements. Follow these steps:

1. Start the Command Center. If it is not already open, choose Start|Programs|IBM DB2|Command Tools|Command Center to open it.

2. In the main panel, connect to the CDLIB database, and enter the following commands in the Command section:

> **INPUT**
> ```
> insert into CATEGORY (CATEGORYID, DESCRIPTION)
> values (1, 'Rock'), (2, 'Classical'), (3, 'Country');
> ```

3. Click the gears button to process the command. The Results screen opens, showing that the command completed successfully.

4. Continue to add data in this way. Return to the Script screen, click the down arrow to recall the command, change the values as appropriate to add another row, and click the gears button again. (You need to connect to the database only once.)

5. To see the data that you've just entered, you can issue a SELECT statement from the Script screen:

> **INPUT**
> ```
> select * from CATEGORY;
> ```

6. Click the gears button to see the data that you've entered (see Figure 9.8).

FIGURE 9.8

Sampling data in the Command Center.

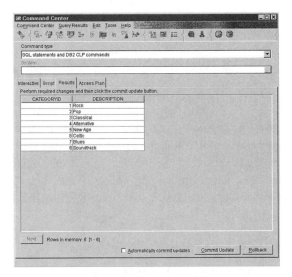

Setting Up Referential Integrity

A database usually isn't a simple table with a list of items, as you've created so far. It's usually made up of many tables, each containing normalized data.

As discussed on Day 8, normalizing helps you avoid redundancies and inconsistencies in your data. The main idea behind normalizing is to reduce tables to a set of columns where all the non-key columns depend on the entire primary key of the table.

Each table is linked to ensure that certain business rules are followed. These rules are normally called *referential integrity*. For example, in the CATEGORY table, you've created a list of music categories. Now create a table that lists the record company associated with an album and another table that lists the albums available on CD for each artist. You can even take this further and add a table that contains graphic files of the band or album cover, audio samples of the CD itself, and even video clips. Each table that you create will contain a certain type of information and will be connected to one or more of the tables with foreign keys.

To see how this is done, create ALBUM, a table that contains the name of the album and its year of release and length, along with relationships to the CATEGORY, RECORDLABEL, ALBUMCOVER, and GROUP tables.

Because you want to add foreign keys to the table as you define it, use the Create Table Wizard:

1. Start the Control Center, if it's not already started.
2. Expand the object folders under the CDLIB database folder until you see the Tables folder. Right-click that folder.
3. Select Create|Table from the pop-up menu to start the Create Table Wizard.
4. On the Name page, enter the following information:
    - Table Schema—Select ADMINISTRATOR from the list of existing schemas.
    - Table Name—For this example, name the table ALBUM.
5. Click Next to continue.
6. On the Columns page of the wizard, select from a list of predefined columns to use for your table. For this example, you want to create columns for ALBUMID, TITLE, RELEASEYEAR, CATEGORYID, RECORDLABELID, ALBUMCOVERID, and LENGTH.
7. Click the Add button to open the Add Column dialog box and fill in the details as follows:

Column Name	Data Type	Nullable
ALBUMID	SMALLINT	No
TITLE	VARCHAR, 45	No
RELEASEYEAR	SMALLINT	No
CATEGORYID	SMALLINT	No
RECORDLABELID	SMALLINT	No
ALBUMCOVERID	SMALLINT	Yes
LENGTH	SMALLINT	Yes

See Figure 9.9 to see all the columns and their characteristics. Click the Keys page to continue.

FIGURE 9.9

The Create Table Wizard's Columns page.

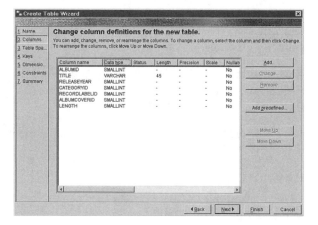

8. On the Keys page, click Add Primary to define a primary key for the new table (see Figure 9.10). From the list of columns in the table, select the columns you want to have as a primary key. In this example, you want to have ALBUMID as the primary key, so move ALBUMID into the Key Columns list and click OK to continue.

FIGURE 9.10

The Create Table Wizard's Define Primary Key dialog box.

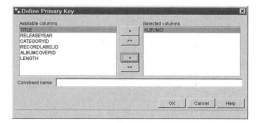

9. On the Keys page, click Add Foreign to add a foreign key to the table (see Figure 9.11). Fill in these fields:

- Table Schema—Specify the name of the schema of the parent key. In this example, the schema for all the tables is ADMINISTRATOR.

- Table Name—Specify the name of the parent table. In this example, you want CATEGORY as the parent table. Choose CATEGORY; its primary key value will appear in the Primary Key box.

- Primary Key—This box is filled in automatically when you select the parent table. The primary key of the CATEGORY table is CATEGORYID, so this appears in the Primary Key box.

- Foreign Key—In the Available Columns box, select columns that you want to define as foreign keys. Each column you select must match a primary key column for the parent table in meaning and data type. In this example, select CATEGORYID to be the foreign key.

- On Delete—From this optional list, specify the action to take place on the dependent table when a row is deleted from the parent table. In this example, the ALBUM table is dependent on the parent table CATEGORY. Suppose that you have Rock listed in the CATEGORY table and decide to delete it. Because you also have a row in the ALBUM table that uses Rock as a category and these rows are linked, you now have to decide what to do with all the rows in ALBUM. Your choices are No Action (the default), Restrict, Cascade, or Select NULL. If you select No Action or Restrict, DB2 will give an error message if you attempt to delete a row in the parent table if there are dependent rows. No rows will be deleted. If you choose Cascade, the row in the parent table is deleted along with any of the dependent rows in dependent tables. If you choose Specify NULL, when the parent row is deleted, any dependent rows will replace all columns with a NULL value if it's allowable. For this example, leave this at the default value: No Action.

- On Update—From this optional list, specify the action to take place on the dependent table when a row of the parent table is updated. Your choices are No Action and Restrict. If you choose No Action or Restrict, an error will occur if you attempt to update a row in the parent table. For this example, use the default value: No Action.

- Constraint Name—In this optional text box, type a name for the constraint that you're defining. If a name isn't entered, one is generated for you. It's useful to have a meaningful constraint name. If an error occurs, the constraint name is used to describe the error condition. A meaningful name helps correct the error.

10. Click OK to add the foreign key.

11. On the Constraints page of the Create Table Wizard, you can add rules to help ensure that only valid data is inserted into the table (see Figure 9.12).

12. Click Add to open the Add Check Constraint dialog box to define a constraint (see Figure 9.13). For example, the column RELEASEYEAR is intended to contain the year the album or CD was released. This date is printed on the back of each CD. Depending on your collection, the release years may range from 1950 to present

day. You can add a check constraint to ensure that only dates in a specific range are
entered.

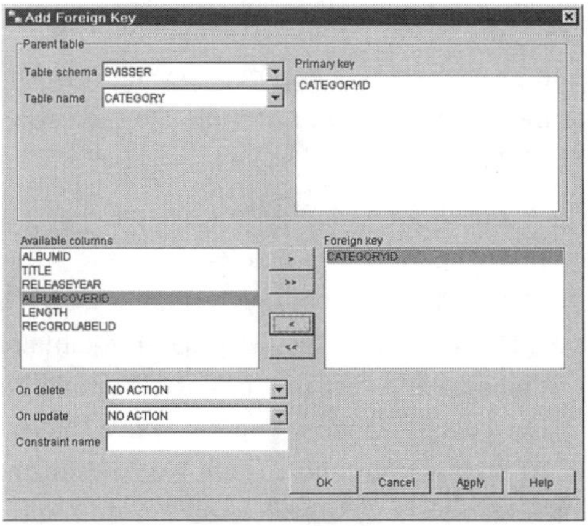

FIGURE 9.11

*The Add Foreign Key
dialog box.*

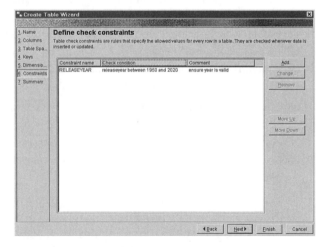

FIGURE 9.12

*The Create Table
Wizard's Constraints
page.*

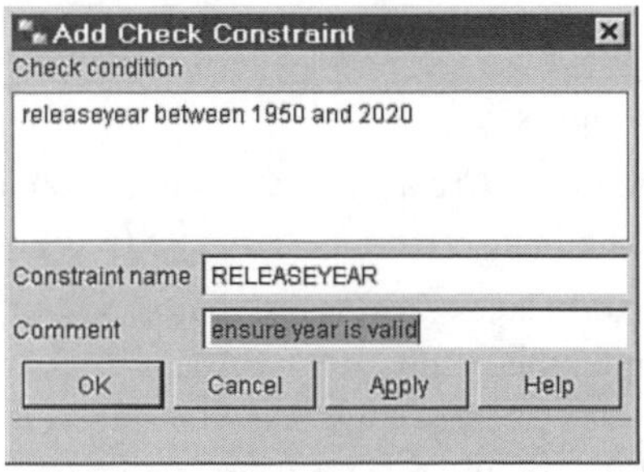

FIGURE 9.13

*The Add Check
Constraint dialog box
launched from the
Create Table Wizard's
Constraints page.*

13. You can define a check constraint that references a single column by specifying that column in the Check Condition box. For example, you can add a check constraint to validate the year entered for the release date of a CD. A check condition of `releaseyear between 1950 and 2020` would be suitable. (In Day 15, "Using System Administration Tools," you'll add a trigger to ensure that a year beyond the current year isn't entered.)

NOTE
Check constraints aren't checked for inconsistencies, duplicate conditions, or equivalent conditions. Therefore, contradictory or redundant check constraints can be defined, resulting in possible errors at execution time.

Although the Constraint Name and Comment text boxes are optional, they're useful. If you don't enter values for these text boxes, the system generates a unique but incomprehensible name for the constraint. If you violate a check constraint condition, having a useful name appear in the message makes it easier to correct the error.

14. You can add multiple check constraints before closing this dialog box. Click Add on the Add Check Constraint dialog box to add the constraint and click Close when you've finished adding constraints.

15. Click Finish to create the table.

Altering Tables

After you create a table, the attributes that you can change are limited. You can do the following:

- Change the size of a column—for example, increase the size of a column defined with the data type VARCHAR.
- Change the comment and the data capture for propagation option.
- Add new columns and change, remove, or rearrange the new columns.
- Add unique, foreign, and partitioning keys for the table.
- Add or drop columns from the primary keys for the table or change the constraint name.
- Add, change, or remove new check constraints.
- Change the lock size, percentage of free space, and other performance-related details.

TIP

> If you're altering a table by adding a foreign key, you need to turn off constraint checking before you alter the table. After you add the foreign key, you need to turn constraint checking back on.

NOTE

> If you turn off constraint checking for a parent table, the foreign key constraints of all its dependent and descendent tables are put in check-pending state.

Right-click the table you want to alter and select Alter from the pop-up menu. The Alter Table dialog box opens. If you want to change an attribute in the table but it isn't in this list, you'll need to create a new table with the new attributes and import the data from the existing table.

Summary

Today you saw how to use the Create Database Wizard, which you launch through the Control Center, to create simple or sophisticated DB2 databases. The wizard prompts you for the required information and creates the database you need.

You use the Create Table Wizard to create tables in an existing database. Again, you're prompted for information about the columns of the table, and the table is created for you.

Referential integrity can be added to your database when you're using the Create Database Wizard.

You can add data to tables in many ways. One way is to use SQL statements to insert the data into the table. Of course, an easier way to add data is using an ODBC application.

What Comes Next?

On Day 10, "Creating Table Spaces," you learn how to create more sophisticated databases that use table spaces to organize the data into partitions.

Q&A

Q **How can you be sure that rows deleted from the parent table do not affect the rows in the dependent tables?**

A When defining a foreign key, specify the action to take place on the dependent table when a row is deleted from the parent table. Your choices are No Action (the default), Restrict, Cascade, or Select NULL. If you select No Action or Restrict, DB2 will give an error message if you attempt to delete a row in the parent table if there are dependent rows. No rows will be deleted. If you choose Cascade, the row in the parent table is deleted along with any of the dependent rows in dependent tables. If you choose Specify NULL, when the parent row is deleted, any dependent rows will replace all columns with a NULL value if it's allowable.

Q **What are the actions you can specify to take place on the dependent table when a row of the parent table is updated?**

A When defining a foreign key, your choices are No Action and Restrict. If you choose No Action or Restrict, an error will occur if you attempt to update a row in the parent table.

Q **If you created a column using the default value of nullable, can you use it as a primary key?**

A Primary keys cannot be nullable. This characteristic cannot be changed after the table is created. If you have already created the table and then decide to change a column from nullable to not null, you will need to re-create the table to do so.

Q **When is a table put into check-pending state?**

A If you turn off constraint checking for a parent table, the foreign key constraints of all its dependent and descendent tables are put into check-pending state.

Workshop

The purpose of the Workshop is to allow you to test your knowledge of the material covered in the lesson. See whether you can successfully answer the questions in the quiz and complete the exercise before you continue with the next lesson. The answers appear in Appendix B, "Answers to Quiz Questions and Exercises."

Quiz

1. Can you define a primary key column to be nullable? Why or why not?
2. What are some differences between the data types VARCHAR and CHARACTER?

3. What are the rules for naming a database?

4. After you create a table, what attributes can change by altering the table?

5. When is data checked to make sure that it complies with rules defined as a check constraint?

Exercise

1. Create the movie database that you designed in Day 8 and the tables that must be created within the database. When you're using the Create Table Wizard, explore the available options in the list of predefined columns.

DAY 10

Creating Table Spaces

The type of data in your database, the size of your database, and your performance needs are some of the considerations that you must take into account when deciding on how your data should be stored. DB2 provides table spaces and buffer pools to give you flexibility in defining how your data is stored.

Today you learn how to create and tune these storage objects for your environment. You will use the Create Table Space Wizard to create table spaces in your database that can be used to store your data. You will also learn how you can separate different types of data to improve performance.

Today you learn the following:

- How to create table spaces
- How to manage your data across multiple table spaces
- How to use the Create Table Space Wizard
- How to create table spaces for indexes and large data
- How to create tables in table spaces
- How to create buffer pools
- How to assign additional space to containers

Managing Your Data in Table Spaces

For databases that are very large, contain large objects such as photos, or require high performance, you need to use advanced methods to store your data. DB2 provides table spaces, containers, and buffer pools for you to define how data is stored on your system.

Databases are logically organized into *table spaces*. Table spaces consist of physical storage devices called *containers*. A single table space can span many containers. A *buffer pool* is an allocation in memory used to cache tables and to index data pages as they are being read from disk or being modified.

You aren't required to create a table space, container, or buffer pool to create tables in a database. You can accept the defaults for each when you create a database and a table in a database. By default when a database is created in DB2, three default table spaces are created. These are

- SYSCATSPACE—Regular table space used to store the system catalog tables.
- TEMPSPACE1—Temporary table space used to sort or reorganize tables, create indexes, and join tables.
- USERSPACE1—Regular table space used to store the table's data and indexes.

Using table spaces to store your data gives you the flexibility to assign portions of a table such as data, indexes, and long field data to different table spaces. This gives you the opportunity to assign different storage devices, depending on the content of each table space. Table spaces can also be backed up and restored as a unit. If you separate your data into table spaces according to how often it's updated, you can then choose to back up the table space containing the more frequently updated data more often.

In Day 9, "Creating Databases and Tables," you learned that the easiest option for choosing space for storing table data is to accept the default table space on the Table Space page in the Create Table Wizard. If you expect the table to be large, you can assign it a separate index space or a separate long space, or both. To create separate spaces for specific data, you use the Create Table Space Wizard.

Using the Create Table Space Wizard

Use the Create Table Space Wizard to create table spaces that contain your data tables. The wizard allows you to define containers as well as the type of management. After you create a table space, you can assign data tables to it. Assign a table to a table space when you create the table.

To create table spaces for your database, follow these steps:

1. Start the Control Center.

2. Expand the folders until you see the objects in the CDLIB database.

3. Right-click the Table Spaces folder. Select Create|Table Space Using Wizard from the pop-up menu. The Create Table Space Wizard appears.

TIP

> The Create Table Space Wizard can also be started by clicking the Create button on the Table Space page of the Create Table Wizard. This allows you to create regular table spaces only.

4. On the Name page (see Figure 10.1), you must type a name for the table space. The name must be different from any other table space in this database and can contain up to 18 characters. For the example, enter CDLIBTS as the name of the table space and click Next to continue.

10

FIGURE **10.1**

The Create Table Space Wizard's Name page.

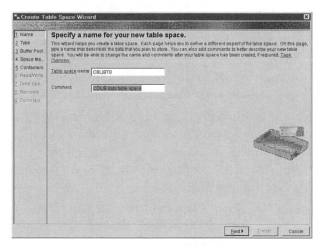

5. On the Type page (see Figure 10.2), decide what type of table space you want to create. Your choices are Regular, Large, System Temporary, or User Temporary. Before you select a type, you should know what data you plan to put in this table space. The type of table space affects the type of space management, containers, and performance options available. You will not be able to change the type after the table space is created.

FIGURE 10.2

*The Create Table
Space Wizard's Type
page.*

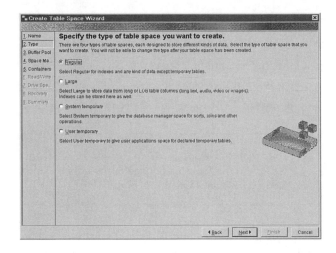

You can choose from among these types:

- Regular—Use this type for all kinds of table data except temporary tables. If you opened the Create Table Space Wizard from the Create Table Wizard, Regular is the only type that can be selected. A database should have at least one regular table space.

- Large—Use this type to create a table space that stores large object data such as images, audio, video, or long text fields. When this type is selected, DB2 uses the high-performance management option for this table space.

- System Temporary—Use this type to create a table space to store system temporary tables. The temporary space is used during sorts, joins, and other operations. You can create more, but in most situations, only a single temporary table space per database is needed. The default temporary table space is called TEMPSPACE1.

- User Temporary—Use this type to create a table space to store declared global temporary tables. User temporary table spaces are not automatically created during database creation.

For this example, choose Regular and click Next to continue.

6. On the Buffer Pool page (see Figure 10.3), you can specify an area in memory that will be used as a cache for the data in this table space. Memory in the buffer pool is read and written in blocks. Page size determines the size of the block. By default, the IBMDEFAULTBP is selected with 250 pages with the size of 4KB pages. From this page, you are also given the opportunity to create a new buffer pool. At this time, choose to accept the default and click Next to continue. Buffer pools are covered in more detail in "Creating a Buffer Pool" later in today's lesson.

FIGURE 10.3

The Create Table Space Wizard's Buffer Pool page.

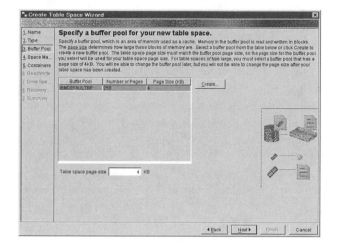

7. On the Space Management page (see Figure 10.4), you control how and where your table spaces are stored. You can choose whether you want the table space to be low maintenance or high performance:

- System-Managed Space (Low Maintenance)—This type of space management is managed by the operating system. A system-managed space (SMS) table space is the easiest type for you to create and manage because it grows automatically, and you can see the database files and their sizes. (If you selected Indexes Only or Long on the second page, you can't select Low Maintenance.)

- In general, small personal databases are easiest to manage with SMS table spaces. Temporary table spaces should be SMS because their size can grow and shrink as needed. This reduces unnecessary temporary space and reduces the possibility of running out of temporary space. You have less control over SMS table spaces.

TIP

If you plan to store many small tables in a table space, consider using SMS for that table space. The database-managed space (DMS) advantages with I/O and space management efficiency aren't as important with small tables. The SMS advantages of allocating space one page at a time, and only when needed, are more attractive with smaller tables. If one of your tables is larger or you need faster access to the data in the tables, consider a DMS table space with a small extent size.

10

- Database-Managed Space (High Performance)—This type of space management provides many tuning options, including predefining the size of each table space and adding containers as your data grows. One advantage of using DMS over SMS space management is that you can separate indexes and long data from the rest of your regular data. You can back up, restore, and tune the performance for each table space separately. In general, a well-tuned set of DMS table spaces will outperform SMS table spaces.

TIP

You may want to use a separate table space for each very large table and group all small tables in a single table space. This separation also allows you to select an appropriate extent size based on the table space usage. This is available only if using DMS table spaces.

- Because the goal is to have three separate table spaces—one for regular data, one for indexes, and one for long data—you must choose Database-Managed Space (High Performance). (Data can be split across several table spaces only by using DMS managed space.) Click Next to continue.

FIGURE 10.4

The Create Table Space Wizard's Space Management page.

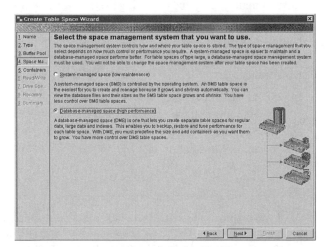

8. On the Containers page, specify where the table space will be stored (see Figure 10.5). A container defines where you want data stored. If you've defined a DMS table space, you must also define a size for the container. By defining multiple containers on separate physical drives, you can improve the performance of your database.

Figure 10.5

The Create Table Space Wizard's Containers page.

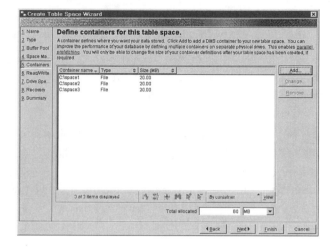

If you don't see any containers in the list, click the Add button to open the Add Container dialog box, which varies depending on the space management selected. For SMS, you need to define only the Container name, drive, and directory for the container. DB2 takes care of the storage for you, increasing storage size when necessary. For DMS, you must define the file size and specify whether the container will be stored in a file or on a raw device:

- File Size—For DMS, you must define the size of the container. You can specify the size in units of megabytes (MB) or 4KB pages. (There are 256 4KB pages in 1MB.) The minimum size of a container is 5 times the extent size of the table space plus one 4KB page. Because the default extent size is 32 4KB pages, the default minimum size for the entire table space is 32 4KB pages multiplied by 5, plus one, equal to 161 4KB pages (approximately 660KB).

- Unit Size—Choose between 4KB pages or MB. If you choose 4KB pages for the unit size of the container, enter a size for page size (4, 8, 16, or 32).

- File—Choose between a file or raw device for the container. Files are easier to use than raw devices but don't perform as well. They are easier to use because DB2 works through the operating system's file system to create and access the data in files.

- Raw—A *raw device* is a large contiguous chunk of disk space. You can use an unformatted partition or an unpartitioned disk as a raw device. It may perform better than a file because DB2 accesses the disk directly.

- Container Name, Drive, and Directory—Choose a name for the container, as well as a drive and directory where the container is to be located. Use a directory that won't be used for anything else. You should specify a filename that doesn't exist because it will be automatically created.

Because you chose High Performance in step 7, the table space is using DMS managed space. Add several containers on a drive where you want to store your data. For example, add containers such as in i:\cdlibts\container1, i:\cdlibts\container2, and i:\cdlibts\container3.

At this point, you can click Finish to create the table space and container. For this example, however, click Next to proceed to the Read/Write and Drive Speed pages.

9. On the Read/Write page (see Figure 10.6), you can get assistance from the wizard as to the extent and prefetch size that you define. Answer the two questions on the page for the wizard to recommend values for extent and prefetch sizes for this table space.

FIGURE 10.6

The Create Table Space Wizard's Read/Write page.

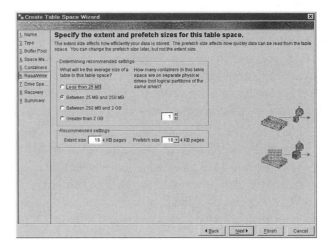

Data for any table is stored on all containers in a table space in a round-robin fashion. The data is balanced across the containers for a given table space. The number of pages that DB2 writes to one container before a different one is used is called the *extent size*. The extent size affects how efficiently your data is stored.

Prefetch size indicates how much data is retrieved from disk in anticipation of its use. To determine the prefetch size, you must know how many containers in the table space are on separate physical drives (as opposed to separate logical partitions on the same drive). Type the number of containers that are on separate drives. This number is multiplied by the extent size to give the recommended prefetch size. The prefetch size recommendation is based on whether you have containers on separate drives; DB2 can prefetch from all those drives at the same time. The prefetch size affects how quickly data can be read from the table space.

To determine the extent size, you must estimate the average size of a table in this table space. You can calculate the size of a table by multiplying the number of bytes in a single row by the number of rows in a table. A rough estimate is all you need. The extent size recommendations are based on smaller tables being more efficiently stored in smaller extent blocks.

You can alter the prefetch size later, but you can't alter the extent size. After you determine the extent and prefetch size for this table space, click Next to continue.

10. On the Drive Speed page, you provide information to help the SQL optimizer choose the best path for a query (see Figure 10.7). Enter actual specifications for your hard drive or answer the questions to come up with approximate specifications.

FIGURE 10.7

Create Table Space Wizard—Drive Speed page.

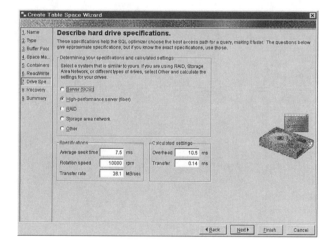

11. On the Recovery page, you specify the dropped table recovery option for your new table space (see Figure 10.8). You can recover a table that has been dropped from your table space by setting this option. Your table space must be of type Regular to enable this option. If you enable the option, you can recover a dropped table by restoring your table space. If you don't enable this option, you must restore your entire database to recover a dropped table. You can change this option after your table space is created, if required.

12. On the Summary page, you review all your choices before the table space is created (see Figure 10.9). Click Finish when you've completed all the pages.

FIGURE 10.8

Create Table Space Wizard—Recovery page.

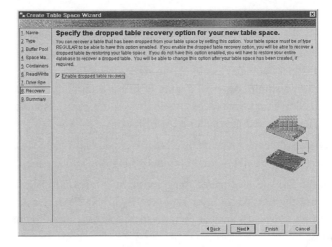

FIGURE 10.9

Create Table Space Wizard—Summary page.

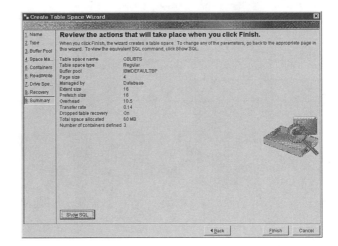

To see the table space that you created, click the Table Space icon. You'll see the CDLIBTS table space listed with the default table spaces already created. To view or change any of the values for your table space, right-click the table space and select Alter from the pop-up menu.

Allocating Additional Space

Capacity for a DMS table space is the total size of containers allocated to the table space. When a DMS table space reaches capacity (depending on the usage of the table space, 90 percent is a possible threshold), you should add more space to it. The database manager then automatically rebalances the tables in the table space across all available containers. During rebalancing, data in the table space remains accessible.

The strategy for adding space to a table space is different for DMS and SMS table spaces. For a DMS table space that has reached capacity, you can either extend or resize the existing containers or add additional containers. You can add another container by following these steps:

1. Start the Control Center.

2. Expand the objects until you see the Table Spaces folder within the database you want to work with.

3. Click the Table Spaces folder to see a list of table spaces in the contents pane.

4. Right-click the CDLIBTS table space in the contents pane and select Alter from the pop-up menu. The Alter Table Space dialog box opens.

5. Click the Table Space tab to open the Table Space page, as shown in Figure 10.10. On this page, you can alter the table space comment, change the buffer pool associated with the table space, and enable table recovery.

FIGURE 10.10

The Table Space tab of the Alter Table Space dialog box.

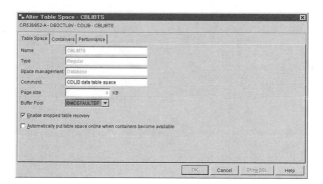

6. Click the Containers tab to open the Containers page, as shown in Figure 10.11.

FIGURE 10.11

The Containers tab of the Alter Table Space dialog box.

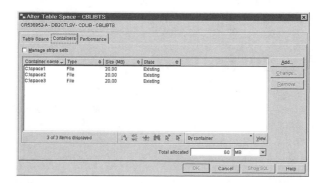

7. Click the Add button to open the Define Container dialog box.

8. If you select the File radio button, enter a size, a name, a drive, and a directory for the new container—for example, i:\container1.

   If you select the Raw Device radio button, enter the size of the new container, and select whether the device is an unformatted partition or an unformatted drive.

9. Click OK to return to the Alter Table Space dialog box.

10. Click the Performance tab to open the Performance page as shown in Figure 10.12. On this page, you can change the values for Prefetch Size, Overhead, and Transfer Rate.

FIGURE 10.12

The Performance tab of the Alter Table Space dialog box.

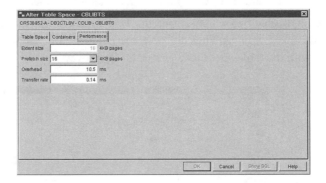

11. Click OK again to have the new container added to the table space.

In general, you can't extend the size of an SMS table space without extending the underlying file system, because SMS capacity depends on the space available in the file system and the maximum size of the file supported by the operating system. You can use the Windows Disk Management facility to extend the file system, or you can use the DB2 redirected restore to back up the table spaces and restore them onto a larger file system. Redirected restore is covered in Day 16, "Backup and Recovery Concepts."

Creating a Buffer Pool

A *buffer pool* is an area of main memory into which database pages are temporarily read and changed. The purpose of the buffer pool is to improve database system performance. Data can be accessed much faster from memory than from disk; therefore, the fewer times DB2 needs to read from or write to a disk, the better the performance.

You can create more than one buffer pool, although for most situations one will suffice. Having more than one buffer pool allows you to tune the performance for different applications.

To create a buffer pool, follow these steps:

1. Right-click the Buffer Pools folder and select Create from the pop-up menu. The Create Buffer Pool dialog box opens as shown in Figure 10.13.

FIGURE 10.13

*Create Buffer Pool
dialog box.*

10

TIP	You can also open the Create Buffer Pool dialog box within the Create Table Space Wizard.

2. Enter a name for the buffer pool. The name can contain up to 18 characters. For this example, use the name BUFFER1.

3. In the Page Size field, select the page size to be used for the buffer pool from the drop-down list. Valid values are 4KB, 8KB, 16KB, and 32KB. The default page size is 4KB. The page size of a table space must be the same as the page size of the buffer pool associated with it.

NOTE	You cannot alter the page size of the buffer pool after you create it. To add more size, you must alter the buffer pool. To change the page size, you must drop and re-create the buffer pool.

4. In the Size in 4KB Pages text box, type the size of the buffer pool in pages. This size can be changed later using the Alter Table Space dialog box.

5. The Use Extended Storage check box indicates that pages being migrated out of this buffer pool will be stored in the extended storage on your computer, if available. To use extended storage, this check box must be selected, and the num_estore_segs configuration parameter must be greater than zero. For our example, do not select this option.

6. Select Use Default Buffer Pool Size to create the buffer pool using the default size of 250 pages. The amount entered in step 4 will be ignored if this option is checked.

7. The default is to create the buffer pool immediately, but you may defer the creation until the next time DB2 is started by selecting the Create Buffer Pool on Database Restart option.

8. Click OK to create the buffer pool.

When you create new table spaces, you can select to have this new buffer pool used rather than the default buffer pool. You can also alter existing table spaces and have them use this new buffer pool.

Creating Table Spaces for Indexes and Large Data

Now that you've learned many of the concepts behind creating a table space, use the Create Table Space Wizard to create two more table spaces—one to contain the indexes and one to contain the long data.

Follow the steps in the "Using the Create Table Space Wizard" section to create a regular table space called CDINDEX to store the indexes associated with CDLIB using these values:

Option	Value
Table Space Name	CDINDEX
Type of Table Space	Regular
Space Management	System
File Size	2MB File
Container	i:\cdindex

Follow these steps to create a large table space to store large objects associated with CDLIB:

1. Start the Control Center.

2. Expand the folders until you see the objects in the CDLIB database.

3. Right-click the Table space folder. Select Create from the pop-up menu. The Create Table Space Wizard opens.

4. Type a name for the table space. The name must be different from any other table spaces on your system and can contain up to 18 characters. For this example, use CDLONG as the name of the table space. Click Next to continue.

5. On the Type page, select the Large radio button. The Large type of table space is used to store data from long or LOB table columns (long text, audio, video, or images). Click Next to continue.

6. On the Space Management page, indicate whether to use system or database management. Large objects are stored in the high performance or DMS type of storage. Because you selected Large on the previous page, the DMS radio button is preselected. Click Next to continue.

7. On the Containers page, click the Add button to open the Define Container dialog box to specify where the table space will be stored. For this example, set the file size to 2MB, click the File radio button, and type names for the containers (such as `i:\cdlibts\container4` and `i:\cdlibts\container5`). Click OK to add the containers and close the Add Containers dialog box.

8. On the Read/Write page, you can specify the extent and prefetch size to use for the table space. For our example, keep the default value.

9. On the Drive Speed page, enter actual specifications for your hard drive or answer the questions to come up with approximate specifications.

10. On the Summary page, review all your selections to make sure that everything is as you want it. Click OK to create the table space you have defined.

In your list of table spaces, you should see CDLIBTS, CDINDEX, and CDLONG. Next you'll create a table that uses these table spaces.

Creating Tables in Table Spaces

Earlier, you created the CATEGORY table by using the Create Table Wizard. Now use the Create Table Wizard to create the ALBUMCOVER table and use the more advanced pages in the wizard to assign the tables to the table spaces and to create foreign keys.

To use the wizard to create a table and assign a table space, follow these steps:

1. Start the Control Center, if it's not already started.

2. Expand the object folders under the CDLIB database folder until you see the Tables folder. Right-click that folder.

3. Select Create from the pop-up menu to start the Create Table Wizard.

10

4. On the Name page, enter the table schema and table name. In the example, you'll create the table ALBUMCOVER, which will be used to store graphics of each album cover. Click Next to continue.

5. On the Columns page, click the Add Predefined button to open the Select Columns dialog box to define the columns for the table. For the ALBUMCOVER table, you want to create two columns: one for the photo and one for the ID.

6. To create a column for the ID, scroll through the list of column categories and select ID NUMBERS. In the Predefined columns list, you'll see a list of columns you can choose from (see Figure 10.14).

FIGURE 10.14

Selecting columns from the ID Numbers column category in the Create Table Wizard's Select Columns dialog box.

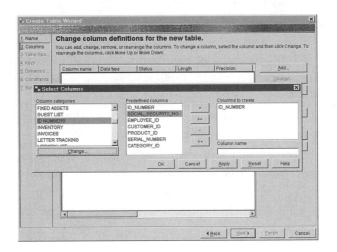

7. Choose ID_NUMBER and click the right arrow to move the column into the Columns to Create List. Click Apply to add this column and remain in the Select Columns dialog box.

8. For the photo column, choose Media from the Column categories list and select the column PHOTO from the Predefined Columns list. Click the right arrow to move the column into the Column to Create list (see Figure 10.15). Click OK to add this column and close the Select Columns dialog box.

9. You'll see that both columns have been added. Select the PHOTO column and click Change. You'll see all the predefined characteristics of this column. In the Name text box, change the name to ALBUMCOVER. In the Length text box, the size is set to 10MB, but change it to 1MB. Click OK. Select the ID_NUMBER column and click Change. In the Name text box, change the name to ALBUMCOV-ERID. Click the Nullable check box to allow this column to be defined as a primary key. Click OK to save the changes.

FIGURE 10.15

Selecting columns from the Media column category in the Create Table Wizard's Select Columns dialog box.

10. Move the ALBUMCOVERID column ahead of the ALBUMCOVER column by selecting ALBUMCOVERID and clicking the Move Up button. The order of the columns doesn't matter, but it's standard practice to have the ID of a column in the first position. Figure 10.16 shows the completed Columns page. Click Next to continue.

FIGURE 10.16

The Create Table Wizard's Columns page.

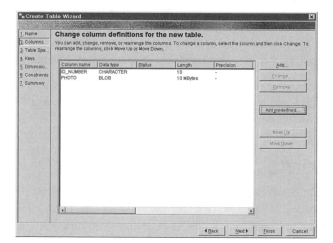

10

11. On the Table Space page, use the drop-down menu to see the list of available table spaces. Use the name of the table space you created for regular data: CDLIBTS. Click Next to continue.

12. On the Keys page, click the Add Primary button to define ALBUMCOVERID as the primary key for the table.

TIP

If ALBUMCOVERID was defined as NULLABLE, you will not be able to select it as the primary key. If that is the case, go back to the Columns page to alter the column and deselect the NULLABLE option.

13. Click the Add Foreign button to define the relationship between the tables ALBUMCOVER and ALBUM: ALBUMCOVER is the parent table, and ALBUM is the dependent table. Because you must define the foreign keys on the dependent table, leave this page blank. Later, you'll have to alter the ALBUM table to specify this foreign key.

14. Because we do not want to create dimensions or check constraints for this table, click on Summary to see the options as they are defined.

15. Click OK to create the table and close the Create Table Wizard.

Summary

Today you saw how to use table spaces, containers, and buffer pools to define how data is stored on your system.

You can create table spaces by using the Create Table Space Wizard (launched through the Create Database Wizard or the Control Center). When creating a table space, you have the option of using low-maintenance or high-performance space management.

A *container* defines where the data will be stored. Table spaces can span more than one container. The database manager attempts to balance the load of the data across the containers.

What Comes Next?

On Day 11, "Accessing the Data," you learn several ways that you can access data in DB2 databases, including ODBC applications such as Lotus Approach, the Control Center, the Command Center, Net.Data applications, and JDBC applications.

Q&A

Q What three table spaces must a database contain?

A A database must contain a table space for the system catalog tables. This is known as the catalog table space and is named SYSCATSPACE. This space is created when the database is created, and it can't be dropped.

The database must contain at least one user table space that contains all user-defined tables. By default, one table space is created to contain user tables and is called USERSPACE1. When you create a table, you specify the table space that you want to use for the data.

The database also contains at least one temporary table space, which contains temporary tables. Temporary tables are necessary for performing tasks such as sorting. By default, one temporary table space is created that's called TEMPSPACE1. Although you can create many temporary table spaces, it's preferable to have as few as possible.

Q When should I use DMS table spaces rather than SMS table spaces?

A SMS table spaces are lower maintenance than DMS table spaces because the size automatically grows as space is needed. SMS table spaces are best suited for temporary data and database catalogs. SMS is also best to use if your database contains many small tables.

DMS table spaces, on the other hand, provide more options for managing your data. With DMS table spaces, you can separate each type of data into a different table space. By separating data, you can back up, restore, and tune the performance for each table space separately. If you're storing long data such as audio or photos, you must use DMS table spaces. This is also true if you want to store your indexes on a separate table space. DMS table spaces are more difficult to maintain because you must predefine the size of each table space and add containers when necessary.

Q How do containers relate to a file?

A When you're creating SMS table spaces, you must specify the number of containers that you want to use for your table space. It's important to identify all the containers that you want to use because you can't add or delete containers after an SMS table space is created. Each container used for an SMS table space identifies an absolute or relative directory name. Each directory can be located on a different file system or physical disk.

Workshop

The purpose of the Workshop is to allow you to test your knowledge of the material covered in the lesson. See whether you can successfully answer the questions in the quiz and complete the exercises before you continue with the next lesson. The answers appear in Appendix B, "Answers to Quiz Questions and Exercises."

Quiz

1. How many buffer pools should you define for each database?
2. At what point in the process do you specify the tables to be stored in a table space?
3. If you plan to store temporary data in your table space, what type of table space should you create?

4. When are buffer pools created?

5. How can you extend the size of an SMS table space?

Exercises

1. At the beginning of Day 9, you created a simple database using the Create Database Wizard. Use the Create Database Wizard to create another database, but this time, use what you learned today to explore the pages that we skipped.

2. One of the most difficult concepts covered in today's lesson is containers. As you go through the lesson and create table spaces and containers, check your file system to see the relationship between your file system and containers.

DAY 11

Accessing the Data

You can view the data in DB2 databases by using the following:

- The Control Center
- The Command Center
- ODBC applications such as Microsoft Access
- JDBC applications such as Java
- Applications written in C, C++, or other programming languages

Each method uses SQL to access the data.

Today you learn how to use each method to view the data in the CDLIB database. Before you can actually access data in any database, you must first have the authority to access the database and the privileges to perform the chosen actions. At a minimum, you must have CONNECT authority on the database. See Day 4, "Getting Started," for details on how to set authorities.

Today you learn the following:

- How to access data through the Control Center
- How to access data through the Command Center

- How to access data using the Command Line Processor
- How to access data through Microsoft Access
- How to access data through Java applications
- How to access data through your own applications

Accessing Data Through the Control Center

The Control Center allows you to view rows of the selected table. By default the first 50 rows are shown. The names of the table's columns are displayed at the top of each column in the Sample Contents window. Each column's contents are displayed below the corresponding column name. You might need to scroll right to see all the columns and scroll down to see all the rows.

To view the contents of the CDLIB database, follow these steps:

1. Open the Control Center, if it's not already started.
2. Expand the objects within the CDLIB database until you see the Tables folder.
3. Click the folder in the main Control Center panel. In the right panel, you'll see all the tables now in the database.
4. Scroll down until you see the ARTIST table. Right-click it and choose Sample Contents from the pop-up menu. You'll see all the columns and up to 50 rows of the ARTIST table (see Figure 11.1).

FIGURE 11.1

The Sample Contents window in the Control Center.

You can only view the data through the Control Center. If you want to modify the data or create more complex queries, you must use one of the other methods described in this lesson.

Accessing Data Through the Command Center

The Command Center is installed automatically with all DB2 Universal Database products on the Windows operating environments. You can use the Command Center to access and manipulate databases from an interactive window. From it, you can

- Issue SQL statements, DB2 commands, and MVS system commands.
- See the execution result of one or many SQL statements and DB2 commands in a result window. You can scroll through the results and save the output to a file.
- Save a sequence of SQL statements and DB2 commands to a script file. You can then schedule the script to run as a task. When a saved script is modified, all jobs dependent on the saved script inherit the new modified behavior.
- Recall and run a script.
- See the execution plan and statistics associated with a SQL statement before execution. You do this by invoking Visual Explain in the interactive window.
- Get quick access to database administrative tools such as the Control Center and the Journal from the main toolbar.
- Display all the command scripts known to the system through the Script Center, with summary information listed for each.
- Access local and remote databases.
- Request command syntax help for DB2 commands and message help for DB2 messages.

The Command Center allows you to enter simple SQL statements to view and manipulate the data in your databases. Follow these steps to view all the rows and columns of the EMPLOYEE table:

1. Start the Command Center by choosing Start|Programs|IBM DB2|Command Line Tools|Command Center. Or, if you already have the Control Center open, simply click the Command Center icon from the toolbar. (The hover help displays when your mouse pointer is on the toolbar icons.)

2. Type your commands on the Interactive page in the Command input area labeled Command (see Figure 11.2). If you want to run multiple commands, you must end

11

each command with a semicolon and then press Enter to start the next command on a new line.

FIGURE 11.2

The Interactive page in the Command Center.

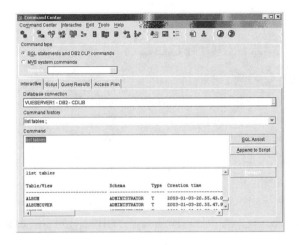

NOTE   In this example we used the DB2 command list tables. Notice that the results of this command are shown in the command results box directly below the Command input area. Results of queries are shown in the Query Results page as you will see in the next example.

3. To connect to the CDLIB database, click the button on the right side of the Database connection field and select the CDLIB database as shown in Figure 11.3. The connect to cdlib command is automatically placed in the Command input area and executed.

4. To issue a SELECT statement, enter the following command in the Command input area:

INPUT   `select * from album;`

NOTE   The semicolon is optional at the end of a single SQL statement but must be used to separate multiple SQL statements within a series.

FIGURE 11.3

The Select Database page in the Command Center.

5. Click the gears button to process the commands. The Command Center shows the results of the query in the Query Results page, in which you'll see all the rows and columns in the ALBUM table (see Figure 11.4).

FIGURE 11.4

The Command Center's Query Results page.

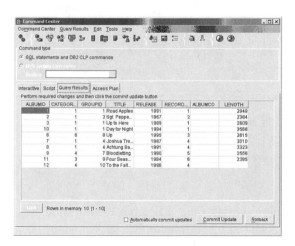

To recall commands or queries that you've typed in interactive mode, return to the Command Center's Interactive page and click the arrow beside the Command History input area.

To save commands entered in interactive mode as scripts, choose Script|Save As from the menu.

> **TIP**
>
> If you want to schedule commonly used SQL statements or DB2 commands, click the Task Center icon on the main toolbar to start the Task Center.

Use the Script page of the Command Center to execute a script previously saved in the Task Center or in a file.

Use the Command Center to interactively create an access plan for any explainable statement when it is executed. An access plan can only be created for one statement at a time.

Click the SQL Assist button on the Command Center's Interactive page to open the Show SQL page for help creating SQL statements of the type SELECT, INSERT, UPDATE, or DELETE. As you make selections, the actual SQL query is built in the SQL Code input area at the bottom of the window as shown in Figure 11.5.

FIGURE 11.5

The Command Center's Show SQL page.

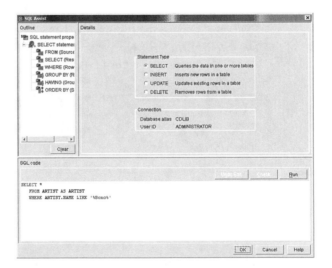

Use the Command Center Options dialog box to customize the settings of the Command Center. You can set the number of items that are kept in the history file, whether commands are automatically committed, the detail of the error message, and whether access plans are automatically created. Figure 11.6 shows an example of the Results page of the dialog box.

FIGURE 11.6

The Command Center Options dialog box.

Using the Command Line Processor

The Command Line Processor is installed automatically with all DB2 Universal Database products. Use the DB2 Command Line Processor to access and manipulate databases from the system command prompt or command files. From it, you can

- Issue SQL statements, DB2 commands, and Windows commands
- Maintain a history file of all requests
- Redirect the output of requests
- Access local and remote databases
- Request command syntax help for DB2 utilities and message help for DB2 messages

Entering Commands

To invoke the Command Line Processor to enter DB2 commands or SQL statements and view their output, choose Start|Programs|IBM DB2|Command Line Tools Command Line Processor.

You can also invoke the Command Line Processor by entering db2cmd at a command prompt and then entering db2.

The prompt for the Command Line Processor looks like this:

```
db2 =>
```

This prompt indicates that you don't type DB2 commands with a db2 prefix; instead, you just type the DB2 command—for example:

```
list node directory
```

To run Windows commands in the Command Line Processor, precede the command with an exclamation mark (!):

```
!dir db2*.log
```

If you need to enter a long command that doesn't fit on one line, use the \ line-continuation character:

```
db2 => select group.name, artist.name from \
db2 (cont.) => group, artist, artistingroup \
db2 (cont.) => where group.groupid = artistingroup.groupid \
db2 (cont.) => and artist.artistid = artistingroup.artistid \
db2(cont.) => order by group.name
```

To exit the Command Line Processor, type terminate.

Entering Commands in a Command Window

To use the Command Line Processor like a Windows command window, where you can enter DB2 commands or SQL statements and view their output, use one of the following methods:

- Choose Start|Programs|IBM DB2|Command Line Tools|Command Window.
- Enter db2cmd at a command prompt.

After you invoke the DB2 command environment, you can enter DB2 commands at the command prompt. You must include the db2 prefix—for example:

```
db2 list database directory
```

Enter Windows commands as usual, without a prefix:

```
dir db2*.log
```

To exit the Command Line Processor, type exit.

Accessing Data Through Microsoft Access

Microsoft Access is a database interface that enables you to use the mouse to access data and search your databases. Use the instructions provided with Microsoft Access to install it. You can install it on the same system where your databases are located or on a remote client.

| TIP | Although these instructions are for Microsoft Access, the instructions would be similar if opening the database in Lotus Approach or other database interface programs. |

To access DB2 databases through Microsoft Access, you must first register the DB2 database that you want to access as an ODBC data source. Follow these steps:

1. Choose Start|Programs|IBM DB2|Set-up Tools Configuration Assistant. The Configuration Assistant opens.

2. Right-click on the database you want to access in the ODBC application (the CDLIB database for this example) and click Change Database to open the Change Database Wizard.

3. Select 4 Data Source to open the Register This Database as a Data Source page. Select the check box and make sure that the As System Data Source radio button is selected (see Figure 11.7). This makes the database source available to all users on the system.

FIGURE 11.7

The Data Source page of the Change Database Wizard.

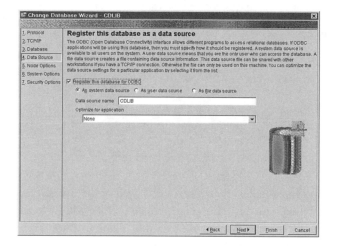

4. Select 1 Protocol to open the Select a Communications Protocol page. Click the protocol that you intend to use for this connection. The settings you can use for the properties are covered in detail in Day 6, "Installing and Configuring DB2 Clients."

5. Click Finish when the information has been added.

6. In the Test Connection dialog box, select the connection type: Standard, CLI, ODBC, OLEDB, JDBC or ADO. Select Standard, enter a valid username and password, and click Test Connection.

7. Exit from the Configuration.

Now that DB2 is registered as an ODBC data source and is started, you're ready to view the tables in the CDLIB database with Microsoft Access. For example, to view the ALBUM table, follow these steps:

1. Choose Start|Programs|Microsoft Access to start Microsoft Access.

2. Click File|Open. In the Open dialog box, select ODBC Databases() from the Files of Type drop-down list.

3. The Select Data Source dialog box opens. Click the Machine Data Source tab to see all system data sources on your computer as shown in Figure 11.8. Double-click the CDLIB entry in the list.

FIGURE 11.8

The Machine Data Source tab in the Select Data Source dialog box.

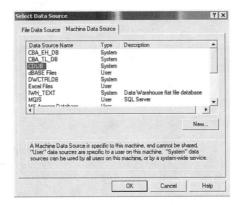

4. In the Link Tables dialog box, click each of the user-created tables in the CDLIB database. Typically, all the user-created tables will have a schema name that is the same as your username—for example, Administrator. Figure 11.9 shows all the user-created tables. Click OK to continue.

FIGURE 11.9

The tables in CDLIB to select in the Link Tables dialog box.

5. The tables will now appear in Access format. Choose the ALBUM table and click Open. The table opens as shown in Figure 11.10.

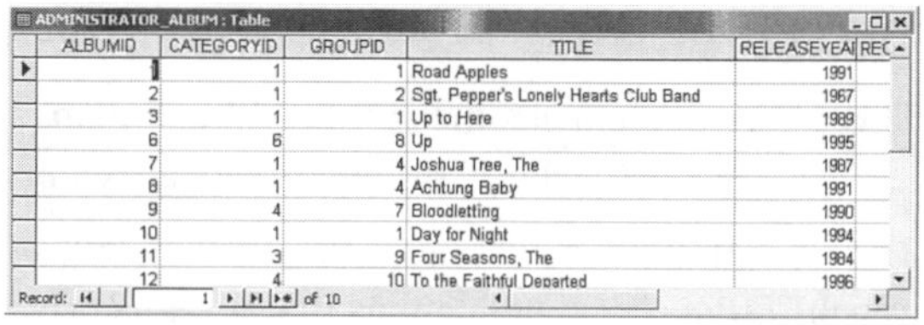

ADMINISTRATOR_ALBUM : Table

ALBUMID	CATEGORYID	GROUPID	TITLE	RELEASEYEAI	REC
1	1	1	Road Apples	1991	
2	1	2	Sgt. Pepper's Lonely Hearts Club Band	1967	
3	1	1	Up to Here	1989	
6	6	8	Up	1995	
7	1	4	Joshua Tree, The	1987	
8	1	4	Achtung Baby	1991	
9	4	7	Bloodletting	1990	
10	1	1	Day for Night	1994	
11	3	9	Four Seasons, The	1984	
12	4	10	To the Faithful Departed	1996	

Record: 1 of 10

FIGURE 11.10

The ALBUM table in Microsoft Access.

6. Use the instructions provided with Microsoft Access to perform additional tasks with the DB2 data.

Accessing Data Through Java Applications

DB2 provides support for Sun Microsystem's Java Database Connectivity (JDBC) API through a JDBC driver that comes with DB2. The JDBC API, similar to the CLI/ODBC API, provides a standard way to access databases from Java code. Your Java code passes SQL statements as function arguments to the DB2 JDBC driver, which then calls the CLI/ODBC driver.

DB2 includes support for the JDBC API as distributed with Java Development Kit (JDK) 1.3. The JDK provides the tools and environment you need to develop Java applications and applets. To access DB2 databases, you need to use the DB2 JDBC driver.

You can use DB2 JDBC support to run the following types of Java programs:

- Java applications that rely on the DB2 Run-Time Client to connect to DB2
- Java applets that don't require any other DB2 component code on the client
- SQLj applications that use JDBC as a foundation for such tasks as connecting to databases and handling SQL errors but can also contain embedded static SQL statements in the SQLj source files

You can also use the Java programming language to develop user-defined functions and stored procedures that run on the server. This process is similar to creating UDFs and stored procedures in any other programming language. After you create and register your Java UDFs and stored procedures, you can call them from applications coded in any supported programming language.

DB2 SQLj support is provided by the DB2 Application Development Client. Along with the JDBC support provided by the DB2 client, DB2 SQLj support allows you to create, build, and run embedded SQL for Java applications, applets, stored procedures, and user-defined functions (UDFs). These contain static SQL and use embedded SQL statements that are bound to a DB2 database.

There are four types of JDBC drivers; all are supported by DB2:

- Type 1—This driver implements the JDBC API and maps it to another data access API such as ODBC. JDBC-ODBC bridge drivers are examples of a Type 1 driver.
- Type 2—The DB2 JDBC application driver enables Java applications to make calls to DB2 through JDBC. Java applications that use this driver must run on a DB2 client, through which JDBC requests flow to the DB2 server. The DB2 JDBC application driver (Type 2) is included in the COM.ibm.db2.jdbc.app package. This driver is recommended for use when the applications require high transaction rates.
- Type 3—The DB2 JDBC Type 3 driver, also known as an applet or net driver, can be loaded by the Web browser along with the applet, or the applet driver can be used in standalone Java applications. The DB2 JDBC Type 3 driver is included in the COM.ibm.db2.net package.
- Type 4—The DB2 JDBC Universal Driver (Type 4) is the latest driver provided by DB2. This driver is included in the com.ibm.db2.jcc package.

To use the class libraries included with DB2 in your own applications, you must include the appropriate import package statements at the top of your source files. You can use the following packages in your Java applications:

- java.sql.*—The JDBC API included in your JDK. You must import this package in every JDBC and SQLj program.
- sqlj.runtime.*—SQLj support included with every DB2 client. You must import this package in every SQLj program.
- sqlj.runtime.ref.*—SQLj support included with every DB2 client. You must import this package in every SQLj program.

To run JDBC and SQLj programs on Windows, the CLASSPATH environment variable is automatically updated when DB2 is installed to include

- "." (the current directory)
- The file sqllib\java\db2java.zip
- The file sqllib\java\db2jcc.jar

To build SQLj programs, the CLASSPATH environment variable is also updated to include the file sqllib\java\sqlj.zip. To run SQLj programs, the CLASSPATH environment variable is also updated to include the file sqllib\java\runtime.zip.

JRE/JDK Support

The Java Runtime Environment (JRE) 1.3.1 is required for running applications and tools on all platforms, except HP-UX, where JRE 1.4 is required. For developing applications, the Java Development Kit (JDK) is required. JRE/JDK is required on all platforms, except 64-bit HP-UX and 64-bit Solaris, where 1.4 is required. You can develop Java programs to access DB2 databases with the appropriate Java Development Kit (JDK) for your platform.

Setting Up the Windows Java Environment

To build Java applications on a Windows operating system with DB2 JDBC support, you need to install and configure the following on your development machine:

- One of the following: IBM Developer Kit and Runtime Environment for Windows, Java 2 Technology Edition, Version 1.3.1; Java Development Kit (JDK) 1.3.1 for Win32 from Sun Microsystems
- DB2 Java Enablement, provided on DB2 Universal Database Version 8 for Windows clients and servers

To run DB2 Java routines (stored procedures and UDFs), you need to update the DB2 database manager configuration on the server to include the path where the JDK is installed on that machine. You can do this by entering the following on the server command line:

```
db2 update dbm cfg using JDK_PATH c:\jdk13
```

where `c:\jdk13` is the path where the JDK is installed.

Java Sample Programs

DB2 provides sample programs to demonstrate building and running JDBC programs that exclusively use dynamic SQL and SQLJ programs that use static SQL. There are separate directories for JDBC and SQLJ samples under the Java samples directory. For the Windows platforms, sample programs are found in the following directories:

- `sqllib\samples\java`—Contains a README file for Java sample programs in all subdirectories
- `sqllib\samples\java\jdbc`—Contains JDBC sample programs
- `sqllib\samples\java\sqlj`—Contains SQLJ sample programs
- `sqllib\samples\java\Websphere`—Contains WebSphere sample programs
- `sqllib\samples\java\plugin`—Contains plug-in example files for the DB2 Control Center
- `sqllib\samples\java\plugin\doc`—Contains javadoc files for the plug-in interfaces

11

Accessing Data Through WebSphere Application Server

The IBM WebSphere Application Server provides a rich application deployment platform with a complete set of application services including capabilities for transaction management, clustering, and connectivity. It is a compliant Java 2 Platform Enterprise Edition (J2EE) server.

In the DB2 and WebSphere Application Server environment, WebSphere Application Server assumes the role of transaction manager, and DB2 acts as a resource manager. WebSphere Application Server implements Java Transaction Service (JTS) and part of Java Transaction API (JTA), and DB2 JDBC driver also implements part of JTA so that WebSphere and DB2 can provide coordinated distributed transactions.

For detailed information about how to configure the WebSphere Application Server with DB2, refer to the WebSphere Application Server InfoCenter at

```
http://www-4.ibm.com/software/webservers/appserv/library.html
```

To enable DB2 to be used by WebSphere Application Server, use the WebSphere Application Server Administrative Console, select Resources, and then under General properties select DB2 JDBC Provider. The classpath for the DB2 JDBC provider must be included in the DB2 driver information.

The default classpath is

```
$(DB2_JDBC_DRIVER_PATH)/db2java.zip
```

Replace this with

```
/IBM/SQLLIB/java/db2java.zip
/IBM/SQLLIB/java/db2jcc.jar
```

Also, under the Session Manager Persistence Settings, select "database" to have DB2 manage its recovery.

Accessing Data Through Your Own Applications

Today you've learned the various types of applications that can access DB2 databases, including ODBC applications, JDBC applications and applets, and WebSphere applications. You can also develop applications by using the DB2 Application Development Client, which includes the following:

- Embedded SQL
- APIs
- Stored procedures
- User-defined functions
- Calls to the DB2 CLI

As mentioned in earlier lessons, DB2 Application Development Clients are shipped with the DB2 Personal Developer's Edition and the DB2 Universal Developer's Edition.

An application on a DB2 client can access a remote database without knowing its physical location. The DB2 client determines the location of the database, manages the transmission of the requests to the database server, and returns the results. In general, to run a database client application, follow these steps:

1. Make sure that the database manager is started on the database server to which the application program is connecting. If it's not, you must issue the db2start command at the server before starting the application.
2. Make sure that you can connect to the database that the application uses.
3. Bind the utilities and the applications to the database before you run the application program.

Binding Database Utilities

You must bind the database utilities (import, export, reorg, the Command Line Processor, and DB2 CLI) to each database before they can be used with that database. In a network environment, if you're using multiple clients that run on different operating systems or are at different versions of DB2, you must bind the utilities once for each operating system/DB2-version combination.

When a database is created, the database manager attempts to bind the database utilities in db2ubind.lst to the database. This file is stored in the \sqllib\bnd subdirectory.

Binding a utility creates a *package*, an object that includes all the information needed to process specific SQL statements from a single source file. The bind files are grouped together in different .lst files in the bnd directory under the installation directory (typically sqllib). Each file is specific to a server.

Follow these steps to bind the database utilities to a database by using the Configuration Assistant (CA):

1. Start the CA by choosing Start|Programs|IBM DB2|Start-Up Tools Configuration Assistant.

2. Right-click the database to which you want to bind the files and choose Bind from the pop-up menu. For our example, choose the CDLIB database. The Bind dialog box opens (see Figure 11.11).

FIGURE 11.11

Files page of the Bind – CDLIB dialog box, launched through the Configuration Assistant.

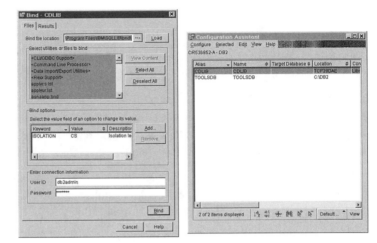

3. In the Bind File Location field, enter the file location of the .lst files.

4. Choose one or more of the utilities or files to bind. You have a choice between:

   - CLI/ODBC Support
   - Command Line Processor
   - Data Import/Export Utilities
   - Rexx Support

5. Click Select All to bind all these files.

6. In the Bind Options section, click Add to open the Add Bind Option dialog box to see a list of available bind options. For our example, choose ISOLATION and set the isolation level to Cursor Stability, as shown in Figure 11.12. Click OK to set this value and close the Add Bind Option dialog box.

7. Enter a username and password to connect to the database. The username must have the authority to bind new packages against this database.

8. Click Bind to have the files bound to the database. The results of the binding step are shown on the Results page (see Figure 11.13).

The db2ubind.lst file contains the list of bind (.bnd) files required to create the packages for the database utilities. The db2cli.lst file contains the list of bind (.bnd) files required to create packages for the DB2 CLI and the DB2 ODBC drivers.

FIGURE 11.12

The Add Bind Option dialog box launched from the Bind – CDLIB dialog box.

FIGURE 11.13

Results page of the Bind – CDLIB dialog box, launched through the Configuration Assistant.

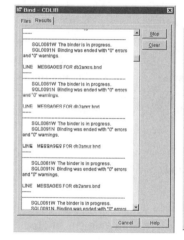

11

Summary

Today you learned several ways to access the data in DB2 databases. Some ways include the Control Center; SQL statements entered in the Command Center; ODBC applications such as Lotus Approach and Microsoft Access; Internet applications created with Java or WebSphere; or applications written in C, C++, or other programming languages.

When accessing data through the Control Center, you can sample the first 200 rows of the selected table. When accessing data through the Command Center, you can enter valid SQL statements.

Before you can use an ODBC application you must register the database to be ODBC-enabled. When this is done, using an ODBC application makes accessing data in a DB2 database simple.

What Comes Next?

On Day 12, "Using SQL," you learn how to use SQL to query data in DB2 databases.

Q&A

Q What's the difference between the Command Center, the Command Line Processor, and the Command Window?

A The main difference between these tools is that the Command Center provides a graphical interface to the command line. When you use the Command Center, you can move between the entry and results pages and save queries or results to files.

The Command Line Processor and Command Window are basically Windows command-line sessions. The Command Line Processor provides several different modes of operation, the most commonly used being interactive mode. When you're in interactive mode, you'll see a DB2 prompt and can enter commands and statements the same as you would in the Command Center (without prefixing the commands with db2).

The Command Window is a Windows command window prepared to accept DB2 commands. All DB2 commands and SQL statements must be prefixed with db2 for the commands to be valid.

Overall, it makes little difference which method you use for commands and statements. Try all three methods and use the one you are most comfortable with. One or two commands can't be entered in the Command Center. If you get an error message that the command isn't known or accepted, try entering the command in the Command Line Processor or the Command Window to see whether you can successfully run the command.

Q How can I register a database to be ODBC-enabled?

A The easiest way to enable a database for ODBC applications is through the Configuration Assistant, which also enables you to optimize the ODBC settings for the application you intend to use.

Q What do I need to create Java applications or applets?

A Java Database Connectivity (JDBC) support is built into each DB2 product. When you have DB2 running, you'll need to download the Java Development Kit (JDK) before you can create Java applications and applets.

Workshop

The purpose of the Workshop is to allow you to test your knowledge of the material covered in the lesson. See whether you can successfully answer the questions in the quiz and complete the exercise before you continue with the next lesson. The answers appear in Appendix B, "Answers to Quiz Questions and Exercises."

Quiz

1. If you are using the Command Center to enter SQL commands, what is one way to get help?

2. What's the main difference between a JDBC applet and a JDBC application?

3. If you get a message that the table you're opening in an ODBC application is read-only, what's the most likely problem?

4. When entering commands in the Command Center, do you need to end each line with a ; (semicolon)?

5. What tool do you need to use to see the execution plan and statistics associated with a SQL statement before execution?

Exercise

1. Microsoft Access is one example of an ODBC-enabled application. If you have access to another ODBC-enabled application, such as Lotus Approach, try to access DB2 data from this application, using the instructions from today's lesson.

11

Day **12**

SQL Concepts

The language of relational database technology is the Structured Query Language (SQL). Invented by IBM in the 1970s, the SQL language continues to evolve and is the only way to access relational database data. The SQL language has three major components:

- Data Maniupulation Language (DML)—Used to select, insert, update, or delete database objects

- Data Definition Language (DDL)—Used to create, modify, or drop database objects

- Data Control Language (DCL)—Used to grant or revoke databases

Today you learn the following:

- How to use the SELECT, UPDATE, INSERT, and DELETE statements
- How to include SQL statements into application programs
- The various programming interfaces supported by DB2

Data Manipulation Language

SQL allows users to access data from relational databases. The data is stored in relational tables, composed of rows and columns. The primary SQL statements used to retrieve or update data are

- SELECT—Queries data from one or more tables
- INSERT—Adds new rows into a table
- UPDATE—Changes existing rows in the table
- DELETE—Removes rows from a table

The SELECT statement is used to retrieve data. The format of this statement is

```
SELECT column name(s)
 FROM table name(s)
 WHERE conditions for rows to meet (if any)
```

```
SELECT column name(s)
 FROM table name(s)
 WHERE conditions for rows to meet (if any)
```

Using the Sample database that is shipped with DB2, the following examples illustrate how SQL can be used to retrieve data.

Selecting Columns

To select all the rows and columns from the ORG table, use the following statement:

```
SELECT *
 FROM ORG
```

This statement produces the following result:

```
DEPTNUMB    DEPTNAME        MANAGER    DIVISION    LOCATION
      10    Head Office         160    Corporate   New York
      15    New England          50    Eastern     Boston
      20    Mid Atlantic         10    Eastern     Washington
      38    South Atlantic       30    Eastern     Atlanta
      66    Pacific             270    Western     San Francisco
      84    Mountain            290    Western     Denver
```

To select the department names and department numbers from the ORG table, use the following statement:

```
SELECT DEPTNAME, DEPTNUMB
 FROM ORG
```

This statement produces the following result:

```
DEPTNAME            DEPTNUMB
Head Office               10
```

```
New England        15
Mid Atlantic       20
South Atlantic     38
Pacific            66
Mountain           84
```

Selecting Rows

To select specific rows from a table, after the SELECT statement, use the WHERE clause to specify the condition or conditions that a row must meet to be selected. A criterion for selecting rows from a table is a *search condition*.

A search condition consists of one or more *predicates*. A predicate specifies a condition that is true or false (or unknown) about a row. You can specify conditions in the WHERE clause by using the basic predicates shown in Table 12.1.

TABLE 12.1   SQL Predicate Functionality

Predicate	Function
x = y	x is equal to y.
x <> y	x is not equal to y.
x < y	x is less than y.
x > y	x is greater than y.
x <= y	x is less than or equal to y.
x >= y	x is greater than or equal to y.
IS NULL/IS NOT NULL	Tests for null values.

When you construct search conditions, be careful to perform arithmetic operations only on numeric data types, and to make comparisons only among compatible data types. For example, you can't compare text strings to numbers.

If you are selecting rows based on a character value, that value must be enclosed in single quotation marks—for example:

```
WHERE JOB = 'Clerk'
```

Each character value must be typed exactly as it exists in the database. If the data value is lowercase in the database and you type it as uppercase, no rows will be selected. If you are selecting rows based on a numeric value, that value must not be enclosed in quotation marks—for example:

```
WHERE DEPT = 20
```

From the STAFF table, select only the rows for Department 20. Specify only the department, name, and job columns:

```
SELECT DEPT, NAME, JOB
 FROM STAFF
 WHERE DEPT = 20
```

This statement produces the following result:

```
DEPT  NAME     JOB
20    Sanders  Mgr
20    Pernal   Sales
20    James    Clerk
20    Sneider  Clerk
```

From the STAFF table, select only the rows from Department 20 and employees who are clerks:

```
SELECT DEPT, NAME, JOB
 FROM STAFF
 WHERE JOB = 'Clerk'
 AND DEPT = 20
```

This statement produces the following result:

```
DEPT  NAME     JOB
20    James    Clerk
20    Sneider  Clerk
```

From the STAFF table, list employees whose commission is not known (NULL):

```
SELECT ID, NAME
 FROM STAFF
 WHERE COMM IS NULL
```

This statement produces the following result:

```
ID    NAME
 10   Sanders
 30   Marenghi
 50   Hanes
100   Plotz
140   Fraye
160   Molinare
210   Lu
240   Daniels
260   Jones
270   Lea
290   Quill
```

From the STAFF table, list employees with more than nine years with the company. Specify the name, salary, and years columns:

```
SELECT NAME, SALARY, YEARS
  FROM STAFF
  WHERE YEARS > 9
```

This statement produces the following result:

```
NAME    SALARY    YEARS
Hanes   20659.80     10
Lu      20010.00     10
Jones   21234.00     12
Quill   19818.00     10
Graham  21000.00     13
```

Sorting Rows

From the STAFF table, list employees in Department 84 ordered by the number of years they have been employed. Specify the name, job, and years columns:

```
SELECT NAME, JOB, YEARS
  FROM STAFF
  WHERE DEPT = 84
  ORDER BY YEARS
```

This statement produces the following result:

```
NAME     JOB     YEARS
Davis    Sales      5
Gafney   Clerk      5
Edwards  Sales      7
Quill    Mgr       10
```

You specify ORDER BY as the last clause in the entire SELECT statement. The columns (numerical or character values) named in this clause can be expressions or any column of the table.

From the STAFF table, list employees in Department 84 by the number of years they have been employed in descending order. Specify the name, job, and years columns:

```
SELECT NAME, JOB, YEARS
  FROM STAFF
  WHERE DEPT = 84
  ORDER BY YEARS DESC
```

This statement produces the following result:

```
NAME     JOB     YEARS
Quill    Mgr       10
Edwards  Sales      7
Davis    Sales      5
Gafney   Clerk      5
```

12

You can order rows in ascending or descending order by explicitly specifying either ASC
or DESC, respectively, within the ORDER BY clause. If neither is specified, the rows are
automatically ordered in ascending sequence.

Removing Duplicate Rows

From the STAFF table, list only the distinct jobs within each department, for department
numbers under 30. Specify the department and job columns:

```
SELECT DISTINCT DEPT, JOB
 FROM STAFF
 WHERE DEPT < 30
 ORDER BY DEPT, JOB
```

This statement produces the following result:

```
DEPT    JOB
10      Mgr
15      Clerk
15      Mgr
15      Sales
20      Clerk
20      Mgr
20      Sales
```

Using Expressions to Calculate Values

From the STAFF table, calculate the salaries of each employee in Department 38 if they
each received an additional $500. Specify the department, name, and salary columns:

```
SELECT DEPT, NAME, SALARY + 500
 FROM STAFF
 WHERE DEPT = 38
 ORDER BY 3
```

This statement produces the following result:

```
DEPT    NAME      3
38      Abrahams  12509.75
38      Naughton  13454.75
38      Quigley   17308.30
38      Marenghi  18006.75
38      O'Brien   18506.00
```

NOTE _____ In the previous example, the column name for the third column is a number.
This is a system-generated number because SALARY + 500 does not specify a
column name.

An expression is a calculation or function that you include in a statement. You can form arithmetic expressions by using the basic arithmetic operations for addition (+), subtraction (-), multiplication (*), and division (/).

The operators can operate on numeric values from several different types of operands; some examples are

- Column names (as in RATE * HOURS)
- Constant values (as in RATE * 1.07)
- Scalar functions (as in LENGTH(NAME) + 1)

Naming Expressions

From the STAFF table, calculate the total compensation for each employee. Produce a report that specifies name, job, and pay columns for employees earning less than $13,000 and order by their compensation.

```
SELECT NAME, JOB, SALARY + COMM AS PAY
 FROM STAFF
 WHERE (SALARY + COMM) < 13000
 ORDER BY PAY
```

This statement produces the following result:

```
NAME        JOB     PAY
Yamaguchi   Clerk   10581.50
Burke       Clerk   11043.50
Scoutten    Clerk   11592.80
Abrahams    Clerk   12246.25
Kermisch    Clerk   12368.60
Ngan        Clerk   12714.80
```

By using the AS clause, you can refer to a particular column name rather than the system-generated number in the ORDER BY clause as you saw in the previous section.

Selecting Data from More Than One Table (Join)

You can use the SELECT statement to produce reports that contain information from two or more tables. This is commonly referred to as a *join*. For example, you can join data from the STAFF and ORG tables to form a new table. To join two tables, specify the columns you want to be displayed in the SELECT clause, the table names in the FROM clause, and the search condition in the WHERE clause. The WHERE clause is optional.

Produce a report that lists the manager's name from the STAFF table and the associated department name from the ORG table (see Figure 12.1):

```
SELECT DEPTNAME, NAME
 FROM ORG, STAFF
 WHERE MANAGER = ID
```

12

FIGURE 12.1

Selecting from the STAFF and ORG tables.

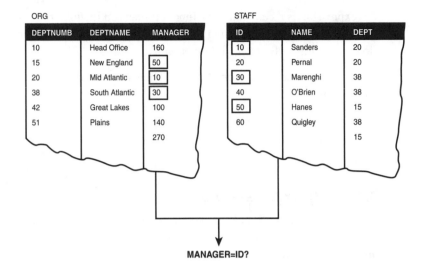

This statement produces the following result:

```
DEPTNAME        NAME
Mid Atlantic    Sanders
South Atlantic  Marenghi
New England     Hanes
Head Office     Molinare
Pacific         Lea
Mountain        Quill
```

Using a Subquery

When you write a SQL SELECT statement, you can place additional SELECT statements within the WHERE clause. Each additional SELECT starts a subquery. A subquery can then, in turn, include another separate subquery, whose result is substituted into the original subquery's WHERE clause. In addition, a WHERE clause can include subqueries in more than one search condition. The subquery can refer to tables and columns different from the ones used in the main query.

Find the division and location from the ORG table of the employee whose ID is 280 in the STAFF table:

```
SELECT DIVISION, LOCATION
 FROM ORG
 WHERE DEPTNUMB = (SELECT DEPT
                    FROM STAFF
                    WHERE ID = 280)
```

This statement produces the following result:

```
DIVISION   LOCATION
Western    San Francisco
```

When you use a subquery, the database manager evaluates it and substitutes the resulting value directly into the WHERE clause.

Column Functions

Column functions operate on a set of values in a column to derive a single result value. The following are just a few examples of column functions available with DB2:

- AVG—Returns the sum of the values in a set divided by the number of values in that set
- COUNT—Returns the number of rows or unique values in a column
- MAX—Returns the largest value in a set of values
- MIN—Returns the smallest value in a set of values

Select the names and salaries of employees whose income is more than the average income and who have been with the company fewer than the average number of years:

```
SELECT NAME, SALARY
 FROM STAFF
 WHERE SALARY > (SELECT AVG(SALARY) FROM STAFF)
 AND YEARS < (SELECT AVG(YEARS) FROM STAFF)
```

This statement produces the following result:

```
NAME       SALARY
Marenghi   17506.75
Daniels    19260.25
Gonzales   16858.20
```

In this example, in the WHERE clause, the column function is stated in a subquery as opposed to being directly implemented (for example: WHERE SALARY > AVG(SALARY)). Column functions cannot be stated in the WHERE clause. This is due to the order of operations. Think of the WHERE clause as being evaluated before the SELECT clause. Consequently, when the WHERE clause is being evaluated, the column function does not have access to the set of values. This set of values is selected later by the SELECT clause. You can use the DISTINCT element as part of the argument of a column function to eliminate duplicate values before a function is applied. Thus, COUNT(DISTINCT WORKDEPT) computes the number of different departments.

12

Scalar Functions

A *scalar function* performs an operation on a single value to return another single value. The following are just a few examples of scalar functions available with DB2:

- ABS—Returns the absolute value of a number
- HEX—Returns the hexadecimal representation of a value
- LENGTH—Returns the number of bytes in an argument (For a graphic string, it returns the number of double-byte characters.)
- YEAR—Extracts the year portion of a datetime value

Select the department names and the length of each of these names from the ORG table:

```
SELECT DEPTNAME, LENGTH(DEPTNAME)
  FROM ORG
```

This statement produces the following result:

```
DEPTNAME         2
Head Office     11
New England     11
Mid Atlantic    12
South Atlantic  14
Pacific          7
Mountain         8
```

Grouping

You can organize rows according to a grouping structure defined in a GROUP BY clause. In its simplest form, a *group* is a set of rows, each having identical values in the GROUP BY columns. The column names in the SELECT clause must be either a grouping column or a column function. Column functions return a value for each group defined by the GROUP BY clause. Each group is represented by a single row in the resultset.

List the maximum salary for each department from the STAFF table:

```
SELECT DEPT, MAX(SALARY) AS MAXIMUM
  FROM STAFF
  GROUP BY DEPT
```

This statement produces the following result:

```
DEPT    MAXIMUM
10      22959.20
15      20659.80
20      18357.50
38      18006.00
42      18352.80
51      21150.00
```

```
66      21000.00
84      19818.00
```

The MAX(SALARY) is calculated for each department, a group defined by the GROUP BY clause, not the entire company.

Using a WHERE Clause with a GROUP BY Clause

A grouping query can have a standard WHERE clause that eliminates nonqualifying rows before the groups are formed and the column functions are computed. You have to specify the WHERE clause *before* the GROUP BY clause.

List the maximum salary for each education level within each department from the EMPLOYEE table. Include only those employees who were hired after 1979:

```
SELECT WORKDEPT, EDLEVEL, MAX(SALARY) AS MAXIMUM
 FROM EMPLOYEE
 WHERE HIREDATE > '1979-12-31'
 GROUP BY WORKDEPT, EDLEVEL
 ORDER BY WORKDEPT, EDLEVEL
```

This statement produces the following result:

```
WORKDEPT    EDLEVEL    MAXIMUM
D21            15      27380.00
D21            16      36170.00
E11            12      15340.00
E21            14      26150.00
```

Using the HAVING Clause After the GROUP BY Clause

You can apply a qualifying condition to groups so that DB2 returns a result only for the groups that satisfy the condition. To do this, include a HAVING clause *after* the GROUP BY clause. A HAVING clause can contain one or more predicates connected by ANDs and ORs. Each predicate compares a property of the group (such as AVG(SALARY)) with either

- Another property of the group, for example:

  ```
  HAVING AVG(SALARY) > 2 * MIN(SALARY)
  ```

- A constant, for example:

  ```
  HAVING AVG(SALARY) > 20000
  ```

List the maximum and minimum salary of each department with more than four employees from the EMPLOYEE table:

```
SELECT WORKDEPT, MAX(SALARY) AS MAXIMUM, MIN(SALARY) AS MINUMUM
 FROM EMPLOYEE
 GROUP BY WORKDEPT
 HAVING COUNT(*) > 4
 ORDER BY WORKDEPT
```

12

This statement produces the following result:

```
WORKDEPT    MAXIMUM     MINIMUM
D11         32250.00    18270.00
D21         36170.00    17250.00
E11         29750.00    15340.00
```

Combining Queries by Set Operators

The UNION, EXCEPT, and INTERSECT set operators enable you to combine two or more outer-level queries into a single query. Each query connected by these set operators is executed, and the individual results are combined. Each operator produces a different result:

- The UNION operator derives a result table by combining two other result tables (for example TABLE1 and TABLE2) and eliminating any duplicate rows in the tables. When ALL is used with UNION (that is, UNION ALL), duplicate rows are not eliminated. In either case, each row of the derived table is a row from either TABLE1 or TABLE2.

- The EXCEPT operator derives a result table by including all rows in TABLE1 but not in TABLE2, and eliminating all duplicate rows. When you use ALL with EXCEPT (EXCEPT ALL), the duplicate rows are not eliminated.

- The INTERSECT operator derives a result table by including only rows that exist in both TABLE1 and TABLE2 and eliminating all duplicate rows. When you use ALL with INTERSECT (INTERSECT ALL), the duplicate rows are not eliminated.

When using the UNION, EXCEPT, and INTERSECT operators, keep the following in mind:

- All corresponding items in the select lists of the queries for the operators must be compatible.

- An ORDER BY clause, if used, must be placed after the last query with a set operator. The column name can only be used in the ORDER BY clause if the column name is identical to the corresponding items in the select list of the queries for every operator.

- Operations between columns that have the same data type and the same length produce a column with that type and length.

List the employees who have a salary greater than $21,000 or have managerial responsibilities and have been working fewer than eight years:

```
SELECT ID, NAME
  FROM STAFF
  WHERE SALARY > 21000
UNION
```

```
SELECT ID, NAME
 FROM STAFF
 WHERE JOB = 'Mgr' AND YEARS < 8
 ORDER BY ID
```

This statement produces the following result:

```
ID_    NAME
 10    Sanders
 30    Marenghi
100    Plotz
140    Fraye
160    Molinare
240    Daniels
260    Jones
```

If you use the ORDER BY clause in a query with any set operator, you must write it after the last query. The system applies the ordering to the combined answer set.

If the column name in the two tables is different, the combined result table does not have names for the corresponding columns. Instead, the columns are numbered in the order in which they appear. So, if you want the result table to be ordered, you have to specify the column number in the ORDER BY clause.

List the employees who have a salary greater than $21,000 but are not managers and have been there for more than eight years:

```
SELECT ID, NAME
 FROM STAFF
 WHERE SALARY > 21000
EXCEPT
 SELECT ID, NAME
 FROM STAFF
 WHERE JOB = 'Mgr' AND YEARS < 8
```

This statement produces the following result:

```
ID_____    NAME
   260     Jones
```

List the employees who have a salary greater than $21,000 and are managers and have been there for more than eight years:

```
SELECT ID, NAME
 FROM STAFF
 WHERE SALARY > 21000
INTERSECT
 SELECT ID, NAME
 FROM STAFF
 WHERE JOB = 'Mgr' AND YEARS < 8
```

12

This statement produces the following result:

```
ID    NAME
140   Fraye
160   Molinare
```

IN, BETWEEN, LIKE, EXISTS, and Quantified Predicates

Additional predicates are available to further qualify rows in a given query. This section reviews some of the additional predicates available.

Using the IN Predicate

Use the IN predicate to compare a value with several other values. For example:

```
SELECT NAME
 FROM STAFF
 WHERE DEPT IN (20, 15)
```

This example is equivalent to

```
SELECT NAME
 FROM STAFF
 WHERE DEPT = 20 OR DEPT = 15
```

You can use the IN and NOT IN operators when a subquery returns a set of values. For example, the following query lists the surnames of employees responsible for projects MA2100 and OP2012:

```
 SELECT LASTNAME
  FROM EMPLOYEE
  WHERE EMPNO IN
(SELECT RESPEMP
  FROM PROJECT
  WHERE PROJNO = 'MA2100'
  OR PROJNO = 'OP2012')
```

The subquery is evaluated once, and the resulting list is substituted directly into the outer-level query. For example, if the preceding subquery selects employee numbers 10 and 330, the outer-level query is evaluated as if its WHERE clause were

```
WHERE EMPNO IN (10, 330)
```

The list of values returned by the subquery can contain zero, one, or more values.

Using the BETWEEN Predicate

The BETWEEN predicate compares a single value to an inclusive range of values (named in the BETWEEN predicate). The following example finds the names of employees who earn between $10,000 and $20,000:

```
SELECT LASTNAME
 FROM EMPLOYEE
 WHERE SALARY BETWEEN 10000 AND 20000
```

This is equivalent to

```
SELECT LASTNAME
 FROM EMPLOYEE
 WHERE SALARY >= 10000 AND SALARY <= 20000
```

The next example finds the names of employees who earn less than $10,000 or more than $20,000:

```
SELECT LASTNAME
 FROM EMPLOYEE
 WHERE SALARY NOT BETWEEN 10000 AND 20000
```

Using the LIKE Predicate

Use the LIKE predicate to search for strings that have certain patterns. The pattern is specified through percentage signs and underscores:

- The underscore character (_) represents any single character.
- The percent sign (%) represents a string of zero or more characters.
- Any other character represents itself.

The following example selects employee names that are seven letters long and start with the letter 'S':

```
SELECT NAME
 FROM STAFF
 WHERE NAME LIKE 'S            '
```

The next example selects employee names that do not start with the letter 'S':

```
SELECT NAME
 FROM STAFF
 WHERE NAME NOT LIKE 'S%'
```

Using the EXISTS Predicate

You can use a subquery to test for the existence of a row that satisfies some condition. In this case, the subquery is linked to the outer-level query by the predicate EXISTS or NOT EXISTS.

When you link a subquery to an outer query by an EXISTS predicate, the subquery does not return a value. Rather, the EXISTS predicate is true if the answer set of the subquery contains one or more rows, and false if it contains no rows.

12

The EXISTS predicate is often used with correlated subqueries. The following example uses a correlation variable "X" so that the subquery can reference a column outside the subquery. This query lists the departments that currently have no entries in the PROJECT table:

```
SELECT DEPTNO, DEPTNAME
  FROM DEPARTMENT X
  WHERE NOT EXISTS
(SELECT *
  FROM PROJECT
  WHERE DEPTNO = X.DEPTNO)
  ORDER BY DEPTNO
```

You may connect the EXISTS and NOT EXISTS predicates to other predicates by using AND and OR in the WHERE clause of the outer-level query.

Quantified Predicates

A quantified predicate compares a value with a collection of values. If a fullselect returns more than one value, you must modify the comparison operators in your predicate by attaching the suffix ALL, ANY, or SOME. These suffixes determine how the set of values returned is to be treated in the outer-level predicate. The > comparison operator is used as an example (the following remarks apply to the other operators as well):

```
expression > ALL (fullselect)
```

The predicate is true if the expression is greater than each individual value returned by the fullselect. If the fullselect returns no values, the predicate is true. The result is false if the specified relationship is false for at least one value. The <>ALL quantified predicate is equivalent to the NOT IN predicate.

To find employees who earn more than their manager, you can use a subquery and the > ALL comparison operator. The SQL statement would be written as

```
SELECT LASTNAME, JOB
  FROM EMPLOYEE
  WHERE SALARY > ALL
(SELECT SALARY
  FROM EMPLOYEE
  WHERE JOB='MANAGER')
```

For a given predicate, expression > ANY (fullselect), this is true if the expression is greater than at least one of the values returned by the fullselect. If the fullselect returns no values, the predicate is false. Note that the =ANY quantified operator is equivalent to the IN predicate.

For any given predicate, where the expression is > SOME (fullselect), SOME is synonymous with the ANY keyword.

Inserting Data

To enter new rows into a table, you use the INSERT statement. This statement has two general forms:

- With one form, you use a VALUES clause to specify values for the columns of one or more rows.
- With the other form, instead of specifying VALUES, you specify a full select to identify columns from rows contained in other tables and/or views. Fullselect is a SELECT statement used in INSERT or CREATE VIEW statements, or following a predicate.

Insert a new department called Headquarters with a department number of S01:

```
INSERT INTO DEPARTMENT VALUES ('S01', 'HEADQUARTERS', NULL, 'A00', NULL)
```

Changing Data

Use the UPDATE statement to change the data in a table. With this statement, you can change the value of one or more columns for each row that satisfies the search condition of the WHERE clause.

Update an employee's telephone extension number:

```
UPDATE EMPLOYEE SET PHONENO = '2779' WHERE EMPNO = '000340'
```

The SET clause specifies the columns to be updated and provides the values. The WHERE clause is optional, and it specifies the rows to be updated. If the WHERE clause is omitted, the database manager updates each row in the table or view with the values you supply.

Deleting Data

Use the DELETE statement to delete rows of data from a table based on the search condition specified in the WHERE clause.

Delete all departments that belong to the MidWest division:

```
DELETE FROM ORG WHERE DIVISION = 'Midwest'
```

The WHERE clause is optional, and it specifies the rows to be deleted. If the WHERE clause is omitted, the database manager deletes all rows in the table or view.

When you delete a row, you remove the entire row, not specific column values from it.

12

Using Views

You may also want to create a view to restrict access. You can define a view so that it includes some or all of the rows in the table. You can create a view, for example, for each individual department manager that allows each manager to look at the salary information for employees. This is done by specifying the department number for each manager when you define each view.

To create a view, use the Control Center as follows:

1. Expand the object until you see the View folder within the CDLIB database.
2. Right-click the View folder and select Create from the pop-up menu.
3. In the Create View dialog box (see Figure 12.2), select a schema for the view from the View Schema drop-down list. For the example, select the DB2ADMIN schema.

FIGURE 12.2

Creating a view.

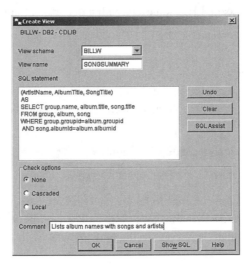

4. In the View Name text box, enter a name for the view—for example, **SONGSUMMARY**. The name must be 18 characters or fewer and must be unique within the view's schema.
5. Enter a SQL statement that defines the view. For example, use the following query to view the songs that appear on an album and the group that released the album:

```
(ArtistName, AlbumTitle, SongTitle)
AS SELECT group.name, album.title, song.title
FROM group, album, song
WHERE group.groupid = album.groupid and
      song.albumid = album.albumid
```

6. In the Check Options section, specify how the constraint conforms to the definition of the view. A row that doesn't conform to the definition of the view is a row that doesn't satisfy the search conditions of the view:

- Use None (the default) if the definition of the view isn't used in the checking of insert or update operations. For this example, stay with the default.
- Select Cascaded if the constraint on a new view inherits the search conditions as constraints from an updatable view on which the new view depends.
- Select Local to specify that the search condition used to create the view is used as a constraint for insert or update operations.

7. Click OK to create the view.

8. To sample the contents of a view, right-click the view you've just created and select Sample Contents from the pop-up menu.

A view provides a means of controlling access or extending privileges to a table by allowing access only to designated columns of a table or access only to a subset of the rows in a table. In Figure 12.3, you see only three columns and only the rows that satisfy the condition of the WHERE clause.

FIGURE 12.3

Sample contents of the SONGSUMMARY view.

12

How SQL Statements Are Invoked

SQL statements are classified as executable or nonexecutable. An executable SQL statement can be embedded in an application program, dynamically prepared and executed, or issued interactively. An *executable statement* can be invoked in four ways:

- Embedded in an application program
- Embedded in a SQL procedure
- Prepared and executed dynamically
- Issued interactively

A *nonexecutable statement* can be embedded only in an application program. These statements are typically placed in the declaration section of the application. Examples of nonexecutable statements are the INCLUDE, INCLUDE SQLDA, and DECLARE CURSOR statements.

Another SQL statement construct is the select-statement. A *select-statement* can be invoked in three ways:

- Included in DECLARE CURSOR and executed implicitly by OPEN, FETCH, and CLOSE (static invocation)
- Prepared dynamically, referenced in DECLARE CURSOR, and executed implicitly by OPEN, FETCH, and CLOSE (dynamic invocation)
- Issued interactively (that is, through the Command Center)

Embedding SQL into Applications

SQL statements can be included in a source program that will be submitted to a precompiler. Such statements are said to be *embedded* in the program. An embedded statement can be placed anywhere in the program where a host language statement is allowed. Each embedded statement must be preceded by the keywords EXEC SQL. When developing DB2 applications, you can code your embedded SQL applications in the C/C++, Java, SQLJ, COBOL, and FORTRAN programming languages.

An application in which you embed SQL statements is called a *host program*. The programming language you use to create a host program is called a *host language*. The program and language are defined this way because they host or accommodate SQL statements. You can embed static or dynamic SQL statements, or a mixture of both, in a host program.

For static SQL statements, you know before compile time the SQL statement type and the table and column names. The only unknowns are specific data values the statement is searching for or updating. You can represent those values in host language variables. You precompile, bind, and then compile static SQL statements before you run your application. Static SQL is best run on databases whose statistics do not change a great deal. Static SQL statements are *persistent*, meaning that the statements last for as long as the package exists. Generally, static SQL statements are well-suited for high-performance applications with predefined transactions. A reservation system is a good example of such an application.

In contrast, dynamic SQL statements are those that your application builds and executes at runtime. An interactive application that prompts the end user for key parts of a SQL statement, such as the names of the tables and columns to be searched, is a good example of dynamic SQL. The application builds the SQL statement while it's running and then submits the statement for processing. Generally, dynamic SQL statements are well-suited for applications that run against a rapidly changing database where transactions need to be specified at runtime. An interactive query interface is a good example of such an application.

When you embed SQL statements in your application, you must precompile and bind your application to a database by following this process:

1. Create source files that contain programs with embedded SQL statements.

2. Connect to a database and then use the PRECOMPILE command on the source file.

   The precompiler converts the SQL statements in each source file into DB2 runtime API calls to the database manager (this modified source file contains host language calls for the SQL statements). The precompiler also produces an access package in the database and, optionally, a bind file, if you specify that you want one created.

   The access package contains access plans selected by the DB2 optimizer for the static SQL statements in your application. The access plans (or package) contain the information required by the database manager to execute the static SQL statements in the most efficient manner as determined by the optimizer. For dynamic SQL statements, the optimizer creates access plans each time you run your application.

   The bind file contains the SQL statements and other data required to create an access package. You can use the bind file to re-bind your application later without having to precompile it first. The re-binding creates access plans optimized for current database conditions. You need to re-bind your application if it will access a different database from the one against which it was precompiled. You should re-bind your application if the database statistics have changed since the last binding or if you create a new index on a table accessed by the application.

3. Compile the modified source files (and other files without SQL statements) using the host language compiler.

4. Link the object files with the DB2 and host language libraries to produce an executable program.

12

5. Use the BIND command on the bind file to create the access package if this was not already done at precompile time, or if a different database is going to be accessed. This command prepares SQL statements stored in the bind file generated by the precompiler and creates a package that is stored in the database.

6. Run the application. The application accesses the database using the access plan in the package.

Declare a cursor named UP_CUR to be used in a C program to update the start date (PRST-DATE) and the end date (PRENDATE) columns in the PROJECT table. The program must receive both of these values together with the project number (PROJNO) value for each row:

```
EXEC SQL   DECLARE UP_CUR CURSOR FOR
                 SELECT PROJNO, PRSTDATE, PRENDATE
                 FROM PROJECT
                 FOR UPDATE OF PRSTDATE, PRENDATE;
```

Declare a cursor named c1 for a C++ program to retrieve all data from the ORG table until all the data is retrieved (a SQL return code of 100 means that no data was found because the cursor will be positioned after the last row of the result table). This demonstrates that an application can use several cursors concurrently; each cursor requires its own set of DECLARE CURSOR, OPEN, CLOSE, and FETCH statements:

```
/* declare cursor */
  EXEC SQL DECLARE c1 CURSOR FOR
    SELECT deptnumb, deptname FROM org WHERE deptnumb < 40;
/* open cursor */
  EXEC SQL OPEN c1;
/* fetch cursor */
  EXEC SQL FETCH c1 INTO :deptnumb, :deptname;
while (sqlca.sqlcode != 100)
  {
    printf("    %8d %-14s\n", deptnumb, deptname);
    EXEC SQL FETCH c1 INTO :deptnumb, :deptname;
  }

  /* close cursor */
  EXEC SQL CLOSE c1;
```

In the preceding example, :deptnumb and :deptname are known as *host variables*. You use host variables to receive data from the database manager or to transfer data to it from the host (that is, C, C++, Java, and so on) program. Host variables that receive data from the database manager are *output host variables*, whereas those that transfer data to it from the host program are *input host variables*.

TIP

> You can use the Declaration Generator utility (db2dclgn) to generate declarations for a given table in a database. It creates embedded SQL declaration source files that you can easily insert into your applications. These source files contain the host variable structures that match the data types and size of the columns referenced from a table. The utility supports the C/C++, Java, COBOL, and FORTRAN languages.

Performance of Static Versus Dynamic SQL Statements

A *static SQL* statement is embedded within an application program. All these embedded statements must be precompiled and bound into a *package* before the application can be executed. When DB2 compiles these statements, it creates an `access plan` for each one based on the catalog statistics and configuration parameters at the time that the statements were precompiled and bound. These access plans are always used when the application is run; they do not change until the package is bound again.

Dynamic SQL statements are SQL statements prepared and executed within an application program each time the program is called. When DB2 runs a dynamic SQL statement, it creates an `access plan` based on current catalog statistics and configuration parameters. This access plan might change from one execution of the statement's application program to the next.

Static and dynamic SQL each come in two types that make a difference to the DB2 optimizer. These types are

- Static SQL containing no host variables—This is an unlikely situation that you may see only for initialization code and novice training examples. This is actually the best combination from a performance perspective in that there is no runtime performance overhead, and the DB2 optimizer's capabilities can be fully realized.

- Static SQL containing host variables—This is the traditional *legacy* style of DB2 applications. It avoids the runtime overhead of a `PREPARE` and catalog locks acquired during statement compilation. Unfortunately, the full power of the optimizer cannot be utilized because the optimizer does not know the entire SQL statement. A particular problem exists with highly non-uniform data distributions.

- Dynamic SQL containing no parameter markers—This is the typical style for random query interfaces (such as the CLP) and is the optimizer's preferred *flavor* of SQL. For complex queries, the overhead of the `PREPARE` statement is usually offset by the improved execution time.

12

- Dynamic SQL containing parameter markers—This is the most common type of SQL for CLI applications. The key benefit is that the presence of parameter markers allows the cost of the PREPARE to be amortized over the repeated executions of the statement, typically a SELECT or INSERT. This amortization is true for all repetitive dynamic SQL applications. Unfortunately, just like static SQL with host variables, parts of the DB2 optimizer will not work because complete information is unavailable. The recommendation is to use *static SQL with host variables* or *dynamic SQL without parameter markers* as the most efficient options.

Developing Windows Applications

You can build and run DB2 applications with a DB2 Application Development Client installed. You can also run DB2 applications on the DB2 Run-Time Client and the DB2 Administration Client. Several examples of how to program C, C++, Java, and COBOL programs in a Windows environment are located in the /sqllib/samples directory.

On Windows operating systems, these are some of the ways to access DB2 databases:

- ActiveX Data Objects (ADO) implemented in Microsoft Visual Basic and Microsoft Visual C++
- Remote Data Objects (RDO) implemented in Microsoft Visual Basic
- Object Linking and Embedding (OLE) Automation Routines (UDFs and stored procedures)
- Object Linking and Embedding Database (OLE DB) table functions
- Develop Microsoft Visual Basic and Visual C++ applications that conform to Data Access Object (DAO) and Remote Data Object (RDO) specifications, and ActiveX Data Object (ADO) applications that use the Object Linking and Embedding Database (OLE DB) Bridge
- Develop applications using IBM or third-party tools such as Weblogic, Excel, Perl, and Open Database Connectivity (ODBC) end-user tools such as Microsoft Access
- JDBC for Java applications and applets
- Applications developed using the DB2 Application Development Client that include embedded SQL, APIs, stored procedures, user-defined functions, or calls to the DB2 Call Level Interface (CLI)

For DB2 for Windows software support updates, visit the DB2 application development Web site:

http://www.ibm.com/software/data/db2/udb/ad

The DB2 CLI is based on Microsoft's Open Database Connectivity (ODBC) specification and is 100% compatible. The DB2 CLI driver also acts as an ODBC driver when loaded by an ODBC driver manager, and it conforms to ODBC 3.51. You do not need to precompile or bind DB2 CLI applications because they use common access packages provided with DB2. You simply compile and link your application. In addition, some DB2-specific extensions have been added to help the application programmer specifically exploit DB2 features.

The DB2 CLI is a C/C++ Application Programming Interface (API) for relational database access that uses function calls to pass dynamic SQL statements as function arguments. It is an alternative to embedded dynamic SQL, but unlike embedded SQL, DB2 CLI does not require host variables or a precompiler.

You can build an ODBC application without using an ODBC driver manager, and simply use DB2's ODBC driver on any platform by linking your application with `db2cli.lib` on Windows operating systems. The DB2 CLI sample programs demonstrate this and are located in the `sqllib\samples\cli` directory.

Before your DB2 CLI or ODBC applications can access DB2 databases, the DB2 CLI bind files that come with the DB2 Application Development Client must be bound to each DB2 database that will be accessed. This occurs automatically with the execution of the first statement, and it is recommend that the administrator bind the bind files from one client on each platform that will access a DB2 database.

Summary

12

Today you saw some of the functionality provided by simple and advanced SQL statements. The Development Center is a graphical IDE that can assist you to build either stored procedures or UDFs. The steps for embedding SQL statements into host programs were examined, and the benefits of using static versus dynamic SQL statements were examined.

What Comes Next?

On Day 13, "Advanced SQL," you will learn how to use the objectlike features of DB2 to simplify application programming.

Q&A

Q What is a SQL predicate?

A A *predicate* is an element of a search condition that expresses or implies a comparison operation. Predicates are included in clauses beginning with WHERE or HAVING.

Q Why should I use views?

A One reason you may want to use a view is to restrict access to certain rows or columns in a database. For example, you have a personnel database that contains each employee with employee salaries. You'll want only authorized people to see the salary for each employee. You might want to set it up so that managers can view the salaries of their own employees, but not the salaries of employees outside their departments. You many also want a single person in the Human Resources department to have access to all salaries in the company. You can also create views so that each employee can see his own salary, but not the salary of anyone else in the company. You can restrict the data in many ways so that sensitive information is available only to those with the proper authority.

Q What is produced from the precompile operation?

A This processes an application program source file containing embedded SQL statements. A modified source file is produced, containing host language calls for the SQL statements, and, by default, a package is created in the database.

Q What is a package?

A A package is an object stored in the database that includes information needed to execute specific SQL statements in a single source file. A database application uses one package for every precompiled source file used to build the application. Each package is a separate entity and has no relationship to any other packages used by the same or other applications. Packages are created by running the precompiler against a source file with binding enabled, or by running the binder later with one or more bind files.

Workshop

The purpose of the Workshop is to allow you to test your knowledge of the material covered in the lesson. See whether you can successfully answer the questions in the quiz and complete the exercise before you continue with the next lesson. The answers appear in Appendix B, "Answers to Quiz Questions and Exercises."

Quiz

1. What are the relative advantages of static versus dynamic SQL?
2. What is produced during the Bind process?

Exercise

1. The better you understand how to use SQL, the more you can leverage your investment in database technology. By understanding what SQL statements can do for your programs, you can manage data far more efficiently than using application program logic to accomplish the same task. Take this opportunity to explore the various options of submitting SQL to the database. Familiarize yourself with the various command-line tools as well as how to store and submit SQL statements using scripts.

12

DAY 13

Advanced SQL

DB2 Universal Database provides several object-oriented functions through SQL that offer the programmer several options on how business logic or rules are implemented in their program. These features include large object support, user-defined types, triggers, and routines. These features offer you many bene-fits, including the ability to reuse code, create objects that more closely imitate the way we think of things, keep objects and functions for use by multiple applications closer to data, and create more flexible applications.

Today you learn the following:

- How to use constraints to implement business rules
- How to create user-defined types to extend the data types supported by the database
- How to implement business rules using triggers
- The benefits of using server-based routines
- How DB2 supports binary large objects
- The benefits of using the DB2 Development Center
- The purpose of the IBM DB2 Relational Extenders and the types of applications they support

Object-Oriented SQL Concepts

DB2 provides several features that can reduce the complexity of the application program. DB2 includes several objectlike features, such as large object support, user-defined types, user-defined functions, and triggers. By having the database provide this functionality to the application, the reuse of server-based database objects can reduce the effort in delivering new applications.

Constraints

Within any business, data must often adhere to certain restrictions or rules. For example, an employee number must be unique. DB2 provides *constraints* as a way to enforce such rules. Developers can use DB2 to enforce these rules rather than code the rule in each application.

DB2 provides the following types of constraints:

- NOT NULL—Prevents null values from being entered into a column.
- Unique—Ensures that the values in a set of columns are unique and not null for all rows in the table. For example, a typical unique constraint in a DEPARTMENT table might be that the department number is unique and not null.
- Check—A database rule that specifies the values allowed in one or more columns of every row of a table.
- Primary key—Each table can have one primary key. A primary key is a column or combination of columns that has the same properties as a unique constraint. You can use a primary key and foreign key constraints to define relationships between tables.
- Foreign key—(Also known as referential integrity constraints.) Enables you to define required relationships between and within tables.

This example creates a table that enforces the following rules: the values of the department number must be between 10 and 100, the valid jobs are Sales or Mgr or Clerk, and every employee with more than 10 years with the company must be making more than $50,000.

```
CREATE TABLE EMPLOYEE
 (ID         SMALLINT NOT NULL,
 NAME        ARCHAR(9),
 DEPT        SMALLINT CHECK(DEPT BETWEEN 10 AND 100),
 JOB         CHAR(5),
 HIREDATE    DATE,
 SALARY      DECIMAL(7,2),
 COMM        DECIMAL(7,2),
 PRIMARY     KEY(ID),
```

```
CHECK       (JOB IN ('SALES', 'MGR', 'CLERK')),
CONSTRAINT  YEARSAL CHECK (YEAR(HIREDATE) > 1993 OR SALARY > 50000))
```

Referential Constraints and Relationships

Referential constraints are established with the FOREIGN KEY clause and the REFERENCES clause in the CREATE TABLE or ALTER TABLE statements. Before creating a referential constraint, consider certain effects from a referential constraint on a typed table or to a parent table that is a typed table.

The identification of foreign keys enforces constraints on the values within the rows of a table or between the rows of two tables. The database manager checks the constraints specified in a table definition and maintains the relationships accordingly. The goal is to maintain integrity whenever one database object references another.

For example, primary and foreign keys each have a department number column. For the EMPLOYEE table, the column name is WORKDEPT, and for the DEPARTMENT table, the name is DEPTNO. The relationship between these two tables is defined by the following constraints:

- There is only one department number for each employee in the EMPLOYEE table, and that number exists in the DEPARTMENT table.

- Each row in the EMPLOYEE table is related to no more than one row in the DEPARTMENT table. There is a unique relationship between the tables.

- Each row in the EMPLOYEE table that has a non-null value for WORKDEPT is related to a row in the DEPTNO column of the DEPARTMENT table.

- The DEPARTMENT table is the parent table, and the EMPLOYEE table is the dependent table.

The SQL statement defining the parent table, DEPARTMENT, is

```
CREATE TABLE DEPARTMENT
  (DEPTNO    CHAR(3)    NOT NULL,
   DEPTNAME  VARCHAR(29) NOT NULL,
   MGRNO     CHAR(6),
   ADMRDEPT  CHAR(3)    NOT NULL,
   LOCATION  CHAR(16),
   PRIMARY KEY (DEPTNO))
```

13

The SQL statement defining the dependent table, EMPLOYEE, is

```
CREATE TABLE EMPLOYEE
  (EMPNO     CHAR(6)    NOT NULL PRIMARY KEY,
   FIRSTNME  VARCHAR(12) NOT NULL,
   LASTNAME  VARCHAR(15) NOT NULL,
   WORKDEPT  CHAR(3),
   PHONENO   CHAR(4),
```

```
PHOTO     BLOB(10m)    NOT NULL,
   FOREIGN KEY DEPT (WORKDEPT)
   REFERENCES DEPARTMENT ON DELETE NO ACTION)
```

By specifying the DEPTNO column as the primary key of the DEPARTMENT table and WORKDEPT as the foreign key of the EMPLOYEE table, you are defining a referential constraint on the WORKDEPT values. This constraint enforces referential integrity between the values of the two tables. In this case, any employees that are added to the EMPLOYEE table must have a department number that can be found in the DEPARTMENT table.

The delete rule for the referential constraint in the employee table is NO ACTION, which means that a department cannot be deleted from the DEPARTMENT table if any employees are in that department.

Although the previous examples use the CREATE TABLE statement to add a referential constraint, the ALTER TABLE statement can also be used.

For another example, the same table definitions are used as those in the previous example. Also, the DEPARTMENT table is created before the EMPLOYEE table. Each department has a manager, and that manager is listed in the EMPLOYEE table. MGRNO of the DEPARTMENT table is actually a foreign key of the EMPLOYEE table. Because of this referential cycle, this constraint poses a slight problem. You could add a foreign key later. You could also use the CREATE SCHEMA statement to create both the EMPLOYEE and DEPARTMENT tables at the same time.

User-Defined Types (UDTs)

A *user-defined type (UDT)* is a named data type created in the database by the user. A UDT can be a *distinct type*, which shares a common representation with a built-in data type, or a *structured type*, which has a sequence of named attributes that each have a type. A structured type can be a subtype of another structured type (called a supertype), defining a type hierarchy.

UDTs support *strong typing*, which means that even though they share the same representation as other types, values of a given UDT are considered to be compatible only with values of the same UDT or UDTs in the same type hierarchy. To compare these different data types, you could write a user-defined function to convert one of the currencies to the other by using the Create Distinct Type dialog box. Open the Control Center, select a database folder, and then expand the Application Objects folder. Right-click the User Defined Distinct Datatypes folder and select Create to diplay the dialog box (see Figure 13.1). The settings shown in Figure 13.1 produce the following distinct type:

```
CREATE DISTINCT TYPE T_CDNDOLLAR AS DECIMAL(5,2) WITH COMPARISONS
```

FIGURE **13.1**

The Create Distinct Type dialog box.

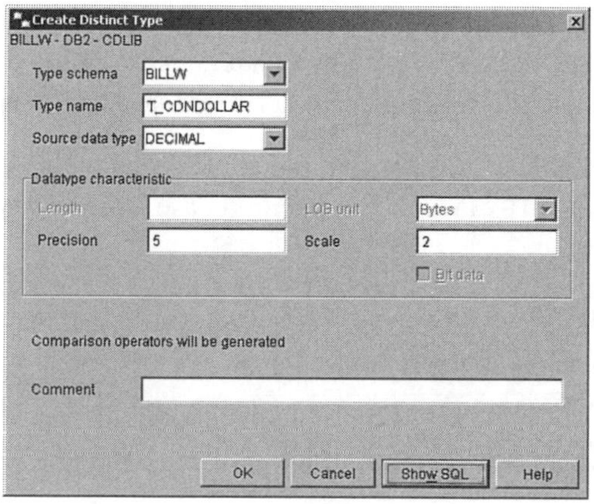

User-Defined Structured Types

A structured type is a user-defined data type containing one or more named attributes, each of which has a data type. *Attributes* are properties that describe an instance of a type. A geometric shape, for example, might have attributes such as its list of Cartesian coordinates. A person might have attributes of name, address, and so on. A department might have attributes of a name or some other kind of ID.

A structured type also includes a set of method specifications. Methods enable you to define behaviors for structured types. Like user-defined functions (UDFs), methods are routines that extend SQL. In the case of methods, however, the behavior is integrated solely with a particular structured type.

A structured type may be used as the type of a table, view, or column. When used as the type for a table or view, that table or view is known as a *typed table* or *typed view*, respectively. For typed tables and typed views, the names and data types of the attributes of the structured type become the names and data types of the columns of the typed table or typed view. Rows of the typed table or typed view can be thought of as a representation of instances of the structured type.

A type cannot be dropped when certain other objects use the type, either directly or indirectly. For example, a type cannot be dropped if a table or view column makes a direct or indirect use of the type.

Triggers

Triggers are more complex and potentially more powerful than constraints. They define a set of actions executed in conjunction with, or triggered by, an INSERT, UPDATE, or DELETE clause on a specified base table. You can use triggers to support general forms of

13

integrity or business rules. For example, a trigger can check a customer's credit limit before an order is accepted, or be used in a banking application to raise an alert if a withdrawal from an account did not fit a customer's standard withdrawal patterns.

A trigger defines a set of actions executed in conjunction with, or triggered by, an INSERT, UPDATE, or DELETE clause on a specified base table or a typed table. Some uses of triggers are to

- Validate input data
- Generate a value for a newly inserted row
- Read from other tables for cross-referencing purposes
- Write to other tables for audit trail purposes

You can use triggers to support general forms of integrity or business rules. For example, a trigger can check a customer's credit limit before an order is accepted or update a summary data table.

The benefits of using a trigger are

- Faster application development—Because a trigger is stored in the database, you do not have to code the actions it does in every application.
- Easier maintenance—After a trigger is defined, it is automatically invoked when the table it is created on is accessed.
- Global enforcement of business rules—If a business policy changes, you only need to change the trigger and not each application program.

The following SQL statement creates a trigger that increases the number of employees each time a new person is hired, by adding 1 to the number of employees (NBEMP) column in the COMPANY_STATS table each time a row is added to the EMPLOYEE table.

```
CREATE TRIGGER NEW_HIRED
 AFTER INSERT ON EMPLOYEE
 FOR EACH ROW MODE DB2SQL
 UPDATE COMPANY_STATS SET NBEMP = NBEMP+1;
```

You can use the Create Trigger Wizard from the Control Center to generate this SQL statement.

A trigger is an object that initiates an action when an UPDATE, DELETE, or INSERT operation is run against a table. You can use triggers that run before such operations in several ways:

- To check for certain conditions before performing a triggering operation.
- To change the input values before they're stored in the table.

- To check or modify values that run before an UPDATE, INSERT, or DELETE in the database. This is useful if you need to transform data from the way the user sees it to some internal database format.

- To run other nondatabase operations coded in user-defined functions.

Similarly, you can use triggers that run after an update or insert in several ways:

- To update data in other tables. This is useful for maintaining relationships between data or in keeping audit trail information.

- To check against other data in the table or in other tables. This is useful to ensure data integrity when referential integrity constraints aren't appropriate, or when table check constraints limit checking to the current table only.

- To run non-database operations coded in user-defined functions. This is useful when issuing alerts or to update information outside the database.

To see how triggers work, create a trigger for the CDLIB sample database to verify that the release year of an album is valid. Follow these steps:

1. Start the Control Center.
2. Expand the objects until you see the Triggers folder within the CDLIB database.
3. Right-click the folder and select Create from the pop-up menu. The Create Trigger dialog box opens (see Figure 13.2).

FIGURE 13.2

The Create Trigger dialog box.

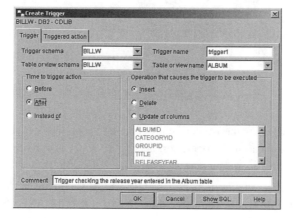

13

4. On the Trigger page, select a schema for the trigger and a schema for the table the trigger will be acting on.

5. Enter a name for the trigger that's fewer than 18 characters and is unique within the schema—for example, trigger1.

6. Select a table for the trigger to act on. For this example, you want the trigger to act on the ALBUM table.

7. Select a time to trigger the action. Select Before to activate the trigger before the UPDATE, INSERT, or DELETE action; select After to activate the trigger after the UPDATE, INSERT, or DELETE action. For this example, select After to have the value entered for RELEASEYEAR verified.

8. Select an operation that causes the trigger to be executed. Your choices are Insert, Delete, or Update of Columns. If you choose Update of Columns, you can select a specific column to trigger the action. For this example, however, select Insert.

9. On the Triggered Action page, you can specify correlation names for old and new rows and temporary tables for old and new rows (see Figure 13.3). Correlation names and temporary tables are necessary when you need to refer to the rows before or after they're updated. For this example, use NEW for the correlation name and CDLIB for the temporary tables.

FIGURE 13.3

The Triggered Action page of the Create Trigger dialog box.

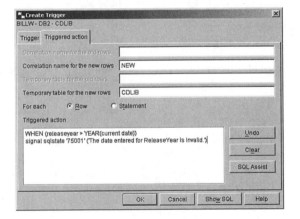

10. Specify whether the trigger is to occur each time the operation acts on a row or just one time after the operation acts on all rows. For this example, to have the trigger occur each time a row is inserted, select the Row radio button.

11. In the Triggered Action list box, enter a SQL statement to define the trigger. The following statement compares the value of the RELEASEYEAR column with the current year, which results in an error if the entered date is greater than the current date:

```
when (releaseyear > YEAR(current date))
signal sqlstate '75001' ('The date entered for ReleaseYear is invalid.')
```

12. Click OK to have the trigger created.

13. To test the trigger, insert a row in the ALBUM table, providing a RELEASEYEAR that's greater than the current year.

Routines (Stored Procedures, UDFs, Methods)

The term *routines* is used by DB2 to refer to stored procedures, UDFs, and methods. Each of these server-based functions is implemented by DB2 in a similar fashion with respect to the client interfaces supported (embedded SQL, CL, and JDBC), and they each employ some of the same parameter styles. Each routine can be invoked by a client or other routines, and each fulfills a different purpose.

Routines are composed of application logic that resides on the database server and can be invoked from a client or other routines. They can be written using SQL or by a number of programming languages. Because routines are database objects, you must register them with a database to invoke them. You can implement three types of routines:

- Stored procedures serve as extensions to clients and run on the database server. They are invoked via the CALL statement and execute multiple SQL statements at the server. Stored procedures can be written using SQL, C/C++, Java, OLE, OLE DB (only for table functions), or COBOL. For SQL-based procedures, a prerequisite will be a supported C compiler at the database server.

- DB2 allows you to create functions beyond what is already provided. A UDF is a scalar function; you pass it a value, and it returns a single value each time it is called. You can also code a row, column, or table function that returns a row, column, and set of data, respectively. UDFs can be written using SQL, C/C++, Java, OLE, or OLE DB (Table UDFs only).

- Defining scalar functions to use with structured types enables the creation of *methods*. The creation of methods is a central concept of object orientation. These can be written using C/C++, Java, or OLE.

Registering Routines

Registering a routine is the act of coupling a custom-built application library with the database. Until the routine is registered, it cannot be invoked as a routine.

For the routine to work properly, it is vital that you register it with the applicable clauses. Choices you made while writing the routine need to be reflected in its registration. For example, there needs to be an exact mapping between the parameters passed from a client application to a routine. To simplify matters, many of the clauses for registering the different types of routines are common.

13

One special consideration of stored procedures is whether to register the procedure as fenced or not fenced. Although not fenced stored procedures will typically perform better because the process executes in the database address space, there are potential integrity issues. If a not fenced stored procedure abends, it could potentially bring down the database manager. For this reason, unless you have thoroughly tested and validated the procedure, the fenced stored procedure is recommended.

To register a routine, issue the CREATE statement with the applicable clauses that correspond to the type of routine you are working with. The statements are as follows: CREATE FUNCTION, CREATE METHOD, CREATE TYPE, and CREATE PROCEDURE.

For the registration of methods, issuing the CREATE TYPE statement is the first step, and issuing the CREATE METHOD statement is the second step. The CREATE METHOD statement only addresses attributes that relate to a method's signature.

After you have registered your routine, you can invoke it from a client application or a calling routine.

SQL Procedures

DB2 allows you to implement application programming logic through the use of SQL procedures. SQL control statements allow you to control logic flow (that is, IF, GOTO, RETURN), declare and set variables, and handle warnings and exceptions. You will require the Application Development Client and a DB2 supported C or C++ compiler on the server to execute SQL-PL procedures.

The DB2 Command Line Processor scripts (those ending with the .db2 extension), in the sqllib\samples\sqlproc directory on Windows, execute CREATE PROCEDURE statements to create stored procedures on the server. Each CLP script has a corresponding client application file of the same name, with an extension denoting its language and application interface: .sqc (for C embedded SQL), .c (for DB2 CLI), or .java (for JDBC).

Before running a CREATE PROCEDURE CLP script, connect to the sample database with the command:

```
db2 connect to sample
```

To execute the CREATE PROCEDURE statement contained in the rsultset.db2 script file, enter the following command:

```
db2 -td@ -vf rsultset.db2
```

Now, the SQL procedure is ready to be called. You can call stored procedures by using the CALL statement from the DB2 Command Line Processor interface. The stored procedure being called must be defined in the catalog.

To use the CALL statement, enter the stored procedure name plus any IN or INOUT parameters, as well as '?' as a placeholder for each OUT parameter.

The parameters for a stored procedure are given in the CREATE PROCEDURE statement for the stored procedure in the program source file. For example, in the SQL procedure source file, whiles.db2, the CREATE PROCEDURE statement for the DEPT_MEDIAN procedure begins as follows:

```
CREATE PROCEDURE DEPT_MEDIAN
(IN deptNumber SMALLINT, OUT medianSalary DOUBLE)
```

To call this procedure, you need to put in a valid SMALLINT value for the IN parameter, deptNumber, and a question mark, '?', for the OUT parameter.

The DEPT_MEDIAN procedure accesses the STAFF table of the sample database. The variable deptNumber is assigned to the DEPT column of the STAFF table, so you can obtain a valid value from the DEPT column—for example, the value "51".

Now, you can enter the CALL statement with the procedure name and the value for the IN parameter, and a question mark, '?', for the value of the OUT parameter. The procedure's parameters must be enclosed in parentheses as follows:

```
db2 call dept_median (51, ?)
```

After running this command, you should receive this result:

```
Value of output parameters
--------------------------
Parameter Name  : MEDIANSALARY
Parameter Value : +1.76545000000000E+004

DB20000I  The SQL command completed successfully.
```

Large Object Support

The VARCHAR and VARGRAPHIC data types have a limit of 32KB of storage. Although this may be sufficient for small to medium size text data, applications often need to store large text documents. They may also need to store a wide variety of additional data types such as audio, video, drawings, mixed text and graphics, and images. DB2 provides three data types to store these data objects as strings of up to 2GB in size. The three large object (LOB) data types are Binary Large Objects (BLOBs), Character Large Objects (CLOBs), and Double-Byte Character Large Objects (DBCLOBs).

13

NOTE	CLOBs can contain either single-byte or double-byte characters. DBCLOBs can contain either 4-byte or double-byte characters.

Each DB2 table may have a large amount of associated LOB data. Although any single LOB value may not exceed 2GB, a single row may contain as much as 24GB of LOB data, and a table may contain as much as 2TB of LOB data.

A separate database location stores all large object values outside their records in the table. There is a large object descriptor for each large object in each row in a table. The large object descriptor contains control information used to access the large object data stored elsewhere on disk. It is the storing of large object data outside their records that allows LOBs to be 2GB in size. Accessing the large object descriptor causes a small amount of overhead when manipulating LOBs. (For storage and performance reasons, you would likely not want to put small data items into LOBs.)

The maximum size for each large object column is part of the declaration of the large object type in the CREATE TABLE statement. The maximum size of a large object column determines the maximum size of any LOB descriptor in that column. As a result, it also determines how many columns of all data types can fit in a single row. The space used by the LOB descriptor in the row ranges from approximately 60 to 300 bytes, depending on the maximum size of the corresponding column.

The LOB-options-clause on CREATE TABLE gives you the choice to log the changes made to the LOB column(s). This clause also allows for a compact representation for the LOB descriptor. This means that you can allocate only enough space to store the LOB, or you can allocate extra space for future append operations to the LOB. The tablespace-options-clause allows you to identify a LONG table space to store the column values of long field or LOB data types.

With their potentially large size, LOBs can slow down the performance of your database system significantly when moved into or out of a database. Even though DB2 does not allow logging of a LOB value greater than 1GB, LOB values with sizes approaching 1GB can quickly push the database log to near capacity. An error, SQLCODE -355 (SQLSTATE 42993), results from attempting to log a LOB greater than 1GB in size. The lob-options-clause in the CREATE TABLE and ALTER TABLE statements allows users to turn off logging for a particular LOB column. Although setting the option to NOT LOGGED improves performance, changes to the LOB values after the most recent backup are lost during roll-forward recovery.

When selecting a LOB value, you have three options:

- Select the entire LOB value into a host variable. The entire LOB value is copied from the server to the client. This is inefficient and is sometimes not feasible. Host variables use the client memory buffer, which may not have the capacity to hold larger LOB values.

- Select just a LOB locator into a host variable. The LOB value remains on the server; the LOB locator moves to the client. If the LOB value is very large and is needed only as an input value for one or more subsequent SQL statements, it is best to keep the value in a locator. The use of a locator eliminates any client/server communication traffic needed to transfer the LOB value to the host variable and back to the server.
- Select the entire LOB value into a file reference variable. The LOB value (or a part of it) is moved to a file at the client without going through the application's memory.

If you do not want to log changes to a LOB, you must turn off logging by specifying the NOT LOGGED clause when you create the table:

```
CREATE TABLE EMPLOYEE
    (EMPNO     CHAR(6)      NOT NULL PRIMARY KEY,
     FIRSTNME  VARCHAR(12)  NOT NULL,
     MIDINIT   CHAR(1)      NOT NULL WITH DEFAULT,
     LASTNAME  VARCHAR(15)  NOT NULL,
     WORKDEPT  CHAR(3),
     PHONENO   CHAR(4),
     PHOTO     BLOB(10M)    NOT NULL  NOT LOGGED)
```

As mentioned, if the LOB column is larger than 1GB, logging must be turned off. (As a rule of thumb, you may not want to log LOB columns larger than 10MB.) As with other options specified on a column definition, the only way to change the logging option is to re-create the table.

Even if you choose not to log changes, LOB columns are *shadowed* to allow changes to be rolled back, whether the rollback is the result of a system generated error, or an application request. Shadowing is a recovery technique where current storage page contents are never overwritten. That is, old, unmodified pages are kept as "shadow" copies. These copies are discarded when they are no longer needed to support a transaction rollback.

NOTE When recovering a database using the RESTORE and ROLLFORWARD commands, LOB data that was NOT LOGGED and was written since the last backup will be replaced by binary zeros.

13

You can make the LOB column as small as possible using the COMPACT clause on the CREATE TABLE statement. For example:

```
CREATE TABLE EMPLOYEE
    (EMPNO     CHAR(6)      NOT NULL PRIMARY KEY,
     FIRSTNME  VARCHAR(12)  NOT NULL,
```

```
MIDINIT    CHAR(1)      NOT NULL WITH DEFAULT,
LASTNAME   VARCHAR(15)  NOT NULL,
WORKDEPT   CHAR(3),
PHONENO    CHAR(4),
PHOTO      BLOB(10M)    NOT NULL   NOT LOGGED   COMPACT)
```

There is a *performance cost* when appending to a table with a compact LOB column, particularly if the size of LOB values is increased (because storage adjustments must be made).

On platforms where sparse file allocation is not supported and where LOBs are placed in SMS table spaces, consider using the COMPACT clause. Sparse file allocation has to do with how physical disk space is used by an operating system. An operating system that supports sparse file allocation does not use as much physical disk space to store LOBs as compared to an operating system not supporting sparse file allocation. The COMPACT option allows for even greater physical disk space "savings" regardless of the support of sparse file allocation. Because you can get some physical disk space savings when using COMPACT, consider using COMPACT if your operating system does not support sparse file allocation.

Development Center

The Development Center can help you develop either stored procedures or UDFs. The stored procedures can by generated as SQL or Java code, whereas the options for UDFs include SQL-based, IBM WebSphere MQSeries, XML, and OLE DB objects. To start the Development Center, either select Programs|IBM DB2|Development Tools| Development Center from the Start menu, or, if you are in the Control Center, choose Tools|Development Center. The Development Center is shown in Figure 13.4.

The Development Center can run as a standalone Integrated Development Environment (IDE) and is targeted to assist the database administrator to manage application development objects. The Development Center can be connected to a database and provides an editor and debugger to test and execute the Java and SQL stored procedures and UDFs.

You can launch the Development Center from the Control Center or from Microsoft Visual Studio, Microsoft Visual Basic, or from IBM WebSphere Studio.

For assistance in developing routines, use the DB2 Development Center. It provides simple interfaces and a set of wizards that help make it easy to perform your development tasks. You can also integrate the DB2 Development Center with popular application development tools, such as Microsoft Visual Studio.

FIGURE 13.4

The Development Center.

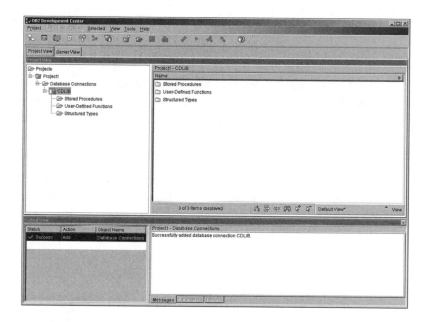

The development of routines involves the following tasks:

1. Register the Routine. This task can occur at any time before you invoke the routine, except in the following circumstances:

    • Java routines that are cataloged on JAR files must be written before they can be registered.

    • Routines that issue SQL statements that refer to themselves must be registered before they are precompiled and bound. This also applies to situations where there is a cycle of references—for example, Routine A references Routine B, which references Routine A.

2. Write the routine.

3. Build (precompile—for routines with embedded SQL, compile, and link) the routine. (See the related links for platform and language-specific build information.)

4. Debug and test the routine.

5. Invoke the routine.

13

DB2 XML Extender

The XML Extender helps you integrate the power of IBM's DB2 Universal Database with the flexibility of XML. DB2's XML Extender provides the capability to store and access XML documents, generate XML documents from existing relational data, and shred (decompose, storing untagged element or attribute content) XML documents into relational data.

XML Extender provides new data types, functions, and stored procedures to manage your XML data in DB2. You also have the ability to decompose and store XML in its component parts as columns in multiple tables. Indexes can be defined over the element or attribute of an XML document for fast retrieval. In addition, text search and section search can be enabled on the XML column or its decomposed part using Text Extenders.

You can also formulate an XML document from your existing DB2 tables for data interchange in a business-to-business environment. Net.Data and XML Extender can be used to generate XML documents from DB2, and these documents can be distributed to consumers for viewing with a browser.

XML Extender provides the following features to help you manage and exploit XML data with DB2:

- Administration tools to help you manage the integration of XML data in relational tables.
- Storage and usage methods for your XML data: XML column, XML collection.
- A Document Type Definition (DTD) repository (DTD_REF) for you to store DTDs used to validate XML data.
- A mapping scheme called the Document Access Definition (DAD) file for you to map XML documents to relational data. DAD files are managed using the XML_USAGE table, created when you enable a database for XML.
- Powerful user-defined functions (UDFs) to store and retrieve XML documents in XML columns, as well as to extract XML element or attribute values. A UDF is a function defined to the database management system and can be referenced thereafter in SQL queries. The XML Extender provides the following types of UDFs:
  - Storage—Stores intact XML documents in XML-enabled columns as XML data types.
  - Extract—Extracts XML documents, or the specified elements and attributes, as base data types.
  - Update—Updates entire XML documents or specified element and attribute values.

XML Extender provides two storage and access methods for integrating XML documents with DB2 data structures: XML column and XML collection. These methods have different uses but can be used in the same application (see Figure 13.5):

FIGURE **13.5**

The XML Extender.

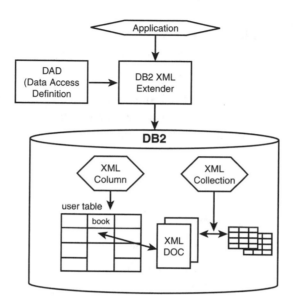

- The XML column method helps you store intact XML documents in DB2. The XML column method works well for archiving documents. The documents are inserted into columns enabled for XML and can be updated, retrieved, and searched. Element and attribute data can be mapped to DB2 tables (side tables), which can be indexed for fast search.

- The XML collection method helps you map XML document structures to DB2 tables so that you can either compose XML documents from existing DB2 data, or decompose XML documents, storing the untagged data in DB2 tables. This method is good for data interchange applications, particularly when the contents of XML documents are frequently updated.

The following is an example of inserting XML data (book_table: id, author, book):

```
INSERT INTO book_table VALUES
➥('444555', 'Gene Roddenberry', DB2XML.XMLDOC(XML_CLOB, 'e:\xml\book.xml'))
```

The following is an example of searching for XML data:

```
SELECT ID FROM  book_table WHERE DB2XML.CONTAINS
➥(book, 'book/toc/title', 'Programming')
```

The following example shows the retrieval of XML data:

```
SELECT DB2XML.CONTENT(book, 'e:\xml\book.xml') FROM book_table WHERE ID='444555'
```

13

DB2 Net Search Extender

The DB2 Net Search Extender adds the power of a fast full-text retrieval engine to Java, DB2 CLI, or Net.Data applications integrated into the DB2 Universal Database.

Net Search Extender provides fast indexing of large data volumes, allows search at high speed with a large number of concurrent users, and stores presorted table columns in main memory at indexing time to avoid expensive database access and paging at search time.

Net Search Extender provides the following features:

- Indexing:
  - One very fast index type (Ngram)
  - Multiple indexes on the same text column
  - Indexing proceeds without locking data
  - Dynamic updating of indexes, reflecting changes in the database
- Searching:
  - Provides stored procedure search and SQL scalar search functions
  - Allows word, phrase, stemmed, or fuzzy search
  - Identifies and restricts searching to sections in the documents that have been marked by special tags
  - Offers a numeric search on a range of values
  - Supports Boolean and wildcard operations
- Search results:
  - Lets you specify how the search results are sorted at indexing time, or user-supplied rank values for sorting
  - Lets you specify search result subsets when large data volumes are searched and large result lists are expected
  - Lets you set a limit on search terms with a high hit count
  - Allows positioning (cursor setting) access on search results

Textual data is a large and valuable source of unstructured information in any enterprise. Adding smart text search capability to your database allows you to make even more informed business decisions according to your specific needs. The DB2 Net Search Extender can be managed right from the DB2 Universal Database Control Center, significantly simplifying basic tasks such as creating a text index. You can even use DB2 Net Search Extender with DB2's built-in federated support to index and search your text data stored in other DB2 and Informix Dynamic Server (IDS) databases. This Extender comes with Java and Net.Data sample applications.

DB2 Spatial Extender

Traditionally, geospatial data have been managed by specialized geographic information systems (GISs) that cannot integrate spatial data with other business data stored in the RDBMS and other data sources. With the addition of object extensions to the RDBMS, GIS intelligence can now be incorporated directly into the database. The Spatial Extender was developed through collaboration with Environmental Systems Research Institute (ESRI), a major developer of GIS systems. The DB2 Spatial Extender can enable users to answer questions that involve spatial data, such as querying to see where best to locate a new retail site, assessing insurance premiums, or where best to test a new product.

The DB2 Spatial Extender system consists of DB2 Universal Database, DB2 Spatial Extender, and, for most applications, a geobrowser. A geobrowser is not required but is useful for visually rendering the results of spatial queries, generally in the form of maps. Databases enabled for spatial operations are located on the server. You can use client applications to access spatial data through the DB2 Spatial Extender stored procedures and spatial queries. You can also configure DB2 Spatial Extender in a standalone environment, which is a configuration where both the client and server reside on the same machine. In both client/server and standalone configurations, you can view spatial data with a geobrowser such as ArcExplorer for DB2 or ESRI's ArcGIS tool suites running with ArcSDE.

You can download a free copy of ArcExplorer for DB2 from IBM's DB2 Spatial Extender Web site at the following address:

`http://www.ibm.com/software/data/spatial/`

The spatial data types supported by DB2 Spatial Extender are implementations of the geometries shown in Figure 13.6.

A superclass called geometry is the root of the hierarchy. The subtypes are divided into two categories: the base geometry subtypes and the homogeneous collection subtypes.

13

Figure 13.6

Hierarchy of geometries supported by DB2 Spatial Extender. Instantiable geometries shown here include examples of how they might be rendered visually.

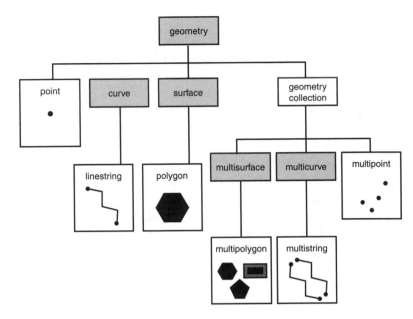

The base geometries include

- Points—Represent discrete features perceived as occupying the locus where an east-west coordinate line (such as a parallel) intersects a north-south coordinate line (such as a meridian). For example, suppose that the notation on a large-scale map shows that each city on the map is located at the intersection of a parallel and a meridian. A point could represent each city.

- Linestrings—Represent linear geographic features (for example, streets, canals, and pipelines).

- Polygons—Represent multisided geographic features (for example, welfare districts, forests, and wildlife habitats).

The homogeneous collections include

- Multipoints—Represent multipart features whose components are each located at the intersection of an east-west coordinate line and a north-south coordinate line (for example, an island chain whose members are each situated at an intersection of a parallel and meridian).

- Multilinestrings—Represent multipart features whose components are linear geographic features (for example, river systems and highway systems).

- Multipolygons—Represent multipart features made up of multisided units or components (for example, the collective farmlands in a specific region, or a system of lakes).

As their names imply, the homogeneous collections are collections of base geometries. In addition to sharing base geometry properties, homogeneous collections have some of their own properties as well.

In the following example, the ST_Area function returns a numeric value that represents the sales area of store 10. The function returns the area in the same units as the units of the coordinate system being used to define the area's location:

```
SELECT db2gse.ST_Area(sales_area)
FROM stores
WHERE id = 10
```

Summary

Today you saw some of the functionality provided by some of the more advanced SQL statements. The Development Center is a graphical IDE that can assist you to build either stored procedures or UDFs. Also, a number of DB2 Relational Extenders were reviewed. They are built using the object relational capabilities of DB2.

What Comes Next?

On Day 14, "Design Considerations," you're introduced to the options you should consider when designing a database or applications.

Q&A

Q What causes a trigger to be activated?

A Every trigger is associated with an event. Triggers are activated when their corresponding event occurs in the database. This trigger event occurs when the specified action, either an UPDATE, INSERT, or DELETE (including those caused by actions of referential constraints), is performed on the subject table.

Q Describe scenarios where you might use BEFORE triggers?

A BEFORE triggers are basically an extension to the constraint subsystem of the database management system. They are useful for performing validation of input data, automatically generating values for newly inserted rows, and reading from other tables for cross-referencing purposes. BEFORE triggers are not used for

13

further modifying the database because they are activated before the trigger event is applied to the database. Note that BEFORE triggers must have a granularity of FOR EACH ROW.

Q Describe scenarios where you might use AFTER triggers?

A AFTER triggers are basically a module of application logic that runs in the database every time a specific event occurs. As a part of an application, AFTER triggers always see the database in a consistent state. Note that they are run after the integrity constraints that may be violated by the triggering SQL operation have been checked. Consequently, you can use them mostly to perform operations that an application can also perform. For example, you can continue to apply modify operations to the database, or perform actions outside the database, such as generating an alert. Note that actions performed outside the database are not rolled back if the trigger is rolled back. Note that AFTER triggers can have a granularity of either FOR EACH ROW or FOR EACH STATEMENT.

Q Describe scenarios where you might use INSTEAD OF triggers?

A INSTEAD OF triggers must have a granularity of FOR EACH ROW, and the subject table must be a view. You can view an INSTEAD OF trigger as a description of the inverse operation of the view it is defined on. For example, if the select list in the view contains an expression over a base table, the INSERT statement in the body of its INSTEAD OF INSERT trigger will contain the reverse expression.

Workshop

The purpose of the Workshop is to allow you to test your knowledge of the material covered in the lesson. See whether you can successfully answer the questions in the quiz and complete the exercise before you continue with the next lesson. The answers appear in Appendix B, "Answers to Quiz Questions and Exercises."

Quiz

1. How does the XML Extender store XML data?
2. What are the advantages of using the Net Search Extender over storing a document as a LOB and using SQL to search the document?
3. What kind of applications need spatial data to resolve their queries?

Exercise

1. Understanding the use of the advanced SQL capabilities of DB2 can improve programmer productivity. By having the database server implement selective func-

tions, business logic only needs to be written once and can be invoked by each application program with access to the database. Performance can also be improved by using stored procedures, thereby reducing network traffic between a given application and the database. Take this opportunity to use SQL to implement new data types, additional constraints, and new server-based functions such as triggers.

13

WEEK 2

DAY 14

Design Considerations

Today you learn what you need to think about when designing your databases or applications, as well as maintaining the system. You learn what resources you should consider when implementing an application. From a programming perspective, you learn the basics of managing data concurrency by understanding row and table-level locking. Also covered are some programming techniques you can use to reduce network traffic between a database client and server. These techniques include using stored procedures, blocking SQL statements, and retrieving groups of rows. Database structures such as indexes also are reviewed to see how they can improve application performance.

The guidelines covered during this lesson should be considered when you are designing your database. You can use some of these tips to help improve performance after your database is designed.

Today you learn the following:

- How much systems resources are required to develop new applications
- General SQL guidelines to ensure optimal application performance
- What factors affect concurrency

- How indexes can optimize data retrieval
- Considerations for complex query applications

System Resources

When you are beginning to develop a new application, consider all available resources in the environment. Enough system resources such as hardware, memory, and disk must be made available before you can expect a given application to perform. Only with the proper system resources available will changes to the database and application have any effect on application performance.

Before tuning any parameters, have fall-back procedures in place so that the former environment can be re-created.

Disk Space Management

Database administrators can physically distribute database data into objects known as *table spaces*. A table space has one or more *containers* (preallocated system files or directories) associated with it. Containers are separate identifiers of storage space to be used by the table space. You learned in detail how to create table spaces in Day 10, "Creating Table Spaces."

Separating data into table spaces provides a number of advantages, including separating different data types and enabling prefetch. Each is described in the following sections.

Separating Different Data Types

When you create a table, consider keeping different types of data, indexes, and large object (LOB) data separate from the rest of the table data. These separate table spaces can possibly be on different media than the rest of the data. This flexibility allows you to choose the table space characteristics and the physical devices supporting those table spaces to best suit the type of data. You can also allocate a table space to a specific buffer pool.

NOTE
> Separating data is possible only if you're using DMS table spaces.

You may, for example, have tables containing infrequently used historical data. As a result, end users may be willing to accept a longer response time for queries executed against this data. In this situation, you could use a different table space for the historic tables and assign this table space to less expensive physical devices with slower access rates.

You may be able to identify some essential tables that require high availability and fast response time. You may want to put these tables into a table space assigned to a fast physical device that can help support these important data requirements.

Indexes stored in a different table space from that used to store other table data can allow for more efficient use of disks by reducing the movement of read/write heads. You can also allocate faster devices to indexes, which can speed index access.

Long column data stored in a different table space allows you to allocate a special device to this type of data. For example, you may choose to store large object data on devices that have a large capacity but may be slow, and store the rest of your data on a faster device.

Enabling Prefetch

Enabling prefetch means that index and data pages are copied into the buffer pool from disk before they are actually needed. This can help improve performance by reducing the time spent waiting for the I/O to complete. By splitting data across devices, the prefetch operations become more effective at improving performance. You learn more about prefetch operations on Day 20, "Tuning DB2 Universal Database Performance."

Large Object Considerations

When using large objects in your database, you have special performance considerations. DB2 Universal Database provides the flexibility for you to

- Access only those portions of a large object that are needed by the application—for example, using the SUBSTR scalar function.
- Use LOB locators to eliminate the need to transport the LOB from the data source server to the application (and possibly back again).
- Use LOB locators to defer or avoid materialization of large objects.
- Choose whether changes to this column will be logged when defining a large object column.

TIP

> You can specify the NOT LOGGED option when you are adding a column using the Create Table dialog box. Day 9, "Creating Databases and Tables," covered the details of using the Create Table Wizard.

14

- Store large object data in separate database partitions specially architected for large object handling.

General System Recommendations

Assuming that there is enough processing power, real memory, and disk, a number of parameters should be examined to exploit the available system resources. Here are some guidelines that will have a significant impact on the performance of a given application:

- Start with 75% of main memory devoted to the buffer pool (buffpage); the buffer pool is typically the most important memory resource.

- Make sure that enough memory is allocated to the sortheap parameter to enable sorts without overflowing to disk reads. This is applicable for query applications. Applications that do not perform queries and that are primarily updating data can consider lowering this parameter.

- Most network devices have delay parameters, and most of them default to values that are bad for distributed databases. To improve performance, locate these parameters and if possible, set them to zero.

- To improve disk performance, place data and indexes on different disks.

- Use SMS table spaces for TEMP table spaces, and use one TEMP table space for a given pagesize.

- Use default of 32 for EXTENTSIZE when you create a table space and set PREFETCH-SIZE to be a multiple of EXTENTSIZE (start with the number of containers as the multiple).

- Place database logs on different disk drives for improved performance. Consider increasing the LOGFILESIZ parameter to minimize the frequency of logs becoming full and reducing the wait time for a usable log.

General SQL Guidelines

DB2 includes a sophisticated cost-based SQL optimizer, which provides superior complex query performance. The purpose of the SQL optimizer is to select the most efficient way to access the data. Relational databases offer many different ways of accessing the data, each with a cost associated with it. The optimizer considers these potential paths, assigns a cost to each one by using its model of the database, and selects the most efficient access path by choosing the one with the lowest estimated overall cost.

The optimizer includes a sophisticated query rewrite phase that transforms queries into forms that can be optimized more effectively. This ensures that you have the fastest route to your data. For example, it adds logically implied predicates, merges views, converts subqueries into joins, and eliminates redundant references to tables.

Stored Procedures

In a database application environment, many situations are repetitive—for example, receiving or returning a fixed set of data or performing the same multiple requests against a database.

A *stored procedure* is a technique that allows an application running on a client to call a procedure stored on a database server. The server procedure executes and accesses the database locally and returns information to the client application. To use this technique, an application must be written in two separate procedures:

- The calling procedure is contained in a client application and executes on the client.
- The server procedure executes at the location of the database on the database server.

Applications using stored procedures have the following advantages:

- Reduced network traffic
- Improved performance of server-intensive work
- Access to features that exist only on the database server

The use of stored procedures is applicable in all DB2 environments. Network traffic will be reduced because only the initial request and final result flow across the network.

Compound SQL

Compound SQL allows you to group several SQL statements into a single executable block. The SQL statements contained within the block (substatements) could be executed individually; however, by creating and executing a block of statements, you reduce the database manager overhead. For remote clients, compound SQL also reduces the number of requests that have to be transmitted across the network.

General SQL Recommendations

Even though there is a sophisticated cost-based optimizer, there are some SQL guidelines that can assist in the performance of the applications. They include the following:

- Select only the columns required by the application and limit the number of rows retrieved by using the appropriate predicate.

14

- Consider using built-in DB2 features to enforce data integrity, such as referential integrity, user-defined data types, column and table constraints.

- For query applications, consider using Advanced Summary Tables to reduce scans and sorts.

- Consider using stored procedures or user-defined functions at the server to reduce network traffic.

- Make sure the statistics in the database catalog are current by executing RUN-STATS after a significant number of updates have occurred to the data.

- Match data types and lengths of host variables and columns ensures the most efficient comparison between values; this avoids the overhead of performing data type conversions.

Managing Concurrency

Whenever you have multiple concurrent users, you have to manage the interaction of their activities. That is, you have to determine to what degree each user appears to be acting independently. What you manage is the degree of independence or isolation of one user from the others. DB2 offers four degrees of isolation, ranging from very isolated to no isolation:

- *Repeatable Read* keeps a lock on all rows accessed by the application program since the last commit point and holds these locks until the next commit point. If the application program reads the same row again, the values will not have changed. The effect of this isolation level is that one application program can prevent other application programs or users from changing tables. As a result, overall concurrency may decrease.

- *Read Stability* keeps a lock on all qualifying rows accessed by the application program until the unit of work is complete. Changes made by other applications can't be read until the changes are committed by those applications. If an application issues the same query more than once, it may be able to read the new or changed rows.

- *Cursor Stability* holds a row lock only while the cursor is positioned on that row. When the cursor moves to another row, the lock is released. If the data is changed, however, the lock must be held until the data is committed. Cursor stability applies only to read data. All changed data remains locked until a COMMIT or ROLLBACK is processed.

- *Uncommitted Read* allows you to view rows without waiting for locks. It applies only to read-only and SELECT statements. For other operations, it performs the same way as cursor stability. An application program using this isolation level reads and returns all rows, even if they contain uncommitted changes made by other application programs. Because this isolation level doesn't wait for concurrency locks, overall performance may increase.

The isolation level is specified at precompile time or when an application is bound to the database. If no isolation level is specified, the default of cursor stability is used. To see the isolation level that is used for a package, select the package folder in the object tree in the Control Center. The right panel provides details on the package, including the isolation level. Figure 14.1 shows the isolation levels set for the packages in the SAMPLE database.

FIGURE 14.1

Isolation level used by packages.

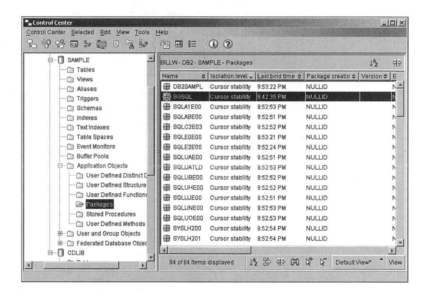

The first command has the option `isolation cs`, and the second has `isolation ur`. These are bind commands that set the isolation levels for the packages. The first command sets the isolation level for the package to cursor stability; the second sets the isolation level for the package to uncommitted read.

Row and Table Locking

Concurrent processing means that multiple processes or applications can access the same database at the same time. DB2 uses *locking* to maintain data integrity during concurrent processing. Locking guarantees that a transaction maintains control over a database row until it has finished and prevents another application from changing a row before the ongoing change is complete.

14

DB2 Universal Database provides *table-level* and *row-level locking*. Row-level locking provides finer granularity and better concurrency support. If extensive changes are required to the database, you may want to avoid contention by using the LOCK TABLE statement in an application instead, to lock the entire table until the transaction is committed or rolled back. Figure 14.2 summarizes the two lock-level methods.

FIGURE 14.2

Row-level and table-level locking.

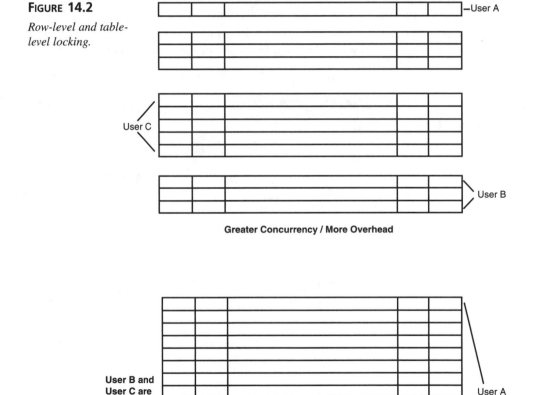

Tables and rows can be locked in share or exclusive mode. If share mode is chosen, other applications can retrieve data as read-only.

DB2 locks a single row as it is accessed, meaning that only the rows being updated, inserted, deleted, or read (unless the isolation level is cursor stability or uncommitted read) are locked. These rows remain locked until the transaction is committed or rolled back. If concurrency is less of a consideration, you can avoid the overhead cost of row-level locking by using the LOCK TABLE statement to lock an entire table. The lock isn't released until the transaction is committed or rolled back.

When the number of locks issued exceeds the capacity specified in the database configuration file, a *lock escalation* condition occurs. During a lock escalation, locks are freed by converting locks on rows of a table into one lock on a table. This is repeated until enough locks are freed by one or more processes to meet the capacity specified in the database configuration file.

DB2 Universal Database uses isolation levels to determine the basic locking scheme for cursors in an application. A *cursor* is a SQL mechanism that enables an application to retrieve a set of rows from the database.

A *deadlock* can occur when two or more transactions are waiting for data locked by the other. A *deadlock detector* is periodically activated in the background to check the locks now in the system to determine whether there's a deadlock situation. If there is, the detector selects a transaction involved in the deadlock and stops it. This transaction will be rolled back, and the other transactions will be able to proceed. The frequency of the deadlock detector activity is controlled by a parameter in the Database Configuration file.

You also can choose to have locks *time out*. If locks haven't been released in the time specified in the timeout interval configuration parameter, the waiting application will time out, and a failure return code will be passed to the application or user.

General Concurrency Recommendations

In general, design applications to minimize the amount of data locked as well as to minimize the duration of the locks. Additional concurrency guidelines include

- COMMIT transactions frequently to promote concurrent access of data by several users, assuming that the unit of work is completed or the data is consistent in the database. For example, for a transaction that withdraws funds from one account and deposits them into another, the COMMIT would not be issued until after the deposit has been completed.

- Monitor the memory allocated to locks (determined by LOCKLIST and MAXLOCKS configuration parameters). If lock escalations occur frequently, increase the values for these configuration parameters.

14

- Consider using a TABLE-level LOCKSIZE for read-only tables.
- Close cursors to release the locks that they hold. You can close a cursor using the CLOSE CURSOR statement that includes the WITH RELEASE statement.

Index Considerations

An index is a table's key value. It provides pointers to the rows in the table, which allows more efficient access by creating a direct path to the data. An index optimizes data retrieval without performing a lengthy sequential search—that is, you can avoid having the entire table scanned when data is queried. An index does not have to be defined for a database table, but it can improve system performance by establishing a high-speed path to frequently accessed information.

You do not decide when an index should be used to improve performance; DB2 makes this decision based on the available table and index information. However, you play an important role in the process by defining keys that create the necessary indexes. It is also important for you to collect statistics on your indexes when you create them and on an ongoing basis.

TIP

> The best index on a table is one that uses high-speed disks, is highly clustered, and is made up of only a few narrow columns.

DB2 provides an Index Wizard to guide you through the creation of an index. The Design Advisor also can be used to find the best indexes for a query or set of queries for an application.

Although indexes typically increase query performance, avoid sorts, and enforce integrity constraints, there are costs for creating indexes. Such costs can include additional disk space, slower INSERT or DELETE operations, because of the updating of the index key that would be required, and slower load operations due to potential rebuilding or appending of data to existing indexes.

General Index Recommendations

Although indexes can improve performance, overhead is involved in maintaining the indexes as well. Create indexes only on those columns you think the application will require. Use the Explain tools to see whether the query is utilizing any given index. Here are some additional guidelines with respect to index usage:

- Use unique or primary indexes where possible to avoid unnecessary sorting by DB2.

- Use a clustered index to improve performance of query applications that retrieve multiple records in index order.

- Consider using multidimensional clustering for query applications that need to support queries requiring various fields in index order.

- Consider creating an index on columns referenced in the joining of tables.

- If you create a multicolumn index, in general, select the first column that is most often referenced by an equal (=) predicate to improve index performance.

Complex Query Application Considerations

DB2 has a number of features that can be used to improve the performance of query applications. For larger databases or more complex query applications, consider using the following:

- Multidimensional clustering—Enables the administrator to define multiple columns that require data to be in a clustering sequence. This feature can also be used to enhance transaction-based applications as well.

- Materialized Query Table (MQT)—A table that can be defined to store a precomputed resultset. No changes are required to existing applications; DB2 can automatically redirect any given query to take advantage of an existing MQT.

Summary

In this lesson, you learned that performance of an application depends on system and database resources. System resources include processing power, memory, and disk. The application can directly impact performance by how it is written to manage concurrency. Database parameters also have to be tuned properly to maximize the use of the available system resources.

When tuning the system, change one parameter at a time: Do not change more than one performance tuning parameter at a time. Even if you are sure that all the changes will be beneficial, you will have no way of evaluating how much each change contributed. You also cannot effectively judge the trade-off you have made by changing more than one parameter at a time. Every time you adjust a parameter to improve one area, you almost always affect at least one other area that you may not have considered. Changing only one at a time allows you to have a benchmark to evaluate whether the change does what you want.

14

What Comes Next?

Day 15, "Using System Administration Tools," will review some useful utilities to help you manage and maintain your database environment.

Q&A

Q What are some of the more important memory resources to tune?

A The buffer pool is probably the most important memory resource to tune. Other important memory parameters include SORTHEAP, LOCKLIST, PCKCACHESZ, DBHEAP, and CATALOGCACHE_SZ.

Q What does prefetching data to the buffer pool mean?

A *Prefetching* pages means that one or more pages are retrieved from disk in the expectation that they will be required by an application. Prefetching index and data pages into the buffer pool can help improve performance by reducing the I/O wait time. In addition, parallel I/O enhances prefetching efficiency.

Q What's a requirement for using table spaces to separate different types of data?

A The two types of table spaces are database managed space (DMS) or system managed space (SMS). If you want to separate different types of data, you must use DMS table spaces. You may want to separate indexes or LOB data into separate table spaces to improve the performance.

Q What are the four degrees of isolation?

A DB2 provides Repeatable Read, Read Stability, Cursor Stability, and Uncommitted Read as ways to control how locks are handled when multiple concurrent users access the same data.

Repeatable Read allows you to lock the rows you're accessing until you commit your changes. This prevents all other users from changing the data in the rows you're accessing until your changes are completed.

Read Stability also locks the data that you're accessing until you complete your changes but allows other applications to change rows that might affect the result table that you create.

Cursor Stability locks the row you're accessing while the cursor is positioned on the row. The lock remains in effect until the next row is fetched or changes are committed.

Uncommitted Read allows an application to access uncommitted changes of other transactions. The application also doesn't lock other applications out of the row it's reading unless the other application attempts to drop or alter the row.

Q **What are some ways to improve performance if I have a large amount of network traffic?**

A Stored procedures can reduce the amount of network traffic. A stored procedure allows an application running on a client to call a procedure stored on the database server. The server executes and accesses the database locally and returns information to the client application.

Row blocking allows a group of rows to be returned from the database in response to a FETCH operation. Without row blocking, each row is transmitted separately.

You can use compound SQL to group several SQL statements in a single executable block. Having a group of statements reduces the number of requests that have to be transmitted across the network.

Workshop

The purpose of the Workshop is to allow you to test your knowledge of the material covered in the lesson. See whether you can successfully answer the questions in the quiz and complete the exercise before you continue with the next lesson. The answers appear in Appendix B, "Answers to Quiz Questions and Exercises."

Quiz

1. When would you use table locking versus row locking?
2. What's a deadlock? How can you break out of a deadlock situation?
3. How can you ensure that your catalog statistics are up-to-date? Why is this important?
4. When should you use the highest level of optimization?

Exercise

1. Today you learned some of the important system and DB2 resources that affect application performance. For this exercise, familiarize yourself with the database parameters that were reviewed and change these parameters to see what effect they have on performance for a given application.

14

WEEK 3

At a Glance

During Week 3, you learn how to use tools to help you administer your databases; back up and recover data; and export, import, load, and replicate data. You also learn how to ensure that you are getting the best performance from your system, and diagnose problems that you may encounter. Here's a day-by-day summary of Week 3:

- Day 15, "Using System Administration Tools"

  This lesson introduces tools such as the Task Center and Journal.

- Day 16, "Recovery Concepts"

  This lesson teaches the very important topic of producing a backup-and-recovery plan for your data.

- Day 17, "Moving Data"

  During this lesson you learn how to export data from a DB2 table, and import and load data into a DB2 table.

- Day 18, "Replicating Data"

  The topic of replicating data from one table to another is covered in this lesson.

- Day 19, "Database Monitoring Tools"

  Performance aids such as Visual Explain, Snapshot Monitor, and Event Monitor are introduced. You learn how you can use these aids to explore the performance of your databases and applications.

- Day 20, "Tuning DB2 Universal Database Performance"

15

16

17

18

19

20

21

During this lesson you learn how to customize configuration parameters to ensure your system is finely tuned for your specific needs.

- Day 21, "Diagnosing Problems"

This lesson gives you guidance on solving problems that you may encounter.

DAY 15

Using System Administration Tools

Today you learn how to use several DB2 tools that simplify administering your database. The following tools will be examined:

- Task Center, which enables you to create and run scripts. You can run scripts immediately or schedule them to run later.
- Journal, which enables you to view the results of the scripts you have run, and keeps history, alert, and message logs that you can review.
- Tools Setting dialog box, which enables you to customize the various DB2 tools.
- License Center, which enables you to check the license information, statistics, registered users, and current users for each of the installed products.

Today you also learn how to perform other important system administration tasks that may not be performed on a day-to-day basis. These tasks include creating indexes on your tables, viewing the directories that store configuration information, and managing a list of contact names.

Using the Task Center

Use the Task Center to schedule tasks, run tasks, and notify people about the status of completed tasks. *Tasks* are actions performed by the types of scripts shown in Table 15.1.

TABLE 15.1   Scripts Used by DB2

Type of Script	Content
DB2 command script	The script contains DB2 commands.
OS command system script	The script contains operating system commands.
Grouping task	The script is part of a group of tasks. This setup enables you to initiate other scripts based on the success of other scripts in the group.

Creating a DB2 Command Script

A mini-application known as a *script* is a set of one or more commands created through the Command Center or the Task Center. Storing commonly used queries and DB2 commands in DB2 command scripts is a way for you to simplify and organize your work. You create groupings for multiple tasks that can be scheduled to run regularly or to be run if another task succeeds or fails. You can have the results emailed to you or to someone else.

Follow these steps to create a DB2 command script:

1. Start the Task Center. Click the Task Center icon on the toolbar of the Control Center, or choose Start|Programs|IBM DB2|General Administration Tools|Task Center.

2. In the Scheduler System box, select a system name that the Task Center will use to determine when to start tasks.

3. Create a task for each script that you want to run. Choose Task|New from the menu. The Task Properties dialog box opens. Figure 15.1 shows the Task page with all the values entered.

4. In the Name field, type a descriptive name for your script. This example uses `CDLIB Report A`.

5. In the Type field, choose the type of task to create. For this example, choose DB2 Command Script.

6. In the Description field, type a description of the purpose of the script.

7. In the Task Category field, click the button on the right side of the field to open the Select Task Categories window. Here, you can organize your list of tasks. The first

time you use this feature, the dialog box will be empty and you will need to create new categories. In the New Task Category field, enter a useful task category name such as Backups. Click the arrow button to move the category into the Selected Task Categories box (see Figure 15.2). Click OK to return to the Task page and continue.

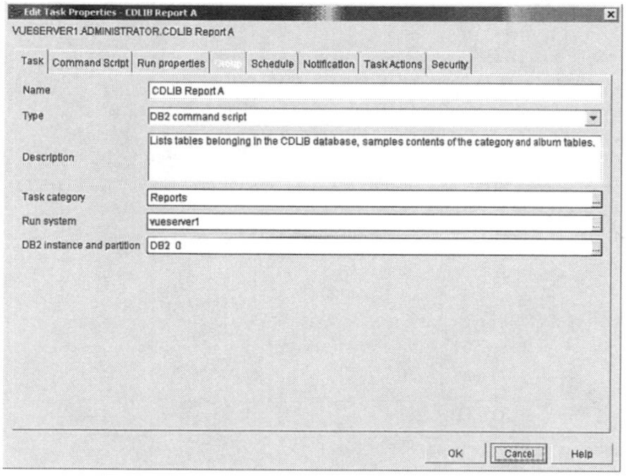

FIGURE 15.1

The Task Center's Task Properties dialog box: Task page completed.

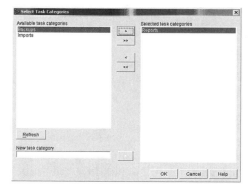

FIGURE 15.2

The Task Center's Select Task Categories window.

8. In the Run System field, select the system on which the task will run. A default system is provided. If you want to change the default, click the button on the right side of the field to open the Select Run System window. From this dialog box, you can choose a system or search for a system (see Figure 15.3). Click OK to return to the Task page and continue.

9. In the DB2 Instance and Partition field, select an instance name to associate with the command script. Click the button on the right side of the field to open the

Select Partitions window. Choose an instance by clicking the arrow next to the instance field. In the Available Partitions box, click the partition to which you want to associate the script and click the right arrow to move the selection into the Selected Partitions box (see Figure 15.4). Click OK to continue.

FIGURE 15.3

The Task Center's Select Run System window.

FIGURE 15.4

The Task Center's Select Partitions window.

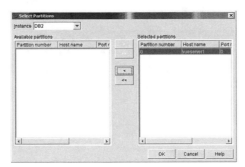

10. Click the Command Script tab of the Task Properties dialog box. Type in the commands that will make up your script. For example, to connect to the CDLIB database, list the tables of the database, and view the contents of the CATEGORY and ALBUM tables, enter the following commands:

```
connect to cdlib;
list tables;
select * from category;
select * from album;
```

11. Ensure the termination character is set to a semicolon (;) to match the commands. Enter a working directory path where the script results can be saved (see Figure 15.5).

FIGURE 15.5

The Task Center's Command Script window.

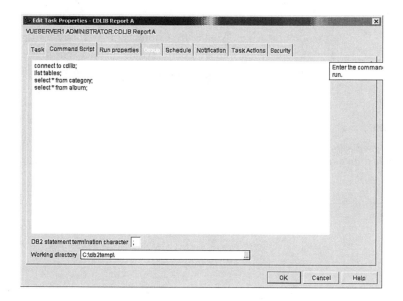

12. On the Run Properties page, shown in Figure 15.6, you can select a success code set or create a success code set to specify conditions required for the task to be successful. If you do not specify a success code set, only a return code of 0 is considered successful. For purposes of this example, keep the default settings.

Click the Stop Execution at the First Return Code That Is a Failure check box to stop the task immediately after receiving a failing return code.

FIGURE 15.6

The Task Center's Run Properties page.

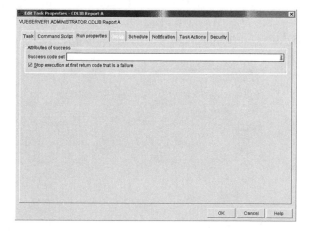

13. On the Schedule page, you provide scheduling options. Setting a schedule is covered in the next section.

14. On the Notification page, you can have the results of the script emailed to you or someone else. (See "Managing Contacts" later today for details on adding people to your contact list.) Or you can have the results sent to the Journal as a message. Click the Notification Type and select Create Journal Message, as shown in Figure 15.7. Click Add to move the option to the List of Notifications.

FIGURE 15.7

The Task Center's Notification page.

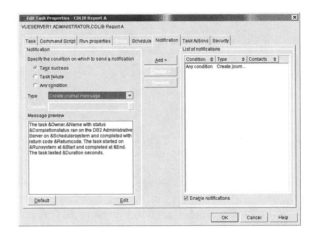

15. On the Task Actions page, you can specify actions that can take place after this script succeeds, fails, or in either case. The actions you can specify include Run Task, Enable Schedule Of, Disable Schedule Of, or Delete This Task. The next section shows you how to set up such actions. Leave this one at its default setting.

16. On the Security page (see Figure 15.8), you can set the Read, Run, and Write privileges for each user. We have indicated that users ADMINISTRATOR and DB2ADMIN can read, run, or write to this script.

FIGURE 15.8

The Task Center's Security page.

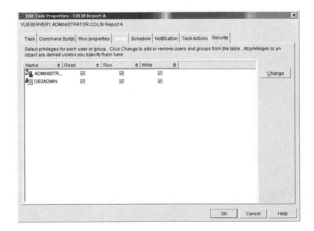

15

17. Click OK to save the script and all its settings. If you need to modify anything, right-click the script and select Edit Task Properties to reopen the notebook.

Importing Scripts

To create a new command script from an existing file, follow these steps:

1. Choose Task|Import from the menu.

2. In the File Browser window, shown in Figure 15.9, choose the IMPORT.SCR file on the CD that accompanies this book that creates the CDLIB database and its tables. Click OK to open the New Task notebook.

FIGURE 15.9

The Task Center's File Browser window.

3. In the Command Script window, make any required changes to the script such as the drive where the .ixf files are located (see Figure 15.10). (Check the CD-ROM that accompanies this book or the directory where you copied them.)

FIGURE 15.10

The Command Script window.

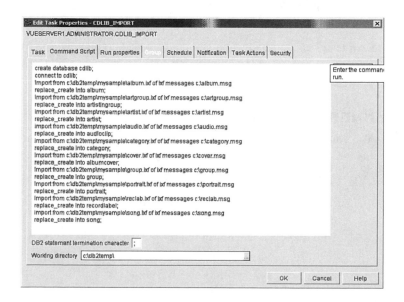

4. On the Task page, enter a new script name, script description, working directory, task category, run system, and instance, and specify that the new script will contain DB2 commands.

5. On the Task Actions page, select the Task Success radio button to indicate that if this script succeeds, the script called CDLIB ReportA that you created in the previous section should be run (see Figure 15.11). Click Add to include this action in the List of Task Actions.

FIGURE 15.11

The Task Center's Task Actions window.

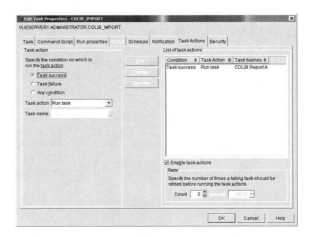

6. Keep the default values for the Run Properties, Schedule, Notification, and Security pages. Click OK to save the script.

Scripts are also created when you create a backup plan by using the Backup Wizard. You can't modify these scripts through the Task Center, but you can run them from the Task Center.

Running Scripts

You can run a saved script or schedule to run it at a later time or date. To immediately run a saved command script, follow these steps:

1. Right-click the CDLIB_IMPORT script and select Run Now from the pop-up menu.

2. In the Run Now window, choose Initiate Show Progress in the Run Options section to see when the script is finished (see Figure 15.12). Type a valid user ID and password and click OK to run the script.

15

3. The Show Progress window opens to show the script as Queued or Running (see Figure 15.13). Set the Refresh Options box to change the frequency that the screen is refreshed. This example is set to 10 seconds. Close the Show Progress window when the script is finished. The Last Success column of the Task Center window shows the status of the script that just ran.

FIGURE 15.12

The Task Center's Run Now window.

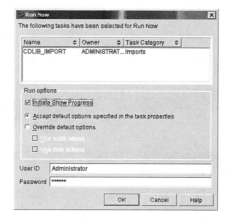

FIGURE 15.13

The Task Center's Show Progress window.

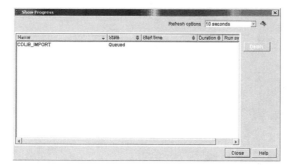

4. To see the results of the script, right-click the script name and choose Show Results from the pop-up menu. The Show Results window allows you to see the time the script started and finished, duration, return code, completion state, and output (see Figure 15.14).

5. Because the Task Actions page indicates that the CDLIB Report A script should be run if the CDLIB_Import script completes successfully, you should see that both scripts ran successfully, as shown in Figure 15.15. Click Close.

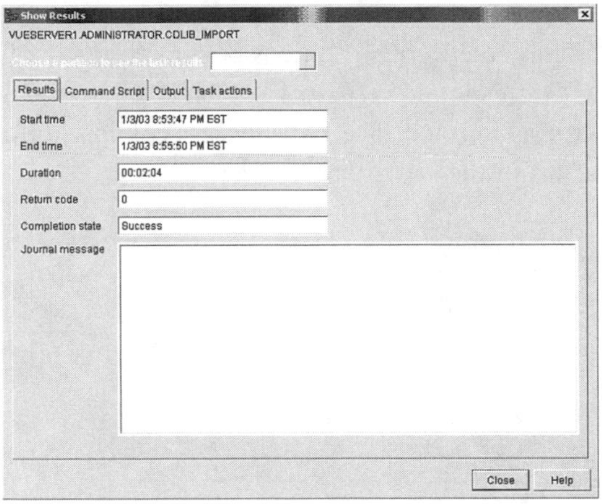

FIGURE 15.14

*The Task Center's
Show Results window.*

FIGURE 15.15

*The Task Center main
window.*

Scheduling Scripts

To schedule a saved script to run every Sunday and Wednesday at 5:30 p.m. for the next
year, for example, follow these steps:

1. Right-click the saved script that you want to schedule to run and select Schedule|
   Change from the pop-up menu.

2. On the Schedule page, enter a Start Date and Start Time; then determine the frequency at which the script will run (see Figure 15.16).

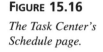

FIGURE 15.16

The Task Center's Schedule page.

15

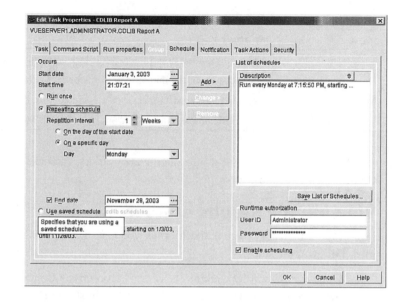

3. In the Occurs section, select one of the following radio buttons to indicate how often the job is to run:

   - Run Once—Choose this option to have the script run as a single job.

   - Repeating Schedule—Choose this option to schedule the job to occur every few hours, weeks, or months. Specify the frequency in the appropriate fields.

   For this example, we chose to have the script run every Monday at 7:30 p.m. until the end of November.

4. In the Runtime Authorization section, type a valid user ID and password.

5. Click Add to have the schedule options added to the List of Schedules window.

6. Click the Save List of Schedules option to give the new schedule a name and description.

7. Ensure Enabled Scheduling is checked. Click OK to have the job scheduled. A job ID is assigned to the job.

The state for this task in the Task Center will now show Pending.

Using the Journal

You use the Journal to view all historical information generated within the Control Center and its components. The Journal maintains several views in an attempt to better organize its data. The views include those shown in Table 15.2.

TABLE 15.2   Journal Views to DB2 Historical Data

View	Enables You To
Task History	View information about the DB2 tasks run on your computer.
Database History	See a history of the database backups performed on your computer.
Messages	See a list of all recent messages associated with DB2.
Notification Log	See notifications generated through the Health Monitor.

The Journal displays historical information about tasks, database actions and operations, Control Center actions, messages, and alerts.

Viewing the Results of a Job

From the Task History page in the Journal, you can view pending, running, and executed jobs. Follow these steps:

1. Open the Journal by clicking the Journal icon on the Control Center's toolbar, or by choosing Start|Programs|IBM DB2|Administration Tools|Journal.

2. From the Scheduler System drop-down box, select the system on which to store and run the command scripts. The default is your local system.

3. To see all tasks organized by name, click View|Saved Views|Overview by Name from the menu (see Figure 15.17). You can also set to view all the columns, events that ended in error, or recent events.

FIGURE 15.17

The Journal's Task History page showing tasks organized by name.

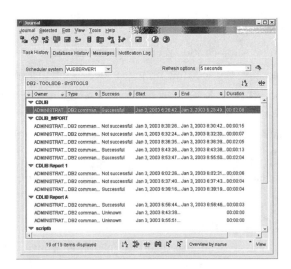

4. To work with any of the tasks listed here, right-click the task and choose one of the following functions:

- Show Results—Opens the Show Results window allowing you to see the results, command script, output, and task actions of the selected task.

- Show in Task Center—Opens the Task Center so that you can view the selected task.

- Edit Task Details—Opens the Edit Task Properties notebook for the selected task.

- Show Statistics—Shows detailed information on the number of times the script has been run and the results as well as the length of time to execute.

- Remove—Removes the task from the list in the Journal.

Use the Journal's Database History page to restore databases, table spaces, or the recovery history of a selected database. You can also view table space information from this page. Figure 15.18 shows an example of the Database History page in the Journal.

FIGURE 15.18

The Journal's Database History page.

NOTE   No entries for a database means that you haven't yet backed up the data in your database. Entries are posted in this log as soon as a backup is performed.

On the Database History page, choose a system, instance, and database for which you want to view the history. With the entries displayed, you can do the following:

- To restore a selected database from a backup image that has been made from this database, right-click it and select Restore from the pop-up menu. The Restore Database Wizard opens. See Day 16, "Recovery Concepts," for information on using this wizard.

- To see a list of table spaces associated with this database, right-click it and select View Table Spaces from the pop-up menu. The View Table Spaces window opens.

On the Journal's Messages page, you can see the messages that are related to your system (see Figure 15.19). Each message (error, warning, or informational) that occurs while operating DB2 is logged in this list. The list indicates the severity of the message, the date and time the message occurred, the message identifier, and the message text.

FIGURE 15.19

*The Journal's
Messages page.*

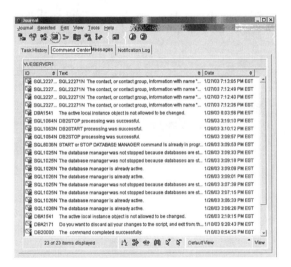

To prune this log when it becomes full, right-click one or more entries and select Remove to remove only the highlighted messages, or select Remove All to remove all entries in the log.

On the Journal's Notification Log page, you can select to see all notifications or only those that were generated through the Health Monitor. Figure 15.20 shows a list of the last 50 messages.

Select an instance for which you want to view the messages by using the drop-down box in the Instance field. In the Notification Log Filter, you can choose to see the Health Monitor notifications only or all notifications. You can also select the number of notifications that should appear in the screen. The default shows 50 messages.

FIGURE 15.20

The Journal's Notification Log page.

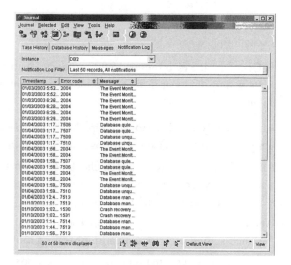

To see the details of a message, right-click the message and choose Show Details. Figure 15.21 shows an example of a message that you might see.

FIGURE 15.21

The Journal's Details of a Notification message.

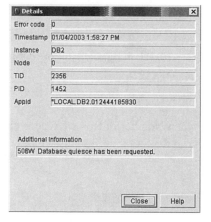

Customizing Tools Settings

You use the Tools Settings notebook to customize settings and set properties for the following:

- Administration tools
- Replication tasks
- OS/390 and z/OS Control Center utility execution options

- Health Center Notification
- The default scheduling schema

On the notebook's General page (see Figure 15.22), you can enable hover help and infopops, automatically start the local instance, define a statement termination character, and set filtering defaults:

- Select the Automatically Display Hover Help check box to enable the help that appears when you put your mouse pointer over an icon in the administration tools.
- Select the Automatically Display Infopops check box to enable the help that appears when you put your mouse pointer over a field or control in the wizards or in windows and notebooks in the administration tools.
- Select the Automatically Start Local DB2 on Tools Startup check box to have the local DB2 instance started each time an administration tool is started.
- Select the Use Statement Termination Character check box to define a character to use at the end of statements in command scripts in the Command Center and Task Center. If you select this check box, the semicolon (;) is used by default to end statements. Optionally, you can define a different character by typing it in the text box.

NOTE

You can't specify the backslash (\) character to continue statements in command scripts.

- Select the Set Filtering When Number of Rows Exceeds check box to define the number of rows to appear in the Sample Contents window and the Command Center window.

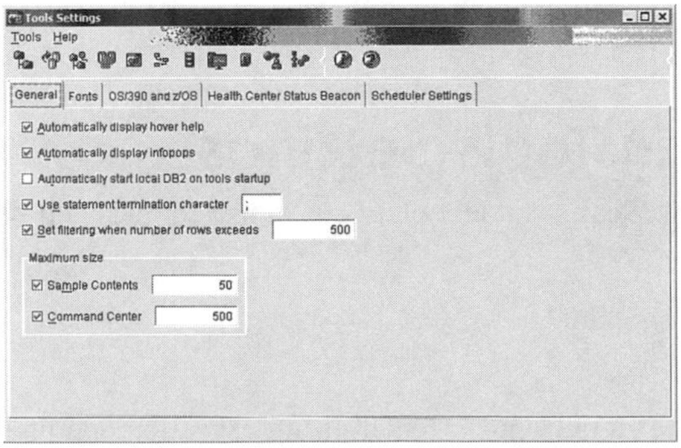

FIGURE 15.22

The Tools Settings notebook's General page.

On the notebook's Fonts page, you can specify the font's type, size, and color for menus and text items (see Figure 15.23).

FIGURE 15.23

The Tools Settings notebook's Fonts page.

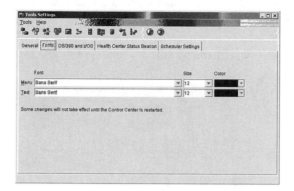

On the notebook's OS/390 and z/OS page, you can make several utility selection options (see Figure 15.24). This topic is beyond the scope of this book.

FIGURE 15.24

The Tools Settings notebook's OS/390 and z/OS page.

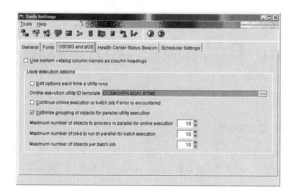

On the notebook's Health Center Status Beacon page, you can select where notifications will take place: through a pop-up menu or through the status line (see Figure 15.25).

FIGURE 15.25

The Tools Settings notebook's Health Center Status Beacon page.

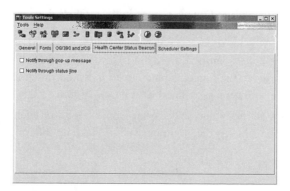

On the notebook's Scheduler Settings page, you can choose whether the scheduling and storage of tasks is to be done locally or on a central system (see Figure 15.26). If you select to have the scheduling centralized, select the centralized system from the drop-down list. If you need to enable another scheduler, select a system and click Create New to open a window where you can create a database for the DB2 Tools Catalog on a cataloged system. If the system you want is not cataloged, you must catalog it first.

FIGURE 15.26

The Tools Settings notebook's Scheduler Settings page.

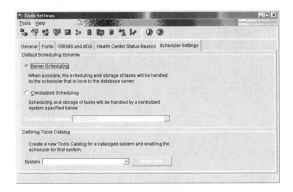

Making Your Database More Useful

There are several ways you can make your databases more useful. One way is to create an index on your table that can improve the performance of selecting data from the table.

Creating Indexes

An *index* is the key value of a table. It provides pointers to the rows in the table, which allows more efficient access by creating a direct path to the data. Also, you can define index keys as unique, thereby preventing duplicate rows from occurring within the table.

An index is created when you create a unique key, a primary key, or a foreign key. You can create an index at the time the table is defined or at any time afterward.

To view the indexes defined on each table in the CDLIB database, follow these steps:

1. Start the Control Center.

2. Expand the objects until you see the Indexes folder. Click that folder to see a list of the indexes in the contents pane. Each index has a name, schema, table schema, table name, and type associated with it (see Figure 15.27).

3. Right-click an index and select Alter from the pop-up menu. In the Alter Index window, you can see the columns used to make up the index, but you can modify

only the comment (see Figure 15.28). If you need to make changes, you must drop
the existing index and re-create it.

FIGURE 15.27

*The Control Center
showing indexes asso-
ciated with the CDLIB
database.*

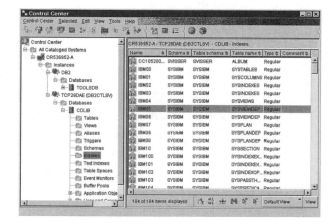

FIGURE 15.28

*The Alter Index win-
dow.*

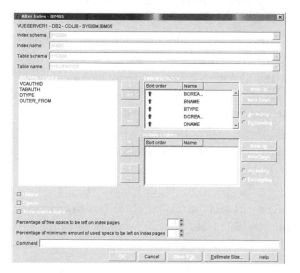

The effectiveness of defining an index depends largely on the type of table access
required. An index is most effective if it matches the way you access your data. Although
the creation of an index usually helps improve performance on large or frequently
updated databases, each index must be kept up to date. Therefore, each insert, update,
and delete request against a table requires an update for the index, if any of the table
columns affected are included in the index definition. Such updates may degrade performance. Thus, you should create indexes carefully, with an understanding of how the data

is stored and used. The simplest recommendation is that you define a key on the table columns you use the most.

To create a new index, follow these steps:

1. Start the Control Center.
2. Expand the objects until you see the Indexes folder.
3. Right-click the Indexes folder and select Create from the pop-up menu.
4. In the Create Index window, complete the following information:

   • Index Schema— From this drop-down list, select a schema. The default schema is the username that you used to log in; use a schema appropriate for your system.

   • Index Name— a name for the index you're creating. The name can be up to 18 characters long. This name must be unique within the index's schema; no other object in the schema can have the same name.

   • Table Schema— From this drop-down list, select the schema that contains the table for which you're creating an index.

   • Table Name— From this drop-down list, select the table in this schema for which you're creating an index.

   • Selected Columns— Select the column or columns that you want to define as part of the index key. Click the arrow to move the column from the Available Columns list box to the Selected Columns list box.

   • Include Columns— Use the Include Columns list box to select additional columns to be included in the index, but not as part of the unique index key. The Include Columns list box is activated when you select the Unique check box.

   • Unique— Select the Unique check box to create a unique index, which prevents the table from containing two or more rows with the same value of the index key. If the table contains rows with duplicate key values, the index is not created.

   • Cluster— Select the Cluster check box to specify that the index is the clustering index of the table. A clustering index cannot be created on a table that is defined to use append mode.

   • Allow Reverse Scans— Select this check box if you want to support both forward and reverse scans of the index.

   • Percentage of Free Space to Be Left on Index Pages— Select a value in this field to specify what percentage of each index page to leave as free space when building an index.

- Percentage of Minimum Amount of Used Space to Be Left on Index Pages—Select a value in this field to specify the threshold for the minimum percentage of space used on an index leaf page.

5. Click OK to create the index.

Working with Directories

DB2 uses three directories to record information for accessing databases. These directories are updated through the normal course of using DB2. You can view the contents of the directories as follows:

- To see the contents of the local database directory or the system database directory, issue the `list database directory` command in the Command Center, as shown in Figure 15.29. The local database and system database directories identify the name, alias, and physical location of each cataloged database.

FIGURE 15.29

The Command Center showing the contents of a local database directory.

- To see the contents of the DCS directory, issue the `list dcs directory` command in the Command Center. The DCS directory contains an entry for each distributed relational database that your system can access. You'll have only a DCS directory if you have DB2 Connect installed.
- To see the contents of the node directory, issue the `list node directory` command in the Command Center. The node directory contains communication information for the client to connect to a remote database server.

Managing Contacts

DB2 allows you to keep an address book of people who can be contacted when tasks are complete. You can set up an email address or pager information for each person. Groups can be created to allow you to send information to more than one person at once. During the installation, you were asked to enter a contact name. If you did, then you have at least one person in the contact list. You can manage the contact list as follows:

1. From the Control Center, click the Contact List icon to open the Contacts window.

2. Click the Add Contact button to add a new name to the list. You are asked to provide a name, email address or pager information, and a description. Click OK to add the name.

3. Click the Add Group button to create a group name. You are asked to provide a name for the group and a description. You can then choose from the list of individuals who will be part of this group. Click OK to add the group.

4. Continue to add groups and individuals as needed. Figure 15.30 shows groups called Managers, DBAs, Programmers, and Users as well as two individuals.

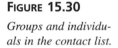

FIGURE 15.30

Groups and individuals in the contact list.

Managing Licenses

The License Center allows you to display the license status and usage information for the DB2 products installed on your computer. If you installed the DB2 product that is included with this book, the License Center will show that you have a short-term license that will expire on the date shown.

To add a license, use the following steps:

1. Open the License Center by clicking the License Center icon on the Control Center.

2. In the System Name field, select the system for which you want to add a new license.

3. Select License|Add to open the Add License window.

4. Select the From a File radio button to add the information from a .lic file. Select the Manual radio button to enter the license information manually.

5. If you chose to add the license from a file, select the file and click Apply to add the license.

6. If you chose to add the license manually, type the product name and password that appear on your license certificate. Click Apply to add the license. Figure 15.31 shows an example of the License page of the License Center.

FIGURE 15.31

The License page of the License Center.

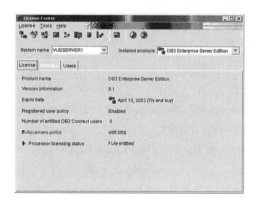

The User page of the License Center allows you to maintain a list of registered users.

The Statistics page of the License Center allows you to use the License Center to configure your system for license monitoring.

Summary

Today you saw that the Task Center allows you to work with saved scripts. A script is a set of one or more commands and is created through the Command Center or the Task Center.

The Journal allows you to view historical information about any scheduled, running, or completed jobs. You also can view the various logs where DB2 stores information.

You can create many objects to make your database more useful. These objects include indexes, contact lists, and license usage statistics.

What Comes Next?

On Day 16, you learn how to develop a backup and recovery plan to protect the data in your database.

Q&A

Q Can I create a script that contains operating system and DB2 commands?

A You can create scripts that contain only operating system commands and scripts that contain only DB2 commands. You can't combine both types of commands in a single script, however. When you're creating a script, be sure to select which type of commands your script contains.

Q Can a script contain scheduling information?

A A script can contain only commands. A script can, however, be scheduled to run at a specified date and time. If you do schedule to run a script, the scheduling information is stored in the properties of the task. Use the Task Center to run the script now, stop the script from running, schedule the script to run, and view the results of the script. If you decide that you need to make changes to the saved script, you can edit it from the Task Center.

Q What's the purpose of the recovery history log?

A The recovery history log contains information about when a backup or recovery was performed for a particular database. If you don't have information in the log, you haven't yet performed a backup or recovery on the data in the database. If you've performed a backup, this information is contained in the log. You can select to restore a backup image while viewing the recovery history log information. This is also the place where you can view the table spaces (if any) associated with the database.

Workshop

The purpose of the workshop is to allow you to test your knowledge of the material covered in the lesson. See whether you can successfully answer the questions in the quiz and complete the exercises before you continue with the next lesson. Answers to quiz questions are provided in Appendix B.

15

Quiz

1. How do you create an index? Why do you want to create an index?

2. What is a unique index?

3. If you don't see hover help while you're using the DB2 tools, how can you turn on this feature?

4. Can you modify scripts that are created as a result of using the Backup Database Wizard?

5. What's the purpose of creating a grouping task?

6. What are the three different types of directories that DB2 uses to record information for accessing databases?

7. What's the purpose of creating a list of contacts?

8. Where can you see the notifications from the Health Center?

Exercise

The Task Center and Journal were introduced in today's lesson. Together, these tools help simplify many of the tasks you'll need to perform as a database administrator. Try out the many options available in these tools to gain an understanding of how you create scripts and what you can do once a script is saved.

DAY 16

Recovery Concepts

When you have data in your database, you must guard against losing this data. DB2 is equipped with tools to help you back up and recover your data.

One advantage of a database management system over storing data in files, is the backup and recovery procedures that can be used to rebuild the database if it becomes damaged in some way. The rebuilding of the database is called *recovery*, and DB2 supports the following types of recovery:

- Crash recovery—The automatic recovery of the database if a failure occurs before all the updates in a given transaction are completed and committed. For example, if a banking transaction involved withdrawing funds from one account and depositing them into another account, DB2 would either roll back the incomplete transaction or complete the transaction, when the crash occurred. The atomicity of the transaction is preserved, meaning that either the whole transaction is committed to the database, or nothing; partial completion of the transaction would not be allowed.

- Version recovery—The restoring of a previous version of the database, using a backup image.
- Roll-forward recovery—The reapplication of transactions recorded in the database log files after a database or a table space backup image has been restored.

Today you learn the following:

- The different logging methods you can use to protect your data
- How to set up a recurring schedule for your backups
- How to verify that your backups are valid
- How to restore your data in case of a database failure
- How to roll forward the transactions logs you have been keeping if you are using the log archiving

Log Management

One aspect unique to database backups is the necessity of considering the database logs. If a database needs to be restored to a point beyond the last backup (either full or incremental), logs are required to roll the data forward to a point of consistency.

DB2 allocates primary and secondary log files to each database created to support recovery operations. Primary log files establish a fixed, preallocated amount of storage to the recovery log files. Enough disk space for the primary log files must be allocated before the database is connected to. Secondary log files are used when the primary log files become full and are allocated one at a time when required.

There are two ways of configuring logging for a DB2 database:

- Circular logging—(the default) Only full, offline backups of the database are allowed. The database must be offline (inaccessible to users) when a full backup is taken. As the name suggests, circular logging uses a "ring" of online logs to provide recovery from transaction failures and system crashes. The logs are used and retained only to the point of ensuring the integrity of current transactions. Only Crash recovery and Version recovery are supported using this type of logging.
- Archive logging—Supports recoverable databases by archiving logs after they have been written to; that is, log files are not reused. Archive logging is used specifically for roll-forward recovery. Enabling the logretain and/or the userexit database configuration parameter results in archive logging. To archive logs, you can choose to have DB2 leave the log files in the active path and then manually archive them, or you can install a user exit program to automate the archiving. Archived logs are logs that were active but are no longer required for crash recovery.

Log files can be characterized as one of the following:

- Active—The log files written to by DB2 that support crash recovery. These files contain information related to units of work that have not yet been committed (or rolled back).

- Archive—The log files that have been written to by DB2 and are no longer needed to support crash recovery. Online archive log files reside in the active log path directory. Offline archive log files do not reside in the active log path directory. They can be moved manually or by an external storage management product.

16

The Configure Database Logging Wizard allows you to specify which logging scheme you want for each database. This wizard allows you to specify various logging options, including

- Logging type—Allows you to change circular logging (the default) to archive logging. Enabling archive logging then allows you the option to perform online backups, table space backups, and recovery to a point in time.

- Logging size—Allows you to specify the number of log files to allocate and their sizes.

- Logging location—Allows you to specify where you want to place the active logs as well as allows you to select whether you want the logs mirrored. The mirrored option is useful for high-availability environments and are often directed to a different location.

To change the default circular logging to archive logging with the Database Logging Wizard, follow these steps:

1. Start the Control Center. Right-click the database you want to back up and select Configure Database Logging from the pop-up menu.

2. Clear the Circular Logging option by selecting the Archive Logging option (see Figure 16.1). This enables you to perform online backups, perform table space backups, and recover to a point in time. Click Next.

3. Indicate whether you want to manually manage what to do with the archive logs after they have been written or allow a user exit to manage the archive logs. Accept the default, Manual Archive Log File Handling, and click Next (see Figure 16.2).

NOTE

You can develop a *user exit program* to automate log file archiving and retrieval. Sample user exit programs are provided for all supported platforms. When a user exit program is invoked, the database manager passes control to the executable file, db2uext2. The user exit sample programs for

DB2 for Windows operating systems are found in the `sqllib\samples\c` subdirectory. Although the samples provided are coded in C, your user exit program can be written in a different programming language.

FIGURE 16.1

Configuration Database Logging Wizard page.

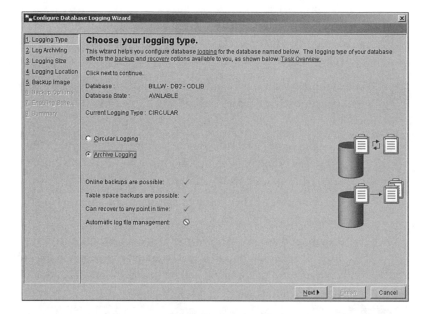

FIGURE 16.2

Log Archiving page.

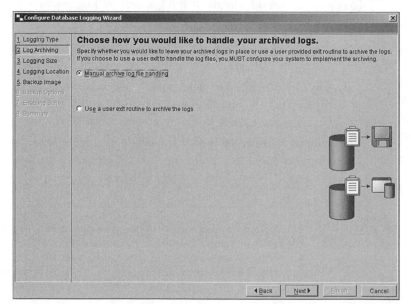

4. On the Logging Size page (see Figure 16.3), the Number of Primary Log Files sets the value for the database configuration `logprimary` parameter. The Number of Secondary Log Files sets the value for the database configuration `logsecondary` parameter. The Size of Each Log File (4K Pages) can range from 4 to 262144, and sets the value for the database configuration `logfilsiz` parameter. Increase the `logfilsiz` value if the database has a large number of updates, deletes, or inserts. If the log is too small, it will fill quickly and will affect system performance. Accept the defaults for this example and click Next.

16

FIGURE 16.3

Logging Size page.

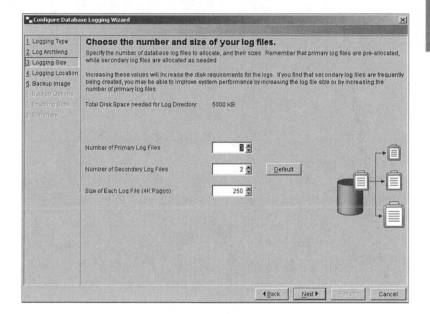

5. The Logging Location page appears (see Figure 16.4). Accept the default for the Active Log Path. You have the option of creating a duplicate active log. This is useful in creating a high-availability environment for your application. Click Next.

6. On the Backup Image page (see Figure 16.5), select a File System to store the backup. In this example, it is `E:\backupdb\`, a directory on a network drive. Click Next.

7. The options page (see Figure 16.6) allows you to select configuration parameters that will influence the performance of the backup operation. Accept the recommended defaults. Click Next.

8. The Scheduling page (see Figure 16.7) allows you to submit the changes to your log configurations immediately or schedule it later. Accept the default value and click Next.

FIGURE 16.4

Logging Location page.

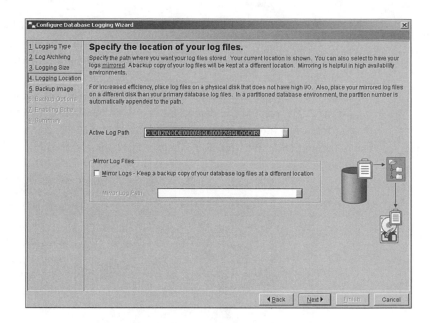

FIGURE 16.5

Backup Image page.

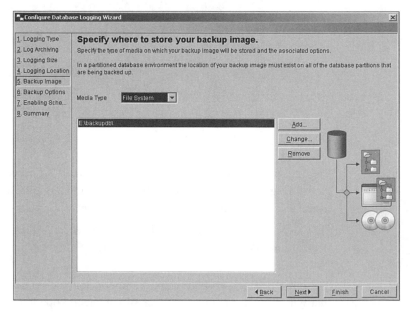

FIGURE 16.6

Backup Options page.

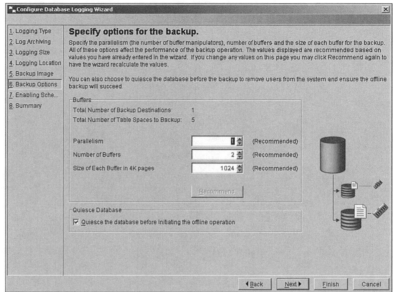

FIGURE 16.7

Scheduling Options page.

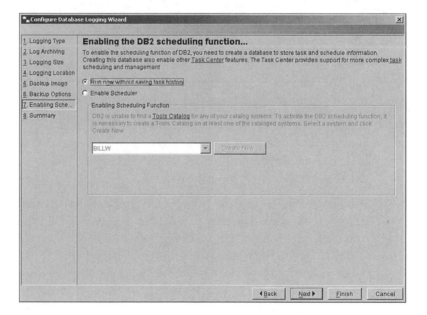

9. The Configure Database Logging Wizard Summary page (see Figure 16.8) summarizes the options you have selected. Click Finish to update your log configurations.

FIGURE 16.8

Summary page.

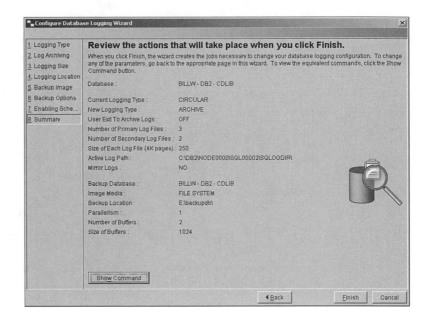

Backing Up Databases

The concept of a database backup is the same as for any other data backup: taking a copy of the data and storing it on a different medium in case of failure or damage to the original. The simplest case of a backup requires shutting down the database to ensure that no further transactions occur and then simply backing it up.

To help you plan for backup and recovery of databases, use the Backup Wizard. It asks you a series of questions, recommends settings, and schedules the backups. It focuses on basic options. To invoke the wizard, right-click on any database in the Control Center and select Backup from the pop-up menu.

Planning for the backup and recovery of your databases is an important topic because the decisions you make now affect your ability to recover your data in the event of a loss. You may encounter media and storage problems, power interruptions, and application failures. So, you will need to back up your database and then rebuild it should it be damaged or corrupted in some way. (Rebuilding the database is called *recovery*. A separate Restore Wizard is available to help with that part of the process.)

DB2 automatically takes care of problems caused by power interruptions. It automatically restarts and returns your database to the state it was in at the time of the last complete transaction. Media and application failures are more severe. The backup plan you create focuses on media failure and application failure.

NOTE | DB2 supports backing up local or remote databases.

Using the Backup Wizard

You should use the Backup Wizard the first time you back up your database. The wizard takes you through the concepts and guides you through what parameters are necessary for the backup operation to proceed.

To back up a database with the Backup Wizard, follow these steps:

1. Start the Control Center.

2. Right-click the database you want to back up and select Backup from the pop-up menu.

3. On the Introduction page of the Backup Wizard (see Figure 16.9), confirm that the name of the database listed is the one you want to create a plan for. The default is to show the database you selected in the previous step. If this is the correct database, click Next; if you want another database instead, choose another database from the Control Center.

FIGURE 16.9

Backup Wizard Introduction page.

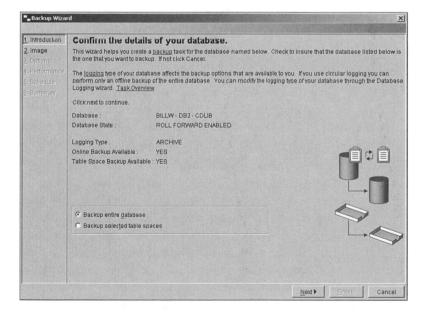

4. DB2 provides a number of choices (File System, Tape, TSM - Tivoli Storage Manager, XBSA a Backup Services API, Vendor DLL for a Windows environment) of where to store the backup image (see Figure 16.10). In this example, a directory on the network will be selected. Choose the File System option and click on the Add button to indicate the directory where the backup will be placed. Click Next to continue.

FIGURE 16.10

Backup Wizard Backup Image page.

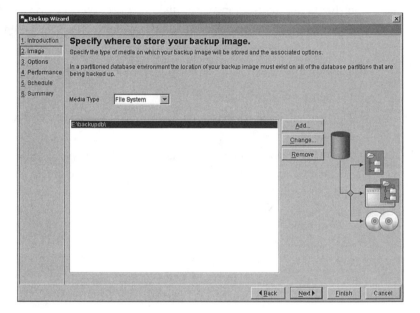

5. On the Backup Options page (see Figure 16.11), decide whether to take a full or incremental backup, as well as whether the backup will be performed online or offline. Choose Full Backup for this example and click Next.

6. On the Backup Performance page (see Figure 16.12), select the number of buffers to be allocated for the backup process. Click Next to continue. On the Restore Data Wizard Performance page, enter the number of buffers to be used for the restore operation. For Parallelism, the default value is 1 and indicates the number of processes or threads spawned during the backup process. For Number of Buffers, the default value is 2 (the valid range is from 1 to 16834). The Size of Each Buffer in 4K pages can range from 8 to 524288; the default value is 1024. The backup buffer size is ideally a multiple of the table space extent size. Accept the defaults on this page and click Next.

FIGURE 16.11

Backup Wizard Options page.

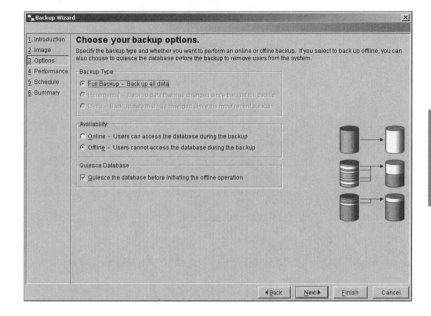

FIGURE 16.12

Performance Options page.

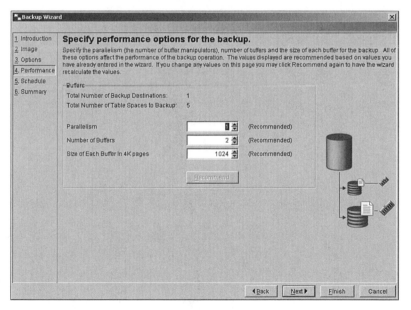

7. On the Backup Scheduling page (see Figure 16.13), you have the option of submitting the backup process now or later by using the Task Center. Keep the defaults for this example and click Next.

FIGURE 16.13

*Backup Wizard
Scheduling page.*

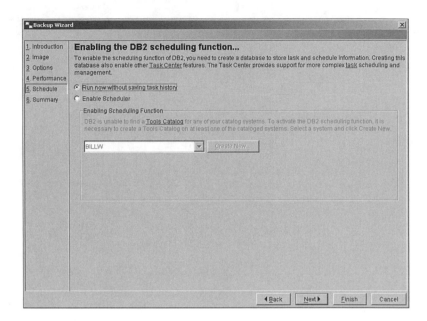

8. The Summary page (see Figure 16.14) reviews the options selected, and the Show Command button lets you see the equivalent SQL command that is produced.

FIGURE 16.14

*Backup Wizard
Summary page.*

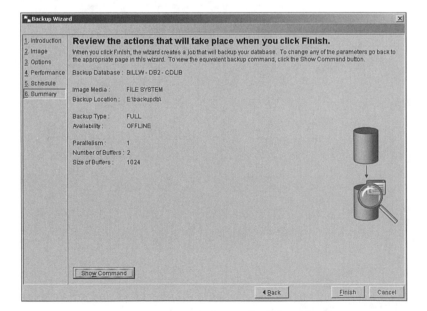

9. Click the Show Command button to display the equivalent SQL command for the actions previously selected (see Figure 16.15). As you gain experience with this operation, you can save the necessary commands and submit these from the Command Line Processor. Click Close to return to the previous panel; then click Finish.

FIGURE 16.15

Backup Wizard Show Command dialog box.

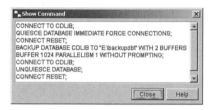

16

When the backup is complete, you will get a message that the data has been backed up successfully. For the complete status of the job, use the Job History page of the Journal. Right-click the job entry for the backup database procedure and choose Show Results from the pop-up menu.

TIP

> To prevent a media failure from destroying a database and your ability to rebuild it, keep the database backup images, the database logs, and the database table spaces on different devices. For this reason, it's highly recommended that you use the NEWLOGPATH configuration parameter to put database logs on a separate device when the database is created.
>
> To change the NEWLOGPATH configuration parameter, right-click the database in the Control Center and select Configure from the pop-up menu. Click the Logs tab and select Change the Database Log Path. Enter a new pathname to change the location of the log files.

Before you have a failure, consider the amount of space you'll require to recover your database. The database restore requires space to hold the backup image of the database and the restored database. The roll-forward operation requires space to hold the backup image of the database, the restored database, and the archived database logs.

Any configuration parameters that must be changed as a result of the plan are done automatically. For example, the LOGARCHIVE database configuration parameter is set to ON for this database if you've changed from the default circular logging to archive logging. If you've selected to use Full Recovery for your database, you must perform a full backup before making any more changes to your database.

If you want to change anything in the plan that you just created (except the schedule), you must delete the entry in the Task Center and redo the steps in the Backup Wizard.

The result of using the Backup Wizard is a script to back up your database that can either execute immediately or later if you selected to use the Task Center to schedule the backup. The time required to perform a backup depends on the amount of data in the database at the time the backup is launched. You can view the progress of the backup on the Running Jobs page of the Journal.

Forcing Users Off DB2

During a backup, you may need to have exclusive access to the database. Follow these steps to force users off the system:

1. Start the Control Center.

2. Right-click on the instance or database you want to back up and select Quiesce from the pop-up menu. In quiesced mode, users are prevented from connecting to the database, which allows the DBA to perform administrative tasks. The UNQUI-ESCE command allows users to connect back to the database.

3. Only users who are not actively performing database functions are forced off the system (that is, connected to the database but not submitting any requests to the database). Users who are actively accessing or changing the data are allowed to complete what they are doing before being forced off.

Recovering Data

No matter how careful you are, disasters can strike your data. You may have to deal with media and storage problems, power interruptions, and application failures. The Restore Database Wizard helps you deal with the basic database recovery. If you find that you have a more complex problem to deal with, use the information covered later on the Restore Database Wizard.

DB2 automatically recovers from system crashes. If your database system crashes due to a software problem or power failure, DB2 automatically restores your database to the state just after the last committed transaction, using a set of logs that recorded every transaction that had not been saved to the hard drive. All committed units of work not written to disk will be redone when the system comes back and the first application connects to a database or when a database is restarted.

Using the Restore Data Wizard

The Restore Data Wizard helps you restore a database to the point in time of the last database backup or the last completed transaction.

Occasionally, you may need to undo something that happened to your database. For example, if an errant application program has damaged your data, you would want to put the database back to the point just before that application was run against it. To do this, use the Restore Database Wizard to perform a full database restore, but in the last step, specify a date and time to which you want to roll forward your database by using the logs.

To use the wizard, follow these steps:

1. Start the Control Center.

2. Right-click the database you want to restore and select Restore|Data Using Wizard from the pop-up menu.

3. On the Restore Data Introduction page (see Figure 16.16), you see the status of your database and the restore alternatives. From the previous exercise of changing the default circular logging to archive logging, you see that the database is roll-forward enabled. Accept the defaults and click Next.

FIGURE 16.16

Restore Data Wizard Introduction page.

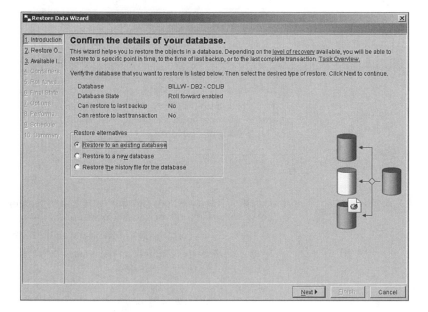

4. On the Restore Objects page (see Figure 16.17), accept the default to restore the entire database. This page appears only after you have created database objects in your database. Click Next.

FIGURE 16.17

Restore Data Wizard Restore Objects page.

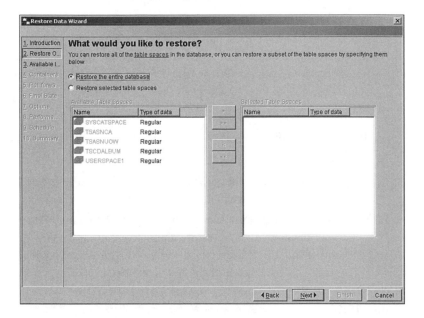

> **NOTE**
>
> You have the option of selectively restoring just table spaces of your database. If you choose to restore a specific table space, the table space is always in roll-forward pending state, and it must be rolled forward. To remove the roll-forward pending state, you need to apply the logs against the table spaces to either a point in time, or to the end of the logs (these options are available with this wizard).

> **NOTE**
>
> Restoring all table spaces is not the same as performing a full restore of the database. When you restore a full database, the following also occurs:
>
> - The recovery history file for the database is restored.
> - The database configuration parameter values are restored to their state at the time of the backup.

5. On the Available Images page (see Figure 16.18), click the desired entry in the Available Backup Images window. Click the > button, and the backup entry will now appear in the Selected Backup Images window. Click Next.

FIGURE 16.18

Restore Data Wizard Available (backup) Images page.

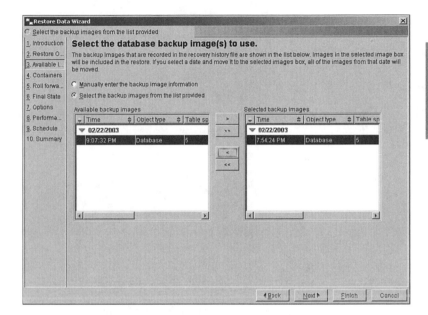

16

6. If you need to back up to another machine with either fewer or more resources, DB2 allows you to redirect the restore to the new machine and containers available (see Figure 16.19). The redirection feature provides considerable flexibility for managing table space containers. In this example, accept the default values and click Next.

7. The Roll Forward page allows you to apply the changes captured in the logs subsequent to the restoration of the backup image (see Figure 16.20). Roll-forward recovery builds on a restored database and allows you to rebuild a database to a specified point in time. For example, if a disk failure occurs on the disk containing your database, you can restore and then roll the database forward to recover the updates as near the point of failure as possible.

If an application problem corrupted your database or accidentally deleted data, you can recover it by restoring the backup image and then performing roll forward to the point in time just before the application destroyed your data. Although you lose all changes made after that point in time, you don't lose the earlier data.

FIGURE **16.19**

*Restore Data Wizard
Containers page.*

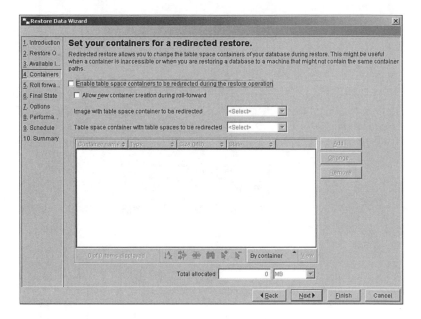

NOTE   With circular logging, roll-forward recovery is not possible: Only crash recovery or version recovery can be done. Thus, the Roll Forward page will not appear if you are using circular logging.

Selecting the Restore Only option will not apply any log changes since the last backup. For this example, select the option to Restore the Database and Roll Forward as Follows. The default for rolling forward is to Roll Forward to the End of the Logs. The Roll Forward to a Point-in-Time options allow you to specify a date and time, either using the server machine's local time setting or Greenwich Mean Time (GMT).

The selection of the Restore the Database and Roll Forward as Follows options also enables the Retrieval of Archived Logs for Rollforward option. The Use Default Log Location Only option directs the roll-forward operation to check for logs in the location specified by the LOGPATH database configuration parameter. If you've moved any logs from the specified location, use the Alternate Locations for Archived Logs option to specify the new location of the logs. You can display the list of available directories by clicking Add. If you do not want to retrieve the archived logs for the roll-forward operation, select the Disable Retrieval of Archived Logs During the Rollforward option.

FIGURE 16.20

*Restore Data Wizard's
Roll-Forward page.*

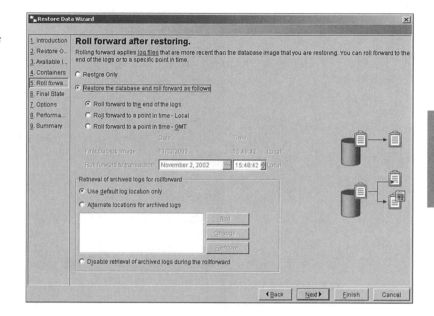

8. On the Final State Page (see Figure 16.21), clear the Leave in Roll-Forward
   Pending State option if you want the database to be usable immediately after the
   restore option. (By default, this check box is selected.) Select the Complete the
   Restore and Return to the Active State option and click Next.

NOTE

One reason why you might want to leave a database in roll-forward pending state is that you want to continue to make changes to the restore
operation.

9. The Restore Options page allows you the option to quiesce the database before
   restoring the database (see Figure 16.22). In quiesced mode, users cannot connect
   from outside the database engine. While the database instance or database is in
   quiesced mode, you can perform administrative tasks on it. After administrative
   tasks are complete, use the UNQUIESCE command to activate the instance and database and allow other users to connect to the database but avoid having to shut
   down and perform another database start. This page also allows you to consider
   restoring database objects that contain references to external data via
   DATALINKS. Accept the default values and click Next.

FIGURE 16.21

Final State page.

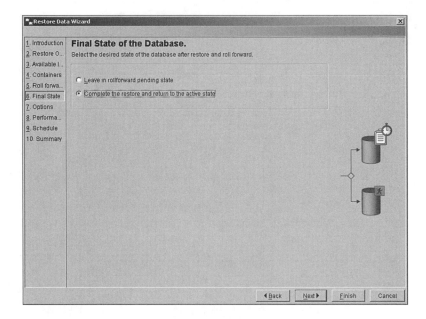

FIGURE 16.22

Restore Options page.

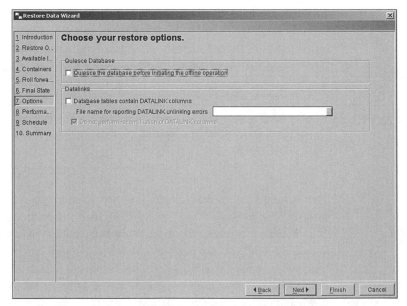

10. On the Restore Data Wizard Performance page (see Figure 16.23), enter the number of buffers to be used for the restore operation. For Parallelism, the default

value is 1 and is good for heavily loaded systems (indicates the number of processes or threads spawned during the restore process). For Number of Buffers, the default value is 2 (the valid range is from 1 to 65535). The Size of Each Buffer in 4K pages can range from 16 to 524288; the default value is 1024. The restore buffer size must be a positive integer multiple of the backup buffer size specified during the backup operation. If an incorrect size is specified, the buffers allocated will be the smallest acceptable size. Accept the defaults on this page and click Next.

FIGURE 16.23

Performance Options page.

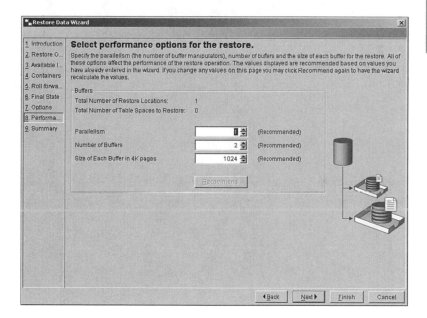

NOTE If you click the Recommend button, DB2 provides values it recommends for each entry that affects performance of the restore operation.

11. The Schedule page allows you to execute the Restore operation immediately or schedule it later (see Figure 16.24). Accept the default value and click Next.

12. The Restore Data Wizard Summary page summarizes the options you have selected (see Figure 16.25). Click Finish to restore the database to an active state.

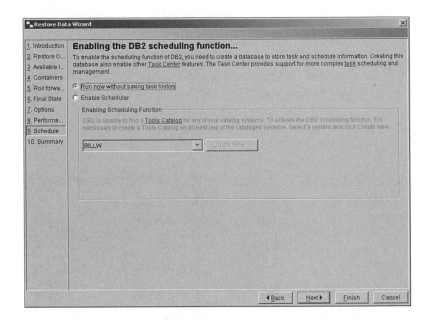

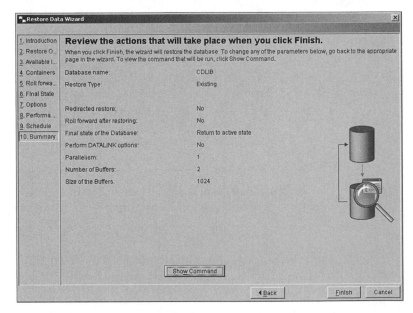

Database History File

Recovery log files and the recovery history file are created automatically when a database is created. These log files are important if you need to recover data that is lost or damaged. You cannot directly modify a recovery log file or the recovery history file; however, you can delete entries from the recovery history file using the PRUNE HISTORY command. You can also use the rec_his_retentn database configuration parameter to specify the number of days that the recovery history file will be retained. The recovery history file is automatically updated whenever any of the following operations occur:

- A database (or table spaces) is backed up.
- A database (or table spaces) is restored.
- A database (or table spaces) is rolled forward.
- A table space is created.
- A table space is altered.
- A table space is quiesced.
- A table space is renamed.
- A table space is dropped.
- A table is loaded.
- A table is dropped.
- A table is reorganized.

The file contains a summary of the backup information that can be used in case all or part of the database must be recovered to a given point in time. The information in the file includes

- The copied part of the database and how it was copied
- The time the copy was made
- The location of the copy
- The last time a restore was done

Every backup operation includes a copy of the recovery history file, which is linked to the database. Dropping a database deletes the recovery history file. Restoring data doesn't overwrite an existing history recovery file.

If the current database is unusable or unavailable and the associated history file is damaged or deleted, you can follow these steps to restore the file:

1. Open the Journal. Click on the Journal option in the Control Center's toolbar or choose Start Programs IBM DB2 General Administration Tools Journal.

2. Click the Database History tab to see the Database History files, as shown in Figure 16.26.

FIGURE **16.26**

*The Journal's
Database History
page.*

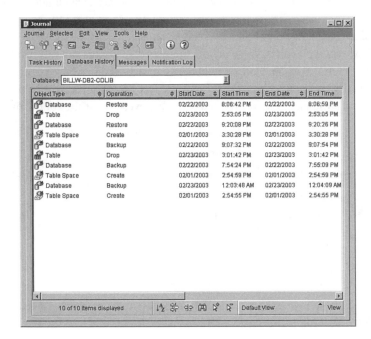

3. In the Restore Database Recovery History Wizard, select an entry, right-click it, and select Restore to invoke the Restore image.

The recovery history file helps you locate information when you've performed a backup. For example, it can help you determine the location of a backup or in which backup a DB2 object can be found. If a backup is moved to different media—say, from disk to tape—this file can be updated to keep track of the new location of the backup.

Every DB2 backup contains a copy of this file, and it can be restored from any backup. If you choose to restore it, use caution to avoid overwriting the database's existing history file.

NOTE

Although the recovery history file is an ASCII file, manually editing the file should be done only at your own risk and isn't recommended.

Log files and the recovery history file are created automatically when a database is created. You cannot modify a log file or the recover history file; however, they are important should you need to use your database backup to recover lost or damaged data.

Summary

16

Today you saw that creating a backup and recovery plan is an important way that you can protect the data in your database. DB2 enables you to save all transaction information into logs, which means that if you do need to recover your data, you can recover right to the point of failure.

Your system is set up for circular logging by default. With this type of logging, you can recover data only to the last full backup you performed. If you need more complete recovery, you must change the default from circular logging to archive logging, which enables you to fully recover your data to the point of failure.

A database recovery strategy should ensure that all information is available when it is required for database recovery. It should include a regular schedule for taking database backups and, in the case of partitioned database systems, include backups when the system is scaled (when database partition servers or nodes are added or dropped). Your overall strategy should also include procedures for recovering command scripts, applications, user-defined functions (UDFs), stored procedure code in operating system libraries, and load copies.

If you're faced with a media failure and have kept backups of your data and logs of the transactions, you can use the Backup Database Wizard or the Restore Database Wizard to fully recover your data.

What Comes Next?

On Day 17, "Moving Data," you learn how to export data from a DB2 database, import data into a DB2 database from another DB2 database or a file, and load large amounts of data into a DB2 database.

Q&A

Q What are the logging methods available for any given database?

A Circular logging is the default behavior when a new database is created. With this type of logging, only full, offline backups of the database are allowed. The database must be offline (inaccessible to users) when a full backup is taken. Circular logging uses a "ring" of online logs to provide recovery from transaction failures and system crashes. The logs are used and retained only to the point of ensuring the integrity of current transactions. Circular logging does not allow you to roll a database forward through transactions performed after the last full backup operation. All changes occurring since the last backup operation are lost. Because this type of restore operation recovers your data to the specific point in time at which a full backup was taken, it is called version recovery.

Archive logging is used specifically for roll-forward recovery. To archive logs, you can choose to have DB2 leave the log files in the active path and then manually archive them, or you can install a user exit program to automate the archiving. Archived logs are logs that were active but are no longer required for crash recovery.

Q What are the active logs used for?

A Active logs are used during crash recovery to prevent a failure (system power or application error) from leaving a database in an inconsistent state. During crash recovery, uncommitted changes recorded in these logs are rolled back. Changes that were committed but not yet written from memory (the buffer pool) to disk (database containers) are redone. These actions ensure the integrity of the database. Active logs are located in the database log path directory.

Q How do you enable roll-forward recovery?

A Archive logging is used specifically for roll-forward recovery. Enabling the `logretain` and/or the `userexit` database configuration parameter will result in archive logging, or you can use the Configure Database Logging Wizard. After you enable archive logging, you must make a full backup of the database.

Q What is *roll-forward pending state*?

A If your database is enabled for archive logging and you use a backup image to restore the data, your database is left in roll-forward pending state. This means that the data has been restored to the level of the backup, but recorded transactions in the log should be applied if you want to recover to the most recently saved transaction. To remove the database from roll-forward pending state, you must use the Roll-Forward tool to restore the data in the logs to a point in time or to the end of the logs.

Q What are the capabilities of the restore function?

A Restore can rebuild a damaged or corrupted database that has been backed up using the DB2 Backup Wizard. The restored database is in the same state it was in when the backup copy was made. The Restore Wizard can also restore to a database with a name different from the database name in the backup image (in addition to being able to restore to a new database).

If, at the time of the backup operation, the database was enabled for roll-forward recovery, the database can be brought to the state it was in prior to the occurrence of the damage or corruption by invoking the roll-forward utility after successful completion of a restore operation.

Workshop

16

The purpose of the Workshop is to allow you to test your knowledge of the material covered in the lesson. See whether you can successfully answer the questions in the quiz and complete the exercise before you continue with the next lesson. The answers appear in Appendix B, "Answers to Quiz Questions and Exercises."

Quiz

1. How can you ensure that you have exclusive access to a database if you want to do a full offline backup of your data?

2. How does using redirected restore give you additional flexibility when using SMS table spaces?

3. How can you use roll-forward recovery to undo an unexpected error?

4. Which database configuration parameters can be tuned to improve the performance of the backup and restore operations?

Exercise

1. Backing up your data is one of the most important things you can do. Of course, at this point, you may not have much data to be concerned about. Take this opportunity to explore the many backup and restore options that you have and spend some extra time understanding the power of the database logs. Use any of the databases on your system (CDLIB, SAMPLE, or your own) for experimentation.

DAY 17

Moving Data

Today, you see how to move data in and out of a DB2 database by importing, loading, or exporting:

- If you want to create a new database, replace data in an existing database, or append to the data in an existing database with data from another source, you use the Import utility.

- If you have a substantial amount of data that you need to move into your database, consider using the Load utility rather than the Import utility.

- If you need to move data from a DB2 database to another source, use the Export utility.

The Import and Load utilities provide similar functions, but the Load utility performs better when large amounts of data are involved. All three utilities support several different file formats, giving you flexibility to choose the format that best suits your environment.

To see how the Export, Import, and Load utilities work, you are going to export the data from the PROJECT table in the SAMPLE database in two formats: IXF and DEL. When you have these files, you'll import the data in the IXF file into a new table, and you'll first modify the data in the DEL file and then load it into a table.

Today you learn the following:

- What data types are supported by DB2 and its utilities
- How to use the Export utility
- How to use the Import utility
- How to use the Load utility
- How to use the Set Integrity Wizard

Exporting Data

You can export data from a table, with the DB2 Export Wizard. The discussion in this section covers how to export data from a table into one of these supported formats:

- Delimited ASCII format (DEL)
- Worksheet format (WSF)
- Integrated exchange format (IXF)

A Delimited ASCII Format (DEL) file is a sequential ASCII file, with each row appearing on a separate line. The columns are separated by a delimiter such as a comma. Each character string is contained within double quotes ("). This file format is commonly used to exchange data with various products that may be using different column delimiters.

Worksheet Format (WSF) is generated or supported by products such as Lotus 1-2-3. Each WSF file represents one worksheet. DB2 uses the following conventions to interpret worksheets:

- Cell values under any column heading are values for that particular column or field.
- Cells in the first row are reserved for descriptive information about the worksheet. This information is optional and is ignored during import.
- Cells in the second row are used for column labels.
- The remaining rows are data rows.

Integrated Exchange Format (IXF) data interchange architecture is a host file format designed to enable the exchange of relational database structure and data. On the workstation, this file format is PC/IXF and is an adaptation of the host IXF format. Use this format when exchanging data between the various versions of DB2.

When you choose an output file for the exported data, make careful notes as to what options you select.

NOTE — You must have SYSADM or DBADM authority, or CONTROL or SELECT privilege for each table participating in the export operation.

Performing a Simple Export

To export data from DB2, follow these steps:

1. Start the Control Center.
2. Expand the objects until you see the Tables folder within the SAMPLE database. Click this folder to see a list of all the tables in the right pane.
3. Right-click the PROJECT table and select Export from the pop-up menu. The Export Wizard opens to the File page, in which you type the path and name of the file that will receive the data (see Figure 17.1). Export the data to a file—for example, e:\california\project.del.

FIGURE 17.1

The Export Wizard's Target page.

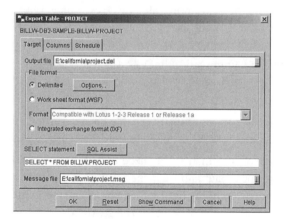

If you don't specify a path, the current working directory is used. If you specify a path, the directory must exist. If the file already exists, its contents are overwritten with the exported data.

4. Choose a format to use for the export: Delimited ASCII Format (DEL), Work Sheet Format (WSF), or Integrated Exchange Format (IXF). For this example, use DEL.

5. If you choose DEL or WSF, you might want to set some additional options:

- For DEL files, select the delimiter characters for columns, character strings, and decimal points. In this example, single quotes were used for column delimiters, double quotes for character string delimiters, and a period for a decimal point (see Figure 17.2).

FIGURE 17.2

The Export Delimited Options page.

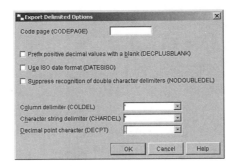

- For WSF files, enter the version and release of the Lotus product to which you're exporting the data.

6. Near the bottom of the Export Table PROJECT dialog box, you will see the SELECT statement that will be used to extract data from the table. By default, all data in the table is extracted. You can add WHERE clauses if you want only a subset of the data. For example, if you only want to export the rows that have Eastern as a division, enter a SQL statement as follows:

```
SELECT * FROM PROJECT WHERE DEPTNO = 'C01'
```

Because two rows in the PROJECT table have department numbers as 'C01,' two rows are exported. The SQL Assist button can step you through the process.

7. The last piece of information you need to add is the location of a message file. As soon as you type a path and filename for the message file, the OK button is activated. (You can't continue until a filename is entered in this field.) For this example, choose a name such as e:\california\project.msg for the message file.

8. Click OK to export the data.

Repeat these steps to export the same data in IXF format. Store the exported data in a file—for example, e:\data\project.ixf; you will import this data later in this lesson.

Specifying Column Names

If you want to specify the column names used in the export file, use the wizard's Columns tab (see Figure 17.3). Click the Add button to open the Add Column Name dialog box. In the Column Name box, type the name of the column you want to add. Click the Add button. The column name appears in the Column Names list, and the Add window remains open. Repeat this step to add as many column names as you want. Click Close to return to the Columns page in the Export Wizard.

This option does not reorder the columns or allow you to export a subset of the data. It simply allows you to change the column name that will be used when importing or loading the data. For example, you may want to change the column names of a table from COL1, COL2, and COL3 to EMPID, FIRST, and LAST to better match the data stored in the column.

FIGURE 17.3

The Export Wizard's Columns page.

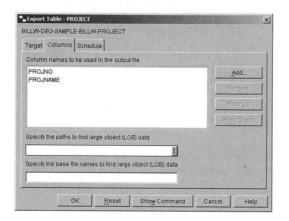

17

NOTE   You can specify column names only for the WSF and IXF formats. If you don't add column names to the list box on the Columns page, the column names in the existing table are used.

Exporting Large Objects (LOBs)

If you want to export tables that include large objects, such as audio or video clips, use the Export Wizard's Columns page to arrange to have the large objects stored in separate files (see Figure 17.4). In the Specify the Paths text box, type the path to the LOB file. Click Add to have the path inserted into the Specify the Paths box. In the Specify the Base File Names text box, type the name of the file that will store the LOBs (don't use a file extension for the filename because a three-digit sequence number is appended to the file). Click the Add button to have the filename added to the list. Repeat this operation for each file you plan to use to store LOBs. Click Close to return to the Large Object page in the Export Wizard. Click OK to perform the export operation.

FIGURE 17.4

The Export Wizard's Large Objects page.

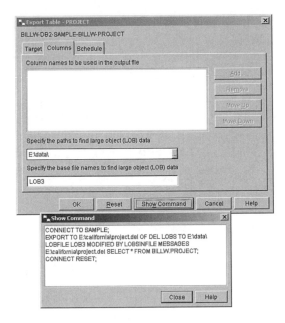

Importing and Loading Data

DB2 provides Import and Load utilities to help you move data into a table from existing sources. Both utilities allow you to load data into tables, but there are some differences. To create a new table with the data you are inserting, you must use the Import utility. You can also replace or add data to an existing table using the Import utility. The Load utility does not allow you to create a new table but does allow you to append to, or replace the data in an existing table. The Load utility is usually faster than the Import utility and is well suited to inserting large amounts into the table. Often tables of data from host database systems are loaded into DB2 databases using the Load utility. Another difference between the two utilities is that the WSF format is supported with the Import utility but is not with the Load utility.

TIP

> To use the import utility to create a new table, you must have SYSADM authority, DBADM authority, or CREATETAB privilege for the database. To replace data in an existing table or view, you must have SYSADM authority, DBADM authority, or CONTROL privilege for the table or view. To append data to an existing table or view, you must have SELECT and INSERT privileges for the table or view.

Importing Data from Files

The DB2 Import utility takes data from an input file and inserts it into a table or a view. An input file contains data extracted from an existing source of data, such as a Lotus 1-2-3 or ASCII file.

DB2 imports file formats generated from the supported sources. Supported formats include non-delimited ASCII format (ASC), delimited ASCII format (DEL), worksheet format (WSF), or integrated exchange format (IXF). The procedure for generating each file varies with the original source.

Non-delimited ASCII format (ASC) is a stream of ASCII characters consisting of data values organized by row and column. Rows are separated on new lines, and each column is defined by a beginning and ending position. The data type of a given column in the ASC file is determined by the type of the target column in the table. This file format can be used for data exchange with applications, including word processors that create flat text files with aligned column data.

A delimited ASCII format (DEL) file is a sequential ASCII file with each row appearing on a separate line. The columns are separated by a delimiter such as a comma. Each character string is contained within double quotes ("). This file format is commonly used to exchange data with a variety of products that may be using different column delimiters.

Worksheet format (WSF) is generated or supported by products such as Lotus 1-2-3. Each WSF file represents one worksheet. DB2 uses the following conventions to interpret worksheets:

- Cell values under any column heading are values for that particular column or field.

- Cells in the first row are reserved for descriptive information about the worksheet. This information is optional and is ignored during import.

- Cells in the second row are used for column labels.

- The remaining rows are data rows.

TIP

For DEL, WSF, and ASC data file formats, define the table, its columns, and data types before importing the file. The Import utility accepts data with minor incompatibility problems, including character data imported with possible padding or truncations, and numeric data imported into different types of numeric fields.

Integrated Exchange Format (IXF) data interchange architecture is a host file format designed to enable the exchange of relational database structures and data. On the workstation, this file format is PC/IXF and is an adaptation of the host IXF format. Use this format when exchanging data between the various versions of DB2.

TIP

> You can create a new database only if IXF format is used. Other formats must be imported into existing tables.

When you have an input file in a supported format, use the Import Wizard to insert data from the file into an existing table. If the table already contains data, you can replace it or append to the existing data with the data in the file. You can also use the Import Wizard to create and populate a new table from an input file, or delete existing rows in the selected table and repopulate it by using data from the input file.

Now it's time to actually import some data. You'll use the data that you exported in IXF format in the preceding discussion and create a new table called NEWORG. First, you need to open the Import Wizard:

1. Start the Control Center.
2. Expand the objects until you see the Tables folder within the SAMPLE database. Select that folder to see a list of tables in the right pane.
3. Right-click any table and select Import from the pop-up menu. The Import Wizard opens (see Figure 17.5).

FIGURE 17.5

The Import Wizard.

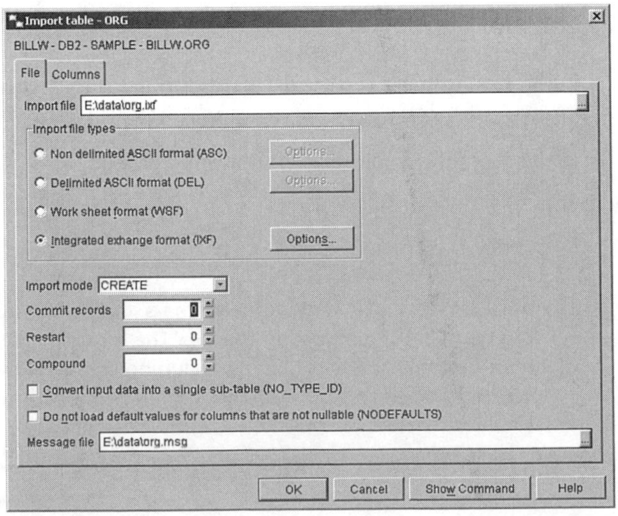

To continue the import process, follow along through the Import Wizard page by page, option by option.

Specifying the Path, Import Format, and Other Settings

On the File page, type the path and name of the file that contains the data you want to import—for example, `e:\data\org.ixf`. If you don't specify the full path, the current working directory is used. Next, select a format to use for the import (ASC, DEL, WSF, or IXF). The options for each file format will be reviewed later in this lesson.

Choose the import mode that you want to use. For this example, select CREATE to create the table definition and the row contents. If the data was exported from a database manager, indexes are also created. The other modes available are as follows:

- INSERT adds the imported data to the table without changing the existing table data.

- INSERT_UPDATE adds the rows of the imported data to the target table, or updates existing rows of the target table with matching primary keys.

- REPLACE can be used only if the table exists. Select it to delete all existing data in the table and insert the imported data. The table and index definitions aren't changed.

- REPLACE_CREATE, available only for IXF input files, deletes all existing data in the table and inserts the imported data without changing the table or index definitions. If the table doesn't exist, this mode creates the table definition and row contents. If the data was exported from a database manager, indexes are also created.

- CREATE, available only for IXF input files, creates the table definition and row contents. If the data was exported from a DB2 table, subtable, or hierarchy, indexes are created. If this option operates on a hierarchy, and data was exported from DB2, a type hierarchy will also be created.

In the Commit records box, specify how often the changes are committed. If you specify 1, the changes to the target table will be committed each time a record is inserted. This reduces the number of lost records if a failure occurs during the import. Keep the default value for this example.

In the Restart box, specify the number of records in the file to skip before the import begins. If an error occurs during an import, you can specify this information to restart the import operation immediately following the last row that was successfully imported and committed. Keep the default value for this example.

In the Compound box, specify whether compound SQL will be used. Compound SQL improves import performance by grouping SQL statements into a block; this option

17

might reduce network overhead and improve response time. Import allows a value between 1 and 100. Keep the default value for this example.

Select the NO_TYPE_ID check box when importing into a single subtable. Typical usage is to export data from a regular table and then to invoke an import operation (using this modifier) to convert the data into a single subtable. Keep the default value for this example.

Select the NODEFAULTS check box if you do not want default values loaded for columns that are not nullable. Keep the default value for this example.

In the Message file text box, type the path and name of the file that will contain the warning and error messages that occur during import. If you don't specify a path, the current working directory is used. For this example, use e:\data\org.msg.

NOTE You can't start the import until a message file is specified.

Click OK to begin the import operation. Check the message file to see whether there were any problems. Use an editor of your choice to view the file, e:\data\org.msg, which is specified on the File page of the Import Wizard.

If you're importing a subset of a table, click the Columns tab to specify column options. The Columns window presents different options depending on the import file type selected and also gives you the option of importing tables with large objects such as audio or video clips. Otherwise, the default action imports columns from the input file to the target table using a one-to-one mapping. (The first column of the input file is imported into the first column of the target table and so on.)

Non-delimited ASCII (ASC) Import Options

By selecting the ASC file format option and then the Columns tab, the Import Table Columns page is displayed (see Figure 17.6). By selecting the Graphical Mapper button on this page, a tool will be displayed that allows you to graphically map (starting and ending locations of the data columns) the relationship between the ASCII input file and the columns of the target table. Alternatively, you can click on the Columns button and type in the start and end positions of the source data columns.

For ASC file formats, the Import Table Columns page lists the following options:

- The Identity Column Behavior box lets you determine whether DB2 automatically generates a numeric value for each row inserted into the table. You have the option to disable this during the import activity by indicating that values are missing or should be ignored. A table can have at most one identity column.

- The Generated Column Behavior box lets you determine whether DB2 generates a value for each row from an expression rather than from an insert or update operation. You also have the option not to generate the value by indicating that values are missing or should be ignored.

- For the Use Defaults for Blanks check box, you can indicate for a specified source column of a target table column to load default values. For ASC files, the NULL indicator is set to yes for the column. If this option is not selected, if a source column contains no data for a row instance, either a NULL is loaded (if the column is nullable) or the utility will reject the row (if the column is not nullable).

- Select the LOB check box if LOBs will be imported, and indicate which file stores the LOBs.

FIGURE 17.6

The Non-delimited ASCII Columns and Graphical Column Mapper page.

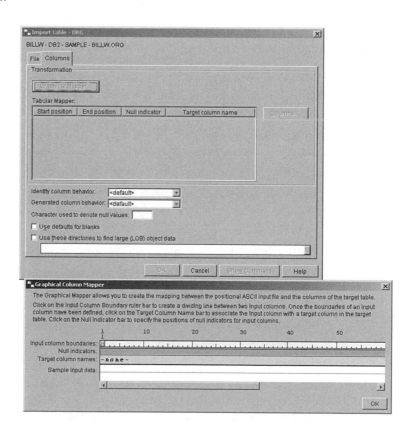

Additional ASC options are available when you click the Options button on the Import Table Files page. The Positional Text Options dialog box appears (see Figure 17.7).

FIGURE 17.7

The (ASC) Positional Text Options page.

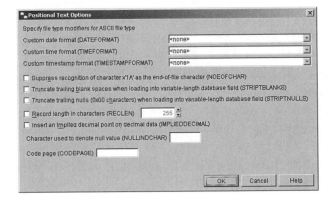

The Positional Text Options page has the following options:

- You have the option to select from a variety of date (DATEFORMAT), time (TIMEFORMAT), and time stamp (TIMESTAMPFORMAT) formats.

- Select the Suppress recognition of character x'1A' as the End-of-File Character check box if you want the character treated as a normal character.

- Select the Truncate trailing blank spaces when loading into variable-length database field check box if you want to drop trailing blanks after the last non-blank character when loading the data into a variable length table column.

- Select the Truncate Trailing Nulls (0x00 Characters) When Loading into Variable-Length Database Field check box to eliminate blank spaces; otherwise, blank spaces are kept.

- Select the Record length in characters check box to specify the number of characters to be read for each row.

- Select the Insert an implied decimal point on decimal data check box to have the column definition imply the location of the decimal point. For example, the value 1701 is loaded into a DECIMAL(8,2) column as 17.01, *not* 1701.00.

- Enter a character 'x' for the Character Used to denote null value box to change a null value to 'x.'

- Enter a code page value for the Code page box if data conversion is required. The value is interpreted as the code page of the data in the output data set. Converts character data to this code page from the application code page during the import operation.

Delimited ASCII (DEL) Import Options

By selecting the DEL file format option and then the Columns tab, the Delimited Columns page is displayed (see Figure 17.8).

For DEL file formats, the Import Table Columns page lists the following options:

- You have the option of selectively picking columns to import into the target table. The selected columns can be picked either by column names or by their position in the input file.

- The Identity Column Behavior box lets you determine whether DB2 automatically generates a numeric value for each row that is inserted into the table. You have the option to disable this during the import activity by indicating that values are missing or should be ignored. A table can have at most one identity column.

- The Generated Column Behavior box lets you determine whether DB2 generates a value for each row from an expression rather than from an insert or update operation. You also have the option not to generate the value by indicating that values are missing or should be ignored.

- For the Use Defaults for Blanks check box, you can indicate, for a specified source column of a target table column, to load default values. For ASC files, the NULL indicator is set to yes for the column. If this option is not selected, if a source column contains no data for a row instance, either a NULL is loaded (if the column is nullable) or the utility rejects the row (if the column is not nullable).

- Select the LOB check box if LOBs will be imported, and indicate which file stores the LOBs.

17

FIGURE 17.8

The Delimited Columns page.

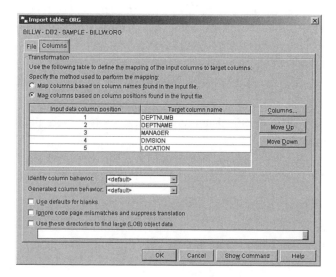

Additional DEL options are available when you click the Options button on the Import Table Files page. The Delimited Options dialog box shown in Figure 17.9 appears:

The Delimited Options page has the following options:

- Enter a code page value for the Code Page box if data conversion is required. The value is interpreted as the code page of the data in the output data set. Converts character data to this code page from the application code page during the import operation.

- Select the delimiter characters to use for columns, character strings, and decimal points. All these choices depend on the input data set.

- Select the Insert an Implied Decimal Point on Decimal Data check box to have the column definition imply the location of the decimal point. For example, the value 1701 is loaded into a DECIMAL(8,2) column as 17.01, *not* 1701.00.

- Select the Suppress Recognition of Character x'1A' as the End-of-File Character check box if you want the character treated as a normal character.

- Select the Prioritize Character String Delimiter Over Record Delimiter check box to accommodate applications that depend on the older priority by reverting the delimiter priorities to character delimiter, record delimiter, column delimiter. The current default priority for delimiters is record delimiter, character delimiter, column delimiter.

- Select the Prefix Positive Decimal Values with a Blank check box instead of a plus (+) sign. The default action is to prefix positive decimal values with a plus sign.

- Select the Preserve Leading and Trailing Blanks in Each Field check box to preserve the leading and trailing blanks in each field of type CHAR, VARCHAR, LONG VARCHAR, or CLOB. Without this option, all leading and trailing blanks that are not inside character delimiters are removed, and a NULL is inserted into the table for all blank fields.

- Select the Suppress Recognition of Double Character Delimiters check box to suppress these delimiters.

- Select the Use ISO Date Format check box to import all date data values in ISO format.

- You have the option to select from a variety of date (DATEFORMAT), time (TIMEFORMAT), and time stamp (TIMESTAMPFORMAT) formats.

WSF Import Options

By selecting the WSF file format option and then the Columns tab, the WSF Columns page is displayed (see Figure 17.10).

FIGURE 17.9

The Delimited Options page.

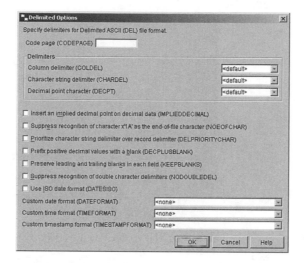

For WSF file formats, the Import Table Columns page lists the following options:

- The Identity Column Behavior box lets you determine whether DB2 automatically generates a numeric value for each row that is inserted into the table. You have the option to disable this during the import activity by indicating that values are missing or should be ignored. A table can have at most one identity column.

- The Generated Column Behavior box lets you determine whether DB2 generates a value for each row from an expression rather than from an insert or update operation. You also have the option not to generate the value by indicating that values are missing or should be ignored.

- For the Use Defaults for Blanks check box, you can indicate, for a specified source column of a target table column, to load default values. For ASC files, the NULL indicator is set to yes for the column. If this option is not selected, if a source column contains no data for a row instance, either a NULL is loaded (if the column is nullable) or the utility will reject the row (if the column is not nullable).

- Select the LOB check box if LOBs will be imported and indicate which file stores the LOBs.

IXF Import Options

By selecting the IXF file format option and then the Columns tab, the IXF Columns page is displayed (see Figure 17.11).

17

FIGURE **17.10**

*The WSF Columns
page.*

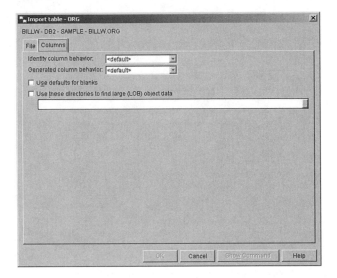

For IXF file formats, the Import Table Columns page lists the following options:

- You have the option of selectively choosing columns to import into the target table. The selected columns can be chosen either by column name or by their position in the input file.

- The Identity Column Behavior box lets you determine whether DB2 automatically generates a numeric value for each row that is inserted into the table. You have the option to disable this during the import activity by indicating that values are missing or should be ignored. A table can have at most one identity column.

- The Generated Column Behavior box lets you determine whether DB2 generates a value for each row from an expression rather than from an insert or update operation. You also have the option not to generate the value by indicating that values are missing or should be ignored.

- For the Use Defaults for Blanks check box, you can indicate, for a specified source column of a target table column, to load default values. For ASC files, the NULL indicator is set to yes for the column. If this option is not selected, if a source column contains no data for a row instance, either a NULL is loaded (if the column is nullable) or the utility will reject the row (if the column is not nullable).

- Select the Ignore Code Page Mismatches and Suppress Translation check box if you want the utility to accept data despite a code page mismatch.

- Select the LOB check box to LOBs will be imported and indicate which file stores the LOBs.

FIGURE 17.11

The IXF Columns page.

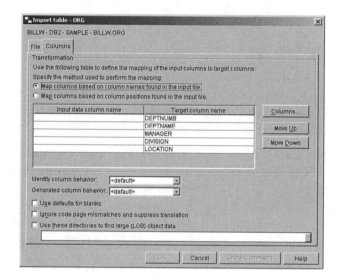

Click the Options button on the Import Table Files page to display the Import IXF File Type Modifiers page (see Figure 17.12).

The Import IXF File Type Modifiers page has the following options:

- Select the Drop Existing Indexes and Create New Ones check box if you want to drop all indexes defined in the table that you selected and to create new ones from the index definitions in the input file. You can use this option only when the contents of a table are being replaced; it can't be used with a view or when columns are inserted.

- Select the Load Each Row Without Checking Target Lengths check box if you want to specify that target fields aren't to be checked and that an attempt be made to load each row. (By default, target fields for fixed-length fields in IXF files are checked to verify that they're large enough for the data.)

- Select the Index Schema check box if you want to specify the schema of the table you are creating. By default, the schema used is the same as the username you used to log in.

Figure 17.12

The IXF Options page – Import IXF File Type Modifiers.

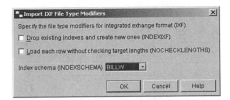

Loading Data

The Load Wizard loads data directly into a DB2 table from one or more files or tapes, or from a cursor. (For example, you might be required to move in data from databases other than DB2.) During load processing, indexes can be built, primary keys can be validated, and statistics generated, all without requiring secondary passes through the data.

The Load Wizard is faster than the Import Wizard but with some functional differences. The Load Wizard is intended for bulk loading of new tables or appending large amounts of data to existing tables. It is common to use the Load utility when moving large amounts of data from DB2 on the mainframe to DB2 systems on the LAN. Load is restartable and recoverable. If a failure occurs while you're loading data, you have the option of continuing the load without starting from the beginning.

If you're using the Load Wizard's INSERT mode for an initial large load of data, create the unique key after loading the data. This avoids the overhead of maintaining the index while the table is being loaded. It also results in the index using the least amount of storage.

If you're using the Load Wizard's REPLACE mode, create the unique key before loading the data. In this case, creation of the index during the load is more efficient than creating the index after the load.

When loading a small amount of data to an existing table, you can improve performance if you use the Import Wizard instead of the LOAD INSERT mode.

NOTE

Users having LOAD authority at the database level, as well as INSERT privilege on a table, can use the LOAD command to load data into a table.

Users having LOAD authority at the database level, as well as INSERT privilege on a table, can LOAD RESTART or LOAD TERMINATE if the previous load operation is a load to insert data.

If the previous load operation was a load replace, the DELETE privilege must also have been granted to that user before the user can LOAD RESTART or LOAD TERMINATE.

> If the exception tables are used as part of a load operation, the user must have INSERT privilege on the exception tables.
>
> The user with this authority can perform the QUIESCE TABLESPACES FOR TABLE, RUNSTATS, and LIST TABLESPACES commands.

To see how the Load Wizard works, first export data from the Sales table in DEL format.

TIP

> You must have an existing table to load the data into. You cannot use the Load Wizard to create a new table.

17

Change some of the data in the SALES.DEL file by using the Notepad. For example, change the cities listed to other cities, such as New York to Toronto.

To load data from the modified SALES.DEL file into the Sales table (created during the import step), follow these steps:

1. Start the Control Center.

2. Expand the objects until you see the Tables folder within the SAMPLE database. Click that folder to see a list of all the tables in the right panel.

3. Right-click on the Sales table. Select Load from the pop-up menu. The Load Wizard opens (see Figure 17.13). Select the type of load operation required; for this example, select the Append data to table option. Click Next.

4. In the Specify Input and Output Files dialog box, specify locations such as files or directories (see Figure 17.14). You should fully qualify the filename. For example, if you want to load data from the file e:\california\sales.del, type the entire name in the text box or use the browse function to select an existing file. Repeat this in specifying a message file. For this example, select DEL as the input file format. Click Next.

5. The Columns page offers a number of options on how to load the data (see Figure 17.15). You define the mapping between the input columns and the target column name of the Sales table.

   The Load Wizard Columns page has the following options:

   • The Identity Column Behavior box lets you determine whether DB2 automatically generates a numeric value for each row that is inserted into the table. You have the option to disable this during the import activity by indicating that values are missing or should be ignored. A table can have at most one identity column.

- The Generated Column Behavior box lets you determine whether DB2 generates a value for each row from an expression rather than from an insert or update operation. You also have the option not to generate the value by indicating that values are missing or should be ignored.

- For the Use Defaults for Blanks check box, you can indicate, for a specified source column of a target table column, to load default values. For ASC files, the NULL indicator is set to yes for the column. If this option is not selected, if a source column contains no data for a row instance, either a NULL is loaded (if the column is nullable) or the utility will reject the row (if the column is not nullable).

- Select the LOB check box if LOBs will be imported and indicate which file stores the LOBs.

FIGURE 17.13

The Load Wizard.

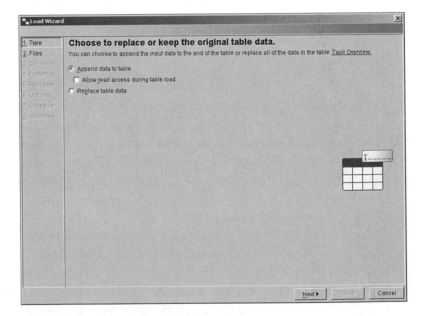

6. Select the defaults and click Next.

7. The Specify Performance and Statistics Collection Options page offers a number of options that include how the building of indexes will be handled, how much space will be left in the table and index pages after the load, and how to update the catalog statistics (see Figure 17.16). Accept the defaults and click Next.

FIGURE 17.14

The Load Wizard Files page.

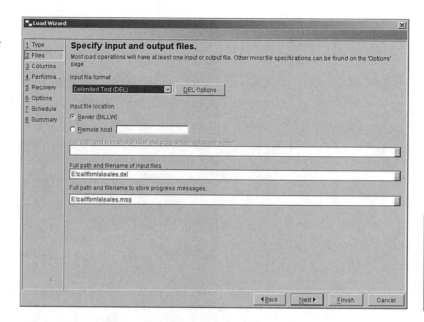

FIGURE 17.15

The Load Wizard Columns page.

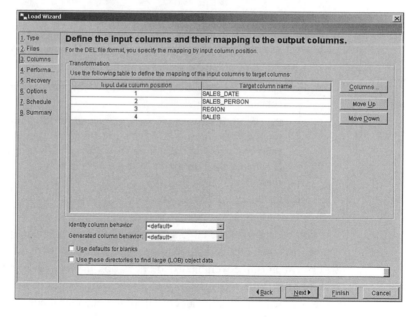

8. On the Recovery page (see Figure 17.17), you can specify how to save a copy of the changes made during the load process. If you do not need to save a copy of the changes, select the Perform an Unrecoverable Load check box to specify that the

load is non-recoverable (that is, when loading LOBs, it is faster to just reload the LOB rather than recover). Accept the defaults and click Next.

FIGURE 17.16

The Load Wizard Performance and Statistics page.

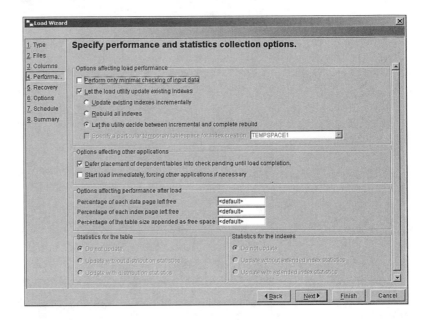

TIP

Forward recovery must be enabled for the database before you can save a copy of the changes.

By default, if forward recovery is enabled for the database in which this table resides and you load data into the table, the table spaces for that table are placed in backup pending state. In this case, the data in the table is not accessible until a table space backup or a full database backup is made.

If you do not want the table spaces to be placed in backup pending state, you can perform a non-recoverable load or create an image copy of the load. Select the Perform an Unrecoverable Load check box if you want to perform the load without jeopardizing the recoverability of all the other tables in the database and without the overhead of building a copy of all the changes made.

Select the Save a Copy of the Input Data check box to specify that a copy of the changes made during the load process be saved.

FIGURE 17.17

The Load Wizard Recovery page.

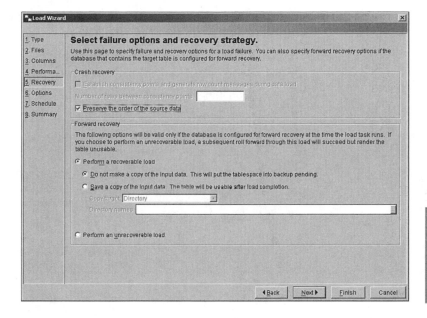

NOTE

If you want to perform a sequence of multiple load operations on a recoverable database, the sequence of operations will be faster if you specify that each load operation is non-recoverable and take a backup at the end of the load sequence than if you invoke each of the load operations with the Perform a Recoverable Load option.

9. On the Set Advanced Options page (see Figure 17.18), you can accept the defaults or change selected parameters that will affect load behavior and performance:

- The Recovery parameter allows you to specify a threshold to limit the number of warning messages during the load operation. If the threshold is exceeded, the load operation ceases.

- The Degree of CPU Parallelism allows you to specify the number of CPUs to dedicate to the load operation. If this parameter is zero or has not been set, the load utility will determine how many CPUs to use (usually the number of CPUs available at runtime).

- The Degree of Disk Parallelism allows you to specify the number of processes or threads dedicated to writing data to disk. If a value has not been selected, the utility selects an intelligent default, based on the number of table space containers and the characteristics of the table.

- The Databuffer Size Used for Transferring Data is the number of 4KB pages that will be used for this internal operation.

- The Base Name for Temporary Files option allows you to select a temporary file that will be used during the load operation.

- The Exception Table option allows you to indicate which table will collect rows that encountered errors during the load.

- The Exception File to Write Rejected Rows option allows you to indicate the file where rejected rows are written to.

- The Suppress All Warnings About Rejected Rows option suppresses any warning messages regarding rejected rows.

10. Accept the defaults and click Next.

FIGURE 17.18

The Load Wizard Advanced Options page.

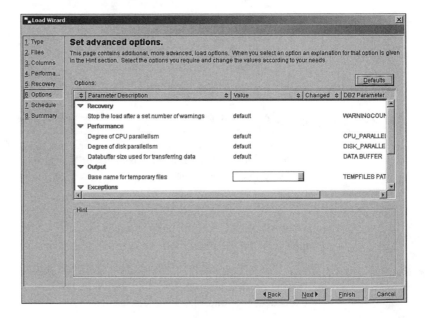

11. On the Enabling the DB2 Scheduling Function page (see Figure 17.19), you have the option of running the load operation now, or scheduling it at a later time. Accept the default and click Next.

12. The Summary page displays the SQL command generated from the Load Wizard (see Figure 17.20). Click Finish to start the load operation. A DB2 Message screen appears indicating that the command completed successfully.

FIGURE 17.19

The Load Wizard Advanced Scheduling page.

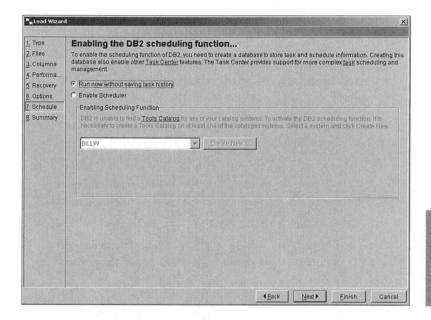

FIGURE 17.20

The Load Wizard Summary page.

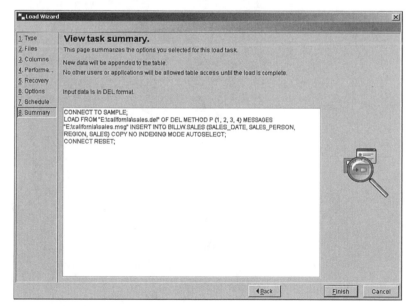

Setting Integrity Constraints

Referential integrity and check constraints on a table are normally enforced automatically. In some situations, you might need to turn on the constraint checking manually for a table. Typically, you need to set constraint checking manually after loading data into a table.

The load operation causes a table to be put into check pending state automatically if the table has check or foreign key constraints defined on it. When the load operation is completed, you can turn on constraint checking for the table.

Use the Set Integrity window to turn off constraint checking for a table and to turn it back on. Follow these steps:

1. Log on as a user with SYSADM or DBADM authority, unless you have CONTROL privilege on the table and on all tables whose foreign keys can be traced back to the primary key of the table. These tables are its dependents and descendants.

2. Start the Control Center.

3. Expand the object tree until you find the Tables folder. Click that folder. The available tables are listed on the right side of the window.

4. Right-click the table you want to set constraints and select Set Constraints from the pop-up menu. The Set Constraints dialog box opens (see Figure 17.21).

FIGURE 17.21

The Set Integrity Wizard.

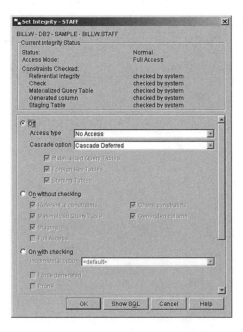

5. To turn off constraint checking, select Off. This puts the table in check pending state. Click OK to turn off constraint checking for this table.

Select On with Checking to turn on constraint checking for referential and check constraints, and to check the table immediately for constraint violations.

Select On Without Checking to turn on constraint checking for a table without checking existing table data. The table can't be a system table.

When you select On with Checking, you can specify an exception table that will collect any row that's in violation of a foreign key or check constraint before it's deleted from the table. Specify an exception table by using the Exception Table Schema and Exception Table Name options. The constraints are turned back on again, and the table is taken out of check pending state, regardless of whether errors are detected. A warning is issued to indicate that one or more rows were moved to the exception table. If you don't specify an exception table and any constraints are violated, only the first violation detected is returned to you. The table is left in check pending state.

When you select On Without Checking, you can use the Referential Constraints and Check Constraints check boxes to specify the constraint type for which you're turning on constraint checking. When you turn on constraint checking without performing the checking, this is recorded in the database catalog. (The value in the CONST_CHECKED column in the SYSCAT.TABLES view is set to U.) This indicates that you've assumed responsibility (over the database management system) for ensuring that the data complies with the constraints. This value remains the same until the table is put back into check pending state or all unchecked constraints for the table are dropped.

Summary

Today you saw that you can export data from a DB2 database to a variety of data formats: delimited ASCII, worksheet, and integrated exchange. You can import data into a DB2 database from an input file by using four formats, and the data can be inserted into either an existing table or a new table.

You can load data into a DB2 database from a file, tape, or named pipe. Loading data can be faster than importing data if you have a large amount of data that needs to be moved.

Informational and error messages are kept during export, import, and load operations, which can be helpful if you run into a problem with the operations.

What Comes Next?

On Day 18, "Replicating Data," you learn how to replicate data from one database to another.

Q&A

Q **If I want to create a new database by importing data, what format should the data be in?**

A The Integrated Exchange Format (IXF) must be used if you want to import into a new table. IXF is a format that contains the relational database structure. This format is recommended when exchanging data between different versions of DB2.

Q **Where are messages kept?**

A When you are setting up the export, import, or load operation, you must indicate the name of the file you want the messages to be kept in. Specify an entire path for the filename. You can't start the operation if you don't indicate a message file.

Q **Can I import flat text?**

A If you use an editor such as Notepad, you can create flat or ASCII text files, and these can be imported. It's easiest if you use delimiters such as commas between each data column. You'll then need to enclose character strings with double quotes ("). If you create a text file like this, you'll import it by using the delimited ASCII format.

Q **What are some of the differences between Import and Load?**

A Although both operations can populate data into a table, some characteristics of Import include the following: Slow when moving large amounts of data, all rows are logged, a backup image is not required (because the import utility uses SQL inserts, DB2 logs the activity, and no backups are required to recover these operations in case of failure). In contrast, Load has the following characteristics: Faster than the import utility when moving large amounts of data (because the load utility writes formatted pages directly into the database), minimal logging is performed, a backup image can be created during the load operation.

Workshop

The purpose of the Workshop is to allow you to test your knowledge of the material covered in the lesson. See whether you can successfully answer the questions in the quiz and complete the exercise before you continue with the next lesson. The answers appear in Appendix B, "Answers to Quiz Questions and Exercises."

Quiz

1. To create a new table by importing IXF data, which import mode should you use?

2. If you want to create a new table, what format should you use? Would you use the Load Wizard or the Import Wizard to create a new table?

3. How do you export only a subset of the data in a table?

4. What must take place before you can save a copy of the changes when using the Load Wizard?

Exercise

1. Use the Export Wizard to export data from the SAMPLE database using the file formats that you did not use during the lesson. Then use the Import and Load Wizards to insert this data into new or existing tables. Try using some available options that weren't used in the lesson.

17

DAY **18**

Replicating Data

DB2 provides integrated replication to enable you to propagate data from a source database to a target database. Today you learn the following:

- What replication environments are supported by DB2
- How to create a replication source and target table
- How to create a subscription set
- How to administer the Capture and Apply programs

Replication Concepts

Replication is the process of propagating data from the source database and using SQL to transform the data as it is applied to tables at the target site. You can use replication to define, synchronize, automate, and manage copy operations for data across your enterprise. You can automatically deliver the data from a host system to target sites. For example, you can copy data on a regular basis from a company's headquarter site to each of the branch offices, even to a personal database residing on each sales representative's laptop.

DB2 uses SQL statements to move data from the source site to the target site. DB2 replication supports a variety of replication environments, including

- One-to-many, where "one" is the source and "many" is the target, a common configuration for distributing data to data marts.
- Many-to-one, where "many" is the source and "one" is the target, a common configuration for consolidating data into a large database or data warehouse.
- Peer-to-peer replication (update-anywhere), where each site can update its data, and replication occurs bi-directionally.
- Replication to many pervasive devices, each having a DB2 database. A common configuration involves a two or three-tiered replication environment.
- Table-based, event-based, or transaction-based replication.
- Heterogeneous replication to support replicating data to and from other relational databases.
- Site-to-site replication, the copying of data to another site to support higher availability and disaster recovery scenarios.

To manage the replication environment, you define source tables known as *replication sources* and specifications for copying changed data known as *replication subscriptions*. Two programs, Capture and Apply, take the changes from a source table, stage them until the target replication program is ready to receive them, and then replicate the changes to one or more target tables (see Figure 18.1).

FIGURE 18.1

The replication environment.

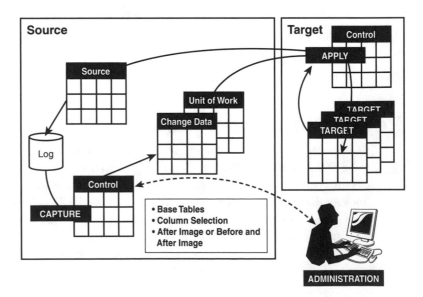

The Capture and Apply programs perform the ongoing replication operations. When your application updates the source table, Capture reads the database log or journal and copies the changes to a staging area for replication at a later time. The Apply program reads the changes and replicates them to the target table.

The Apply program can be used to make a variety of target tables. They are classified as follows:

- Base Aggregate—This target table contains the aggregated data for a user table based on SQL column functions and GROUP BY filters that you define.
- Change Aggregate—This target table contains aggregated data based on changes recorded for a source table.
- Point-in-time—This target table matches the source table, with a time stamp column added.
- Staging table—This consistent-change-data table can be used as the source for updating data to multiple target tables.
- User copy—This target table is a complete or partial copy of the source table, optionally with transformed columns or new columns.
- Replica—This target table is an updateable copy of all or a portion of the source table. It is used only for update-anywhere replication scenarios.

With the Replication Center, you can do the setup required for replication by using the Define as replication source and Define subscription actions. Administrators can perform the following tasks from the Replication Center:

- Define replication sources
- Define replication subscriptions
- Create control tables and target tables
- Specify SQL to enhance data during the apply process
- Perform replication operations, including Start Capture, Apply, Analyzer, and Trace
- Monitor the major replication programs: Capture and Apply dynamically or review historical data

The Capture program reads the replication control tables for current registration information and stores its status in these tables. Any database that will act as a Capture control server must contain the Capture control tables.

The Replication Center includes a Launchpad that will help the user create the replication environment. The Launchpad also provides a graphical representation indicating where the Source, Control, and Change Data tables are placed and where subscription sets are applied. You can choose not to have this window appear each time you start the

18

Replication Center by checking the option Do Not Show the Launchpad Agent When the Replication Center Opens (see Figure 18.2).

FIGURE 18.2

Replication Center Launchpad.

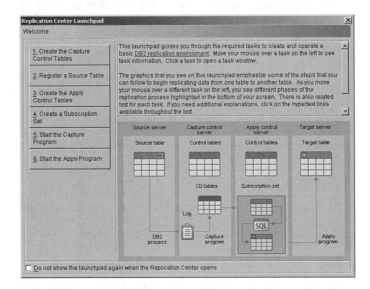

Creating a Replication Environment

The following example follows the six steps of the Replication Center Launchpad; however, the steps are executed directly from the Replication Center. The following six steps set up the CDLIB database as the Capture server and the SAMPLE database as the Target server:

- Step 1: Create the Capture control tables.
- Step 2: Register a Source table.
- Step 3: Create the Apply control tables.
- Step 4: Create a subscription set.
- Step 5: Start the Capture program.
- Step 6: Start the Apply program.

Step 1: Create the Capture Control Tables

To create the Capture control tables, follow these steps:

1. Start the Replication Center from the Control Center, expand the Replication Definitions folder, right-click the Capture Control Servers folder, and select Create Capture Control Tables|Quick.

2. In the Select a Server window, you can select which database you want the control tables for the Capture server; select CDLIB (see Figure 18.3). You then see the Create Control Tables – Quick – Server Information window; select the Host Sources for Replication and Capture Changes to Those Sources check box (see Figure 18.4). Click Ok.

FIGURE 18.3

Selecting a database server.

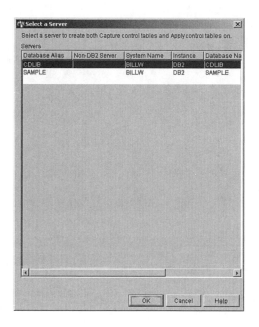

3. In the Create Control Tables - Quick - Replication Details window, accept the default values and click Next (see Figure 18.5).

4. In the Create Control Tables - Quick - Table Spaces window, enter the table space specification for the TSASNCA table space. For example, set the buffer pool to IBMDEFAULTBP. For this scenario, accept the default Capture schema, ASN (see Figure 18.6).

After you select the options for the TSASNCA table space, highlight the TSAS-NUOW table space and enter the desired page and buffer pool options. Enter a valid user ID and password in the Run Now or Save SQL window (Figure 18.7) and click OK to run the SQL script immediately. In the DB2 Message window, you should see a message that the script ran successfully on the CDLIB server.

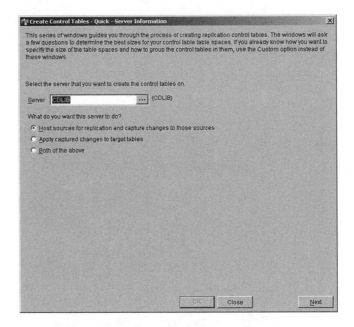

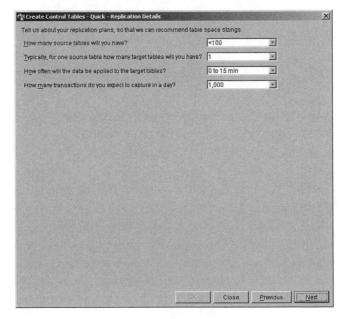

FIGURE 18.6

Creating the table spaces.

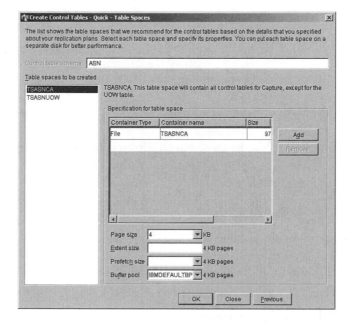

FIGURE 18.7

Run Now or Save SQL window.

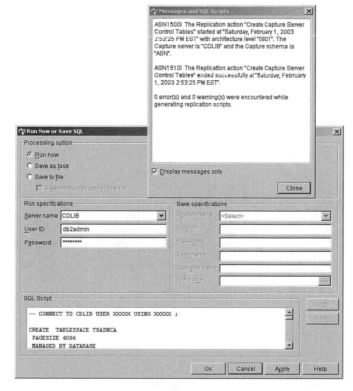

18

NOTE

> The Capture program reads the DB2 log for log records that include changes to registered tables. The log must be an archive log so that DB2 will not reuse the log file before the Capture program can read the log. The DB2 default is circular logging, so you must change this setting to archive logging.

If the CDLIB database has not been enabled for log archiving, you can either right-click the CDLIB database and select Enable Database for Replication, or use the Configure Database Logging Wizard.

Step 2: Register a Source Table

DB2 offers a number of options when you're registering a source table. Allowable sources for replication include a DB2 table, a non-DB2 relational table through a nickname, a subset of the data in a table (DB2 or non-DB2 relational), a view over a single table (DB2), and a view that represents an inner join of two or more tables (DB2).

You need to select tables on the source server from which to copy data and register them as replication sources. You can choose what data is captured from that source and repeat this process until you have registered all the tables or views required. To register a table as a replication source, follow these steps:

1. Expand the Replication Definitions folder, then the Capture Control Servers folder, and then the CDLIB database folder. Right-click the Registered Tables folder and select Register Tables.

2. In the Add Registerable Tables window, click Retrieve All to list in the CDLIB database all the tables that you can register as replication sources (see Figure 18.8). Select the ALBUM table and click OK. The Register Tables window opens (see Figure 18.9).

3. In the Register Tables window, click the CD Table tab, accept the defaults for this example, and click OK (see Figure 18.10).

NOTE

> Each source table has a corresponding CD table where the captured changes are stored.

FIGURE 18.8

Add Registerable Tables window.

FIGURE 18.9

The Register Tables window's Definition page.

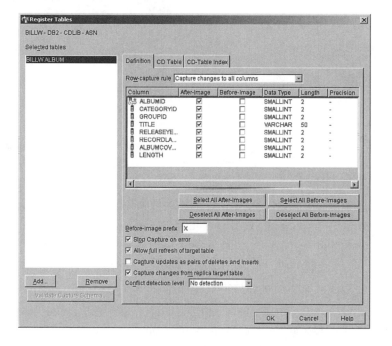

18

4. The Run Now or Save SQL window (see Figure 18.11) shows the result of generating the SQL script that will create the Capture control tables. Click OK to execute the generated SQL statement; if any errors occur, they are displayed in the Message and SQL Scripts window.

The contents pane for the CDLIB database folder should now show ALBUM as a registered table. The ALBUM table is now defined as a replication source. When you ran the

SQL script, the Replication Center created the CD table and CD-table index for this replication source, and it updated the Capture control tables.

FIGURE **18.10**

The Register Tables window's CD Table page.

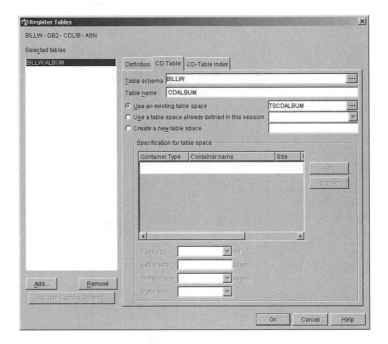

Step 3: Create the Apply Control Tables

The Apply program reads the replication control tables for current subscription-set information and stores its status in these tables. Any database that will act as an Apply control server must contain the Apply control tables.

To create Apply control tables, follow these steps:

1. Expand the Replication Definitions folder. Right-click the Apply Control Servers folder and select Create Apply Control Tables|Quick.

2. In the Select a Server window, you can select which database you want the control tables for the Apply server; select SAMPLE (see Figure 18.12). You then see the Create Control Tables – Quick – Server Information window; select the Apply Captured Changes to Target Tables check box (see Figure 18.13). Then click Next.

3. In the Create Control Tables - Quick - Replication Details window, accept the default values and click Next (see Figure 18.14).

Figure 18.11

Run Now or Save SQL.

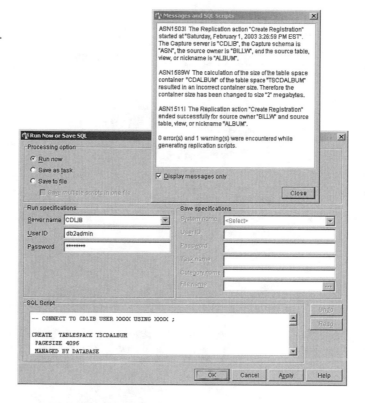

Figure 18.12

Select a database server for the Apply control tables.

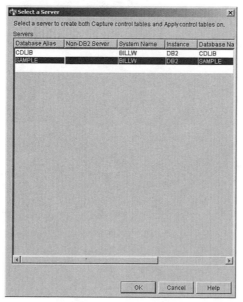

18

FIGURE **18.13**

*Create Control Tables
– Quick – Server
Information window.*

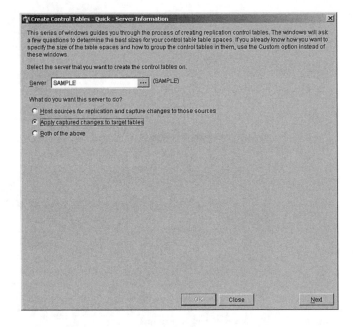

FIGURE **18.14**

Replication details.

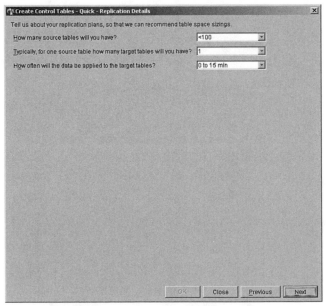

4. In the Create Control Tables - Quick - Table Spaces window, enter the table space specification for the TSASNAA table space (see Figure 18.15). For example, set the buffer pool to IBMDEFAULTBP. Click OK.

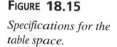

FIGURE 18.15

Specifications for the table space.

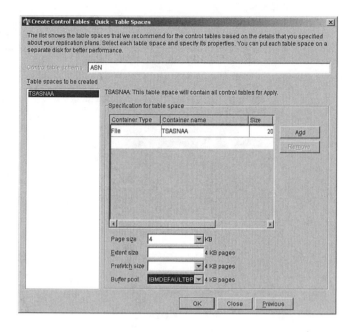

5. Enter a valid user ID and password in the Run Now or Save SQL window and click OK to run the SQL script immediately. In the DB2 Message window, you should see a message that the script ran successfully on the SAMPLE server. Click Close. If any errors occur, they are displayed in this window (see Figure 18.16). Click the Close button to close the window.

6. Expand the Apply Control Servers folder. The SAMPLE database should be displayed under that folder.

Step 4: Create a Subscription Set

After you register the source table, you need to create a subscription set. A *subscription set* defines a relationship between the replication source database (CDLIB in this scenario) and a target database (SAMPLE in this scenario). A subscription-set member defines a relationship between the replication source table (ALBUM in this scenario) and one or more target tables (this scenario has only one, called ALBUMCOPY).

To create a subscription set and a subscription-set member, follow these steps:

1. Expand the Replication Definitions folder, then the Apply Control Servers folder, and then the SAMPLE folder. Right-click the Subscription Sets folder and select Create.

FIGURE **18.16**

Run Now or Save SQL.

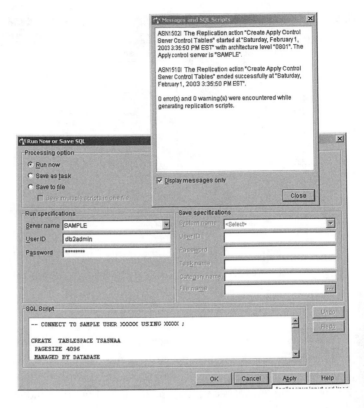

FIGURE **18.16**

Run Now or Save SQL.

2. In the Set Information page of the Create Subscription Set window, enter the following information (see Figure 18.17):

   • In the Set Name field, enter **MUSICSUB**. This string identifies the subscription set and must be unique for a particular Apply qualifier.

   • In the Apply Qualifier field, enter **MUSIC1** (the qualifier is case sensitive). This string identifies the replication definitions that are unique to the instance of the Apply program that will run this subscription set.

   • Click the Browse button for the Capture Control Server Alias field. In the Select a Capture Control Server window, select the CDLIB database and click OK.

   • Click the Browse button for the Target Server Alias field. In the Select a Target Server window, select the SAMPLE database and click OK.

   • Select the Activate the Subscription Set check box.

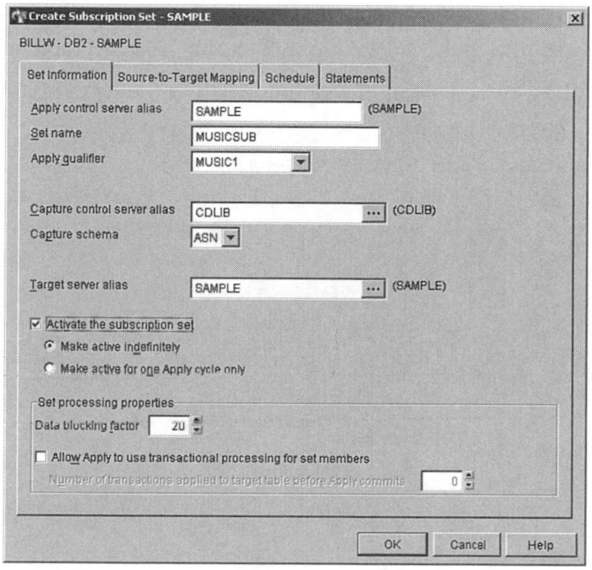

FIGURE 18.17

FIGURE 18.17

The Create Subscription Set window's Set Information page.

3. Click the Source-to-Target Mapping page of the Create Subscription Set window (see Figure 18.18). Click Add to add a registered source to the subscription-set member.

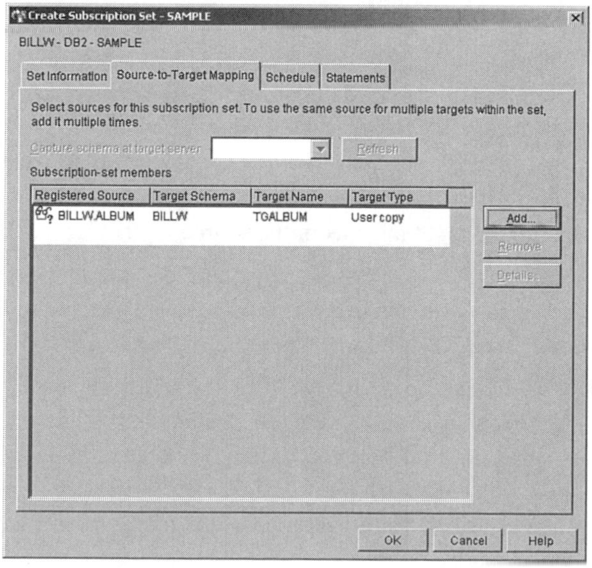

18

FIGURE 18.18

The Create Subscription Set window's Source-to-Target Mapping page.

4. In the Add Registered Sources window, click Retrieve All to display all registered sources in the CDLIB database. Select the ALBUM table and click OK.

5. Click the Source-to-Target Mapping page of the Create Subscription Set window. In the Target Name field, change the name of the target table from TGALBUM by typing **TGALBUMCOPY** over the default name (see Figure 18.19).

FIGURE 18.19

Specifying a target name.

6. Click Details to open the Member Properties window. From this window, you can define the properties for the subscription-set member. You don't need to make any changes to the Column Selection or Column Mapping pages of the Member Properties window because you want to replicate all columns and create the same columns in the target table as in the source table. Click OK.

7. The Replication Center tries to create an index to improve performance (see Figure 18.20). You can override this feature and select your own index. Accept the recommendation, the IXTGALBUMCOPY index, and click OK.

8. In the Row Filter page of the Member Properties window, shown in Figure 18.21, enter the following clause in the WHERE statement field: **RELEASEYEAR > 2000**. This WHERE clause indicates that you want to replicate only those rows that meet certain criteria—in this case, that the ALBUM number is greater than 2000. When you use this WHERE clause, the target table contains three rows instead of all nine rows. Click OK.

FIGURE 18.20

The Member Properties window's Target-Table Index page.

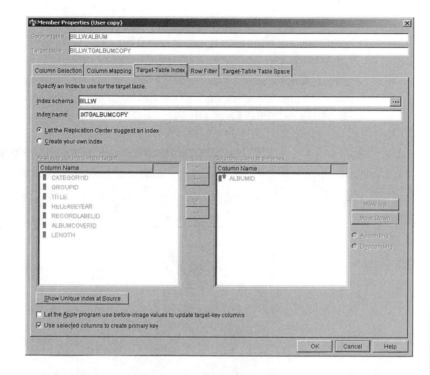

FIGURE 18.21

The Member Properties window's Row Filter page.

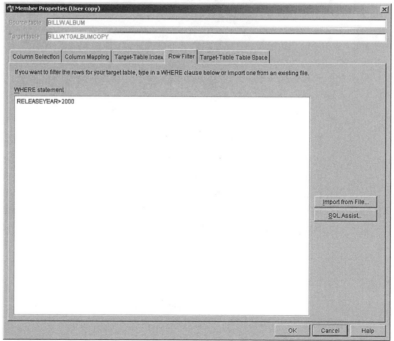

18

9. In the Target-Table Table Space page of the Member Properties window, you must specify information for the new TSTGALBUMCOPY table space (see Figure 18.22).

    In the Specification for Table Space area, click the Container Name field to specify the container name for the TSTGALBUMCOPY table space. Set the buffer pool to IBMDEFAULTBP. Click OK to close the Member Properties window.

FIGURE 18.22

The Member Properties window's Target-Table Table Space page.

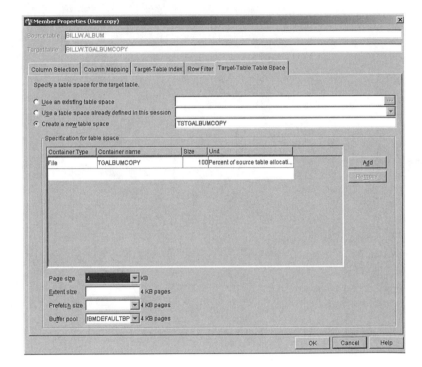

10. In the Schedule page of the Create Subscription Set window, the number of minutes of the Use Relative Timing option is currently set to 20 so that the Apply program will process this subscription set every 20 minutes (see Figure 18.23). You can change how often the Apply program executes by using the spin button on the Minutes field in the Frequency of Replication Area to select a different interval. Keep the default values for Start Date, Start Time, Time-Based, and Use Relative Timing. Click OK.

11. In the Statements page of the Create Subscription Set window (see Figure 18.24), click Add to open the Add SQL Statement or Procedure Call window (see Figure 18.25).

FIGURE 18.23

The Create Subscription Set window's Schedule page.

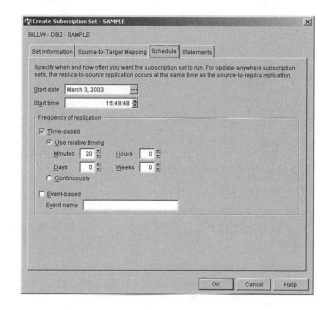

FIGURE 18.24

The Create Subscription Set window's Statements page.

18

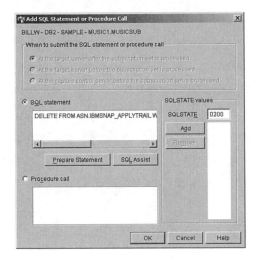

FIGURE 18.25

Add SQL Statements or Procedure Call window.

Use this window to define the SQL statements that will be processed when the subscription set is run. In the Add SQL Statement or Procedure Call window, enter the following information:

- In the SQL Statement field, enter

  ```
  DELETE FROM ASN.IBMSNAP_APPLYTRAIL WHERE LASTRUN
       < (CURRENT TIMESTAMP - 7 DAYS)
  ```

  This statement deletes any records in the Apply trail table that are older than seven days.

  The Apply program will execute the SQL statement that you added at the target server after the subscription set is processed. The SQL statement must run at the target server because the Apply control server and target server are co-located and the Apply trail table is in the Apply control server.

- In the SQLSTATE field, enter **02000** and click Add. This SQL state indicates that the "row not found" error is acceptable and that the Apply program should ignore it. You can define up to 10 SQL states that you want the Apply program to ignore for this subscription set.

Click OK to close the Add SQL Statement or Procedure Call window. Click OK to close the Create Subscription Set window.

12. Click Close on the Message window. This window shows the result of generating the SQL script that will update the Apply control tables and create the target table. If any errors occur, they are displayed in this window. Click OK on the Run Now or Save SQL window to run the SQL script immediately. In the DB2 Message

window, you should see a message that the script ran successfully at both the SAMPLE and CDLIB servers (see Figure 18.26). Click Close.

FIGURE 18.26

Run Now or Save SQL.

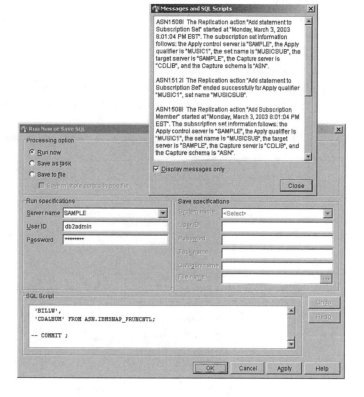

18

Step 5: Start the Capture Program

In the previous steps, you registered the replication source and created the subscription set. Now you must start the Capture and Apply programs to perform the initial full refresh for the target table and begin change-capture replication.

NOTE

Optionally, you can do the full refresh of the target tables yourself. The Replication Center provides the Manual Full Refresh option to update the Apply control tables when you initially populate the target tables outside of replication. You may want to use this option if the target table is large.

To start the Capture program, follow these steps:

1. From the Replication Center, expand the Operations folder. Select the Capture Control Servers folder. The CDLIB database should be displayed in the contents pane for Capture control servers. Right-click the CDLIB database and select Start Capture. In the Start Capture window (see Figure 18.27), select the CAPTURE_PATH keyword. In the Directory in Which to Store Log File field, enter the directory in which you want the Capture program to write its output, including work and log files. You do not need to change any of the other keywords for the Capture program. Click OK on the Start Capture window.

FIGURE 18.27

Start Capture window.

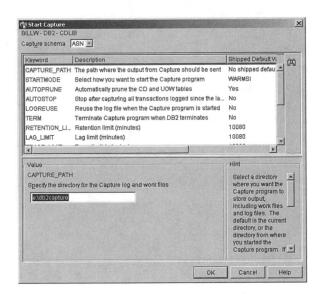

2. Click OK on the Run Now or Save Command window to run the command immediately (see Figure 18.28). In the DB2 Message window, you should see a message that the command ran successfully (see Figure 18.29). Click Close. The Capture program is now running but will not begin capturing changes for registered tables until the Apply program completes a full refresh for all registered tables.

Step 6: Start the Apply Program

To start the Apply program, follow these steps:

1. From the Replication Center, expand the Operations folder, then the Apply Control Servers folder, and then the SAMPLE folder. Select the Apply Qualifiers folder. The MUSIC1 Apply qualifier for subscription set should be displayed in the

contents pane for Apply qualifiers. Right-click the MUSIC1 Apply qualifier and select Start Apply.

FIGURE 18.28

Run Now or Save Command window.

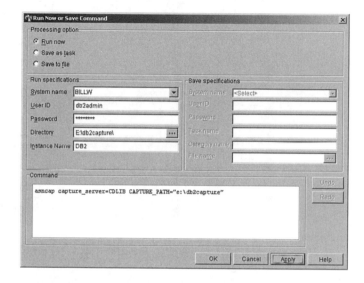

FIGURE 18.29

DB2 Message window.

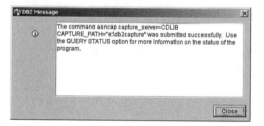

2. In the Start Apply window (see Figure 18.30), enter the following information:

   • Select a system on which to run the Apply program from the System list in the Where to Start Apply area. For this example, BILLW was selected.

   • Select the APPLY_PATH keyword. Enter a value for the directory in which the Apply program will store its log and work files. For this example, the directory e:\db2apply was selected. Click OK.

3. Do not change any of the other keywords for the Apply program. If necessary, type a valid user ID and password for the system on which you will run the Apply program in the Run Now or Save Command window (see Figure 18.31). Click Apply to run the command immediately. In the DB2 Message window, you should see a message that the command ran successfully.

FIGURE 18.30

Start Apply window.

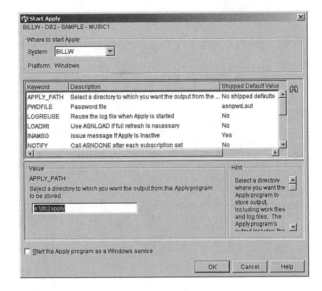

FIGURE 18.31

Run Now or Save Command window.

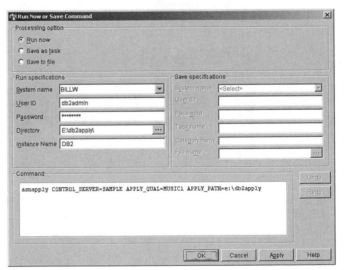

Replication Operations

The Replication Center provides a graphical monitor that allows you to monitor the Capture and Apply programs. You can set alert thresholds so that you are notified if any of these conditions are reached; these alerts are also logged. The process is similar when you use Health Center: You can identify contacts to be e-mailed when the alert conditions are met.

Here are the steps to monitor the main activities occurring during replication:

1. Create the monitor control tables by right-clicking the Monitor Control Servers after expanding the Operations Folder and selecting the Create Monitor Control Tables option.

2. The monitor control tables can exist on the same systems where the Capture or Apply servers are located, or on a separate server. In this example, select the SAMPLE database, where the Apply server is located (see Figure 18.32. Click OK.

FIGURE 18.32

Select a database server.

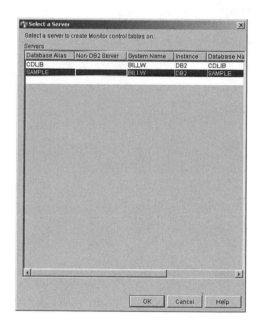

3. Accept the defaults for the Table Space Properties options and Index Name options, select the default buffer pool, and click OK.

4. When the Messages and SQL Scripts window appears, click Close. When the Run Now or Save SQL window becomes active, click Apply (see Figure 18.33). You then see a message indicating whether the changes have been applied correctly.

5. Return to the Replication Center and right-click the Monitor Control Servers folder. Then click Add.

6. You can choose to monitor the Capture Control Server, the Apply Control Server, or both. For this example, select to monitor the Apply Control Server (the SAMPLE database) and click OK (see Figure 18.34).

FIGURE 18.33

Run Now or Save SQL window.

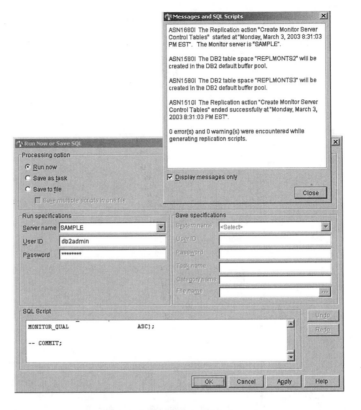

FIGURE 18.34

Add Monitor Control Servers window.

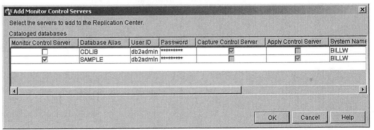

7. The SAMPLE database icon appears in the Monitor Control Servers folder. Right-click the Monitor Qualifiers so that you can select thresholds to monitor. Select the option Select Alert Conditions for Apply Qualifiers or Subscription Sets (see Figure 18.35).

8. Enter the Monitor qualifier (BILLW in this case) and select the Apply control server you want to monitor (the SAMPLE database in this example). Click Add and then the Retrieve All button to see the list of available subscriptions to monitor, select MUSICSUB, and then click OK (see Figure 18.36).

FIGURE 18.35

Monitor Qualifiers folder.

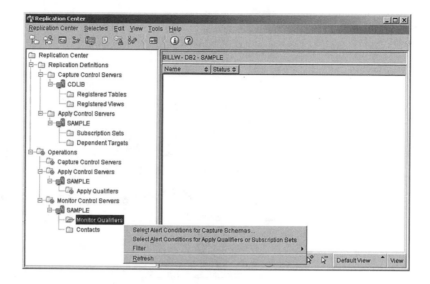

FIGURE 18.36

Add Subscription Sets window.

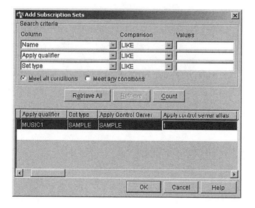

9. Select which error conditions you want someone to be alerted to. You can specify a different contact for each alert condition. The contact box on the bottom of the window allows you to identify a person's email or pager ID for the alert (see Figure 18.37). Click OK.

10. A Messages window indicates that the alert condition has been specified for the Apply Server and a list of which alerts to monitor. Click Close on this window and then click Apply on the Run Now or Save SQL window to run the script. Error alerts on the MUSICSUB subscription are sent to the person you identified— Shirley, in this case (see Figure 18.38).

FIGURE **18.37**

Select Alert Conditions.

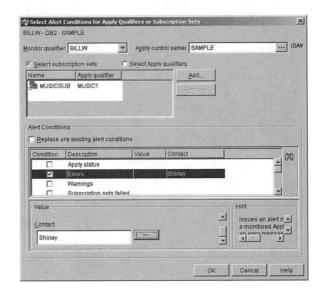

FIGURE **18.38**

Run Now or Save SQL window.

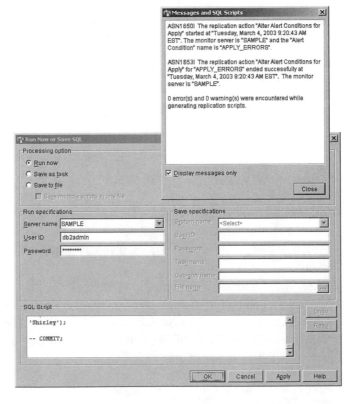

Summary

Today you saw that you can replicate data from one database to another. When the replication is set up, logs are used to record data transactions. These logs are then used to update the replica database, minimizing the amount of copying that needs to be done to keep the databases synchronized.

You used the Replication Center to define the replication sources and the subscription actions. When these actions are set up, you use the Capture and Apply programs outside the Control Center to read and replicate the changes.

You can set up many different types of replication. You can choose to have the entire contents of the database copied or just the changes.

You have the option of setting up a more advanced scenario in which the source database is replicated to many sites and any changes made to the replicated databases at these individual sites are then captured and replicated back to the source database.

What Comes Next?

On Day 19, "Database Monitoring Tools," you will examine the major utilities to monitor and maintain the health of your database system.

18

Q&A

Q How are changes to the source data captured?

A Each source table has a corresponding Change Data (CD) table where the captured changes are stored. The CD table is created by the Replication Center when you define a replication source table. You can choose to capture a subset of the source table columns. You can also capture the values before the change is made (called *before-image* columns) with the values after the change is made (called the *after-image* columns).

Q When do I need to worry about conflict detection?

A Conflict detection is necessary only when you're using update-anywhere replication. Update-anywhere replication means that you've replicated your table to many sites and these changes can be replicated back to the source database. Conflict detection is necessary to ensure that changes made to the same data at two separate sites don't jeopardize the integrity of the data.

Q What is a subscription set?

A A subscription set is one or more source table–to–target table mappings. The source-to-target mappings are called *subscription members*. A subscription set has only one source server and one target server. Each subscription set has an apply qualifier with it. An Apply program is started with an apply qualifier, and that Apply program will process all the sets with a matching apply qualifier. An apply qualifier can have many sets. Each set has zero or more members.

Workshop

The purpose of the workshop is to allow you to test your knowledge of the material covered in the lesson. See whether you can successfully answer the questions in the quiz and complete the exercises before you continue with the next lesson. Answers to quiz questions are provided in Appendix B.

Quiz

1. What are the possible sources of data that can be registered for replication?
2. Where must the Capture program be run? Where must the Apply program be run?
3. What is *capture before-image*? When would you use this option?

Exercise

When you have the replication set up as described in this lesson, add data to the ALBUM table to see that the data is replicated to the ALBUMCOPY table.

WEEK 3

DAY 19

Database Monitoring Tools

DB2 provides several tools to help you determine your specific performance requirements. You will learn how to use the following tools:

- Health Monitor, which enables you to monitor a DB2 instance by allowing you to create alerts and notifications if an alert threshold is exceeded

- Database System Monitor, a collecton of APIs that enable you to gather information on what's occurring in the system, either at a single point in time (snapshot monitoring) or over a period of time (event monitoring)

- Visual Explain, which enables you to graphically see the access plan the DB2 optimizer has selected for a given SQL statement

- RUNSTATS, which allows you to collect statistics about the physical organization of data in the tables or indexes

- Reorg, which enables you to reorganize your table or index data into a sequential order to allow for faster retrieval of data

These tools help you find out what is going on in your databases and can help you tune the performance on your system. You can find out specifics about who is using the database, how many statements are being issued, and which exact SQL statements are being entered.

Health Monitor

The Health Monitor is a tool that runs on the server; it constantly monitors the health of the instance, even without user interaction. If the Health Monitor finds that a defined threshold has been exceeded (for example, the available log space is not sufficient), or if it detects an abnormal state for an object (for example, an instance is down), it raises an alert. When an alert is raised, two things can occur:

- Alert notifications can be sent by email or to a pager address, allowing you to contact whoever is responsible for a system.
- Preconfigured actions can be taken. For example, a script or a task (implemented from the Task Center) can be run.

A *health indicator* is a system characteristic that the Health Monitor checks. The Health Monitor comes with a set of predefined thresholds for these health indicators. The Health Monitor checks the state of your system against these health-indicator thresholds when determining whether to issue an alert. Using the Health Center, commands, or APIs, you can customize the threshold settings of the health indicators and define who should be notified and what script or task should be run if an alert is issued. The following are the categories of health indicators:

- Application concurrency
- Database management system
- Database
- Logging
- Memory
- Package and catalog caches
- Sorting
- Table space storage

You can start the Health Monitor by selecting IBM DB2|Monitoring Tools|Health Center, or you can start the Health Monitor from the Tools menu in the Control Center. After you right-click the Sample database from the Health Center, select Configure, and then select Database Object Health Indicator Settings, you will see the window shown in Figure 19.1.

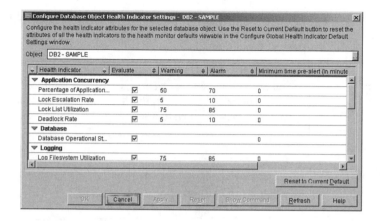

FIGURE 19.1

The Health Monitor's Configure Database Object Health Indicator Settings window.

Database System Monitor

The Database System Monitor is a set of commands and APIs used to provide a wide variety of statistical information about the operation of the database manager, and activity information such as counters and other measurements of database processing. This information can be used to help you

- Better understand how the database manager works
- Improve database and application performance
- Tune configuration parameters
- Determine the source and cause of problems
- Understand user and application activity within the database manager

The information gathered by the monitor is generated by the internal components of the database manager. The monitor begins recording the database manager level of information when DB2 is started and records until DB2 is stopped. The monitor begins recording database information when the first connection is made to the database and records until the last application disconnects from it. Application information is recorded from the time an application connects to a database and is recorded until it disconnects.

Some basic monitoring information is always collected, and you can also selectively collect other statistical information. This flexibility is important because additional monitoring increases overhead, which can have an impact on performance.

You can run the Database System Monitor commands from any of the command-line tools to quickly gather statistical information. Applications can be written to take advantage of the rich set of APIs and to provide some automated analysis of the vast amount of monitor data available from the Database System Monitor. The Command Center in

19

Figure 19.2 demonstrates how this command-line tool can be used to issue a database command.

NOTE

You need either SYSADM, SYSCTRL, or SYSMAINT authority to issue the following commands: UPDATE MONITOR SWITCHES, GET MONITOR SWITCHES, or GET DATABASE MANAGER MONITOR SWITCHES.

FIGURE 19.2

GET MONITOR SWITCHES

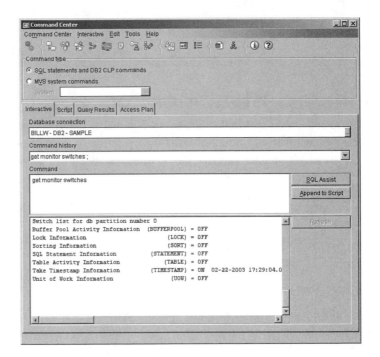

There are two monitoring methods of extracting information collected by the Database System Monitor: *event* and *snapshot*. Event monitoring is used to query the operational status of a database over a period of time. Snapshot monitoring is used to query the operational status of a database at any particular point in time.

The snapshot monitor and event monitor can help you gather information about your databases. You can choose to enter Database System Monitor commands at a command prompt, write your own applications with the Database System Monitor APIs, or simply use the tools that are provided with DB2, all to perform the same basic functions. For both Snapshot and event monitors, you have the option of storing monitor information in files or SQL tables, viewing it on the screen, or processing it with a client application.

The snapshot monitor and event monitor provide the following benefits:

- Comprehensive, flexible data collection—More than 200 performance attributes are supported, including buffer pool and I/O, lock and deadlock, sorting, communication, agent, and logging information. Data is shown for database managers, databases, table spaces, tables, buffer pools, connections, transactions, and SQL statements.

- Easy-to-use, intuitive viewing—Snapshot data can be viewed in real time with easy-to-read graphs or textual views conveniently organized into logical groups. Details and summary views are provided, with the ability to access more detailed information.

- Powerful data analysis capabilities—You can customize measurements by allowing spreadsheet-like formulas. Rather than monitor an absolute measurement, for example, you can monitor a ratio calculated from two related measurements.

TIP

You also can use the Windows Performance Monitor to monitor database and system performance. Windows also provides performance information on CPU usage, memory utilization, disk activity, and network activity.

Event Monitoring

You can create an event monitor to record data about the occurrence of specific milestones for a period of time. An *event monitor* allows you to collect information about transient events that would be difficult to monitor through snapshots, such as deadlocks, transaction completion, and completion information that includes how long a transaction took or how much CPU a statement used. This information is presented as a report on the activities occurring in the database.

Monitoring a database manager event results in information being returned when that event occurs. The information provides a good summary of the activity of a particular event—for example, a database connection or a SQL statement.

You use the Event Analyzer to view the information collected by an event monitor and stored in event files. The Event Analyzer is used with an event monitor file to provide information about database events that have taken place. For example, you can use an event monitor to record information on database activities, such as connections, transactions, statements, and deadlocks. After the event monitor creates its file, you can look at the collected performance information by using the Event Analyzer.

19

You can create event monitors that help you manage your databases and the applications that connect to them. For example,

- You can analyze deadlocks by collecting deadlock information.
- You can enable usage accounting by gathering data at the connection or application level.
- You can improve capacity planning. You can use statistical data collected for database objects and applications in trend analysis to predict future project needs.
- You can tune applications—by analyzing connection and transaction data or by analyzing SQL statement event data—with a focus on heavy SQL statements.
- You can tune databases by using data collected on database objects, such as buffer pools, table spaces, and tables. This tuning can include an evaluation of configuration parameters and sort activity.

Creating an Event Monitor

Use the Create Event Monitor window to create an event monitor that will collect performance information on database activities in a file. Follow these steps:

1. Start the Control Center.
2. Expand the object tree until you find the database that you want to monitor—for example, the CDLIB database.
3. Right-click the database and then select Monitor Events from the pop-up menu. The Event Monitor window opens.
4. In the Create Event Monitor window shown in Figure 19.3, specify a name for the event monitor you're creating in the Name text box. This new event monitor can't have the same name as any existing monitor and must be fewer than 18 characters in length. Blank spaces aren't allowed in the name. For this example, use `CDLIBEVENT`.

FIGURE 19.3

The Create Event Monitor window.

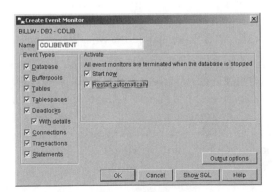

5. Select one or more of the Event Types check boxes to indicate the types of events that you want to monitor (for this example, select all the check boxes):

- Database—Records a database event when the last application disconnects from the database.

- Bufferpools—Records the number of reads and writes, and time taken.

- Tables—Records a table event for each active table when the last application disconnects from the database.

- Table Spaces—Records a table space event for each active table space when the last application disconnects from the database.

- Deadlocks (the default)—Records a deadlock event whenever a deadlock occurs.

- Connections—Records a connection event when an application disconnects from the database. To control monitoring, use a filter to specify the conditions that will generate connection events.

- Transactions—Records a transaction event whenever a transaction completes (a commit or rollback). To control monitoring, use a filter to specify the conditions that will generate transaction events.

- Statements—Records a statement event whenever a SQL statement finishes executing. To control monitoring, use a filter to specify the conditions that will generate statement events.

6. In the Activate section, indicate when you want this monitor to start. The default is Start Now, for monitors to start as soon as they're defined. Keep the Start Now check box selected for this example.

If you start a statement event monitor after a statement starts, the monitor will start collecting information when the next SQL statement starts. As a result, the event monitor won't return information about statements that the database manager is executing when the monitor was started. This is also true for transaction and connection information.

Select Restart Automatically to have monitoring automatically restarted when the database starts. Candidates for auto-started monitors might include monitors that collect statistical data for tuning or those gathering information for usage accounting systems. When the database is stopped, any running event monitor is terminated; only auto-started monitors restart when the database comes back online.

19

TIP

> You can create any number of event monitors, turning them on or off as required. This flexibility allows you to maintain a collection of various event monitors and enables you to turn on an appropriate subset of monitors to achieve your desired monitoring. The maximum number of active event monitors for a database at any given time is 32.

7. In the Show SQL window, you can see the SQL that will be used to create a table for the Event Monitor where you can query later (see Figure 19.4).

FIGURE 19.4

SQL for creating an event monitor.

Click the Output Options button on the Create Event Monitor dialog box to view the Output Options dialog box (see Figure 19.5). In the Data Integrity section, indicate the type of file I/O you want. Event monitors have two I/O buffers: blocked or nonblocked file I/O. The default is blocked file I/O.

FIGURE 19.5

Output Options dialog box.

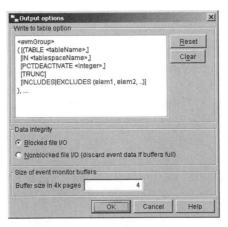

If you select Blocked File I/O, and both I/O buffers are full, the database agents wait for the event monitor to write one of its buffers to disk before attempting to write new data to the buffer. If you select Nonblocked File I/O, the database agents don't wait for the monitor to write to disk; if both buffers are full when an event occurs, the event data is discarded.

TIP

Blocked I/O provides better data integrity, but nonblocked I/O provides better performance because database activities don't slow down due to waits.

Stopping an Event Monitor

To stop an event monitor, follow these steps:

1. From the list of monitors in the Event Monitors window, select the event monitor that you want to stop (see Figure 19.6).

FIGURE 19.6

The Monitored Periods View window.

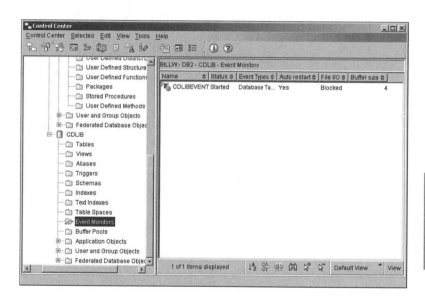

2. Right-click the selected event monitor and choose Stop Event Monitoring from the options.

Viewing Monitored Events

Event data is available at different times depending on the event type. To view event monitor files, follow these steps:

1. From the list of monitors in the Event Monitors window, click the event monitor that you want to view. Right-click the selected event monitor and select Analyze Event Monitor Records to start the Event Analyzer.

2. Choose Selected|Open As from the menu. The monitored database objects appear
   in a list. Because you selected to have all objects monitored when you created the
   sample event monitor, you can select from Connections, Deadlocks, Deadlock
   Connections, Overflows, Transactions, or Statements. When you select one of these
   options, you see the details recorded for that event. For this example, click
   Statements to see the SQL statements (see Figure 19.7).

FIGURE 19.7

*The Event Analyzer
window.*

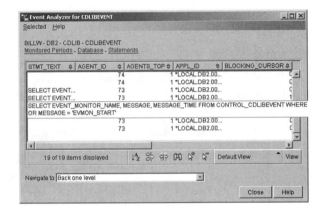

3. To see how an existing event monitor was defined, choose Selected|View
   Definitions from the menu. The selections in the View Definitions window were
   made when the monitor was created (see Figure 19.8).

FIGURE 19.8

*The View Definitions
window.*

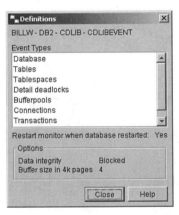

Snapshot Monitoring

Taking a snapshot of data gives you information for the point in time that the snapshot
was requested. This information provides a picture of the current state of all activity in a

database instance. Use the snapshot monitor when you have a problem that's occurring now or if you want to query the status of a database at a particular instance in time. You can analyze long-running transactions for which you may want interim information before they are complete.

Some snapshots provide cumulative information in the form of *counters*, to cover activity from the time monitoring started to the time the snapshot was requested. Other information is returned only if that particular event was complete before the snapshot was requested.

With the snapshot monitor, for a given point in time, a snapshot is returned for a performance variable. The snapshot monitor displays these points for comparison over time. Each point on the graph represents a data value. This information can be used to

- Detect performance problems
- Analyze performance trends
- Tune database instance and database configuration parameters
- Analyze the performance of database applications

Performance information is available for the following database objects:

- Database instances
- Databases
- Tables
- Table spaces
- Database connections

Use the following command to take a snapshot of a database manager instance:

```
> db2 get snapshot dbm
```

This command lists data regarding the state of the database instance at a single point in time.

Using Visual Explain

The Visual Explain tool graphically shows you the access plans for explained SQL statements. You can use the information available from the graph to tune your SQL queries for better performance.

19

An access plan graph shows details of the following:

- Tables, their associated columns, and indexes
- Operators such as table scans, sorts, and joins
- Tables spaces and functions

You can also use Visual Explain to do the following:

- View the statistics used at the time of optimization. You can then compare these statistics to the current catalog statistics to help you determine whether rebinding the package might improve performance.
- Obtain information about each operation in the access plan, including the total estimated cost and number of rows retrieved.
- Model the effects of performing various tuning techniques by comparing before and after versions of the access plan graph for a query.
- Determine whether an index was used to access a table. If an index wasn't used, Visual Explain can help you determine which columns might benefit from being indexed.
- View the access plan chosen by the database manager's optimizer for a given SQL statement.
- Tune SQL statements for better performance.
- Design application programs and databases.
- View all the details of the access plan, including the statistics in the system catalogs.
- Decide whether to add an index to a table.
- Identify the source of problems by analyzing the access plan or performance of SQL statement execution.
- Use the portable snapshot function to view snapshots from any remote DB2 server.
- Display access plans for parallel and SMP systems.

Producing an Access Plan Graph

Follow these steps to produce an access plan graph by using the Command Center:

1. If the statistics in the system catalog table aren't current, update them with the RUNSTATS operation. See the later section "Collecting Statistics" for information on updating statistics.

2. Right-click the SAMPLE database and select the Explain SQL option. The Explain SQL Statement window opens (see Figure 19.9). Enter the following sample query that uses the SAMPLE database:

```
select s.id, s.name, o.deptname, salary+comm
from org o, staff s
where
    o.deptnumb = s.dept and
    s.job <> 'Mgr' and
    s.salary+s.comm  > all(select st.salary*.9
                           from staff st
                           where st.job='Mgr')
    order by s.name
```

This query lists the name, department, and earnings for all non-manager employees who earn more than 90% of the highest-paid manager's salary.

FIGURE 19.9

Explain SQL Statement window.

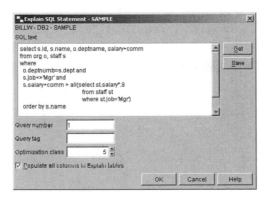

3. Click OK to see whether the statement is accurate. If the statement is accurate, you see some columns of data. (Visual Explain will not work if the SQL statement is not valid.) The explain tables will be automatically created the first time you execute a dynamic explain.

The access plan shows that a number of table scans, hash joins, and nested loop joins are used to access the data (see Figure 19.10). Performance of this query would likely increase with the addition and use of indexes.

To see the statistics being used for the ORG table, double-click the BILLW.ORG table node in the graph. The Table Statistics window opens (see Figure 19.11).

4. Use the zoom slider to see details of the graph. Double-click a node in the graph to see details.

19

FIGURE **19.10**

The access plan graph.

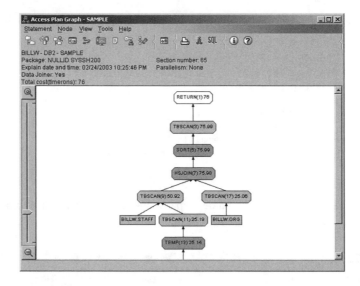

FIGURE **19.11**

The Table Statistics window.

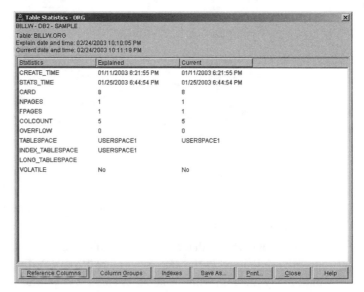

TIP

To view table statistics, you need, at a minimum, the SELECT privilege on the explain tables and system catalog tables. To view statistics for multiple tables in a graph (or indexes, if any), select each table node by clicking it (the color changes); then right-click and select Show Statistics from the pop-up menu.

You can perform some other tasks while viewing the table statistics:

- To display a list of referenced columns, as in Figure 19.12, click the Reference Columns button.
- To save the contents of the window to a file, click the Save As button.
- To print the contents of the window, click the Print button.

FIGURE 19.12

The Referenced Columns Statistics window.

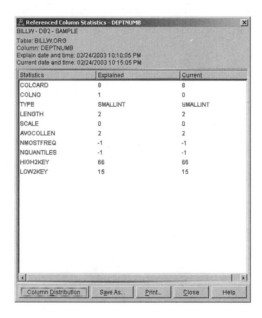

Analyzing an Access Plan Graph

The Table Statistics window displays the statistics shown in Table 19.1.

TABLE 19.1 Table Statistics

Statistic	Description
CREATE_TIME	The date and time that the table was created.
STATS_TIME	The last time a change was made to any recorded statistic for the table. If the statistics are out of date, the optimizer uses default values, which can result in an inefficient access plan. Use the RUNSTATS command to update the statistics and then rebind the package.
CARD	The number of rows in the table. If the cardinality is zero, ensure that you used RUNSTATS after making your table updates.
NPAGES	The number of pages of the table that contain one or more rows.

19

TABLE 19.1 continued

Statistic	Description
FPAGES	The number of columns in the table.
OVERFLOW	The number of overflow pages used by the table.
TABLESPACE	The name of the table's primary table space.
INDEX_TABLESPACE	The name of the table space that contains all indexes for the table.
LONG_TABLESPACE	The name of the table space that contains all long data (LONG or LOB column types) for the table.

An *operator* is either an action that must be performed on data, or the output from a table or an index, when the access plan for a SQL statement is executed. Examples of operators include DELETE, FETCH, FILTER, GRPBY, and INSERT.

To view the details for an operator, double-click an operator node in the diagram to open the Operator Details window (see Figure 19.13). To view detailed information in the window, select Full; to view less detailed information, select Overview. The following sections explain the details shown in this window.

FIGURE 19.13

The Operator Details window.

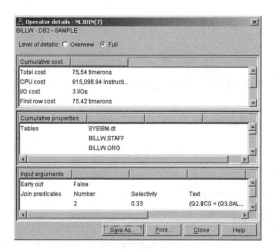

Cumulative Costs

The costs shown in the Operator Details window represent the estimated cumulative costs up to and including the point where the action represented by the operator is performed. These costs are estimated by the optimizer:

- The CPU Cost shows the estimated cumulative CPU cost (in number of instructions).

- I/O Cost shows the estimated cumulative input/output (I/O) cost (in number of seeks and page transfers).

- Total Cost shows the estimated cumulative cost of executing the current access plan (in *timerons*, a combination of CPU and I/O cost).

- First Row Cost shows the estimated cumulative effort (in timerons) required to produce the first row in the set of rows that result when the action represented by the operator is performed.

Cumulative Properties

Several properties are included in the Cumulative Properties section of the Operator Details window:

- Tables lists the tables that have been accessed thus far in the access plan.

- Columns lists the columns that have been accessed thus far in the access plan.

- Order Columns shows the columns on which this stream is ordered. They can be ascending (ASC) or descending (DESC). A value of −1 indicates that they aren't ordered.

- Predicates shows the set of predicates applied (including an estimate of their selectivity). A *predicate* is a condition placed on the data, usually in the form of a comparison operation. Predicates are included in clauses beginning with WHERE or HAVING.

  Selectivity refers to the probability that any row will satisfy a predicate, making it true. A highly selective predicate (with a selectivity of 10% or less) is desirable. Such predicates return fewer rows for future operators to work on, thereby requiring less CPU and I/O to satisfy the query.

- Cardinality shows the estimated number of rows to be returned. If the value is zero, the table appears empty to the optimizer, and you should rerun RUNSTATS.

- Total Buffer Pool Pages Used shows the estimated number of pages in the buffer pool that will be required during processing of this operator and its inputs.

Input Arguments

The arguments in the Input Arguments section of the Operator Details window affect the operator's behavior. The details vary depending on the type of operator and the level of detail chosen. For example, if you're using the DELETE operator, the Deleted Table item shows the name of the table from which the rows are to be deleted. Information regarding other operators is available in the online help.

19

Collecting Statistics

Statistics describe the physical and logical characteristics of a table and its indexes. You must collect table and index statistics periodically for each table. DB2 uses these statistics to determine a good way to access the data. If the data has changed significantly, to the extent that the information last collected no longer reflects the actual table data, performance may begin to deteriorate when users are accessing data.

You should rebind application programs that use static SQL after collecting statistics because the SQL optimizer may choose a different access plan given new statistics. In particular, you should rebind those programs that reference tables for which new statistics are available.

Use the Run Statistics window to update system catalog statistics on the data in a table, data in the table's indexes, or data in the table and indexes. The optimizer uses these statistics to choose which path will be used to access the data. In general, you should update statistics if extensive changes have been made to the data in the table.

To collect statistics, follow these steps:

1. In the Control Center, click the Tables icon to see a list of tables available.

2. In the contents pane, right-click the table for which you want to collect statistics and select Run Statistics from the pop-up menu.

3. In the Run Statistics notebook, shown in Figure 19.14, you can specify the level of statistics you want to gather for the table. In this example, accept the default values. Click the Column Groups tab.

4. Specify any groups of columns you want by clicking the Create button, which opens a window that allows you to specify which columns you want included in the group (see Figure 19.15). Accept the default in this example and click the Index tab.

5. You can collect statistics on any existing indexes on the table (see Figure 19.16). Accept the defaults and click the Options tab.

6. You have the option of running the utility while allowing read and write access to the tables (see Figure 19.17). Accept the default and click the Schedule tab.

7. Accept the default Run Now Without Saving Task History and click OK to run the utility (see Figure 19.18).

FIGURE 19.14

The Run Statistics notebook's Column window.

FIGURE 19.15

The Run Statistics notebook's Column Groups window.

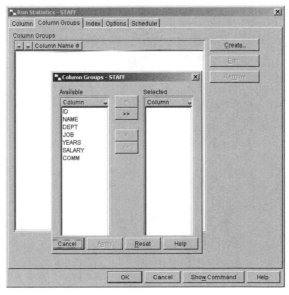

19

The Run Statistics notebook's Index window.

The Run Statistics notebook's Options window.

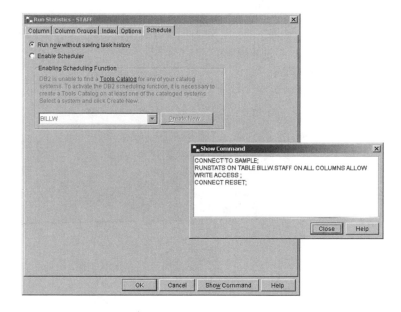

FIGURE 19.18

The Run Statistics notebook's Schedule window.

Reorganizing a Table

You can reorganize a table immediately or schedule it for a specific date and time. When you reorganize a table, the table data is rearranged into a physical sequence, usually according to a specified index. As a result, SQL statements on that data can be processed more efficiently. Also, the reorganization process removes unused, empty space from the table, and the reorganized table is stored more compactly.

Use the following instructions to reorganize your table immediately:

1. Before you reorganize tables, collect the statistics of the data as described in the preceding section.

2. In the Control Center, click the Tables icon to see a list of tables available.

3. In the contents pane, right-click the table you want to reorganize and select Reorganize from the pop-up menu. The Reorganize Table dialog box opens (see Figure 19.19). Accept the defaults for this example.

TIP

It's generally recommended that you specify a temporary SMS table space. If the table you're reorganizing resides in a DMS table space, and you think the temporary space will fit in the same table space, don't specify a table space in this combo box. The reorganization runs faster in this case.

19

> Specifying a DMS table space as the temporary table space isn't generally recommended. If you specify a DMS table space in this field, you can reorganize only one table in that table space at a time.

FIGURE 19.19

The Reorganize Table dialog box.

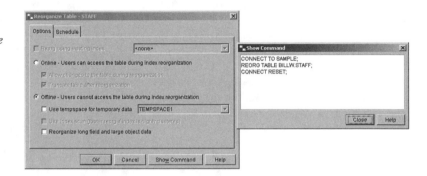

4. Click OK to reorganize the table immediately.

   Alternatively, click Schedule to open the Schedule window to schedule the reorganization for a specific time or date.

> **TIP**
>
> You may want to schedule this activity because reorganizing data can be time-consuming and users won't be able to access the table being organized.

5. When the tables are reorganized, collect the statistics again as explained earlier in the section "Collecting Statistics." Doing so provides the most up-to-date statistics for the data so that you can get the fastest access to it based on the new organization of the data and indexes.

> **TIP**
>
> You may want to issue the REORGCHK command, which calculates the statistics on the database and provides a recommendation if the tables or indexes, or both, need to be reorganized.

You should rebind applications that use static SQL after collecting statistics because the SQL optimizer may choose a different access plan given the new statistics. In particular, you should rebind those programs that reference tables for which the new statistics are available. (See Day 10, "Accessing the Data.")

Storage Management Tool

The Storage Management tool, available through the Control Center, displays a snapshot of the storage for a particular database or table space (see Figure 19.20). This tool monitors indicators also available through the Health Monitor.

FIGURE 19.20

Storage Management tool.

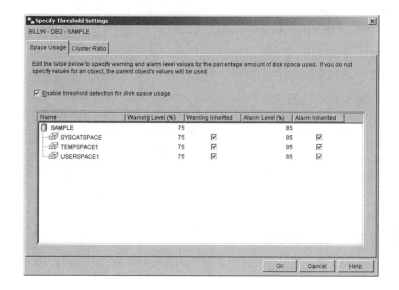

Statistical information can be captured periodically and displayed depending on the object chosen:

- For table spaces, information is displayed from the system catalogs and database monitor for tables, indexes, and containers defined under the scope of the given table space.
- For databases or database partition groups, information is displayed for all the table spaces defined in the given database or database partition group.
- For databases, information is also collected for all the database partition groups within the database.

You can use the Storage Management tool displayed in this view to monitor various aspects of your storage, such as space usage for table spaces, and capture cluster ratios of indexes for table spaces.

You can also set thresholds for data skew, space usage, and index cluster ratio. A warning or alarm flag alerts you if a target object exceeds a specified threshold.

Summary

Today you saw that DB2 provides Database System Monitor commands and APIs that allow you to find out more about the operation of the database manager. You can use this information to gain a better understanding of how the database manager works, to tune configuration parameters, or to determine the source and cause of problems.

The snapshot monitor and the event monitor are tools that enable you to identify and analyze performance problems and to identify exception conditions based on thresholds.

Visual Explain graphically shows you the access plans for explained SQL statements. By using the Visual Explain tool, you can view the statistics used during optimization, determine whether an index was used to access a table, and view all the details of the access plan, including statistics in the system catalogs.

You can collect information to update system catalog statistics on the data in the table. The optimizer uses these statistics to choose which path to use when accessing data.

What Comes Next?

On Day 20, "Tuning DB2 Universal Database Performance," you learn how to improve the performance of your system by adjusting the configuration parameters, using directory caching, and tuning I/O operations.

Q&A

Q When do I use an event monitor versus a snapshot monitor?

A Use the event monitor when you want a good summary of the activity of a particular event. When you use event monitors, data is returned when the event occurs. An example of an event is a database connection.

A snapshot monitor, on the other hand, provides a picture of the current state of all activities in a database instance. When you use a snapshot monitor, data is returned for the point in time that the snapshot was requested. You would typically use a snapshot monitor when you're experiencing a problem right now. An object that you might want to get snapshot information about is a database.

Q Can I create more than one event monitor at a time?

A You can start up to 32 event monitors at a time. Each monitor can be turned on and off as required. This flexibility gives you the opportunity to achieve your desired monitoring.

Q When using snapshot monitoring, where can I find out whether a performance variable exceeded its threshold?

A The Performance Details page gives you details on exceeded thresholds. Typically, you get to the Performance Details page through the Alert Center. If you selected to have an event recorded in the Alert Center each time a threshold is exceeded, the Alert Center automatically opens, showing you the object that has exceeded a threshold. Double-click the object to see the performance details. You can also view the performance details directly through the Control Center.

Workshop

The purpose of the workshop is to allow you to test your knowledge of the material covered in the lesson. See whether you can successfully answer the questions in the quiz and complete the exercises before you continue with the next lesson. The answers to the quiz questions are provided in Appendix B.

Quiz

1. What do you need to create an access plan graph?
2. What's an operator? How is it shown on an access plan graph?
3. When is it recommended that you collect statistics and reorganize a table?
4. What should you do immediately following a Run Statistics or a Reorganize Table operation?

Exercise

Create several event monitors and snapshot monitors for your database. Change the performance variables to make it easier to exceed the thresholds. Perform several actions on the database to cause the thresholds to be exceeded. Look at the graphs and data provided. Create an access plan graph, and then perform a Run Statistics and Reorganize Table operation on the table you're querying and re-create the access plan graph. Did any of the values change?

19

Create an access plan graph and determine whether an index is used when accessing the data. Create several indexes on the table and rerun the access plan graph to see whether any of the new indexes are used.

DAY 20

Tuning DB2 Universal Database Performance

This lesson covers the ways you can improve database performance. You will learn how to improve database performance by administering the following:

- Database manager configuration parameters, which enable you to control your database environment
- Database configuration parameters, which enable you to control a specific database
- Configuration Advisor, which enables you to direct DB2 to set several configuration parameters to understand your database environment

You can further tune your environment with environment variables and registry values. Today you learn how to set these values and whether you need to set a value at an instance or global level.

DB2 provides the Configuration Advisor to help you determine how many of your configuration parameters should be set. This lesson guides you through using this tool to tune the performance of your system.

Also covered today are several input/output (I/O) tuning considerations. You can create additional buffer pools and set configuration parameters to ensure I/O tasks are performed in parallel.

Controlling Your DB2 Environment

Registry values, environment variables, and configuration parameters control your database environment.

DB2 configures its operating parameters by checking for variable values according to the following search order:

- The environment variable settings
- Profile registry values set with the db2set command in the instance-level profile
- Profile registry values set with the db2set command in the global-level profile

See the later section "DB2 Registry Values and Environment Variables" for descriptions of the subset of registry values and environment variables that you may want to adjust.

Controlling the DB2 Profile Registry

You can update DB2 registry values for an instance, provided that you have system administration (SYSADM) authority for that instance. Use the db2set command to update DB2 registry values without rebooting your system. The DB2 registry applies the updated information to DB2 server instances and DB2 applications started after the changes are made.

The DB2 profile registry stores DB2 registry values. The *levels* of registry values are as follows:

- DB2 instance-level profile—Contains instance-level variable settings and overrides. Values defined in this level override their settings in the global level.
- DB2 global-level profile—Contains system-wide variable settings. Any variable not defined at the instance level is evaluated at the global level.

To modify registry variable values, you can use the Control Center or the db2set command. The syntax of the db2set command is as follows:

- To set a parameter for the current instance, use db2set
  `registry_variable_name=new_value`.
- To set a parameter's value for a specific instance, use db2set `registry_variable_name=new_value -i instance-name`.

▼
- To set a parameter at the global profile level, use db2set
  registry_variable_name=new_value =new *value* -g.

NOTE   Some parameters, including DB2SYSTEM and DB2INSTDEF, always default to the global-level profile. You cannot set them at the instance profiles.

- To delete a parameter's value at a specified level, you can use the same command syntax to set the parameter but specify nothing for the parameter value. For example, to delete the parameter's setting at the global level, use the following command:

  db2set *registry_variable_name*=new_value = -g

- To explicitly unset a parameter's value at a specified level and prevent evaluation of the parameter at the next level, use this command:

  db2set *registry_variable_name* = -null -i *instance-name*

  The -null option enables you to set the value of a parameter globally but unset the value for a specific instance. For example, you can set DB2COMM to TCPIP at the global level. If you have four instances on your system, you can set three of the instances to default to the global setting but use -null to unset DB2COMM on the fourth instance.

- To evaluate the parameter's value in the current session, use

  db2set *registry_variable_name*

- To evaluate the parameter's value at all levels, use

  db2set *registry_variable_name* -all

- To view a list of all values defined in the profile registry, use

▲
  db2set -all

DB2 Registry Values and Environment Variables

20

Table 20.1 shows a subset of the DB2 registry values and environment variables. These are what you are most likely to need to know about to get up and running. Each has a brief description; some may not apply to your environment.

TIP   To view a list of all supported variables, use the following command:
db2set -lr

TABLE 20.1   DB2 Registry Values and Environment Variables

Parameter	Values	Description
General		
DB2DBDFT	Default not set	Specifies the database alias name of the database that will be implicitly connected to when applications are started and no implicit connect has been done. This keyword is ignored if it's set.
DB2DISCOVERYTIME	Default=40 seconds, minimum=20 seconds	Specifies the amount of time that SEARCH discovery will search for DB2 systems.
DB2INSTDEF	Default=DB2	Sets the value to be used if DB2INSTANCE isn't defined.
System Environment		
DB2INSTANCE	Default=db2instdef	The environment variable used to specify the instance that's active by default.
DB2INSTPROF	Default not set	The environment variable used to specify the location of the instance directory, if different than DB2PATH.
DB2PATH	Default=x:\sqllib	The environment variable used to specify the directory where the product is installed.
Communications		
DB2COMM	Default=null, to specify values=any combination of TCPIP, NETBIOS, APPC, NPIPE	Specifies the communication managers that start when the database manager is started. If this parameter isn't set, no DB2 communication managers are started at the server.
DB2NBADAPTERS	Default=0, range=0–15; multiple values should be separated by commas	Used to specify the local adapters to use for DB2 NetBIOS LAN communications. Each local adapter is specified with its logical adapter number.

Configuration Parameters

DB2 has been designed with an extensive array of tuning and configuration parameters. Configuration parameters affect the operating characteristics of a database or database management system. The parameters' default values may be sufficient to meet your needs; however, you may not be able to achieve maximum performance with these default values. Specifically, you may need to modify the default parameter values if your environment has any of the following:

- A large amount of memory (greater than 2GB)
- Large databases (greater than 100GB)
- Large numbers of connections
- High performance for a specific application
- Different machine configuration/use
- Unique query or transaction loads or types

Each transaction processing environment has one or more unique aspects within it; these differences may have a profound impact on the performance of DB2 when using the default configuration. For this reason, you're strongly advised to take the time to customize DB2 for your environment.

Database Manager Configuration parameters exist on servers and clients. However, only a subset of the Database Manager Configuration parameters can be set on a client. Database Configuration parameters can be set only on the server and affect only a specific database.

Setting Database Manager Configuration Parameters on a Client Instance

You can control Database Manager Configuration parameters on a client instance by using the Configuration Assistant.

To access the client settings, choose Start|Programs|IBM DB2||Set-up Tools| Configuration Assistant. In the Configuration Assistant window, click the Client Settings button. Figure 20.1 shows the Client Settings dialog box of the Configuration Assistant.

Follow the hints provided with the Configuration Assistant in the Client Settings dialog box to modify the Database Manager and Database Configuration parameters for your environment. For each parameter that you select, recommendations for setting the parameter appear in the hint section of the panel.

20

FIGURE 20.1

The Client Settings dialog box.

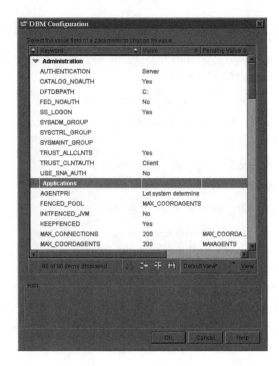

Setting Database Manager Configuration Parameters on a Server Instance

To control Database Manager Configuration parameters on a server instance, follow these steps:

1. In the Control Center, expand the object tree until you see the instance you want to configure. For example, to configure the default instance, look for DB2.

2. Right-click the instance you want to configure and select Configure from the pop-up menu. The Configure Instance notebook opens (see Figure 20.2).

   The DBM Configuration panel contains the following sections: Administration, Applications, Communications, Diagnostic, Environment, Miscellaneous, Monitor, Parallel, and Performance. Within each section you see the configuration parameters that correspond to each category. Select a parameter to be able to change its value.

3. Click Help to see a description of the parameter you've selected. Click Defaults to have each parameter value set to its default value.

4. Click a parameter to see the hint text to help you set the value.

FIGURE 20.2

Configuring Database Manager parameters.

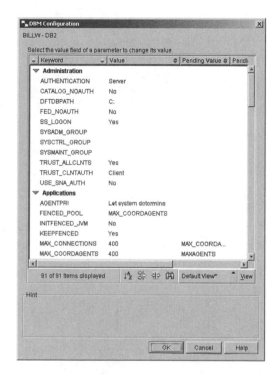

5. Click OK after you finish changing the parameter values. The changes will take effect when you restart the instance.

TIP

You can choose to allow DB2 to select certain values for Database Manager and Database parameters by using the following command:

`update dbm cfg variable_name=automatic`

If you set a parameter to automatic, DB2 automatically adjusts the parameter to reflect current resource requirements.

20

Setting Database Configuration Parameters on a Server Instance

To control Database Configuration parameters on a server instance, use the Control Center as follows:

1. In the Control Center, expand the object tree until you see the database that you want to configure—for example, the SAMPLE database.

2. Right-click the database you want to configure and select Configure from the pop-up menu. The Database Configuration window opens (see Figure 20.3).

FIGURE 20.3

*The Database
Configuration window.*

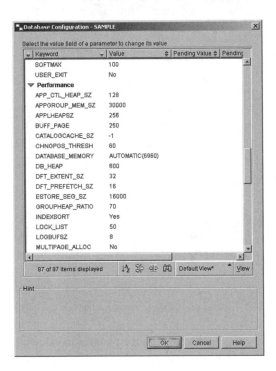

The Database Configuration window contains the following sections: Environment, Performance, Applications, Logs, Recovery, and Status. Within each section you see the configuration parameters corresponding to each category. Select a parameter to be able to change its value. You also see a hint that may help you set the parameter.

3. Click Help to see a description of the parameter you've selected. Click Defaults to have each parameter value set to its default value. You also see a hint that may help you set a value for the parameter.

4. Click OK after you finish changing the parameter values. The values will take effect when you restart the database.

Summary of Configuration Parameters Covered in This Book

All the configuration parameters introduced in this book are as follows:

- LOGRETAIN—Activates archive logging when set to YES. When archive logging is activated, a full offline backup is required. If LOGRETAIN is turned off, logging reverts to circular, and the online logs are automatically deleted. Set this parameter on the server in the Control Center at an instance level.

- DISCOVER—Determines whether you can search the network for databases. On the server, update the Administration Server's configuration file in the command-line processor as follows:

```
update admin cfg using discover [ DISABLE | KNOWN | SEARCH ]

db2admin stop
db2admin start
```

On the client, update this parameter in the Configuration Assistant.

- DISCOVER_COMM—Determines the protocol used during discovery functions. On the server, update the Administration Server's configuration file in the command-line processor as follows:

```
update admin cfg using discover_comm [ NETBIOS | TCPIP ]

db2admin stop
db2admin start
```

On the client, update this parameter in the Configuration Assistant.

- DISCOVER_INST—Determines whether clients can discover databases in the instance. Set this parameter on the server in the Control Center at an instance level.

- DISCOVER_DB—Determines whether a database is available to be discovered by clients. Set this parameter on the server in the Control Center at an instance level.

- DB2DISCOVERYTIME—Specifies that the searched discovery wait 35 seconds for a response from servers. Set this parameter on the client in the Configuration Assistant.

- LOGPATH—Specifies the location in which the roll-forward operation should check for logs.

20

Using the Configuration Advisor

The DB2 Configuration Advisor helps you tune performance and balance memory requirements for a single database per instance by suggesting which configuration parameters to modify and providing suggested values for them.

NOTE

> Many configuration parameters come with default values but may need to be updated to achieve optimal performance for your database. In most cases, the values recommended by the Configuration Advisor will provide better performance than the default values because they're based on information about your workload and your own particular server. Note, however, that the values are designed to improve the performance of, though not necessarily optimize, your database system. You should think of them as a starting point on which you can make further adjustments to obtain optimized performance.

Follow these steps to use the Configuration Advisor:

1. In the Control Center, right-click the database for which you want to configure performance and select Configuration Advisor from the pop-up menu. CDLIB is used in this example.

2. On the Introduction page of the Configuration Advisor (see Figure 20.4), verify you are working with the correct database and then click Next.

FIGURE 20.4

The Configuration Advisor's Introduction page.

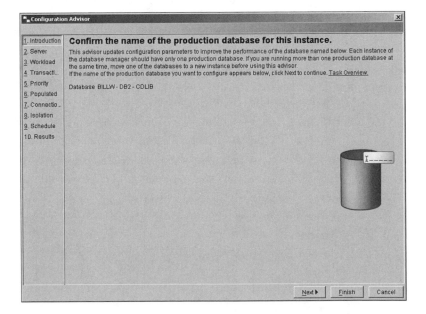

TIP	Ensure that each instance of the database manager has only one production database. Tuning a system with more than one production database per instance running concurrently is difficult.

3. On the Server page (see Figure 20.5), use the slider to indicate the portion of the server's memory (RAM) that can be used by this database (not including the operating system). If other applications are running on this server, set the slider to less than 100%.

FIGURE 20.5

The Configuration Advisor's Server page.

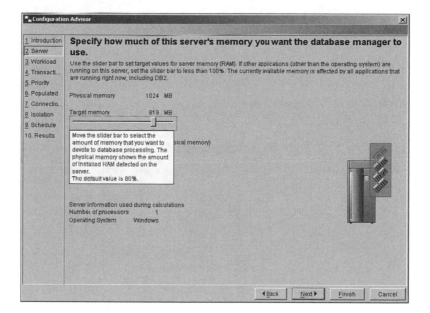

4. On the Workload page (see Figure 20.6), select the option that best reflects your database workload type:

    - If there are many queries of the data, select Queries (Data Warehousing).

    - If the data is updated frequently, select Transactions (Order Entry).

    - If the data is updated and queried frequently, select Mixed.

5. On the Transactions page (see Figure 20.7), indicate the approximate number of SQL statements in a single unit of work (between commits) that best reflects the activity in your database. Also, estimate the number of transactions per minute running in your database. If you aren't sure which value to use, accept the default provided by the Configuration Advisor.

20

FIGURE 20.6

The Configuration Advisor's Workload page.

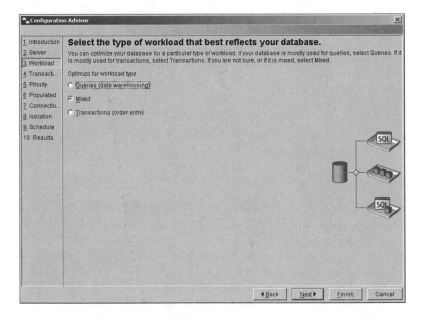

FIGURE 20.7

The Configuration Advisor's Transactions page.

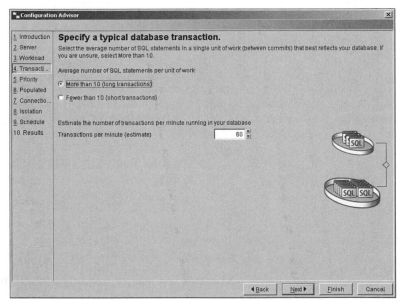

6. On the Priority page (see Figure 20.8), indicate whether it's more important to optimize transaction performance or the time required to recover the database.

FIGURE 20.8

The Configuration Advisor's Priority page.

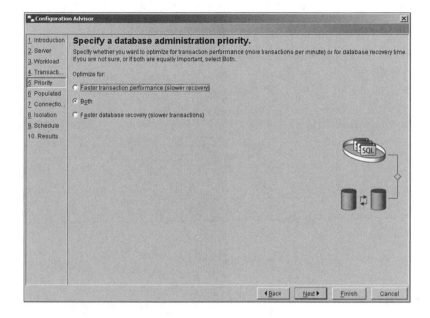

7. On the Populated page (see Figure 20.9), indicate whether the database contains production data. If this database is new, you should rerun the Configuration Advisor after you insert data.

FIGURE 20.9

The Configuration Advisor's Populated page.

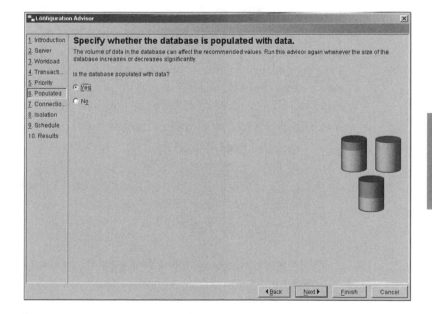

20

8. On the Connections page (see Figure 20.10), estimate the number of applications likely to connect to this database. You can indicate an approximate value for local and remote applications.

FIGURE 20.10

The Configuration Advisor's Connections page.

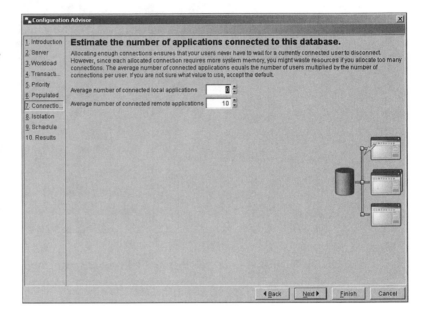

9. On the Isolation page (see Figure 20.11), select an isolation level that best reflects your applications. The isolation level determines the number of locked rows and lock duration when users read or change data. DB2 uses locking to maintain data integrity during concurrent processing. Locking guarantees that a transaction maintains control over a database row until it has finished and prevents another application from changing a row before the ongoing change is complete.

You can select from the following isolation levels:

- Repeatable Read—Select this option if you expect to have many locks of long duration.

- Read Stability—Select this option if you expect to have few locks of long duration.

- Cursor Stability—Select this option if you expect to have many locks of short duration.

- Uncommitted Read—Select this option if you expect to have no locks.

FIGURE 20.11

The Configuration Advisor's Isolation page.

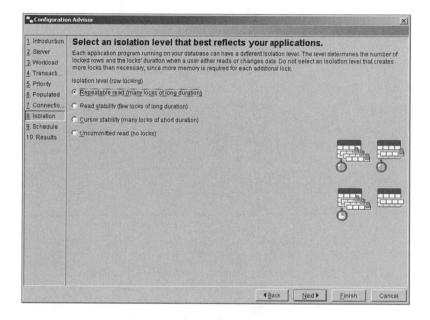

10. On the Schedule page (see Figure 20.12), you can choose to execute the changes immediately or at a later time.

FIGURE 20.12

The Configuration Advisor's Schedule page.

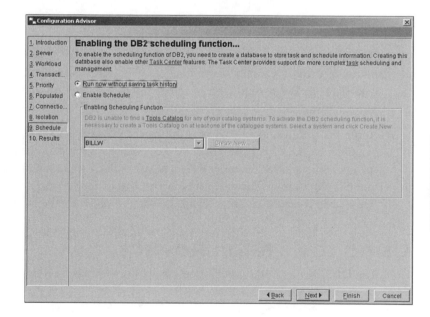

20

11. On the Results page (see Figure 20.13), you can review the performance configuration recommendations. If you want to change any values, return to the preceding pages to make the changes. Click Finish when you're satisfied with the changes that will be made to your configuration parameters.

FIGURE 20.13

The Configuration Advisor's Results page.

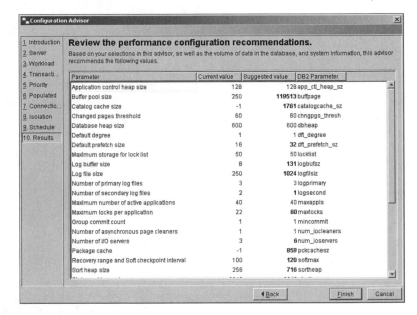

For database configuration parameter updates to take effect, all applications must first disconnect from the database; the changes will take effect only at the first connect to the database. For Database Manager Configuration parameter updates to take effect, you must first stop and then restart the instance.

Rerun the Configuration Advisor if the size of the database significantly increases (for example, by more than 20%) or if the machine characteristics change (for example, more memory is available). Increasing the size of the database or adding memory to your system can significantly change the recommendations for various performance values, and you should rerun the Configuration Advisor to take advantage of these changes.

Using the Design Advisor

The DB2 Design Advisor helps you tune performance by recommending indexes based on the query workload.

Follow these steps to use the Design Advisor:

1. In the Control Center, right-click the database for which you want to configure performance and select Configuration Advisor from the pop-up menu. The SAMPLE database is used in this example.

2. On the Introduction page of the Design Advisor (see Figure 20.14), click Next.

FIGURE 20.14

The Design Advisor's Introduction page.

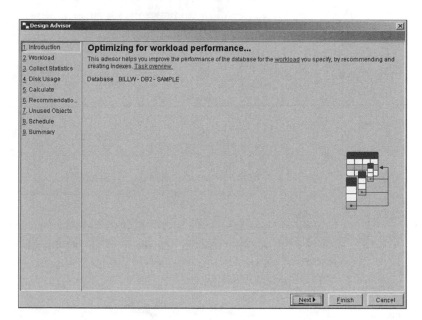

3. On the Workload page, first enter a Workload name; this example uses QueryWorkLoad1. Click Add. An Add SQL Statement window appears (see Figure 20.15). Type in the query that represents the workload of a given application; for this example, enter

```
Select count(*) from sales where region = ?
```

Enter a name to represent this SQL statement; in this case, enter **query1**. Enter the frequency this workload is submitted to the database; for this example, enter **1000** and then click OK.

20

NOTE

> The Workload Performance Wizard uses the frequency number to judge the importance of the statement. If an SQL statement is more important or more critical than some of the other SQL statements in the workload, even though it is run less frequently, specify a frequency that is higher than that of the other statements in the workload.

FIGURE 20.15

The Design Advisor's Workload page and the Add SQL Statement window.

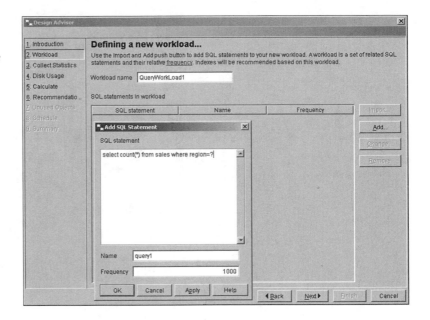

You should now see that QueryWorkLoad1 has one entry, query1, making up its workload (see Figure 20.16). You can now add additional SQL statements that represent the application by clicking Add. In this example, limit the workload to one SQL statement. Click Next.

FIGURE 20.16

The Design Advisor's Defining a New Workload page.

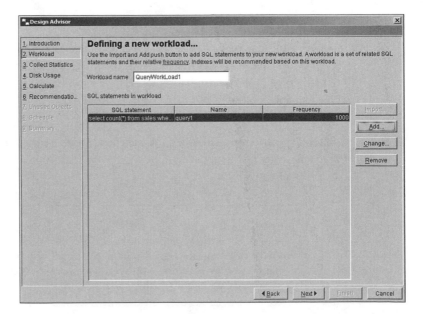

4. The Collect Statistics page asks for the tables involved in the SQL statements (see Figure 20.17). By having accurate statistics, DB2 will choose an appropriate access path. Click the table titled Sales and then the > button. Click Next.

FIGURE 20.17

The Design Advisor's Collect Statistics page.

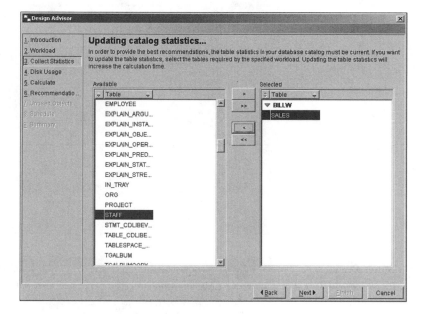

5. On the Disk Usage page, you can select which table space to create recommended indexes and whether you want to set a maximum size for the potential indexes (see Figure 20.18). For this example, accept the defaults and click Next.

6. The Calculate page gives you the option to have DB2 begin calculating its recommendations immediately or later (see Figure 20.19). In this example, accept the default and click Next.

7. The Recommendations page shows that for the query workload given, DB2 recommends the creation of one index (see Figure 20.20). You can see the SQL statement by clicking Show SQL. (DB2 recommends that an index be created on the Region column in the Sales table. Also, two entries under the Workload Performance Improvement section give you an estimate on the performance gains of creating the recommended index.) Click Next.

8. On the Unused Objects page, you can choose to delete indexes that are not relevant with the current workload being examined (see Figure 20.21). However, the indexes may be relevant to other applications and should not be deleted unless you are sure that deleting them will have no impact on other SQL workloads. Accept the default and click Next.

20

FIGURE 20.18

*The Design Advisor's
Disk Usage page.*

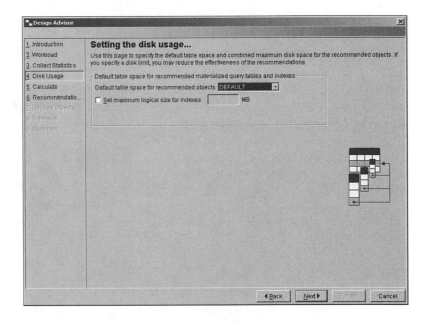

FIGURE 20.19

*The Design Advisor's
Calculate page.*

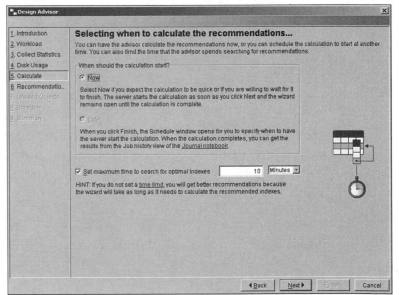

9. On the Schedule page, you can choose to execute the recommendations immediately or later (see Figure 20.22). Accept the default and click Next.

10. The Summary page shows that the recommendation for this workload is to create one index (see Figure 20.23). Accept the recommendation by clicking Finish.

FIGURE 20.20

The Design Advisor's Recommendations page.

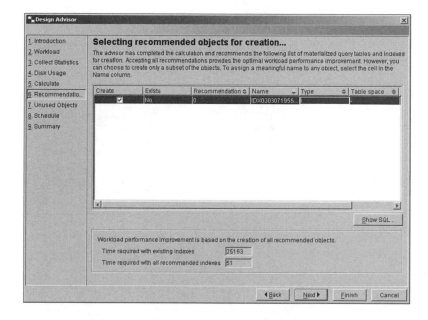

FIGURE 20.21

The Design Advisor's Unused Objects page.

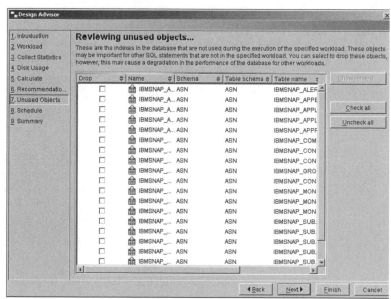

20

FIGURE 20.22

The Design Advisor's
Schedule page.

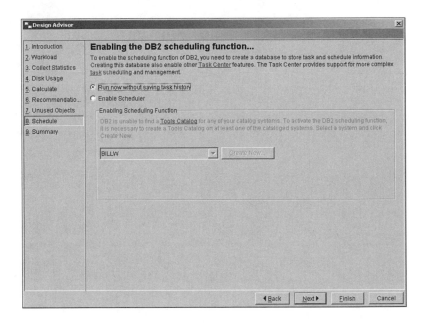

FIGURE 20.23

The Design Advisor's
Summary page.

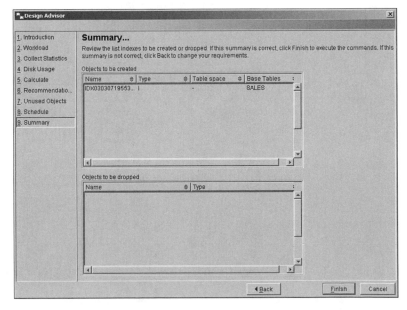

Input/Output Performance

Typically, performing I/O is the slowest function a database needs to complete. DB2 provides several features to eliminate I/O bottlenecks, including

- Prefetching data pages into memory in anticipation of the pages being needed
- Performing I/O in parallel by prefetching several pages of data at a time
- Fetching block-related pages during the prefetch
- Validating constraints after loading data instead of while the data is being loaded
- Creating more than one buffer pool to store data pages and set configuration parameters to ensure that data pages are written to disk in a timely manner

Indexes

Indexes can dramatically increase performance by reducing the need for table scans or the number of columns retrieved for a given query. Indexes perform best when the values are unique (high cardinality) and are placed on fast disk devices. The Index Wizard can assist you in creating an index.

To use the Index Wizard, open the Control Center and right-click the Indexes folder. Then select the Create option to display the Create Index window (see Figure 20.24). This example creates an index on the Staff table, by selecting the ID column for an index. You can consider the following options when creating an index:

- Unique—Creating a unique index can improve query performance by potentially avoiding sorts.
- Cluster—This index parameter can assist insert performance by having the new inserted rows clustered according to an index. Insert performance is improved, page splits are reduced, and the need for reorganizing data is reduced.
- Allow reverse scans—Indexes can be defined in ascending or descending order. This parameter allows index scans to occur in the reverse direction from the way the index was defined; otherwise, the index is not used if the query is requesting the data in reverse order of the defined index.
- Free space—This parameter specifies the PCTFREE keyword value as a percentage of how much free space should remain on the index page, to allow for inserts to be applied later. This can improve performance for applications that will insert data.
- Minimum Amount of Used Space—The parameter specifies the MINPCTUSED keyword value as a percentage of the index page. When this threshold is exceeded, DB2 will automatically try to determine whether two adjacent leaf pages can be merged. This process is known as *online index defragmentation*.

20

The following are some recommendations you should keep in mind when creating indexes:

- Be selective about which columns you choose to create an index because there will be overhead for applications that update data.
- Select columns that are used often to join tables.
- For tables defined with referential integrity, creating indexes on the foreign keys improves the performance of delete and update operations on the parent table.
- If your index is made of multiple columns defining a partial index, specifying a subset of the existing index generally does not improve performance.

FIGURE 20.24

Create Index window.

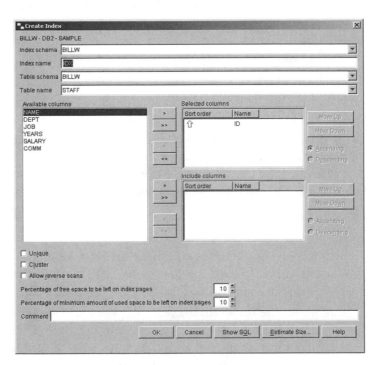

Buffer Pools

Each table is associated with a buffer pool. When you create a table space, the default buffer pool (IBMDEFAULTBP) is used. You can modify the size of the default buffer pool.

The default of one buffer pool will usually suffice, but for a higher level of database tuning, you can create additional buffer pools and assign table spaces to individual buffer pools. For example, you could create four buffer pools, one each for catalogs, temporary space, indexes, and data. The extended buffer pool allows DB2 to take advantage of large amounts of memory.

You can create additional buffer pools in the Control Center by right-clicking the Buffer Pools folder and selecting Add from the pop-up menu. Day 9, "Creating Table Spaces," provides details on creating buffer pools.

To alter the size of a buffer pool beyond what's recommended by the Configuration Advisor, select the Buffer Pool folder from the object list in the Control Center. Right-click IBMDEFAULTBP and select Alter from the pop-up menu. Modify the Size in 4KB Pages field and click OK. The change will take effect the next time the database is started.

Asynchronous Buffer Writer

To read or modify data, pages of data are moved from disk to the buffer pool. If a page has been modified, it should be written back to the disk. The purpose of the buffer writers is to write out most changed pages to disk, so regular database agents always find empty slots and don't have to hold the transaction to write pages out. This means that agents won't wait for additional I/O, and queries should run faster. The buffer writers run in parallel with the database agents.

Pages are written from the buffer pool to disk when the percentage of space occupied by changed pages in the buffer pool has exceeded the value specified by the CHNGPGS_THRESH database configuration parameter. You can also configure the number of page cleaners that are used for the database. Page cleaner agents perform I/O that would normally be done by database agents. As a result, your applications can run faster because transactions are not forced to wait while their database agents write pages to disk. To set the number of page cleaner agents, use the NUM_IOCLEANERS database configuration parameter.

Row Blocking

DB2 Universal Database uses row blocking to provide transmission of data in blocks, instead of one row at a time. A *block* is a group of rows returned from a local or remote database in response to a FETCH request from an application. Performance is usually enhanced by reducing the number of requests made against the database manager.

There are three types of row blocking:

- UNAMBIGUOUS—Causes blocking for read-only requests
- ALL—Causes blocking for read-only and ambiguous requests
- NO—Does not block any requests

20

Row blocking is specified at precompile time or when an application is bound to the database. If no blocking method is specified, the default UNAMBIGUOUS is used. To see the isolation level used for a package, select the package folder in the object tree in the Control Center. The right panel provides details on the package, including the blocking type used:

- The Database Manager Configuration parameter aslheapsz specifies application support layer heap size for local applications.
- The Database Manager Configuration parameter rqrioblk specifies the size of the communication buffer between remote applications and their database agents on the database server.

To specify row blocking, follow these steps:

1. Use the values of the aslheapsz and rqrioblk configuration parameters to estimate how many rows are returned for each block. In both formulas orl is the output row length in bytes.

   Use the following formula for local applications:

   ```
   Rows per block = aslheapsz * 4096 / orl
   ```

   The number of bytes per page is 4096.

   Use the following formula for remote applications:

   ```
   Rows per block = rqrioblk / orl
   ```

2. To enable row blocking, specify an appropriate argument to the BLOCKING option in the PREP or BIND commands.

   If you do not specify a BLOCKING option, the default row blocking type is UNAMBIG. For the command-line processor and call-level interface, the default row blocking type is ALL.

Prefetching Data Pages

Prefetching data pages into the buffer pool can help improve performance by reducing the time spent waiting for I/O to complete. To *prefetch* pages means that one or more pages are retrieved from disk in anticipation of their use. Prefetching is started when DB2 determines that sequential I/O is appropriate and prefetching may help to improve performance. There are two types of prefetch:

- Sequential prefetch—Reads consecutive pages into the buffer pool before the pages are required by the application. When the access plan looks sequential, the DB2 engine automatically begins sequential prefetch. Having DB2 activate or deactivate sequential prefetching as necessary is known as *sequential detection*. To specifically enable sequential prefetching, set the SEQDETECT database parameter in the database configuration file to yes.

- List prefetch, or list sequential prefetch—Provides a way to access data pages efficiently, even when the data pages needed aren't consecutive.

If access to the tables includes many queries or transactions that process large quantities of data, prefetching data from the tables may provide significant performance benefits. A DMS table space using multiple device containers in which each container is on a separate disk offers the best potential for efficient prefetching.

Parallel Input/Output

Many I/O operations can be performed in parallel on behalf of a single query. This can improve application response time, especially when the application performs a table scan. You enable parallel I/O for a database by setting the NUM_IOSERVERS configuration parameter that controls the number of prefetch servers created. This parameter is set in the database configuration file. Configuring enough I/O servers can greatly enhance the performance of queries. Having extra I/O servers does not hurt performance because these extra servers are not used and their memory pages are paged out.

Big Block Reads

Using big block reads allows several disk pages to be read by using a single I/O operation. Reading several disk pages at a time reduces the CPU usage and elapsed time for I/O, and improves query response time. Big block reads are used by the database manager every time prefetch is done. They may also be used for list prefetch if multiple pages being read belong to the same table space extent. DB2 determines when it is necessary to use big block reads.

Summary

Today you saw that DB2 provides registry values, environment variables, and configuration parameters to help you control your database environment.

Configuration parameters affect the entire database environment or affect only a specific database. Database Manager Configuration parameters affect the entire database system as a whole, whereas Database Configuration parameters affect only a single database.

The Configuration Advisor helps you tune the performance of your system by suggesting which configuration parameters you should modify.

Input/output performance is usually the slowest function a database needs to complete.

20

DB2 provides several features, including indexes, buffer pools, asynchronous buffer writers, row blocking, prefetching, parallel input/output, and big block reads to help you eliminate bottlenecks in your system.

What Comes Next?

On Day 21, "Diagnosing Problems," you learn the basics in troubleshooting your DB2 system.

Q&A

Q What are the two levels of registry values?

A The DB2 instance-level profile contains settings for the instance. The DB2 global-level profile contains settings that control the entire system. The values set in the instance-level profile override values in the global-level profile. You set these values by using the db2set command.

Q How do I update configuration parameters?

A To update configuration parameters on your client system, use the Configuration Assistant. To update configuration parameters on your server system, use the Control Center. Both tools group the different types of configuration parameters on separate tabbed pages and provide hints to help you determine the best value for the parameter. On the server, you can also use the Configuration Advisor to help you decide whether parameters should be changed.

Q What must be done for configuration parameter changes to take effect?

A For Database Manager Configuration parameters to take effect, all applications must first disconnect from the database. The changes will take place when the next application connects to the database. For Database Configuration parameters to take effect, you must first stop and then restart the instance.

Workshop

The purpose of the workshop is to allow you to test your knowledge of the material covered in the lesson. See whether you can successfully answer the questions in the quiz and complete the exercises before you continue with the next lesson. Answers to quiz questions are provided in Appendix B.

Quiz

1. How many buffer pools should you define for your system?
2. When do you need to change your configuration parameters?
3. Can database configuration parameters be set on the client?
4. If you expect to have no locks on the data, which isolation level should you use?

Exercise

Use the Configuration Assistant and Control Center to view the current settings of the various configuration parameters. Read the provided hint text to understand the purpose of the parameters. When you have a good understanding of the settings, run the Configuration Advisor to see whether any changes are recommended.

20

WEEK 3

DAY 21

Diagnosing Problems

Today you learn how to find the cause of an error you may have encountered.
You will learn the following:

- How to use the DB2 Information Center
- What error logging facilities are provided by DB2
- How to use the tracing facilities to understand how to troubleshoot DB2

If an error is encountered, DB2 provides an error message, such as SQL30081,
that you can look up in the Messages Reference. The Message Reference provides guidance as to what caused the error message you encountered and possible solutions to the problem. Additionally, the DB2 Web site provides tips and
techniques to solve commonly reported problems.

Today you also learn how to determine if you have corrupt data in your database and how the DB2DART tool can help you correct many corruption problems.

Accessing Documentation

The DB2 Information Center enables you to access the information you need to take full advantage of DB2 Universal Database. The DB2 Information Center also documents major DB2 features and components, including replication, data warehousing, metadata, and DB2 extenders. By clicking the flashlight icon, you can search the documentation by keyword.

To access the DB2 Information Center from a browser, as shown in Figure 21.1, you must use one of the following browsers:

- Microsoft Explorer, version 5 or later
- Netscape Navigator, version 6.1 or later

FIGURE 21.1

The DB2 Information Center.

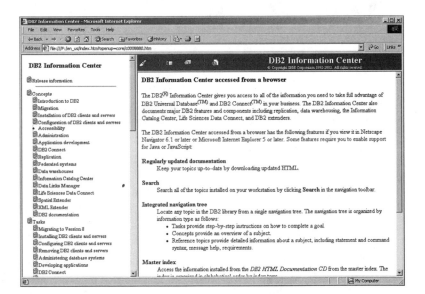

Online Messages

DB2 provides online help that contains error-message information about the cause of errors and the user action to take. See the DB2 Message Reference manual for a listing of the different types of error messages you can get using DB2. To access the help, try the following:

- When using a DB2 tool, click the Help button to activate the help.
- For a description of SQL codes and other messages, type **? *message*** from the Command Center, where *message* is the SQL code or message number.

- For a description and the syntax of DB2 commands, type **? command**, where *command* is the name of the command.

- For a description of any DB2 error message, open the DB2 Information Center to access the Messages manual and click the range where the error code falls.

  The error message text contains information on the possible causes for the problem and provides several suggestions on how the problem can be resolved. Figure 21.2 shows an example of the message text you see for SQL30081.

FIGURE 21.2

Message text for error message SQL30081.

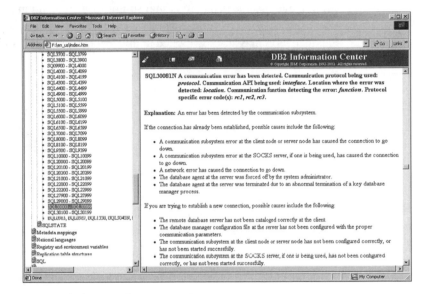

Error-Logging Facilities

DB2 writes two different logs to write error information.

Administration Notification Log

When significant events occur, DB2 writes information to the administration notification log. The information is intended for use by database and system administrators. For Windows installations, all administration notification messages are written to the event log.

Many notification messages provide additional information to supplement the SQL-CODE that is provided. The type of administration notification messages that are written to the administration notification log are determined by the NOTIFYLEVEL configuration parameter.

21

You can set the NOTIFYLEVEL parameter to the following values:

- 0 – No Administration Notification Messages Captured. (This setting is not recommended).
- 1 – Severe Errors Only. Only fatal and unrecoverable errors are logged. To recover from some of these conditions, you may need assistance from DB2 service. (Usually, only IBM can fix severe errors.)
- 2 – All Errors. Logged conditions require immediate attention from the system administrator or the database administrator. If the condition is not resolved, it could lead to a fatal error. Notification of very significant, non-error activities (for example, recovery) may also be logged at this level. This level captures Health Monitor alarms.

NOTE   An *error* means that DB2 fails to process the input. A *warning* indicates that the input was processed successfully but that some problems occurred.

- 3 – All Errors and Warnings. Logged conditions are non-threatening and do not require immediate action but may indicate a non-optimal system. This level captures Health Monitor alarms, Health Monitor warnings, and Health Monitor attentions. This setting is the default, and recommended that you start with this setting.
- 4 – Informational messages.

The default NOTIFYLEVEL is usually sufficient for normal DB2 operation. However, during the initial setup of DB2, or when errors are occurring, you can update the NOTIFYLEVEL to 4 to gather as much information as possible. You must set NOTIFYLEVEL to at least a value of 2 or higher for the Health Monitor to send any notifications to the contacts defined in its configuration.

To update NOTIFYLEVEL to 4, use the Control Center to update the instance diagnostic parameters, or enter the following command from any of the command-line tools:

```
UPDATE DBM CFG USING NOTIFYLEVEL 4
```

DB2 Diagnostic Log

Diagnostic information about errors is recorded in the db2diag.log file. This information is used for problem determination and is intended for DB2 customer support. You can use the DIAGPATH configuration variable to direct where these errors are written to.

Error-Logging Facilities

DB2 provides two ways of checking the internal integrity of DB2 objects. The internal or architectural integrity of the database objects is a requirement for the normal operations of DB2.

Inspect Command

The Inspect command enables you to check the pages of the database for their architectural integrity. You can use this command to check the structures of table objects and table spaces. You can execute this command while users are connected to the database.

The inspect check processing writes out unformatted inspection data results to the result file. The file is written out to the diagnostic data directory path. If no errors are found by the check processing, the result output file will be erased at the end of the inspect operation. If errors are found by the check processing, the result output file will not be erased at the end of the inspect operation.

Database Analysis and Reporting Tool

Use the Database Analysis and Reporting Tool (DB2DART) to verify that the architectural integrity of a database is correct. This tool confirms that

- The control information is correct.
- There are no discrepancies in the format of the data.
- The data pages are the correct size and contain the correct column types.
- Indexes are valid.

You must run this tool on the DB2 server where the database resides. Also, be sure that the database does not have any active connections before you run this tool.

To use DB2DART, enter **db2dart** and the name of the database you're checking; for example, to check the SAMPLE database, enter **db2dart sample**. A report about the integrity of the data is created in a file named sample.rpt. Figure 21.3 shows the result of running DB2DART against the SAMPLE database.

21

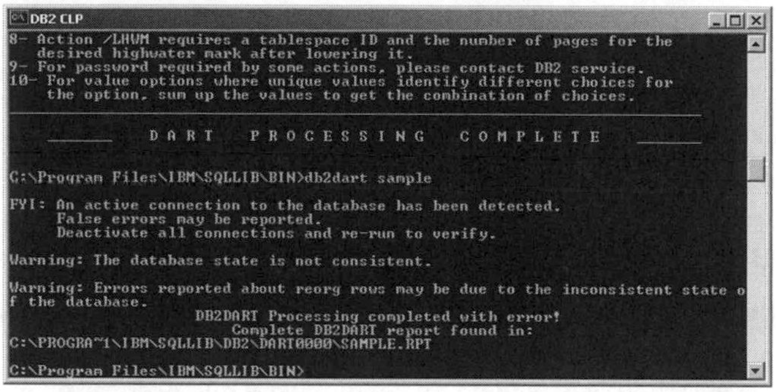

FIGURE 21.3

Results of running DB2DART for the SAMPLE database.

Configuration Files

Many DB2 configuration files kept on your system can be useful if you have a problem you want to debug, such as the following:

- The Database Manager Configuration file contains the overall configuration information for your system. To produce a listing of this file, enter **get dbm cfg > dbm.cfg** from the Command Center. View the dbm.cfg file to see the configuration settings for your system.

- The Database Configuration file contains the configuration information for an individual database. To produce a listing of this file, enter **get db cfg > db.cfg** from the Command Center. View the db.cfg file to see the configuration settings for one of your databases.

- The CLI configuration file contains keywords to set the environment when using the CLI driver. The file, db2cli.ini, is located in the sqllib directory where you installed DB2.

- The odbc.ini file contains the ODBC keywords to set the environment when you are using ODBC applications. The file is located in the same drive where Windows is installed. If you optimized the settings for the ODBC application you use, you may have the db2cli.opt file in the sqllib directory that contains all these optimized settings.

- If you performed imports, exports, or loads, you'll have files that contain operational information. You choose a name and a location for these files when you set up the import, export, or load operation. Day 17, "Moving Data," discusses these three operations.

Tracing Facilities

The DB2 CLI and DB2 JDBC drivers offer comprehensive tracing facilities. (A *tracing facility* is provided by most software vendors for problem determination; it records what is happening in the system at a very granular level.) By default, these facilities are disabled and use no additional computing resources. When enabled, the trace facilities generate one or more text log files whenever an application accesses the appropriate driver (DB2 CLI or DB2 JDBC). These log files provide detailed information about the following:

- The order in which CLI or JDBC functions were called by the application
- The contents of input and output parameters passed to and received from CLI or JDBC functions
- The return codes and any error or warning messages generated by CLI or JDBC functions

DB2 CLI and DB2 JDBC trace file analysis can benefit application developers in a number of ways. First, subtle program logic and parameter initialization errors are often evident in the traces. Second, DB2 CLI and DB2 JDBC traces may suggest ways of better tuning an application or the databases it accesses. For example, if a DB2 CLI trace shows a table being queried many times on a particular set of attributes, an index corresponding to those attributes might be created on the table to improve application performance. Finally, analysis of DB2 CLI and DB2 JDBC trace files can help application developers understand how a third-party application or interface is behaving.

Trace Configuration

The configuration parameters for both DB2 CLI and DB2 JDBC tracing facilities are read from the DB2 CLI configuration file db2cli.ini, located in the \sqllib path. You can override the default path by setting the DB2CLIINIPATH environment variable. An additional db2cli.ini file may be found in the user's profile (or home) directory if any user-defined data sources are defined using the ODBC Driver Manager. This db2cli.ini file overrides the default file.

To view the current db2cli.ini trace configuration parameters from the command-line processor, issue the following command:

```
db2 GET CLI CFG FOR SECTION COMMON
```

21

You can modify the db2cli.ini file to configure the DB2 CLI and DB2 JDBC trace facilities in three ways:

- Use the DB2 Configuration Assistant if it is available.
- Manually edit the db2cli.ini file using a text editor.
- Issue the UPDATE CLI CFG command from the command-line processor.

For example, the following command issued from the command-line processor updates the db2cli.ini file and enables the JDBC tracing facility:

```
db2 UPDATE CLI CFG FOR SECTION COMMON USING jdbctrace 1
```

DB2 CLI Trace

When an application using the DB2 CLI driver begins execution, the driver checks for trace facility options in the [COMMON] section of the db2cli.ini file. These trace options are specific trace keywords that are set to certain values under the [COMMON] section in the db2cli.ini file.

NOTE   Because DB2 CLI trace keywords appear in the [COMMON] section of the db2cli.ini file, their values apply to all database connections through the DB2 CLI driver.

The following DB2 CLI trace keywords can be defined:

- TRACE
- TRACEFILENAME
- TRACEPATHNAME
- TRACEFLUSH
- TRACEREFRESHINTERVAL
- TRACECOMM
- TRACETIMESTAMP
- TRACEPIDTID
- TRACEPIDLIST
- TRACETIME
- TRACESTMTONLY

DB2 CLI trace keywords are read from the db2cli.ini file only once at application initialization time unless the TRACEREFRESHINTERVAL keyword is set. If this keyword is set, the TRACE and TRACEPIDLIST keywords are reread from the db2cli.ini file at the specified interval and applied, as appropriate, to the currently executing application.

The TRACE keyword determines whether any of the other DB2 CLI trace keywords have an effect. If this keyword is not set or set to the default value of 0, the DB2 CLI trace facility is disabled. If this keyword is set to 1, the DB2 CLI trace facility is enabled and the other trace keywords are considered:

```
TRACE = 0 | 1
```

By itself, the TRACE keyword has little effect except to enable the DB2 CLI trace facility processing. No trace output is generated unless one of the TRACEPATHNAME or TRACEFILE-NAME keywords is also specified.

The TRACEFILENAME parameter specifies the fully qualified name of the log file to which all DB2 CLI trace information is written:

```
TRACEFILENAME = <fully_qualified_trace_file_name>
```

If the file does not exist, the DB2 CLI trace facility tries to create it. If the file already exists, new trace information for the current session, if any, is appended to the previous contents of that file.

The TRACEFILENAME keyword option should not be used with multiprocess or multi-threaded applications because the trace output for all threads or processes will be written to the same log file, and the output for each thread or process will be difficult to decipher. Furthermore, semaphores are used to control access to the shared trace file; they could change the behavior of multithreaded applications. There is no default DB2 CLI trace output log filename.

The TRACEPATHNAME parameter specifies the fully qualified pathname of the directory to which all DB2 CLI trace information is written:

```
TRACEPATHNAME = <fully_qualified_trace_path_name>
```

The DB2 CLI trace facility tries to generate a new trace log file each time an application accessing the DB2 CLI interface is run. If the application is multithreaded, a separate trace log file is generated for each thread. A concatenation of the application process ID and the thread sequence number is automatically used to name trace log files. There is no default path to which DB2 CLI trace output log files are written, and the path specified must exist at application execution time (the DB2 CLI driver does not create the path).

21

NOTE | If both TRACEFILENAME and TRACEPATHNAME are specified, the TRACEFILENAME keyword takes precedence and TRACEPATHNAME is ignored.

The TRACEFLUSH keyword specifies how often trace information is written to the DB2 CLI trace log file:

```
TRACEFLUSH = 0 | <any positive integer>
```

By default, TRACEFLUSH is set to 0, and each DB2 CLI trace log file is kept open until the traced application or thread terminates normally. If the application terminates abnormally, some trace information that was not written to the trace log file may be lost.

To ensure the integrity and completeness of the trace information written to the DB2 CLI trace log file, the TRACEFLUSH keyword can be specified. After n trace entries have been written to the trace log file, the DB2 CLI driver closes the file and then reopens it, appending new trace entries to the end of the file. Each file close and reopen operation incurs significant input/output overhead and can reduce performance considerably.

TIP

> The smaller the value of the TRACEFLUSH keyword, the greater the impact DB2 CLI tracing has on the performance of the application. In general, tracing has a negative impact on performance because of the overhead on the system that is created. Extensive tracing should be considered only to troubleshoot a specific problem.

Setting TRACEFLUSH to 1 has the most impact on performance but ensures that each entry is written to disk before the application continues to the next statement.

Setting TRACEREFRESHINTERVAL to a positive integer value n other than the default value of 0 causes the DB2 CLI trace facility to reread the TRACE and TRACEPIDLIST keywords from the db2cli.ini file at the specified interval (every n seconds). The DB2 CLI trace facility then applies those keywords, as appropriate, to the trace that is currently executing:

```
TRACEREFRESHINTERVAL = 0 | <any positive integer>
```

The remaining DB2 CLI trace configuration keywords determine what information is written to the DB2 CLI trace log files.

The following is the TRACECOMM parameter:

```
TRACECOMM = 0 | 1
```

Setting TRACECOMM to the default value of 0 means no DB2 client/server communication information will be included in the DB2 CLI trace. Setting TRACECOMM to 1 causes the DB2 CLI trace to show

- Which DB2 CLI functions are processed completely on the client and which DB2 CLI functions involve communication with the server
- The number of bytes sent and received in each communication with the server
- The time spent communicating data between the client and server

Setting TRACETIMESTAMP to a value other than the default of 0 means the current time stamp or absolute execution time is added to the beginning of each line of trace information as it is being written to the DB2 CLI trace log file. Setting TRACETIMESTAMP to 1 prepends the absolute execution time in seconds and milliseconds, followed by a time stamp. Setting TRACETIMESTAMP to 2 prepends the absolute execution time in seconds and milliseconds. Setting TRACETIMESTAMP to 3 prepends the time stamp:

```
TRACETIMESTAMP = 0 | 1 | 2 | 3
```

Setting TRACEPIDTID to the default value of 0 means process and thread ID information will not be added to each line in the DB2 CLI trace. Setting TRACEPIDTID to 1 means process and thread ID information will be included in the trace:

```
TRACEPIDTID = 0 | 1
```

Setting TRACEPIDLIST to its default of no value, or leaving it unset, means all processes accessing the DB2 CLI driver interface will be traced by the DB2 CLI trace facility. Setting TRACEPIDLIST to a list of one or more comma-delimited process ID values restricts the CLI traces generated to the processes appearing in that list:

```
TRACEPIDLIST = <no value> | <pid1,pid2, pid3,...>
```

Setting TRACETIME to its default value of 1, or leaving it unset, means the elapsed time between CLI function calls and returns will be calculated and included in the DB2 CLI trace. Setting TRACETIME to 0 means the elapsed time between CLI function calls and returns will not be calculated and included in the DB2 CLI trace:

```
TRACETIME = 0 | 1
```

Setting TRACESTMTONLY to its default value of 0 means trace information for all DB2 CLI function calls will be written to the DB2 CLI trace log file. Setting TRACESTMTONLY to 1 means only information related to the SQLExecute() and SQLExecDirect() function calls will be written to the log file. This trace option can be useful in determining the number of times a statement is executed in an application:

```
TRACESTMTONLY = 0 | 1
```

The following is a sample db2cli.ini file trace configuration using these DB2 CLI keywords and values:

21

```
[COMMON]
trace=1
TraceFileName=\temp\clitrace.txt
TRACEFLUSH=1
```

The CLI trace keywords are NOT case sensitive. However, path and filename keyword values may be case sensitive on some operating systems (such as Unix). If either a DB2 CLI trace keyword or its associated value in the db2cli.ini file is invalid, the DB2 CLI trace facility ignores it and uses the default value for that trace keyword instead.

ODBC Driver Manager Trace

It is important to understand the difference between an ODBC driver manager trace and a DB2 CLI driver trace. An ODBC driver manager trace shows the ODBC function calls made by an ODBC application to the ODBC driver manager. In contrast, a DB2 CLI driver trace shows the function calls made by the ODBC driver manager to the DB2 CLI driver *on behalf of the application*.

An ODBC driver manager might forward some function calls directly from the application to the DB2 CLI driver. However, the ODBC driver manager might also delay or avoid forwarding some function calls to the driver. The ODBC driver manager may also modify application function arguments or map application functions to other functions before forwarding the call on to the DB2 CLI driver.

Reasons for application function call intervention by the ODBC driver manager include

- The Microsoft cursor library maps calls such as SQLExtendedFetch() to multiple calls to SQLFetch() and other supporting functions to achieve the same result.
- ODBC driver manager connection pooling usually defers SQLDisconnect() requests (or avoids them altogether if the connection is reused).

For these and other reasons, application developers may find an ODBC driver manager trace to be a useful complement to the DB2 CLI driver trace.

For more information on capturing and interpreting ODBC driver manager traces, refer to the ODBC driver manager documentation. On Windows platforms, refer to the Microsoft ODBC 3.0 Software Development Kit and Programmer's Reference, also available online at http://www.msdn.microsoft.com/.

DB2 JDBC Trace

When an application using the DB2 JDBC driver begins execution, the driver also checks for trace facility options in the db2cli.ini file. As with the DB2 CLI trace options, DB2

JDBC trace options are specified as keyword/value pairs located under the [COMMON] section of the db2cli.ini file.

The following DB2 JDBC trace keywords can be defined:

- JDBCTRACE
- JDBCTRACEPATHNAME
- JDBCTRACEFLUSH

The JDBCTRACE keyword controls whether other DB2 JDBC tracing keywords have any effect on program execution. Setting JDBCTRACE to its default value of 0 disables the DB2 JDBC trace facility. Setting JDBCTRACE to 1 enables it:

JDBCTRACE = 0 | 1

By itself, the JDBCTRACE keyword has little effect and produces no trace output unless the JDBCTRACEPATHNAME keyword is also specified.

The value of JDBCTRACEPATHNAME is the fully qualified path of the directory to which all DB2 JDBC trace information is written:

JDBCTRACEPATHNAME = <fully_qualified_trace_path_name>

The DB2 JDBC trace facility attempts to generate a new trace log file each time a JDBC application is executed using the DB2 JDBC driver. If the application is multithreaded, a separate trace log file is generated for each thread. A concatenation of the application process ID, the thread sequence number, and a thread-identifying string are automatically used to name trace log files. There is no default path name to which DB2 JDBC trace output log files are written.

The JDBCTRACEFLUSH keyword specifies how often trace information is written to the DB2 JDBC trace log file:

JDBCTRACEFLUSH = 0 | 1

By default, JDBCTRACEFLUSH is set to 0, and each DB2 JDBC trace log file is kept open until the traced application or thread terminates normally. If the application terminates abnormally, some trace information that was not written to the trace log file may be lost.

To ensure the integrity and completeness of the trace information written to the DB2 JDBC trace log file, the JDBCTRACEFLUSH keyword can be set to 1. After each trace entry has been written to the trace log file, the DB2 JDBC driver closes the file and then reopens it, appending new trace entries to the end of the file. This guarantees that no trace information is lost.

21

> **CAUTION**
>
> Each DB2 JDBC log file close and reopen operation incurs significant input/output overhead and can reduce application performance considerably.

The following is a sample `db2cli.ini` file trace configuration using these DB2 JDBC keywords and values:

```
[COMMON]
jdbctrace=1
JdbcTracePathName=\temp\jdbctrace\
JDBCTRACEFLUSH=1
```

JDBC trace keywords are NOT case sensitive. However, path and filename keyword values may be case sensitive on some operating systems (such as Unix). If either a DB2 JDBC trace keyword or its associated value in the db2cli.ini file is invalid, the DB2 JDBC trace facility will ignore it and use the default value for that trace keyword instead. Enabling DB2 JDBC tracing does not enable DB2 CLI tracing. Some versions of the DB2 JDBC driver depend on the DB2 CLI driver to access the database. Consequently, Java developers may also want to enable DB2 CLI tracing for additional information on how their applications interact with the database through the various software layers. DB2 JDBC and DB2 CLI trace options are independent of each other and can be specified together in any order under the [COMMON] section of the db2cli.ini file.

Updating DB2 Products

DB2 provides product updates through fix packs (also known as FixPaks, patches, updates, or PTFs). DB2 provides an Internet and FTP site that you can use to download the latest fix. Download the latest DB2 FixPak from the IBM DB2 UDB and DB2 Connect Online Support Web site at
`www.ibm.com/software/data/db2/udb/winos2unix/support`.

After you download a fix pack, use its readme file (`readme.txt`) for prerequisite and installation instructions.

Handling Insufficient Space

If the space required to install selected components exceeds the space found in the path you specify for installing the components, the setup program issues a warning about the insufficient space. You can continue with the installation; however, it will stop when no more space is available. At this time, you have to manually stop the setup program if you can't free up space.

Summary

Today you saw how DB2 provides several problem-determination tools, including an Internet link to DB2 information, product fixes, certification news, and technical notes.

Online messages can help you debug your own problems. Several logs track various kinds of information during the operation of DB2.

Tools are also available to verify the integrity of your databases, and trace tools help you gather additional information in case of a problem you can't diagnose on your own.

Many configuration files are available to help you determine how your system was configured.

What Comes Next?

The appendixes come next. Appendix B contains the answers to all quiz questions covered in the book (no peeking allowed for today's quiz!).

Q&A

Q What message logs are kept by DB2?

A DB2 uses the administration notification log to log significant events; this log is intended to be used by database or system administrators. The db2diag.log is used to record more detailed diagnostic information and is intended to be used by DB2 customer support.

Q If I suspect that I have corrupted data in my database, what tool should I use to check and possibly fix the problem?

A Use the DB2 Database Analysis and Reporting Tool (DB2DART) to verify the architectural integrity of your database. This tool can help discover and correct possible data corruption problems.

Q How can I look at the current configuration of my system?

A There are three main configuration files: the Database Configuration file, the Database Manager Configuration file, and the Administration Configuration file. The easiest way to view these configuration files is through DB2 commands:

```
get dbm cfg > dbm.cfg
get db cfg for SAMPLE > sample.cfg
get admin cfg > admin.cfg
```

21

Workshop

The purpose of the workshop is to allow you to test your knowledge of the material covered in the lesson. See whether you can successfully answer the questions in the quiz and complete the exercises before you continue with the next lesson. Appendix B contains the answers to the quiz questions.

Quiz

1. How do you get fixes for the DB2 products?
2. When would you do a trace on your system?
3. What type of information is available on DB2 Web sites?
4. What parameter must be set to get more detailed information in the administration log?

Exercise

Browse through the various logs to see whether you have any errors. Look through the online Messages Reference to get a description of the problem and to see whether it suggests any actions to overcome the problem. Look at the configuration files set up for your system and database and see whether you understand how these values are set. Look through the online information to get an understanding of each parameter you can set.

PART 4

Appendixes

A

B

Appendix A

Getting Certified

Now that you've read this book, how can you be sure that you've "learned DB2 Universal Database in 21 Days"? The easiest way to verify this to yourself and the world is to take and pass one or more of the DB2 certification exams. After studying from this book, you should now be able to pass Exam 700: DB2 UDB V8.1 Family Fundamentals.

The best thing about passing Exam 700 is that it will earn you a certification. Yes, one exam, one certification. By passing Exam 700, you will earn an IBM Certified Database Associate certification.

What Is Certification?

What is *certification*? Certification is a tool to help objectively measure your performance on a given job at a defined skill level. The DB2 certification program consists of a series of multiple choice exams that you can take to confirm to yourself and to your employer (or potential employer) that you have mastered the skills required for a particular job role.

DB2 certification exams reflect the critical tasks required for a job, the skill levels of each task, and the frequency that a task needs to be performed.

Although the questions on the exam are multiple choice, they require that you have a fair amount of knowledge about DB2, especially hands-on knowledge. The more experience you have working with the product, the easier it will be for you to pass the exams.

Benefits of Becoming Certified

Doing what it takes to get certified can be hard work, but rewards await you.

Certification may accelerate your career potential by validating your professional competency and increasing your ability to provide solid, capable technical support. As a certified professional, you will receive the certification mark associated with your role to acknowledge you as a technical professional. The certification mark is for the exclusive use of the certified individual and may be used on business cards, on resumes, in advertisements, and in business literature. You will also receive a certificate of completion and a wallet-size certificate.

In addition to assessing job skills and performance levels, professional certification may also provide benefits for you personally, for your employer and company, and for business partners and consultants. At a personal level, professional certification

- Helps you prepare for a change in your career
- Helps you manage your career
- Helps you stay current with new technology
- Creates advantages in interviews
- Assists in salary increases and/or corporate advancement
- Increases your confidence in your skills
- Helps you stay competitive in your current job
- Promotes credibility and competence among your colleagues and clients
- Provides a map for you to continually build your skills

For an employer or company, professional certification

- Measures the effectiveness of training
- Reduces course redundancy and unnecessary expenses
- Provides a fair and adequate reflection of an employee's skills
- Provides an accurate measure of technical knowledge of staff

- Helps manage professional development
- Aids as a hiring tool
- Contributes to competitive advantage
- Increases credibility among clients
- Increases employee productivity
- Increases employee morale and loyalty

For business partners and consultants, certification

- Provides independent validation of technical skills
- Increases credibility among clients
- Creates competitive advantage and business opportunities
- Enhances prestige of the team
- Fulfills requirements to join various business partner programs

Am I Ready to Take the Exam?

If you have read this book and completed all the exercises, you are most likely prepared to take the exam. To be sure, take the free online DB2 Family Fundamentals assessment exam. All DB2 assessment exams are posted on the IBM Certification Exam (ICE) Tool (`certify.torolab.ibm.com`). The assessment exams are much like the real certification exam in terms of style, difficulty, and procedure, except that you can take them from the comfort of your own home (or office) and can look up the answers if you need more help.

If you can take the assessment exam without looking up answers and score 75% or greater, you have an excellent chance of passing the real exam. Although the assessment exam contains fewer questions than the real exam, the set of questions presented to you in the assessment exam changes each time you take the exam. Therefore, you should take the assessment exam as often as you want.

If you are not happy with your score, you'll need to study some more. Use the score report that you get after taking the assessment exam to figure out which areas you need to work on. Reread the appropriate chapter(s) and try the related exercises and quizzes. Retry the assessment exam to make sure that you've learned all that you need to know to pass the exam.

Taking a Certification Exam

Now it is time to take the real certification exam. IBM exams can be taken at Prometric or VUE testing centers in many locations throughout the world. To find a location near your home or office, check these Web sites: www.2test.com or www.vue.com/ibm. Schedule your exam either online or by calling the testing center. You'll need a credit card to pay for the exam. Make sure that you make it to your appointment because they'll still charge you if you miss it. When you go to the testing center to take the exam, you'll need two pieces of identification with photos and signatures to prove that you are who you say you are.

Certification exams are timed and must be proctored. There is usually enough time allotted for you to complete the exam, so take your time and make sure that you understand each question prior to answering. Each screen of the exam tells you the number of questions and time remaining. You can mark the questions that you are unsure about and review them before ending the exam. Most questions require a single answer, but a few require two answers. Read the instructions with the question and review the summary screen to make sure that you've fully answered each question.

The number of questions on an exam and the passing score for an exam depend on the exam, and these details are presented to you on the first screen before you begin your exam. For Exam 700, you must answer 54 questions and must score 61% or greater to pass the exam. That means 32 questions must be answered correctly. Make sure that you answer each question on the exam; you are not penalized for answering incorrectly.

When you end your exam, you are presented with a score report telling you whether you passed. A printed report will be given to you by the proctor, allowing you to see your score by section. Although you can use this report as proof that you've passed your exam, you may want to wait for the certificate instead. An email will be sent to you indicating how you can download your certificate or order a paper copy.

In summary, follow these steps to make your study time most effective:

1. Read and understand the exam objectives.
2. Take an assessment exam to find the areas where you need to focus.
3. Study using any of the recommended training resources.
4. Retake the assessment exam to make sure that you've retained the knowledge.
5. Call Prometric or VUE to schedule your exam.

IBM Certified Database Associate DB2 UDB V8.1 Family Fundamentals

The IBM Certified Database Associate certification role is an entry level DBA or a user of any of the DB2 family of products. This individual is knowledgeable about the fundamental concepts of DB2 Universal Database V8 through either hands-on experience or formal and informal education.

The database associate should have an in-depth knowledge of basic to intermediate tasks required in day-to-day administration, understand basic SQL (Structured Query Language), understand how DB2 Universal Database V8.1 is packaged and installed, know how to create databases and database objects, and have a basic knowledge of database security and transaction isolation.

Certification Requirements

Passing Exam 700 - IBM DB2 UDB V8.1 Family Fundamentals earns you an IBM Certified Database Associate certification and provides you with the prerequisite for all intermediate DB2 certifications. Earning this certification proves that you can use data in any of the DB2 family of servers: DB2 on Linux, Unix, Windows, iSeries, or zSeries.

Exam Objectives for Exam 700, DB2 UDB V8.1 Family Fundamentals

Exam 700 requires knowledge of the DB2 components required for your system, an understanding of the tools available with the products, and an understanding of the authorities and privileges required to access data. Further, you must have knowledge of the basic SQL, DML, and DDL to work with DB2 data as well as knowledge of data types and referential constraints to work with the basic DB2 objects (tables, views, and so on). Finally, you must understand basic isolation levels, locking methods, and database concurrency.

Exam 700 contains a total of 54 questions. Candidates are required to score 61% or better to pass the exam. Here are the detailed exam objectives mapped to the chapters of this book:

- **Planning – 15%**

  Knowledge of DB2 UDB products (client, server, and so on). See Day 1.

  Knowledge of DB2 tools such as DB2 Extenders, Configuration Assistant, Visual Explain, Command Center, Control Center, Relational Connect, Replication Center, Development Center, and Health Center. See several lessons in this book, especially Day 1 and Day 2.

Knowledge of data warehouse and OLAP concepts. See Day 1.

Knowledge of non-relational data concepts, such as extenders. See Day 1 and Day 13.

- **Security – 9%**

Knowledge of restricting data access. See Day 7.

Knowledge of different privileges. See Day 7.

- **Accessing DB2 UDB Data – 15%**

Ability to identify and locate DB2 UDB servers. See Day 5 and Day 6.

Ability to create and manipulate DB2 UDB objects. See Day 9 and Day 10.

Ability to create basic DB2 UDB objects. See Day 9 and Day 10.

- **Working with DB2 UDB Data – 31%**

Knowledge of transactions. See Day 14.

Given a DDL SQL statement, knowledge to identify results. See Day 12.

Given a DCL SQL statement, knowledge to identify results. See Day 12.

Given a DML SQL statement, knowledge to identify results. See Day 12.

Ability to use SQL to SELECT data from tables. See Day 12.

Ability to use SQL to SORT or GROUP data. See Day 12.

Ability to use SQL to UPDATE, DELETE, or INSERT data. See Day 12.

Ability to call a procedure. See Day 13.

- **Working with DB2 UDB Objects – 19%**

Ability to demonstrate usage of DB2 UDB data types. See Day 9.

Given a situation, ability to create table. See Day 9.

Knowledge to identify when referential constraints should be used. See Day 9.

Knowledge to identify methods of data validation. See Day 9.

Knowledge to identify characteristics of a table, view, or index. See Day 9.

- **Data Concurrency – 11%**

Knowledge to identify factors that influence locking. See Day 14.

Ability to list objects on which locks can be obtained. See Day 14.

Knowledge to identify characteristics of DB2 UDB locks. See Day 14.

Given a situation, knowledge to identify the isolation levels that should be used. See Day 14.

Beyond Exam 700

After you have passed Exam 700, you will have earned an IBM Certified Database Associate – DB2 UDB V8.1 Family certification and be able to increase your skills and earn other certifications for other job roles as shown in Figure A.1. The DB2 certification program has certification exams that map to three job roles:

- Database administrators—Those responsible for performing the day-to-day administration of DB2 instances and databases.

- Application developers—Those responsible for creating application programs that access or manipulate the data in DB2 databases.

- Solution designers—Those responsible for using specialized applications in conjunction with DB2 such as business intelligence or content management.

Database Administrator Role

The database administrator job role has two levels: database administrator and advanced database administrator. You are required to first earn a Database Associate certification before taking these certifications. Choose one or more of the following certifications:

- IBM Certified Database Administrator – DB2 UDB V8.1 for Linux, Unix, and Windows. See Exam 701 for details.

- IBM Certified Database Administrator – DB2 UDB V8.1 for z/OS. See Exam 702 for details.

- IBM Certified Advanced Database Administrator – DB2 UDB V8.1 for Linux, Unix, and Windows. See Exam 704 for details.

Solution Designer Role

The solution designer job role is an intermediate job role and requires that you first earn a Database Associate certification. Choose from one or more of the following certifications:

- IBM Certified Solutions Designer – DB2 UDB V8.1 Business Intelligence. See Exam 705 for details.

- IBM Certified Solutions Designer – DB2 Content Manager V8. See Exam 442 for details.

Application Developer Role

The application developer job role is an intermediate job role and requires that you first earn a Database Associate certification:

- IBM Certified Application Developer – DB2 UDB V8.1 Family (see Figure A.1). See Exam 703 for details.

FIGURE A.1

Certification roadmap for DB2 Universal Database V8.1.

**IBM DB2 Universal Database V8.1
Certification Roadmap**

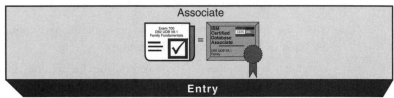

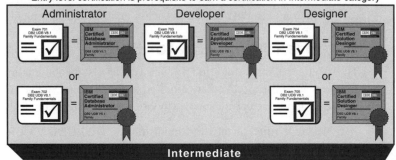

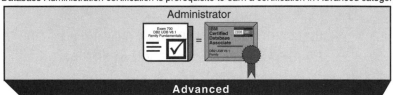

APPENDIX B

Answers to Quiz Questions

Day 1

1. *What's a local application? What's a remote application?*

   When you're running an application on the server where the database is located, it's referred to as a local application. The application could be using the Control Center, the command line, or an ODBC application. If you're running an application on the server but accessing a database located on a different machine, you're running a remote application. If you are on a client machine, you can run only remote applications because you can't have databases on a client machine.

2. *What are the two ways to use Java Database Connectivity to access DB2 data?*

   You can create JDBC applications or applets to access DB2 data. If you're using an applet, all you need is a Java-enabled browser and the applet on your system. If you're using an application, you must have the DB2 Run-Time Client installed on your system, along with the application. A Web browser and Web server aren't required when using JDBC applications.

3. *What's the name of the DB2 product feature that provides a parallel, multinode database environment?*

   The product feature that provides a parallel, multinode environment is known as the DB2 Database Partitioning Feature. It provides the capability of the database to be partitioned across multiple, independent computers by a LAN. It is available to use with DB2 Enterprise Server Editions, can handle extremely large databases, and can improve performance by adding more processing power to a given database operation. The DB2 Database Partitioning Feature exploits large-scale SMP and multinode (MPP/Cluster) configurations.

4. *Name the interfaces that you can use when creating applications with the DB2 Application Development Client.*

   When using the DB2 Application Development Client, you can create applications containing embedded SQL in a program written in languages such as C, C++, COBOL, Call Level Interface (CLI), ODBC, OLE DB, SQLJ, JDBC, and DB2 APIs. This gives you a great deal of flexibility to create the application with the tools that best suit your environment.

5. *DB2 Workgroup Server Edition (WSE) and DB2 Enterprise Server Edition (ESE) are largely the same, except for two differences. What are the differences? When would you use one edition over the other?*

   DB2 WSE is licensed on a per-user basis, whereas DB2 ESE is licensed for an unlimited number of users. DB2 WSE and DB2 ESE are both available for the AIX, HP-UX, Linux, Solaris, and Windows platforms.

   DB2 ESE includes all the features provided in the DB2 WSE, plus support for host connectivity, providing users with access to DB2 databases residing on iSeries or zSeries platforms. The DB2 Database Partitioning Feature can only be installed on DB2 ESE.

   The DB2 Workgroup Server Edition is ideal for smaller departmental applications or for applications that do not need access to remote databases on iSeries or zSeries. For access to host databases, large numbers of users, very large databases, complex workloads, or increased parallelism use the DB2 Enterprise Server Edition.

Day 2

1. *What's the advantage of using a view?*

   By using views, you can set up different presentations of the same data. Each view is derived from the actual table data, but each user will see a subset of the data. The main benefit to using views is that they allow you to control the access your users have to restricted data.

2. *Give some reasons why you would want to define a primary key for a table.*

   Defining a primary key on a table allows you to guarantee that each row in the table is unique. Defining a primary key can improve performance as well, because table access is quicker if each row is uniquely identified. If you're using an ODBC application to update your data, you need to have a primary key defined for the table. An index created automatically for the primary key helps DB2 find an efficient path to the data.

3. *What is the difference between unique keys and primary keys?*

   Unique keys are optional; no two of its values are the same or null. This constraint is enforced by the database manager when data is inserted or updated. A table can have multiple unique keys. Unique keys are defined when the table is created or altered.

   A primary key is a special kind of unique key that uniquely identifies a row of a table. The columns of a primary key can't contain null values. A table can have only one primary key.

4. *What's an instance? What's the advantage of using an instance?*

   An instance is a logical database manager environment. Having an instance allows you to catalog databases and set specific configuration parameters to the environment. For example, you can set up a test environment and a production environment by creating two instances. You can change the catalog information and the configuration parameters in the test instance without affecting the data in the production instance. Using instances can also help you protect access to sensitive information, because each instance has a separate assignment of authorized users.

5. *What's the difference between static and dynamic SQL?*

   When you write a SQL statement for an application program and know the entire statement, including the SQL statement type (UPDATE, INSERT, and so on) and the table and column names that the statement acts on, you're using static SQL. Static SQL is a SQL statement that's fully written in an application program before the program is compiled. Dynamic SQL is a statement that the application builds and

B

executes at runtime. Generally dynamic SQL is used in an interactive program where the user is prompted for key parts of the SQL statement.

Day 3

1. *What's the one difference concerning the default instance when using the Custom install type rather than the Typical install type?*

   If you do a Typical install, you're prompted only for a few key items needed during the installation; you can't select which program components are installed, nor can you customize the protocol information. If you do a Custom install, you must answer many prompts to determine exactly which components to install on your system.

2. *Under what circumstances would you need to manually invoke the installation program?*

   You need to manually invoke the installation program if you want to install a language other than US English on your system. Also, if the installation program doesn't start automatically when you insert the CD-ROM, you'll need to manually start it.

3. *How do you know which subcomponents are installed on your system when using the Custom install type?*

   The Select the Features You Want to Install dialog box allows you to click on a feature category to see the subcomponents that will be installed.

4. *When would you want the default instance to start automatically each time you boot your system?*

   If you're planning to use DB2 each time you boot your system, select to have the DB2 instance started automatically (to reduce the number of steps you need to perform each time you boot your system). If you'll use DB2 only occasionally, select to have it manually started.

5. *What installation steps can be deferred until the installation of the product is complete?*

   The contact information for Health Center notifications can be deferred until after installation is complete. The DB2 Tools catalog must be prepared before using tools such as the Task Center or Scheduler. Preparing this catalog can be deferred until after the product is installed.

Day 4

1. *Why would you want to create and use a schema?*

   Using a schema helps you group database objects under a single name. If you don't create a schema, any database objects you create will, by default, be stored under a schema name that's the same as your username. If your database will be shared with several people in your organization, you are best off creating a schema with a generic name such as the department name and creating all related objects within this schema. If everyone uses their default schema, you may end up with many related objects having different schema names.

2. *What authority do you need to create databases?*

   You must have SYSADM authority to create a database. SYSADM authority—the most powerful authority used within DB2—is given to all users in the Administrators group.

3. *What's the name of the tool that you use to view the DB2 product library?*

   The DB2 Information Center is the tool provided with DB2 products for you to view DB2 product information. The DB2 Information Center also requires that a Web browser be installed on your system because the product information is provided in HTML format.

4. *What are the two ways you can start administration tools such as the Task Center?*

   You can start administration tools such as the Task Center through the General Administration Tools folder or through toolbar icons in the Control Center.

5. *What is the default authentication type, and what is required to connect to a database instance created with this authentication type?*

   A database is created in an instance through one of two different authentication types: CLIENT or SERVER. If an authentication type isn't specified when the instance is created, the default SERVER authentication is used. If the authentication type is SERVER, you must enter a valid username and password on the server system.

Day 5

1. *What properties can you change if you're modifying the TCP/IP protocol?*

   You can change the service name and the port number associated with the TCP/IP protocol. You can't change the hostname because it's a systemwide parameter.

2. *Do you configure communications for an entire instance or for each individual database?*

   Communications is defined on an instance basis. Each database within this instance takes on these communication properties.

3. *What three configuration methods are available with the Configuration Assistant?*

   You can use the Configuration Assistant to search your network for databases, to use a profile generated from a server system, or to manually enter database and protocol information.

4. *What's the command that you use if you want to view the configuration parameters set for the DB2 Administration Server?*

   To view the configuration file for the DB2 Administration Server, enter the command `get admin cfg`.

5. *What drive and subdirectory structure is created when you create an instance?*

   When you create an instance, a subdirectory with the same name as the instance is created under the `SQLLIB` directory in the path where DB2 is installed. (If you set the `DB2INSTPROF` environment variable, the instance subdirectory is created in the directory specified by this variable.)

6. *What's the command to use if you want to change the ownership of the DB2 Administration Server after it's created?*

   To change the ownership of the DB2 Administration Server, use the command `db2admin setid` and provide a username and password.

7. *How do you change the instance that's started as a default?*

   Set the `db2instdef` Registry value to define the instance to start by default.

8. *What types of information can you export to a profile from a server workstation?*

   You can export information about instances on the server system and databases within each instance. The information for each instance includes the protocol information required to connect a client to databases in that instance.

9. *If you don't want your clients to be able to search the network for databases, how can you turn off this option?*

   To turn off the search capabilities, you must set the `DISCOVER` parameter to `DISABLE` on the client and the server.

10. *What protocols are supported by the `SEARCH` discovery method?*

    The DB2 Administration Server must be set up to use NetBIOS or TCP/IP for the `SEARCH` discovery method to work.

11. *What profile registry values can be used to tune the search discovery on the client?*

You can set the DB2DISCOVERYTIME parameter to tune the search discovery.

Day 6

1. *When should the client's DISCOVER parameter be set to SEARCH?*

It's set to SEARCH when you want the client to search the network for available databases.

2. *Why would you want to register a database for ODBC?*

You need to register your database for ODBC when you want to use ODBC applications such as Microsoft Access.

3. *If you can't connect to the server, what's the most likely problem?*

Before you can make a connection between a server and a client, the database manager on the server must be started. Start the database manager by issuing the db2start command at the server.

4. *What types of information can you export to a profile from a client workstation?*

You can export database connection information, CLI and ODBC settings, database manager configuration settings, CLI and ODBC common parameters, and APPC configuration information.

5. *What are the three types of clients you can choose from, and when would you use each?*

The three types of DB2 clients are DB2 Run-Time Client, DB2 Administration Client, and DB2 Development Client.

Use the DB2 Run-Time Client if you use an application to access the database on a remote server and you do not need to use tools such as the Control Center or Command Center. Use the DB2 Administration Client if you want to use the DB2 tools to access and administer DB2 databases. Use the DB2 Development Client to build applications or stored procedures.

B

Day 7

1. *If you want to create databases and assign authorities to other users, what authority should you have?*

SYSADM authority is required to create databases and to assign authorities to other users. Because this is the highest level of authority, be cautious when assigning SYSADM authority to users.

2. *Describe the importance of implicit versus explicit privileges.*

   You can grant implicit privileges to a user to run an application that performs actions on database objects, and the user will obtain the privileges necessary to perform the actions while running the application. This means that you can grant your users explicit privileges to execute applications, and they will be implicitly granted the privileges they need to manipulate the database objects.

3. *What authorities are granted to all users when a database is created?*

   The following database privileges are automatically granted to PUBLIC: CRE-ATETAB, BINDADD, CONNECT, IMPLICIT_SCHEMA, and SELECT privilege on the system catalog views.

4. *What is the default for the Trusted Clients option? What does this mean?*

   The default for the Trusted Clients option (CLIENT) is to trust all clients. This means that you'll allow all clients to access the database even if they don't have reliable local security systems built into the client. If it is set to SERVER, the user ID and password will be validated at the server.

Day 8

1. *What different types of relationships can you represent in a table?*

   You can have one-to-one, one-to-many, and many-to-many relationships represented in a table.

2. *Where are foreign keys defined?*

   Foreign keys are defined on the dependent table and rely on the data in the parent table. A foreign key references a primary key or a unique key in the same or another table. A foreign key assignment indicates that referential integrity is to be maintained according to the specified referential constraints.

3. *Why should you normalize your tables?*

   You should normalize your table to avoid redundancies and inconsistencies in your data.

4. *Is it a good idea to use a phone number as a primary key? Why or why not?*

   Using a phone number as a primary key isn't a great idea, mainly because a phone number may not be unique (you may have several people sharing a phone, for example). Also, phone numbers change as people move or if the phone company needs to change the area code.

5. *What data types should be used for data such as photos or movies?*

   GRAPHIC and BLOB data types are meant for binary data such as photos and movies.

Day 9

1. *Can you define a primary key column to be nullable? Why or why not?*

   Primary keys must not be nullable. There must be a value for each primary key column, and each row must be unique. If the column contained a null value, it would be impossible to reference the row.

2. *What are some differences between the data types VARCHAR and CHARACTER?*

   The VARCHAR and CHARACTER data types hold the same types of data, but VARCHAR is more efficient. Suppose that you create two 10-character columns, defining one column as VARCHAR and the other as CHARACTER. Ten bytes are reserved for the CHARACTER column regardless of the data inserted into the column. For the VARCHAR column, only the amount of space required to store the data is used for the column. CHARACTER columns are a fixed-length and can contain up to 254 bytes per column. VARCHAR columns are variable-length and can contain up to 4,000 bytes per column.

3. *What are the rules for naming a database?*

   The name you choose for the database must be different from any other database stored on the same drive. The name must contain eight or fewer characters, be one of A–Z, 0–9, @, #, or $, and can't begin with a number. If your database will be used outside North America, do not use special characters in the name to avoid potential code-page problems.

4. *After you create a table, what attributes can change by altering the table?*

   After you create a table, the attributes that you can change are limited. You can change the comment, the data capture for propagation option, the lock size, percentage of free space, and other performance-related details.

   When altering a table, you may also add new columns and change, remove, or rearrange the new columns; add unique, foreign, and partitioning keys for the table; add or drop columns from the primary keys for the table or change the constraint name; or add, change, or remove new check constraints.

5. *When is data checked to ensure that it complies with rules defined as a check constraint?*

   Rules defined as check constraints are checked when data is inserted into the database or when an attempt to update data is made. Constraint checking can be turned off to add foreign keys to your table. After you add the foreign key, you need to turn constraint checking back on.

B

Day 10

1. *How many buffer pools should you define for each database?*

   You can define as many buffer pools as you want, but usually one buffer pool is sufficient.

2. *At what point in the process do you specify the tables to be stored in a table space?*

   When you create a table, you have the option of defining a table space for the table to reside in. If you don't specify a table space, the default table spaces are used.

3. *If you plan to store temporary data in your table space, what type of table space should you create?*

   Temporary data can be stored in system temporary table spaces and user temporary table spaces. It cannot be stored in table spaces of type regular or large. System temporary table spaces are for database manager operations such as sorts and joins. User temporary table spaces should be created if you are storing declared global temporary tables.

4. *When are buffer pools created?*

   The default is to create the buffer pool immediately, but you may defer the creation until the next time DB2 is started by selecting the Create Bufferpool on Database Restart option.

5. *How can you extend the size of an SMS table space?*

   In general, you can't extend the size of an SMS table space very easily, because SMS capacity depends on the space available in the file system and the maximum size of the file supported by the operating system. You can use the operating system commands to move the files to a larger file system, or you can use the DB2 redirected restore to back up the table spaces and restore them to a larger number of containers.

Day 11

1. *If you are using the Command Center to enter SQL commands, what is one way to get help?*

   Use the SQL Assist function of the Command Center to help create SQL statements of the type: SELECT, INSERT, UPDATE, or DELETE. As you make selections, the actual SQL query is built in the SQL code at the bottom of the window.

2. *What's the main difference between a JDBC applet and a JDBC application?*

To run a JDBC applet, all you need is a Java-enabled browser; to run a JDBC application, you need to have DB2 Run-Time Client installed on your system, but you don't need a browser.

3. *If you get a message that the table you're opening in an ODBC application is read-only, what's the most likely problem?*

Most likely you'll need to define a unique index on the table before you can open it in read/write mode.

4. *When entering commands in the Command Center, do you need to end each line with a ; (semicolon)?*

If you're entering a single command, you don't need to end the command with a semicolon. If you have a series of commands, you must end each command with a semicolon, except the last command in the series.

5. *What tool do you need to use to see the execution plan and statistics associated with a SQL statement before execution?*

You do this by invoking Visual Explain in the interactive window in the Command Center.

B

Day 12

1. *What are the relative advantages of static versus dynamic SQL?*

The key advantage of static SQL, with respect to persistence, is that the static statements exist after a particular database is shut down, whereas dynamic SQL statements cease to exist when this occurs. In addition, static SQL does not have to be compiled by the DB2 SQL compiler at runtime, whereas dynamic SQL must be explicitly compiled at runtime (for example, by using the PREPARE statement). Because DB2 caches dynamic SQL statements, the statements do not need to be compiled often by DB2, but they must be compiled at least once when you execute the application.

You may want to use dynamic SQL when:

- You need all or part of the SQL statement to be generated during application execution.
- The objects referenced by the SQL statement do not exist at precompile time.
- You want the statement to always use the most optimal access path, based on current database statistics.
- You want to modify the compilation environment of the statement—that is, experiment with the special registers.

2. *What is produced during the Bind process?*

Binding is the process that creates the package the database manager needs to access the database when the application is executed. Binding can be done implicitly by specifying the PACKAGE option during precompilation, or explicitly by using the BIND command against the bind file created during precompilation.

3. *Write a sample INSERT statement that takes all the data from one table and inserts it into another table (assuming the same data types and column names).*

```
INSERT INTO T2
SELECT *
FROM T1
```

Day 13

1. *What options can you use to store XML documents with the XML Extender?*

XML Extender provides two storage and access methods for integrating XML documents with DB2 data structures: XML column and XML collection. These methods have different uses, but can be used in the same application.

The XML column storage access method allows you to manage your XML documents using DB2. You can store XML documents in a column of XML type, and you can query the contents of the document to find a specific element or attribute. You can associate and store a DTD in DB2 for one or more documents. Additionally, you can map element and attribute content to DB2 tables, called *side tables*. These side tables can be indexed for improved performance, but are not indexed automatically. The column used to store the document is called an XML column. It specifies that the column is used for the XML column access and storage method.

The XML collection is defined in a DAD file, which specifies how elements and attributes are mapped to one or more relational tables. The collection is a set of columns, associated with a DAD file, that contain the data in a particular XML document or set of XML documents. You can define a collection name by enabling it and then refer to it by name when issuing a stored procedure to compose or decompose XML documents, called an *enabled XML collection*. The collection is given a name so that it is easily run with stored procedures when composing and decomposing the XML documents.

2. *What are the advantages of using the Net Search Extender over storing a document as a LOB and using SQL to search the document?*

The Net Search Extender allows you to choose from among word, phrase, boolean, fuzzy, wildcard, proximity, and free-text searches, or use the thesaurus support to search within sections of structured documents, including XML and HTML documents. In-memory search is provided for high performance and scalability needs.

3. *What kind of applications can benefit from having access to spatial data?*

By enabling any organization to enhance its understanding of its business, leverage the value of existing data, and build sophisticated new applications, DB2 Spatial Extender can help users answer many types of questions. Some examples are selecting a retail site location (Do the demographics fit our targeted customer base?), assessing and insurance risk (Is this home location within our risk parameters?), and selecting a location to market test a new product (In which region should we test-market this new product?).

Day 14

1. *When would you use table locking versus row locking?*

Use table locking if you want to lock the table while you make extensive changes to it and want to ensure that no other users have access to it while you're making the changes. Use row locking if it's important that many users have access to data in the table at the same time.

2. *What's a deadlock? How can you break out of a deadlock situation?*

A deadlock occurs when two or more transactions are each waiting for data locked by the other. You can break out of a deadlock situation by using the deadlock detector, which will run periodically to determine whether there's a deadlock and will stop one of the transactions in the deadlock. You can also use lock timeouts to have locks released in a specified time limit.

3. *How can you ensure that your catalog statistics are up-to-date? Why is this important?*

Catalog statistics are updated when you perform the Run Statistics operation. This is important because the optimizer uses the statistics to find the most efficient path to the data in your tables. If you've made significant changes to your data without updating the statistics, the optimizer won't be able to find the most efficient path to your data, and performance may suffer.

4. *When should you use the highest level of optimization?*

The highest level of optimization should be used with very complex SQL statements.

B

Day 15

1. *How do you create an index? Why do you want to create an index?*

   An index is created automatically when you define a unique key, a primary key, or a foreign key. You also can define an index when the table is defined or at any time afterward. Creating an index produces pointers to rows in the table and allows more efficient access by creating a direct path to the data.

2. *What is a unique index?*

   Create a unique index to prevent the table from containing two or more rows with the same value of the index key. If the table contains rows with duplicate key values, the index is not created.

3. *If you don't see hover help while you're using the DB2 tools, how can you turn on this feature?*

   Use the Tools Settings dialog box to turn on hover help. (Hover help is turned on by default.) To get to the Tools Settings dialog box, click the Tools Settings icon on the toolbar in the Control Center.

4. *Can you modify scripts created as a result of using the Backup Database Wizard?*

   No, you can't. You can, however, run the script or schedule the script. If you need to make changes beyond the schedule, you must create a new script.

5. *What's the purpose of creating a grouping task?*

   Creating scripts within a group of tasks allows you to initiate other scripts based on the success of other scripts in the group. You create groupings for multiple tasks that can be scheduled to run on a regular schedule or to be run if another task succeeds or fails.

6. *What are the three different types of directories that DB2 uses to record information for accessing databases?*

   The three directories are local database directory or system database directory, DCS directory, and node directory. The local database and system database directories identify the name, alias, and physical location of each cataloged database. The DCS directory contains an entry for each distributed relational database that your system can access. You'll have a DCS directory only if you have DB2 Connect installed. The node directory contains communication information for the client to connect to a remote database server.

7. *What's the purpose of creating a list of contacts?*

   DB2 allows you to keep an address book of people who can be contacted when tasks complete. You can set up an email address or pager information for each person. Specify the person to contact when defining a script in the Task Center.

8. *Where can you see the notifications from the Health Center?*

The Notification Log page in the Journal allows you to see the notification messages issued by the Health Center.

Day 16

1. *How can you ensure that you have exclusive access to a database if you want to do a full offline backup of your data?*

If you try to perform a full offline backup of your database while users are still attached to it, you'll get an error. To gain exclusive access to the database, use Force Applications. You'll maintain exclusive access to the data during the entire time it takes to perform the offline backup.

2. *How does using redirected restore give you additional flexibility when using SMS table spaces?*

If you're using SMS table spaces, you must define the size of the containers when the table space is defined, and you can't change the size of the containers. You can redefine the layout of the table space containers by using redirected restore.

3. *How can you use roll-forward recovery to undo an unexpected error?*

If you know the precise time the error occurred, you can restore your database and then roll forward your logs until the moment before the error occurred. This means that your data will be back to the state it was in just before the error.

4. *Which database configuration parameters can be tuned to improve the performance of the backup and restore operations?*

Setting the parallelism parameter and memory parameters (number of buffers and size of each buffer) are the main database configuration parameters that will affect the performance of backup and restore. You can update the configuration parameters either using the Backup and Restore Wizards or through the Control Center.

Day 17

1. *To create a new table by importing IXF data, which import mode should you use?*

You must use the CREATE import mode to create a new table when importing IXF data.

2. *If you want to create a new table, what format should you use? Would you use the Load Wizard or the Import Wizard to create a new table?*

Integrated exchange format (IXF) is used to create a new table; the DEL, ASC, and WSF formats can be used only to import data into an existing table. IXF format is

B

the format used by database managers. Load doesn't support creating a new table; the table must exist before you can load data into it. To create a new table, use the Import utility.

3. *How do you export only a subset of the data in a table?*

   Click the Columns tab in the Export dialog box to specify only a subset of the columns to export. Exporting a subset of columns is supported only when using WSF or IXF formats.

4. *What must take place before you can save a copy of the changes when using the Load Wizard?*

   Forward recovery must be turned on to enable you to save a copy of the changes when using the Load utility. On the Copy Options page of the Load Wizard, specify that a copy of the changes be saved.

Day 18

1. *How can you set some defaults when using the quick method of defining replication sources?*

   To save time when registering replication sources, you can set up a source object profile ahead of time for the Capture control server. When you register a table, the Replication Center then uses the defaults that you defined in the source object profile instead of the Replication Center defaults. This can save you time when registering because you can overwrite the defaults once instead of having to select each table one at a time and change the default settings manually.

2. *Where must the Capture program be run? Where must the Apply program be run?*

   Run the Capture program from the Replication Center or a command line on the server where the source database is located. Run the Apply program from the Replication Center or a command line on the server where the target database is located.

3. *What is capture before-image? When would you use this option?*

   The capture before-image option in replication allows you to save the column in the source table before it's updated. This option is useful for recovery and auditing.

Day 19

1. *What do you need to create an access plan graph?*

   Before you can create an access plan graph, you need to have a working SQL statement.

2. *What's an operator? How is it shown on an access plan graph?*

An operator is an action that must be performed on the output from a table or index. Examples include DELETE, FETCH, FILTER, GRPBY, and INSERT. The rectangular boxes in the graph are operators.

3. *When is it recommended that you collect statistics and reorganize a table?*

You should collect statistics when the data in your tables changes significantly. You should also collect statistics after a table is reorganized. Tables should be reorganized to remove all the unused space and to write the table and indexes in contiguous pages.

4. *What should you do immediately following a Run Statistics or a Reorganize Table operation?*

Following a Run Statistics or Reorganize Table operation, you should rebind application programs that use static SQL.

Day 20

1. *How many buffer pools should you define for your system?*

Usually one buffer pool is sufficient, but you can create additional buffer pools for a higher level of database tuning.

2. *When do you need to change your configuration parameters?*

Usually the default values defined for the configuration parameters are sufficient to suit your needs, but to achieve maximum performance for your system, you should analyze and tune these parameters by using the Configuration Advisor.

3. *Can database configuration parameters be set on the client?*

Database configuration parameters exist only on the server where the database is located. On the client, you can set database manager configuration parameters.

4. *If you expect to have no locks on the data, which isolation level should you use?*

Use the uncommitted read isolation level if you expect to have no locks on your data.

Day 21

1. *How do you get fixes for the DB2 products?*

You can see the fixes available for the various DB2 products on the www.ibm.com/software/data/db2/udb/winos2unix/support site. Each fix pack comes with a readme file describing the problems the fix pack fixes. After you read through the information provided, you can download the fix pack to your system and install it on your system.

2. *When would you do a trace on the DB2 instance?*

   You would do a trace on your system if you're having a problem and are requested by DB2 Support personnel to gather trace information to help debug the problem.

   The DB2 trace command (`db2trc`) controls the trace facility of a DB2 instance or the DB2 Administration Server. The trace facility records information about operations and formats this information into readable form. Enabling the trace facility may impact your system's performance. As a result, only use the trace facility when directed by a DB2 Support technical support representative.

3. *What type of information is available on DB2 Web sites?*

   The DB2 Web site contains the entire DB2 library in HTML format, many tips and techniques to help you use the product, frequently asked questions, fix pack information, and information on how to become a certified user of DB2.

4. *What parameter must be set to get more detailed information in the administration log?*

   The `DIAGLEVEL` parameter in the database manager configuration file can be set to the level 4 to capture additional diagnostic information in the `db2diag.log` file.

INDEX

Symbols

A

SMS (system managed space), 52, 233, 247

SYSCATSPACE, 52, 230, 246

system temporary table spaces, 232

TEMPSPACE1, 53, 230, 247

user temporary table spaces, 232

USERSPACE1, 52, 230, 246

viewing, 238

triggers, 46-47

UDTs (user-defined types), 45-46

data sources, 257-258

data types, 194-195, 215

binary strings, 39

BLOB, 195

CHARACTER, 195

character strings, 39

choosing, 209

CLOB, 195

DATE, 195

date/time, 39

DBCLOB, 195

DECIMAL, 195

defined, 38

design issues, 322-323

distinct types, 39

DOUBLE, 195

GRAPHIC, 195

graphic strings, 39

INTEGER, 195

LOB, 39-41

LONG VARCHAR, 195

LONG VARGRAPHIC, 195

numbers, 39

SMALLINT, 195

strong typing, 46

supertypes, 300

TIME, 195

TIMESTAMP, 195

UDTs (user-defined types), 45-46, 300-301

VARCHAR, 195

VARGRAPHIC, 195

Data Warehouse Center, 17, 97

database administrator certification, 531

Database Analysis and Reporting Tool (DB2DART), 511

Database Authorities dialog box, 185

Database Configuration dialog box, 137

Database Configuration file, 57, 128-129, 512

database connection services (DCS), 50

Database History page (Journal), 348-349, 385-386

database managed space (DMS), 52, 234, 247

Database Manager, 33, 56, 126-128, 480-483, 512

Database System Monitor, 453-455

database utilities, binding, 263-264

databases (relational), 33. *See also* **tables**

accessing, 249-250

Command Center, 251-254

Command Line Processor, 255

Control Center, 250-251

DB2 Application Development Client, 262-264

directories, 357

JDBC (Java Database Connectivity), 259-261

Microsoft Access, 256-259

WebSphere Application Server, 262

aliases, 213

backing up, 370

Backup Wizard, 371-372, 375-376

forcing users off system, 376

buffer pools, 230-232, 240-242

calculated values, 274-275

cataloging, 169

DOUBLE data type, 195

Double-Byte Character Large Objects, 307

DRDA (Distributed Relational Database Architecture), 10, 19

drivers (JDBC), 260

duplicate rows, removing, 274

dynamic SQL statements, 61, 291-292

E

Edit menu commands, 105

editing
   passwords, 99
   tables, 225-226
   user privileges, 114

embedded SQL. *See* SQL (Structured Query Language)

enabling prefetch, 323

Enabling the DB2 Scheduling Function page (Load Wizard), 414

encapsulation, 42

entering commands
   Command Center, 252
   Command Line Processor, 255-256
   Command Window, 256

Enterprise Server Edition (DB2), 9, 12

enumerating groups, 186

environment variables, 260

Environmental Systems Research Institute (ESRI), 315

error logging
   administration notification log, 509-510
   diagnostic log, 510

ESRI (Environmental Systems Research Institute), 315

evaluating registry parameters, 479

Event Analyzer, 98, 455

event monitors, 455-456, 474
   creating, 456-459
   stopping, 459
   viewing monitored events, 459-460

exams (certification)
   benefits of certification, 526-527
   defined, 525-526
   IBM Certification Exam (ICE) Tool, 527
   preparation, 527
   testing procedures, 528

EXCEPT operator, 280, 282

Exception File to Write Rejected Rows option (Load Wizard), 414

Exception Table option (Load Wizard), 414

exclamation mark (!), 256

executable statements, 287

EXISTS predicate, 283-284

Explain SQL Statement window, 463

Export Profile command (Configure menu), 164

Export Server Profile dialog box, 138

Export Table – PROJECT dialog box, 394

Export Wizard, 393-394

exporting
   client profiles, 164-166
   column names, 394-395
   Export Wizard, 393-394
   LOBs (large objects), 395
   required authorities/privileges, 393
   server profiles, 138
   supported file formats, 392-393

Express Edition (DB2), 9, 12

expressions, 274-275

extent sizes, 236-237

EXTERNALROUTINE privilege, 113

F

file reference variables, 41

files
   administration notification log, 509-510
   configuration files, 56-57, 512

X-Z

Your Guide
to Computer
Technology

www.informit.com

Sams has partnered with **InformIT.com** to bring technical information to your desktop. Drawing on Sams authors and reviewers to provide additional information on topics you're interested in, **InformIT.com** has free, in-depth information you won't find anywhere else.

ARTICLES

Keep your edge with thousands of free articles, in-depth features, interviews, and information technology reference recommendations—all written by experts you know and trust.

POWERED BY

ONLINE BOOKS

Answers in an instant from **InformIT Online Books'** 600+ fully searchable online books. Sign up now and get your first 14 days **free**.

CATALOG

Review online sample chapters and author biographies to choose exactly the right book from a selection of more than 5,000 titles.

     www.samspublishing.com

Wouldn't it be great

if the world's leading technical publishers joined forces to deliver their best tech books in a common digital reference platform?

They have. Introducing **InformIT Online Books** powered by Safari.

POWERED BY Safari

InformIT Online Books

informit.com/onlinebooks

■ **Specific answers to specific questions.**
InformIT Online Books' powerful search engine gives you relevance-ranked results in a matter of seconds.

■ **Immediate results.**
With InformIt Online Books, you can select the book you want and view the chapter or section you need immediately.

■ **Cut, paste, and annotate.**
Paste code to save time and eliminate typographical errors. Make notes on the material you find useful and choose whether or not to share them with your workgroup.

■ **Customized for your enterprise.**
Customize a library for you, your department, or your entire organization. You pay only for what you need.

Get your first 14 days FREE!

InformIT Online Books is offering its members a 10-book subscription risk free for 14 days. Visit **http://www.informit.com/onlinebooks** for details.

What's on the CD-ROM

The companion CD-ROM contains chapter examples and a trial version of DB2 V8.1 Workgroup Server Edition.

Windows Installation Instructions

1. Insert the disc into your CD-ROM drive.
2. From the Windows desktop, double-click the My Computer icon.
3. Double-click the icon representing your CD-ROM drive.
4. Double-click on start.exe. Follow the on-screen prompts to finish the installation.

NOTE

> If you have the AutoPlay feature enabled, start.exe will be launched automatically whenever you insert the disc into your CD-ROM drive.

License Agreement

By opening this package, you are also agreeing to be bound by the following agreement:

You may not copy or redistribute the entire CD-ROM as a whole. Copying and redistribution of individual software programs on the CD-ROM is governed by terms set by individual copyright holders.

The installer and code from the author(s) are copyrighted by the publisher and the author(s). Individual programs and other items on the CD-ROM are copyrighted or are under an Open Source license by their various authors or other copyright holders.

This software is sold as-is without warranty of any kind, either expressed or implied, including but not limited to the implied warranties of merchantability and fitness for a particular purpose. Neither the publisher nor its dealers or distributors assumes any liability for any alleged or actual damages arising from the use of this program. (Some states do not allow for the exclusion of implied warranties, so the exclusion may not apply to you.)

NOTE

> This CD-ROM uses long and mixed-case filenames requiring the use of a protected-mode CD-ROM Driver.